THE GREATER WAR
1912–1923

General Editor
ROBERT GERWARTH

Asia and the Great War

A Shared History

XU GUOQI

OXFORD

UNIVERSITY PRESS

Great Clarendon Street, Oxford, OX2 6DP,
United Kingdom

Oxford University Press is a department of the University of Oxford.
It furthers the University's objective of excellence in research, scholarship,
and education by publishing worldwide. Oxford is a registered trade mark of
Oxford University Press in the UK and in certain other countries

© Xu Guoqi 2017

The moral rights of the author have been asserted

First Edition published in 2017

Impression: 1

Published in the United States of America by Oxford University Press
198 Madison Avenue, New York, NY 10016, United States of America

British Library Cataloguing in Publication Data
Data available

Library of Congress Control Number: 2016943270

ISBN 978–0–19–965819–0

Printed in Great Britain by
Clays Ltd, St Ives plc

For Jay Winter
and Chuck Hayford

Foreword

The First World War was a test of the legitimacy both of the states which waged it and of their control of dependencies and colonies throughout the world. Losing the war meant regime change at home and the loss of colonies abroad. Whatever the outcome, the war launched in 1914 signaled a reconfiguration of the imperial world. If we add the force of the revolutionary events of 1917—the Russian revolutions, the second of which took Russia out of the war, and the American entry into the war—then it is apparent that global power was in the melting pot throughout the conflict.

At the peace conference of 1919, the old imperial powers attempted to stabilize or fortify their imperial power. But everyone could see that the Great War had unleashed both American and Russian alternatives to European domination of the imperial world. Russia was not even represented at the peace conference, and American leadership sank under the failure of Wilson to secure Senate consent to the Paris Peace Treaty. The Great Powers engaged in a mad rush at Versailles to build a durable peace, but instead, they had set in motion forces which one day would destroy the old order entirely. The Paris Peace Treaty has its defenders as the least worst alternative at the time, but I am not one of them.

What kind of 'peace' emerged from Paris in 1919? Violence throughout the globe continued, and in some cases, for instance, in Turkey and Russia, savage civil wars continued until the early 1920s. With respect to the colonial world, there was violent unrest in Egypt, Palestine, Iraq, India, and Korea. Mustafa Kemal Ataturk's abolition of the caliphate left parts of Islam adrift, uncertain as to where Muslim authority lay, and uncomfortable with the supine set of local rulers chosen by the British and the French to do their bidding. The Muslim brothers emerged from this crisis in Islam in the later 1920s. They are with us still.

At the same time, there was a move towards converting colonies into Mandates of the new League of Nations. That body was committed to the ultimate development of many colonies into formally independent states. Outside of Europe, the first to join the ranks of sovereign states was Iraq in 1922, but doubts remained as to whether the imperial powers (then as now) intended to create a set of reconfigured dependencies, or, if you prefer, Potemkin villages, with the scaffolding but not the substance of independence.

Elsewhere in Asia, colonial power was reinforced or refashioned after 1918, through force and fiat in India, Vietnam, Indonesia, the Malaysian peninsula, and in Polynesia. It would take another fifty years for the façade of empire to fall, and even then, first French, British, and Dutch interests, and then American interests, found subtle and not so subtle ways to maintain their hold over these societies and their resources. How different the post-imperial world order of the fourth quarter of the twentieth century was from the imperial world order which preceded it is a matter of considerable dispute and discussion.

There is an abundant literature about the imperial history of these turbulent decades surrounding the Great War. But Xu Guoqi's new and path-breaking book on the First World War in Asia goes beyond conventional wisdom. What sets his book apart is that it is the first scholarly work to tell the story of the Great War from an Asian perspective. At its core is a deep and important account of the war-related transformation of the Sino-Japanese conflict, and its ramifications for the future development of the imperial project in Asia and beyond.

Xu Guoqi's book starts with the Sino-Japanese conflict in the two decades before the outbreak of 1914, and offers us a clear narrative of both nations' competing and contradictory visions of the future of Asia in the war period and beyond. He thereby provides the groundwork for a better understanding of the whole of Asia's colonial history, under the new order of self-determination, overshadowed by the old (though reconfigured) order of imperial power, Japanese as well as British and French.

Japan's "21 demands" of 1915 disclosed in no uncertain terms the thrust of her imperial ambitions in China, which was to become a "vassal state" while the Great Powers were otherwise engaged in destroying each other's armies and in liquidating their resources in doing so. For China, entering the war and securing a place in the international arena of the Allies was not a choice but a vital necessity; her national existence required no less. Xu Guoqi brings alive both the subtleties of Japanese diplomacy and the counter-moves of China, in particular their decision to send a Chinese Labour Corps to the Western Front. On this topic, Xu Guoqi is the recognized authority, and here he places this move in the context of China's assertion of her place among the nations at war, and her right to help shape the future of her region and beyond.

There was a clear power imbalance between China and Japan during and after the war. But what drives this narrative is the paradox that on the one hand, Japan could not effectively conquer China, or find sufficient lackeys through whom they might rule, and on the other hand, China could not effectively resist Japanese power. This bloody and unstable equilibrium dominated events in the early twentieth century; it came to an end violently only in 1945.

From this Asian perspective, Xu Guoqi offers us a telling account of the instabilities inherent in imperial power in the aftermath of the war. What he offers us is a vision of a shared history, *une histoire croisée*, rather than separate and several national histories. All were struck by transnational forces eroding, reconfiguring, or tearing apart colonial authority. Among them was a sense among some Asians that the European slaughter of the Great War had undermined any claim of the West to have a *mission civilisatrice*. Hegemonic European power took another big knock in the 1929 world economic crisis, but it still would take another world war and a further massive hemorrhage of assets and resources for the British and French, alongside others, to realize that they could not afford to retain their imperial dependencies forever.

Such a recognition of the limits of imperial power was hardly visible in 1918. The Great War was an imperial war from start to finish. But change to that reality required the wartime recognition among Asian peoples that the only way they could emerge as fully free states was by developing multiple instruments of power, political, diplomatic, economic, and military, and by using them. Among the human tragedies of the first half of the twentieth century is that Japan and China used these instruments primarily against each other. All of Asia, indeed, the whole world, suffered in this age of iron, before the dreams of independence, so movingly described in this book, could be realized. Xu Guoqi's powerful study of Asia and the Great War illuminates that dark story in important and enduring ways.

Jay Winter
Yale University and Monash University

May 2016

Acknowledgments

This book would not have been written had Jay Winter not invited me to contribute a chapter on Asia and the Great War for his Cambridge History of the First World War. It is Jay who has played a significant role in keeping me in the field of First World War studies for many years. My first book on *China and the Great War* was accepted by Jay for publication in his series Studies in the Social and Cultural History of Modern Warfare from Cambridge University Press over one decade ago. Jay not only gave me advice on how to write this book, he was willing to sacrifice his precious time to write a foreword to grace this humble volume. I would like to use this opportunity to express my profound appreciation to him for shaping my and many others' understanding of the Great War. I am deeply grateful to Robert Gerwarth, who persuaded me to undertake this volume for the series on the Greater War under his general editorship for Oxford University Press and kindly invited me to spend my sabbatical time at his Centre for War Studies at the University College Dublin to work on this book in 2012. The Centre was a wonderful and stimulating place with many great scholars with whom I could test my ideas. I have to thank John Horne of Trinity College Dublin, who not only happily introduced me to the college's great collections, but also spent many hours discussing our shared interest in war studies at his beautiful house in Dublin over drinks and meals. Thanks also go to Kate Darian-Smith, Antonia Finnane, and Ara Keys, who made my brief stays at the University of Melbourne in 2014 and 2015 both joyful and rewarding.

In writing this book, I was inspired by, and am deeply indebted to, many scholars, especially Gordon Johnson, Prasenjit Duara, Michael Adas, Akira Iriye, Erez Manela, Fred Dickinson, Jay Winter, Robert Gerwarth, John Horne, Santanu Das, Marilyn Lake, Kimloan Vu-Hill, Richard Fogarty, Alan Kramer, Radhika Singha, Naoko Shimazu, and many others. I benefited enormously from their works, which provided the perspective and historical foundation for this book to be based on. I have borrowed ideas from so many of them that I am afraid I may fail to give proper acknowledgment to each of them.

Gordon Johnson, Jay Winter, Fred Dickinson, Robert Gerwarth, Chuck Hayford, and Terre Fisher read the whole or part of the manuscript and offered penetrating and brilliant advice and much needed corrections. The anonymous reader of the manuscript also provided great suggestions and constructive criticisms. Although I am not able to accept all of their suggestions, their indispensable feedback has definitely made this book better. Of course, I personally take responsibility for whatever shortcomings this book might have. Robert Faber and Cathryn Steele of Oxford University Press not only gently kept me on track from time to time to make sure I could finish the book on time, but more importantly, they provided much needed and crucial support and had confidence in me and this book.

The Radcliffe Institute for Advanced Study at Harvard University deserves special thanks. The Institute provided a great intellectual base for me to finish my two previous books. When I was working on this volume, the Institute once again invited me back by giving me two summer fellowships which were crucial for this book's timely completion. Moreover, the Institute kindly hired the following brilliant Harvard students to help me with this project: Noel de Sa e Silva, Gina Kim, Fatoumata Fall, Andrew Lee, and Cassandra Euphrat Weston. These students helped me in finding sources in many different languages. I am delighted to express my gratitude for their indispensable assistance, although it took me longer to wrap up this book than their time to finish Harvard degrees. I also would like to express my deep appreciation for two great officers of the Institute: Sharon Bromberg-Lim, Associate Director, and Associate Dean Judith E. Vichniac, Radcliffe Fellowship Program. Both have always made my stay at the Institute fruitful and joyful.

I thank Xu Han, Lee Chi-Chang, and Chen Shuan (all three received doctoral degrees from the University of Tokyo), who provided great help in locating Japanese sources and translations. I am very grateful to my colleagues Janet Borland and Charles Schencking, who offered assistance with cheer whenever I had problems with Japanese language and sources. Thanks also go to Wu Lin-Chun, Izumi Hirobe, and Jan Schmidt, who provided crucial assistance when I worked on this book. I had the good fortune to give lectures related to the subject of this book at the Imperial War Museum, London, Harvard University, University of Melbourne, University of Manchester, University of Geneva, Free University Berlin, University of Vienna, Fudan University, Cambridge University, Peking University, Capital Normal University, and Jinan University in Guangzhou, among other places. I benefited enormously from the audience's comments, criticisms, and suggestions. I have to express my deep gratitude to Oliver Janz, who invited me to be an East Asia co-editor for his "1914–1918-online: International Encyclopedia of the First World War," which gave me the opportunity to work closely with my fellow historians from Asia and other parts of the world; this experience has advanced my understanding of Asia and the war.

I am extremely grateful to my colleagues at the University of Hong Kong for providing stimulating and generous support when I worked on this book. I am happy to acknowledge support from the Hong Kong Government University Research Council's grant (HKU 752013) and the University of Hong Kong's basic research grant. My colleagues at the University of Hong Kong kindly gave me a best output award and outstanding researcher award which provided me with much needed financial resources for this book's research and writing. I am grateful also for both the sabbatical and research leaves that the university granted me to pursue this project.

Lastly, my deep gratitude to my family. Winston Churchill once commented on the process of writing a book with the following: "Writing a book is an adventure. To begin with it is a toy, then an amusement. Then it becomes a mistress, and then it becomes a master, and then it becomes a tyrant and, in the last stage, just as you are about to be reconciled to your servitude, you kill the monster and fling him out to the public." During all of these cycles, my wife and children have always provided great support when I have been working on this book over a long period of time. Their love, support, and encouragement have sustained me finally to finish this rather challenging project in a timely fashion. I owe them great appreciation for all the happiness and fulfillment with which they have blessed me.

Contents

Contents

List of Abbreviations

BA	British National Archives, Kew Gardens
Columbia Library	Rare Book and Manuscript Library, Columbia University, New York
FRUS	United States Department of State Papers relating to the *Foreign Relations of the United States*
ILC	Indian Labour Corps
INC	Indian National Congress
IWM	Imperial War Museum, London
KNA	Korean National Association
LC, Leeds	Liddle Collection (1914–18), Special Collections, University of Leeds Library
NA	National Archives, College Park, MD
NKYA	New Korea Youth Association
Quai d'Orsay	Archive of the French Foreign Ministry, Paris
Vincennes	Service Historique de l'Armée de Terre, *Château de Vincennes*
YMCA	Young Men's Christian Association
YMCA Archives	Kautz Family YMCA Archives, University of Minnesota Libraries, Minneapolis, MI

List of Abbreviations

Introduction

In the beginning, British imperial poet Rudyard Kipling saw the Great War as a conflict between civilization and chaos, and helped his son John gain a commission in the Irish Guards. Kipling had written the poem "If" for John, opening with lines that would be memorized by British children and army officers alike, "If you can keep your head when all about you | Are losing theirs and blaming it on you," and ending with the bracing "you'll be a man, my son."[1] John disappeared during the Battle of Loos in 1915, presumed killed. In a poem only recently discovered, "The Gambler," Kipling wrote: "Three times wounded | Three times gassed | Three times wrecked, I lost at last." Another fragment reads: "This was a Godlike soul before it was crazed. No matter. The grave makes whole."[2] In "Epitaphs of the War," he wrote bitterly: "If any question why we died | Tell them, because our fathers lied."[3] Clearly, even then Kipling had mixed voices and ambiguous feelings about the war.

One hundred years after its outbreak, the world is still consumed by frustration and fascination with the war's origins, effects, and implications. *The Economist* wrote in 2014 that some 25,000 books and scholarly articles have been written on the Great War. Those few years of the wartime have been scrutinized from every possible aspect and perspective, from the war's wider significance for international order to incidents known only to locals. And more books are coming.[4]

The distinguished First World War scholar Jay Winter recently argued eloquently that language defines the memory of war, and the Great War continues to exert its grip most powerfully in "Anglosphere" countries. In Commonwealth War Graves Commission cemeteries, tombstones of the First World War deceased have the inscription "Not glory, but a purpose." It seems to Winter that "glory" got a bad name in the UK during the war. But the Great War is spoken of in many languages. In France, the language of glory was still part of the vernacular during and even after the war.[5] More recently, commentators have been ready to see analogies between

---

[1] Thomas Pinney, ed., *Cambridge Edition of the Poems of Rudyard Kipling* (Cambridge: Cambridge University Press, 2013), 2: 756–7.

[2] Pinney, ed., *Cambridge Edition of the Poems of Rudyard Kipling*, 3: 2111.

[3] Pinney, ed., *Cambridge Edition of the Poems of Rudyard Kipling*, 2: 1144.

[4] No Author, "100 Years after 1914, Still in the Grip of the Great War," *The Economist*, March 29, 2015, 20.

[5] For a detailed discussion of the meaning of the war, see Jay Winter and Antoine Prost, *The Great War in History: Debates and Controversies, 1914 to the Present* (Cambridge: Cambridge University Press, 2005) and Jay Winter, ed., *The Legacy of the Great War: Ninety Years On* (Columbia, MO: University of Missouri Press, 2009).

the Balkans of a century ago and China and Japan, or even more pointedly, the Middle East, where the political chattering classes see the gathering clouds of a crisis comparable to 1914. Those debates will doubtless continue.

THE GREAT WAR ECHOES THROUGH ASIA TODAY

In Asia, serious academic discussion and debate about the Great War have only just started. Research on the war's impact there and Asians' contributions has been insufficient, especially from Asian perspectives. While we now have solid and insightful works on individual nations such as Japan, India, and China, there is no single volume that shines a light on Asia's collective involvement and the war's impact on its societies. Moreover, no volume in any language explores the experiences Asian countries shared as they became embroiled, with divergent results, in the war and its repercussions. One can argue that, given the relevance and importance of the Great War to Asian countries, it was as defining an event there as elsewhere. But as we commemorate the centenary of the war, our knowledge of this part of the story remains at best limited. Many questions await our attention and many more, doubtless, have not yet been formed.

The significance of the Great War to today's Sino-Japanese relations only becomes clear when we understand what happened to China and Japan over the course of that conflict and in the generation leading up to it. I will argue that the Sino-Japanese War of 1894–5 laid the foundation and provided the motivations for China and Japan's scramble to participate in the European conflict. The war may have concluded long ago, but its spirit still haunts Asians in many distorting ways. William Faulkner's quip, "The past isn't dead. It isn't even past," seems to describe perfectly the effects of the war in Asia.[6]

Commentators, scholars, and politicians have begun to use First World War analogies when discussing China's current relations with Japan. In January 2014, Japanese Prime Minister Shinzo Abe told an audience at Davos, Switzerland, that the rivalry between China and Japan is similar to that between Germany and Britain before the First World War, implying that differences in national interest and diplomacy could supersede close trade ties, with China taking the role of Germany. The Chinese, of course, are not pleased with this comparison. Chinese Foreign Minister Wang Yi declared at a March 2014 news conference held during the annual meeting of the National People's Congress: "2014 is not 1914, still less 1894. . . . Instead of using Germany before the First World War as an object lesson, why not use Germany after the Second World War as a role model?" But this same foreign minister responded to a question from a Japanese reporter on the deterioration of China–Japan relations with a warning: for China, on two issues of principle—history and territory—"there is no room for compromise."[7]

---

[6] William Faulkner, *Requiem for a Nun* (New York: Random House, 1951), 92.
[7] Edward Wong, "China's Hard Line: 'No Room for Compromise,'" *The New York Times*, March 8, 2014, A4.

Fritz Stern, a German-American historian, calls the Great War "the first calamity of the 20th century, the calamity from which all other calamities sprang."[8] Its implications extend beyond China and Japan. The existence of two Koreas today is the result of the Second World War and Cold War, which grew directly out of the international pecking order established after the First World War. The greater problem of territorial tensions among Asian nation-states is another clear offshoot. The Indians and Chinese went to war in 1962 over border disputes, and people in both countries remain concerned that clashing interests will lead to another war. Disputes between Vietnam and China over South China Sea questions have often brought them into diplomatic or military clashes. The possibility of war in Asia exists today and reminds us of past relations there, especially during the First World War, which set the stage for Japan's fifteen-year (1931–45) incursion into China, the rise of communism in China, Korea, and Vietnam, and India's long journey to independence. Asians may not be aware of the Great War, but that war nonetheless shaped their modern fate in significant ways.

With both contemporary realities and the broad lack of historical understanding in mind, this book is designed to highlight Asians' multilayered involvement in and perspectives on the "great seminal catastrophe" of the twentieth century. This is long overdue. The war played a powerful role across the region, shaping national aspirations and development, foreign relations, and Asians' perceptions of themselves and the world. As Asia becomes increasingly influential in world affairs and the global economy, and as Asians continue to develop their national identities and possible new directions for national development, the role of the First World War may provide a key to many important issues puzzling us now.

KEY THEMES

Although it is titled *Asia and the Great War*, this book does not cover everything to do with the Great War and considers primarily the experiences of China, India, Japan, Korea, and Vietnam. Turkey is an Asian nation and was critically important in the Great War, but its story deserves its own volume.[9] Still, as A. E. Duchesne noted, Turkey played an indirect role in the story to be told here: It was important to India, since it could threaten Egypt and negatively influence British control of India.[10]

---

[8] Quoted from David Fromkin, *Europe's Last Summer: Who Started the Great War in 1914?* (New York: Vintage, 2005), 6.

[9] For recent works on the Ottoman Empire and the First World War, see Mustafa Aksakal, *The Ottoman Road to War in 1914: The Ottoman Empire and the First World War* (Cambridge: Cambridge University Press, 2008); Robin Prior, *Gallipoli: The End of the Myth* (New Haven: Yale University Press, 2009); Michael Reynolds, *Shattering Empires: The Clash and Collapse of the Ottoman and Russian Empires, 1908–1918* (Cambridge: Cambridge University Press, 2011); Donald Bloxham, *The Great Game of Genocide: Imperialism, Nationalism, and the Destruction of the Ottoman Armenians* (Oxford: Oxford University Press, 2005).

[10] A. E. Duchesne, *Asia and the War*. Oxford Pamphlets No. 59 (London: Oxford University Press, 1914), 3–4.

Other relevant East Asian regions such as Singapore,[11] Thailand (Siam), and Malaysia were all affected and even got involved in one way or another.[12] Unfortunately, they must be excluded due to space and thematic constraints. Instead, I examine cases that are most representative. The book focuses on one rising power (Japan), one country desperately trying to use the war to change its national fate (China), one British colony (India), one French colony (Indochina or Vietnam), and one Japanese colony (Korea). These five nations have long interacted and are related in many ways. Japan, China, Korea, Vietnam, and India as neighbors shared certain common cultural roots based in pre-modern China's imperial reach and the spread of Buddhism, through which they developed a flickering but certain sense of commonality. India and China maintained strong if sometimes indirect cultural contact. Buddhism, was introduced to China from India in late antiquity, and many Chinese poems, plays, and novels, both folk and elite, are steeped in Buddhism, and the language is rich with expressions translated from Indian culture. Buddhism from Korea and China soon became an important part of Japanese society, culture, and politics. Aside from the transmission of Buddhism, Japan had embraced and incorporated cultural knowledge from China in its literature, pre-modern political culture, and even the tea ceremony. Elites in Korea and Vietnam wrote in classical Chinese and their kingdoms remained Chinese tributary states until the late nineteenth century. In more recent times, they all tried to use the Great War to promote national development or international prestige, or both. Ironically, another uniting

---

[11] For instance, the surprise mutiny of Indian Army's 5th Light Infantry (made up entirely of Muslim troops) in Singapore on 15 February 1915 seems to be relevant to Asia and the Great War from the perspectives of both Singapore and India. In the confused fighting across the island during the mutiny, five Chinese and Malays died, but most of those killed were British men, targeted on the golf courses, and in cars and carriages by the rioting Indian soldiers. Japanese historian Sho Kuwajima suggested there might have been a connection between "pan-Islamism" and the anti-war feeling of the Indian soldiers through the mutiny. In the book *The Mutiny in Singapore: War, Anti War and the War for India's Independence*, Kuwajima demonstrated that there was deep Japanese involvement in the Indian mutiny and that Japan helped the British in the suppression of the mutiny, along with France and Russia. The history of the Indian mutiny in Singapore illustrated the international system for the suppression of the aspirations of Asian people for freedom. Kuwajima thus concluded that "In this sense, the suppression of the Mutiny was a part of the First World War." The mutiny offered the people of Singapore or the people of Asia "a chance to reconsider the First World War and freedom." For details, see Sho Kuwajima, *The Mutiny in Singapore: War, Anti War and the War for India's Independence* (New Delhi: Rainbow, 2006), 43, 91, 173. For more details on this topic, see Tim Harper, "Singapore, 1915, and the Birth of the Asian Underground," *Modern Asian Studies*, 47:6 (2013), 1782–811; R. W. E. Harris and Harry Miller, *Singapore Mutiny* (Singapore: Oxford University Press, 1984); Gajendra Singh, *The Testimonies of Indian Soldiers and the Two World Wars: Between Self and Sepoy* (London: Bloomsbury, 2014), 129–56.

[12] The Malaysian Sikhs were involved in the Great War through the Malay State Guides in Aden and the Singapore mutiny. However, a serious study of their participation in the war is still missing. Some institutions, such as the Centre of Hidden Histories at the University of Nottingham, are now funding research on this topic. Thailand's King Rama VI sent a 1,300-man Siamese expeditionary force to France in 1918 and a few of his soldiers even died there, though not as combat casualties. As Brendan and Suthida Whyte argue, Siamese involvement in the war was viewed at home as a crucial step towards its acceptance as an equal by other nations and important to its national development. See Brendan and Suthida Whyte, "The Inscriptions on the First World War Volunteers Memorial, Bangkok," *Journal of the Siam Society*, 96 (2008), 175–91; Brenda Whyte, "The Role of Siam in World War One," *Strategy and Tactics*, 245 (2007), 34–6.

force was the Eurocentric worldview that considered them all colored people, though Indians were distinct from the Chinese, Japanese, Vietnamese, and Koreans. By studying these countries and their peoples' responses to the First World War, I hope this book will convey how the war significantly shaped their thinking about themselves and the international system in the twentieth century, in addition to launching issues that continue to worry the region and the world at large.

The treatment of these five countries is not perfectly balanced for two reasons. First, the three colonial peoples (Indians, Koreans, and Vietnamese) did not control their own war policies or even their own fates, and thus they were not free to generate the discussions, debates, and independent policies around the war and the postwar world order as did the Chinese and Japanese. Second, the existing scholarship on these five countries varies greatly. We certainly need more research on Vietnam and Korea. In other words, this volume both highlights the dearth of research on some areas of the history and suggests directions for future research. Moreover, out of concern for thematic coherence, this book will largely focus on the Western Front and the experiences of the peoples who are my focus here. Many other important areas and issues, such as Indians in the Middle East and Africa, the Chinese in Russia, and the Chinese military intervention in Siberia will have to be left largely untouched.

Besides its narrow geographical focus, this book is intended more as a rumination on the shared journey and the war's impact on these Asian nations than a comprehensive narrative. In other words, the subtitle of this book—"A Shared History"—will actually serve as a true focus of this book. It moves beyond the national or even international level by trying to present history from non-national and transnational perspectives. I hope it will provoke response and stimulate debate. I also attempt to highlight the history that Asians and Westerners shared through their experiences of the Great War. I focus on the themes of expectations, observations, sufferings, and frustrations among Asians—these were to some extent shared by Europeans. As I have argued elsewhere, "Shared experiences or past encounters are something different from a shared journey, which presumes a common destination and mutual interest despite possible difficulties, challenges, and tribulations along the way."[13] But even given their many differences, the Chinese, Japanese, Indians, Vietnamese, and Koreans did indeed interact on many levels and had many things in common in their experiences of the Great War.

To weave together the diplomatic, social, political, cultural, and military histories of my key subjects in a comparative way, this book draws on primary sources such as personal letters, diaries, memoirs, and state records, as well as the latest secondary literature in English and Asian languages. It is a daunting undertaking to treat systematically all the major Asian combatant states and their experiences in the war, based heavily on materials from Asia. It will also address the crucial issue of how war experiences shaped the postwar search for modern national identities and new places for people of the region within a reconfigured world order.

---

[13] See Xu Guoqi, *Chinese and Americans: A Shared History* (Cambridge, MA: Harvard University Press, 2014), 1–22.

Like any study, this project has benefited enormously from existing scholarship, and I will highlight the most exciting research on the topic so far by scholars in Asia and the rest of the world. Contrary to conventional treatments of the Great War, discussion here will make clear how the conflict in Europe engaged Asians diplomatically, socially, politically, culturally, and even militarily. Unlike existing scholarship on Asia, I introduce an international/transnational history narrative of the Great War into our collective reflection on the war's legacy. I will also demonstrate how this war affected Asian countries in surprising and important ways. For example, Japan's interest in the European war was related to its ambition to subjugate China, while China's goal to enter the war, and especially the postwar peace conference, grew from its determination to keep Japan out. It has been fairly argued that a full understanding of either China or Japan requires bringing the other into account.[14] This observation rings especially true in the case of their engagement in the First World War, and perhaps with some variations a similar case can be made for all five nations under consideration. For instance, Koreans clearly wanted to use the Great War to break away from Japanese colonial rule, while the Vietnamese wanted to seek the assistance of the Chinese and Koreans to gain national independence.

The Great War marked a turning point in the national history of Asian countries: while Japan used the war strategically to join the ranks of the major Powers, China, India, Korea, and Vietnam all experienced the emergence of new movements propagating national self-determination and national renewal. But why was the European war viewed as an opportunity for the realization of those ambitions? Why did China eventually enter the war on the same side as Japan, its greatest rival in the region? While the Chinese voluntarily sent about 140,000 workers to France to help the Allied side, many Indians and Vietnamese soldiers and laborers went west to answer their respective colonial masters' call. What role did the European carnage and struggle play in India's eventual independence and democracy, and how did it plant the seeds of the eventual conversion of China and Vietnam to communism? Thousands of Asians died in the conflict, but was it worth it?

For most Asians, the journey to France was one of hardship and suffering. Seasickness, disease, poor conditions, and bad food were major complaints. Despite the fact that they went to support the British or French, or both, Chinese, Indians, and Vietnamese all suffered from European racism while in France. Kipling himself expressed the common imperial mixture of duty and contempt in his "The White Man's Burden" when he referred to Asians as "new-caught sullen peoples, | Half devil and half child." They were sunk in "sloth and heathen folly" and could only earn his respect when they met the standards of "manhood" invented by Kipling and his peers.[15]

---

[14] Joshua A. Fogel, *Articulating the Sinosphere: Sino-Japanese Relations in Space and Time* (Cambridge, MA: Harvard University Press, 2009), 1.

[15] Of course, one has to keep in mind that Kipling was a deeply ambivalent man on many issues and often spoke in many different voices.

Despite the hardships and racism, the Asians' experiences and direct contact with Westerners in Europe gave rise to new perceptions about Eastern and Western civilizations. In addition to the substantial human resources Asians contributed, they provided other important assistance to the Allied side as well. Although it is difficult to say whether Korea, India, or Vietnam benefited materially from the war due to their colonial status, both China and Japan did achieve certain economic advantages. Asian participation had made the war truly great and worldwide in scope, but more importantly, it contributed to the political development and identity of peoples across the region. The excitement among the war's Asian participants at the prospects of the postwar peace conference further indicates the war's importance there.

The five nations under consideration here shared soaring expectations for the war and humiliating disappointments in its aftermath. I will argue that those expectations and frustrations, and the disappointments of the postwar peace conference, were a striking collective experience, although few scholars have attempted comparative studies from this perspective. All five countries were enthusiastic about the new world order laid out in Woodrow Wilson's "Fourteen Points" speech. The relatively weak Chinese, Indians, Koreans, and Vietnamese hoped to gain an equal voice in their national destinies. And the Japanese expected that the Paris Peace Conference would seal their long-cherished aspirations to be recognized as the dominant Asian power and give their recently gained interests in China the international stamp of recognition. More importantly, the Japanese hoped that Western Powers would finally accept Japan as a full equal. The first ambition largely succeeded, though the Japanese were insulted by the hot protests of Chinese and Korean students, intellectuals, businessmen, and diplomats; the second was sorely disappointed.

The rejection of the racial equality provision Japan introduced to the treaty negotiations "contributed to deepening Japan's sense of disillusionment" on three other fronts: the continued Eurocentric bias of the League of Nations, the increasing Anglo-American solidarity in East Asia and the Pacific, and the 1924 US Alien Immigration Act.[16] Western responses to the provision blatantly demonstrated that Japan still did not enjoy equal footing with its Western counterparts. Japan remained outside the white power club and continued to share second-class status with fellow Asians, and this disillusionment may help account for her later go-alone policy and expansionist drive into China.

To make matters worse, Japan was experiencing something of a national identity crisis. While the Chinese found the nineteenth-century world order terribly wrong, unfair, and hostile, Japan had seen herself as the "pioneer of progress in the Orient" for successfully adopting the material advances of Western civilization with special determination to emulate Germany. But the war and new world order forced Japan to conclude that it might have followed the wrong model—after all, Germany was now a denounced and defeated nation.

---

[16] Naoko Shimazu, *Japan, Race, and Equality: The Racial Equality Proposal of 1919* (London: Routledge, 2009), 171.

   Chinese disappointment in Paris was much deeper, since China had pinned so
many hopes on the postwar world. The Chinese had been preparing for the peace
conference since 1915, because they knew their weak and disrespected country had
little other leverage with the Great Powers. With its official declaration of war
against Germany and the large Chinese Labour Corps sent to Europe to support the
Allies, China had earned its place at the conference, but only as a third-rank nation
having two seats, while Japan had five. In hindsight, Japanese success at the
conference automatically meant failure for China. Even so, the Chinese capitalized
on the opportunity and managed to inject substantially new content and perspectives into conference discussions. But they realized neither their dream of equality
among nations nor their desire to recover Shandong from Japan.

   For colonial India, Korea, and Indochina, Wilson's national self-determination
ideas generated great excitement. In 1919, Nguyen Ai Quoc (literally "Nguyen
who loves his country") first made his presence known in Paris. This largely
unknown Vietnamese from the colony would later become famous under the
name Ho Chi-minh. Ho was very active in Paris, and in September 1919 he
even had an audience with Albert Sarraut, the recently returned Governor-General
of Indochina. Sources suggest that many of Ho's ideas in 1919 were inspired by his
contacts with Korean nationalists in the United States and France; Ho is believed to
have borrowed heavily from the Korean independence movement.[17] The Great
War may not have had a significant impact on Korea, nor did it cause Koreans
significant economic hardship, but the ideas espoused in connection with the
postwar peace conference set up high expectations. The Indian nationalist
movement went through a sea change thanks to the war. The Indian National
Congress had been a pillar of the empire until 1914, but once the war was over,
it became a determined enemy. One can argue that India's experience in the
Great War and at the peace conference set it on the path toward full independence after the Second World War. From the perspective of shared experiences,
these Asian countries had all looked to the First World War to shake up
their variously uncomfortable status quo, but they all wound up disappointed
and disillusioned. Like India, Korea and Vietnam would have to wait until
after the Second World War to shake off colonialism and claim national self-
determination.

   Elites in all five nations were deeply affected by American President Woodrow
Wilson's blueprint for a new world order, which created a climate for national and
international debates about Asia's place in the postwar world. The shared disappointment over the Paris peace negotiations marked an important turning point for
Asia's relations with the West. These countries began a search for alternative paths
to independence, a process that set the stage for future conflicts, most notably
between Japan and China.

   Asia in the year 1919 in the wake of the European war was fundamentally
different from the Asia of 1914—socially, economically, intellectually, culturally,

---

[17] Sophie Quinn-Judge, *Ho Chi Minh: The Missing Years*, 1919–1941 (Berkeley: University of
California Press, 2003), 11–18.

and ideologically.[18] Erez Manela has written an excellent book on Wilson's ideas for the new world order and their impact on the Chinese, Indians, Koreans, and Egyptians. Inspired by and building from Manela's incisive arguments, this book emphasizes Asians' own ideas about the shape of the postwar world and the internal voices and forces that drove their responses to the postwar reality and efforts for change and transformation, with a special focus on the push from Asians themselves. I pay special attention to "Asian values" advocated by forceful thinkers such as Rabindranath Tagore in India and Liang Qichao in China, as well as many others in Japan. The broadly defined years of the Great War coincided with a period of tremendous change within Asia, as the old Confucian civilization began to collapse and China struggled to become a nation and sought to assume equal relations with the West. With the Great War, India started its long journey to independence and China embarked on a new journey, namely that of internationalization and national renewal. While China and Vietnam eventually followed communism after the war, the Great War led to the emergence of a Japan that had been transformed by the war and eventually took up military force to challenge the West.

The idea of a shared history across Asia in this period makes perfect sense: the war itself later came to be called a "world war" and it brought together people who would have otherwise had little chance to encounter each other. And not only was the Asian elite's experience of the war and national development shared in the sense that they gained inspiration locally and internationally—even the most marginalized of their countrymen, the workers and foot soldiers recruited from among the poor in China, India, and Indochina shared experiences of personal contact with foreign places and cultures, often under dire circumstances. I argue that although these nations and their respective connections with the war differed in many respects, there are strong parallels among them that add up to a collective journey.

Just how did the various Asian involvements make the Great War not only a true "world" war, but also a "great" war? How did the war generate forces that would transform Asia both internally and externally? Asian involvement in the First World War is a unique chapter in both Asian and world history. Asian participation transformed the meaning and implications of the broader conflict. We must consider why Asian elites viewed themselves as victims of the existing world order both before and during the war, and why those elites became both excited and anxious when news of the war's outbreak reached them. While the European powers, as Christopher Clark concludes, "were sleepwalkers, watchful but unseeing, haunted by dreams, yet blind to the reality of the horror they were about to

---

[18] Due to space constraints and thematic limitations, this book briefly mentions the war's economic impacts in Japan and Vietnam but does not discuss economic aspects in China, India, and Korea. There is enough evidence of the war's significant economic impact (both positive and negative) in all these countries. The major European powers' focus on the war resulted in their having less control on their colonial nations' economic development, such as in India and Vietnam, and contributed to economic growth in both nations. Wartime was a golden period especially for China and Japan, which benefited substantially in the areas of trade, shipping, and overall economic growth. Moreover, the Great War had fundamentally weakened European powers economically and even turned them into debtor countries to the United States. This development had further weakened Western control over Asia.

bring into the world," China and Japan quickly developed plans for their response to the conflict.[19] The First World War was in fact a defining moment that shaped worldviews and developments across Asia.

The Chinese twentieth century started with the broadly defined period of the Great War from 1895 to 1919. China's responses to and engagement in the war fully symbolized the beginning of China's long journey toward internationalization and brought China as a nation into the world. Its involvement in the war also brought China back into the larger world history of the twentieth century. Just as in the era of the Great War, China today is still searching for its new national identity and answers to the questions "What is China and who is Chinese?" Thanks to the aftermath of the Great War, China became a communist country, and in theory it still is. China today is both progressive and backward in the sense that when the Chinese people demand democracy and full integration into the world, the communist dictatorship tries hard to chain them in with censorship and political suppression. During the Great War and May Fourth Movement, the Chinese believed that "Mr. Democracy" and "Mr. Science" could save China. Today's China is still in urgent need of these two ministers, although the Chinese cry for freedom is much more muted compared to the widespread political activism and rise of public opinion during the earlier period. China's social transformation and cultural and political revolutions coincided with a war that provided the momentum and opportunity for China to redefine its relations with the world by injecting itself into the war effort. The war signaled the collapse of the existing international system and the coming of a new world order, an obvious development that fed China's desire to change its international status. The young republic's weakness and domestic political chaos provided strong motivation to enter and alter the international system.

The positions of Indochina and British India as colonies differed from those of China and Japan as independent states. In the Indochinese case, the outbreak of the war in Europe did not command much attention, and the discussions and deliberations regarding the impact of the war on the country were limited and inconsequential. But the Indochinese, like the Chinese, had been deeply affected by the ideas of social Darwinism at the turn of the twentieth century, which spurred them to seek a new direction for their country. Like Indochina, India's involvement in the war was largely a by-product of its inclusion in an empire, not a decision made with India's own interest in mind. India's colonial master at first did not imagine it would need Indian help. The fighting, after all, was primarily between European peoples. But the British soon realized that they would have to mobilize Indian resources if they hoped to survive the conflict. Indian involvement, even under British direction, was important to Indians for both their national development and external relations. The war thus opened some Indians' eyes to the outside world and allowed them to dream and set high expectations, as world politics were changing and their so-called mother country was engaged in a major war.

---

[19] Christopher Clark, *The Sleepwalkers: How Europe went to War in 1914* (New York: HarperCollins, 2013), 562.

Robert Gerwarth and Erez Manela wrote recently that:

> The First World War is hardly a neglected subject of historical research. Yet—understandably perhaps, given the centrality of the fighting in Western Europe—most of the literature produced over the past ninety years has focused on the events on the Western Front and their impact on Britain, France and Germany. Most of these histories proceed within two main assumptions: first that the war began with the sounding of the "guns of August" in 1914 and ended with the Armistice of 11 November 1918. Second, that the war was primarily one of nation-states, and that it was largely a European affair.[20]

This volume takes off from that thesis. The importance of Asia's non-nation-states in the Great War seems obvious. But though we know that personal, social, and transnational ideals and ideas played rather differently in Asia than in Europe, little has been written about how they fed into the aspirations and activities of those non-nation-states. I tease out these connections by examining the role of laborers from China and fighting men from India and Indochina in the war and within Western civilization. Apart from recounting the actual fighting that took place in China—notably the clashes that occurred in Chinese territories when German military forces stationed there were attacked by the British and Japanese—attention will be paid to the hundreds of thousands of Asian men who served (and often died) on the Western Front. One of the key ambitions of this book is to unearth and document the authentic voices of those men, whose lives and contributions in that conflict have been largely ignored. I will ask why India, Indochina, and China all sent men to Europe to help on the Allied side. What were the different experiences of those men in Europe in terms of their daily lives and work, their treatment, and their contributions to the war effort? Rather than being a standard military or diplomatic history, this book also presents the social, cultural, and international history of the Asian participation and response to the war.

Among the countries that participated in the war, China's involvement was perhaps the most unusual. The program to send Chinese laborers marked the first time in modern history that the Chinese government took the initiative in affairs distant from Chinese shores. Since the Great War was total war, fought on both the battlefield and the home front, it consumed massive numbers of fighting forces and other human resources. Staged in the West as a terrible trench war, the enormous human resources contributed by the Chinese, Indians, and Indochinese must be counted an important part of the war effort.

At the same time, the circumstances in each of these countries changed dramatically. During the war years, China struggled to come together as a nation and India started its long journey to independence. While China and Indochina would eventually follow a socialist path, in Japan, the war gave rise to a new sense of national pride that would eventually lead the Japanese to adopt military methods and challenge the West outright. Asian involvement in the war gave the Allied side

---

[20] For details on this point, see Robert Gerwarth and Erez Manela, "Introduction," in Robert Gerwarth and Erez Manela, eds., *Empires at War: 1911–1923* (Oxford: Oxford University Press, 2014), 1–16.

both moral prestige and a strategic and human resources advantage. The upshot of the First World War across Asia contained tragedy, paradoxes, and contradictions. The conflict was about imperial ambitions, but China destroyed its own empire in the course of becoming a republic and a nation-state. Japan used the war to strengthen its claim to empire status, while the Korean, Indian, and Indochinese experience inspired them to work toward throwing off their imperial masters and becoming independent.

The war produced defeats and victories. China had joined the side of victors but saw few rewards. Japan was a victor whose status in the world improved substantially, but its gains lit the fuse for its future destruction. The Great War brought about an end to the nineteenth-century world system and presented an opportunity for a general reordering of world affairs. Educated Asians understood that the Great War represented the moral decline of Europe, but the postwar world system could not dislodge the entrenched Powers and would deliver little in the war's immediate aftermath beyond collective disappointment.

CHAPTER SKETCHES: ASIAN INVOLVEMENTS AND THE SHARED JOURNEY

James Joll, in his classic book on the origins of the First World War, wrote that the conflict marked "the end of an era and the beginning of a new one."[21] This observation applied in Asia as well. Japan and China, with their strong expectations of imminent advantage, and India and Indochina, out of both colonial duty and budding nationalism, all became involved in the European war almost immediately. In terms of actual fighting, only the Indians and Indochinese took part by sending military forces. Japan's meager military support for its Allies made sense since its true motive was expanding its interests in China, not defeating Germany.[22] Because its true focus was China, the Japanese war effort immediately shifted once it had acquired formerly German Qingdao to concentrate on extending its reach across China. Chapter 1 sketches the situation in North Asia at the beginning of the Great War. The 1894 Sino-Japanese War made Japan a major power in the region and an empire with its first colony in Taiwan, which China was forced to cede. That war also laid the groundwork for Japan to acquire a second colony by forcing China to abandon suzerainty in Korea, traditionally a Chinese tributary state. Japan seemed bound for a major international military game as the new power in East Asia. By defeating China, Japan had become a rising Asian power. It was determined to become a leading global player and China's master while the European colonial powers were distracted by the war at home. Chapter 1 also reviews the battle for Qingdao to explain how the European war brought fighting to China and the parts the Indians, Chinese, and Japanese all played in that battle.

---

[21] James Joll, *The Origins of the First World War* (London: Longman, 1984), 1.
[22] Japan, however, provided crucial naval assistance to the Allied war effort during the war.

Chapter 2 focuses on how China and Japan each used the Great War to serve their own national and international interests. It argues that one cannot fully understand the importance of the First World War to Japan without realizing the central place of China in Japan's strategic participation. And if China was key to Japanese involvement, it follows that concern with Japanese intentions also drove China's efforts to enter the war. Chapter 2 goes further, to examine how the Chinese and Japanese war policies were intertwined. It highlights the strategic role and experiences of the Chinese Labour Corps in France. The 1911 Revolution forced the Chinese to pay new attention to changes in the world system, and the Great War was the first major event to engage the imagination of Chinese social and political elites. Changes in the Chinese worldview and the destabilizing forces loosed by the war set the stage for China to have a hand in world affairs, even though there seemed to be no immediate impact on China itself.[23] Chapter 2 pays special attention to issues such as how the Chinese and Japanese used the Great War to achieve national objectives; and how the Great War shaped the directions these two key Asian nations would take in the twentieth century. It will further argue that the Chinese and Japanese entry into the war followed much thinking and careful planning and reflected strategic calculation and long-term thinking. More importantly, their roads to war and experiences both during the war and in the postwar world can best be understood as two sides of the same coin.

Chapter 3 deals with India's contributions of military men and support labor. About 1.2 million Indian men arrived in France during the First World War either as soldiers or laborers to work under their colonial masters near the imperial motherland. This chapter explains how war experiences helped shape Indian understandings of their country's national fate and gave them new perspectives on British and on Western civilization. Race issues emerge here, too, through the perspectives of both Indian laborers and soldiers, and the British. There exists a large literature on India and the Great War, but my discussion spotlights the kinds of experiences Indians shared with fellow Asians. To do this, I focus more on the underprivileged classes and individual voices, and rely on comparisons between the Indian story and that of other Asian nations.

Chapter 4 discusses Indochinese involvement and the war's impact on the eventual national awakening. During the war, the colonies of Tonkin, Cochin China, and Annam, which make up present day Vietnam, contributed nearly 100,000 soldiers and laborers to serve with the French against the Germans. It explores how their contributions and experiences shaped their collective thinking about the history and prospects of their homeland as a nation and as a colony, and their collective dreams for independence. Special attention will be paid to people like Ho Chi-minh, their observations and reflections on the Great War,

---

[23] For the most recent study on the Great War and its long-term impact on Japan, see Frederick Dickinson, "Toward a Global Perspective of the Great War: Japan and the Foundations of a Twentieth-Century World," *American Historical Review*, 119:4 (October 2014), 1154–83; Frederick Dickinson, *World War I and the Triumph of a New Japan, 1919–1930* (Cambridge: Cambridge University Press, 2013).

emerging Indochinese nationalism, and why the war was a turning point for colonial Vietnam.

Chapter 5 studies the war's impact on Korean national independence movements. Unlike India, Japan, Vietnam, or China, the war had little direct impact on the population of the Korean peninsula. Koreans did not get involved in war, nor were they much interested in it. Nonetheless, the war marks a turning point in Korean history because it gave rise to Wilsonian promises of a new world order to be worked out after the war. When Korean nationalists learned of President Woodrow Wilson's Fourteen Points address and his subsequent declarations in January 1918, they were, like the Chinese and Indians, thrilled at the prospect and its implications for the future of Korea. Many Korean nationalists recognized "the Wilsonian moment" as an unprecedented opportunity for Korea and decided to take quick action to make the most of it. Chapter 5 emphasizes the extraordinary journey Koreans shared with fellow Asians to shape their own national development.

Chapter 6 examines the roles of the Japanese and Chinese delegates and lobbyists at the Paris Peace Conference. Although few scholars pay much attention to their role, this chapter argues that even the Japanese were eager to help shape a new world order after the war. They expected the postwar settlement to seal their position as the dominant Asian power and recognize Japan's developing interests in China. Japanese leaders hoped that Western Powers would see Japan as an equal now that "proud, confident, rich Europe had torn itself to pieces."[24] The overriding Chinese goal, of course, was to recover what Japan had taken away and was determined to keep. Chapter 6 further explains how the Chinese and Japanese each were disappointed by the peace negotiations and the resulting Treaty of Versailles.

Chapter 7 follows the handling of Japan's racial equality provision as that unfolded at the Paris Peace Conference. It argues that the Japanese greeted their victories in Paris with mixed feelings. True, Japan was one of the top five Powers at the peace conference, but its proposal for legal racial equality in the postwar world order was bluntly rejected, even ignored. When the delegation returned home, crowds protested their failure on the provision. Still, the Japanese saw no contradiction in treating Koreans as inferior people both in Japan and in Korea, so the problem was a complicated one. The race issue is certainly a painful shared history among the Japanese and their fellow Asians; all of them faced discrimination during their time in Europe, never mind dealing with the colonials at home. When Japan faced a choice between promoting international racial equality and making territorial gains, it went with the latter, since the former had proved difficult for Japanese elites to accept, much less achieve.

Chapter 8 concentrates on the boundary-crossing movement of ideas and the development of pan-Asianism during and after the war. Many Asians, probably most, saw the Great War as simply a war of white people, a European war, and a war between Western countries. But they got involved, and the war and its

[24] Margaret MacMillan, *Paris 1919: Six Months that Changed the World* (New York: Random House, 2002), xxv.

aftermath forced them to think about who they were and what kind of positions they held in the world. Indians, Chinese, and Japanese were all consumed with rethinking the relationship between Asia and the West, between Eastern civilizations and Western civilizations, and what direction they should move in after the war. The war and its destruction had discredited the moral values of Western civilization, and what happened at the Paris Peace Conference fundamentally diminished Asians' expectations and respect for the Western Powers. Chapter 8 addresses the cultural effects and civilizational significance of the Great War for Asians.

* * *

Today, memory, forgetfulness, and even willful amnesia around the Great War in Asia betray the still preliminary state of efforts to capture its significance.[25] Western images and perceptions of Asians and Asian countries and their involvement with the war are likewise muddled. Due to the traumatic political histories of China and Vietnam, the colonial legacy in India and Korea, and the war responsibility issues in Japan, views of the Great War in these participating nations have been distorted. This book is meant to be a step in recovering memories of the war and re-evaluating the war in its Asian contexts. I hope to thereby advance the process of recovering its broader "world" significance and meanings.

---

[25] For an excellent study on the memory of the war in general, see Jay Winter, *Remembering War: The Great War between Memory and History in the Twentieth Century* (New Haven: Yale University Press, 2006).

PART I

THE GREAT WAR AS SHARED HISTORY IN CHINA AND JAPAN

1

The Great War Comes to Asia, 1895–1914

From Shimonoseki to Qingdao

"The Guns of August" in Europe echoed immediately in Asia. German concessions in and around Qingdao, a key city in Shandong, tantalized China, which wanted to regain them, and troubled Great Britain, which initially wanted to keep them out of Japanese hands. The two powers most concerned were Germany, which wanted to retain its colonial territory, and Japan, which wanted to acquire them. The outbreak of war in Europe thus ignited war fever half a world away. A battle involving many nations soon erupted in German-held Qingdao and was quickly settled in favor of Japan. The war's only battle on Eastern Asian soil was a multinational contest with roots in the previous generation and consequences for the following ones. This chapter explores why this peninsula in China's northeast became a battleground and how Japan took advantage of the European conflict to raise its international strategic position, bolster its domestic regime, and establish a dominant position in China.

THE WAR BEFORE THE WAR

The Sino-Japanese War of 1894–5, the first modern conflict between China and Japan, was at the root of their participation in the Great War. Having witnessed the humiliation of the Qing Manchu Empire after the Opium War in the 1840s, Japanese reformist elites decided to join the Western system and launch the Meiji Restoration of 1868. In less than a generation, Japan turned into a Western-style nation, even following the pattern of expansion and empire building with the acquisition of Okinawa and the Ryukyu Islands. The new elites became so confident that they eagerly took on the Qing Empire, formerly the economic and cultural giant of the region. The military campaign that began in 1894 soundly defeated China within a year. This made Japan the major power in East Asia and an empire with its first colony, Taiwan, which China was forced to cede. That war also laid the groundwork for Japan to acquire a second colony when it forced China to abandon Korea, traditionally a Chinese tribute state. Meiji Japan considered its control of Korea "a serious matter for Japan's National Polity," as General Terauchi Masatake, the Japanese Governor-General of Korea, would later declare.[1] In another

---

[1] Dickinson, "The Japanese Empire," in Gerwarth and Manela, eds., *Empires at War*, 200.

upshot of that war, the Chinese government was forced to pay Japan an indemnity of 360 million yen, which not only defrayed Japan's war expenses (about 247 million yen), but also provided funds for the construction of the Yawata Iron Works, the first modern factory built in the Meiji era.[2]

Yet the sweet victory led to a sour confrontation. Nineteenth-century European diplomacy maintained a balance of power by a series of shifting alliances. When one power seemed about to become predominant, its allies would make new treaties or agreements to prevent it. There were no major wars in Europe after the Treaty of Vienna in 1815 and this relative stability allowed the European powers to turn their attention to renewed overseas expansion. This "diplomacy of imperialism" structured international relations when Japan became an imperial power in 1895, but alliances between the nations of the Entente and the future Central Powers were beginning to solidify rather than shift. From that moment, Japan was determined to join the world as a leading player in international politics and seemed bound to take part in a major military gambit.

But Western countries resisted allowing Japan to upset the balance of power in East Asia. In what came to be known as the Triple Intervention, Russia, France, and Germany "advised" Japan that it should not take control of the Liaodong Peninsula even though the Treaty of Shimonoseki had awarded it. This infuriated the Japanese, who became determined to find a way to take action against Germany. One Japanese newspaper's headline, "Wait for another time," clearly conveyed this sentiment.[3] And as Baron Katō, the Japanese foreign minister, explained to an American journalist in 1915:

> Germany is an aggressive European Power that had secured a foothold on one corner of the province of Shan-tung [Shandong]. This is a great menace to Japan. Furthermore, Germany forced Japan to return the peninsula of Liao-tung [Liaodong] under the plausible pretense of friendly advice. Because of the pressure brought to bear on us, Japan had to part with the legitimate fruits of war, bought with the blood of our fellow countrymen. Revenge is not justifiable, either in the case of an individual or a nation; but when, by coincidence, one can attend to this duty and at the same time pay an old debt, the opportunity certainly should be seized.[4]

In preparation for its showdown with Germany, Japan achieved a major diplomatic coup in 1902 when it signed an alliance treaty with Britain. In theory, the Anglo-Japanese alliance required Japan to remain in "strict neutrality" should Great Britain become involved in a war with another Power. But for Japan, the 1902 treaty, which was renewed in 1911 for another ten years, actually set the diplomatic stage for its eventual entry into the Great War. On the basis of the Anglo-Japanese alliance, Japan managed to insert itself on the Allied side when war broke out in

[2] Akira Iriye, *China and Japan in the Global Setting* (Cambridge, MA: Harvard University Press, 1992), 19.

[3] S. C. M. Paine, *The Sino-Japanese War of 1894–1895: Perceptions, Power, and Primacy.* (Cambridge: Cambridge University Press, 2003), 290.

[4] Samuel G. Blythe, "Banzai—and Then What?" *The Saturday Evening Post*, 187:47 (1915), 54.

1914. Against this background, one might say that Japan had been preparing for this opportunity since its war with China in 1895.

Germany's role in the Triple Intervention revealed its own ambition to expand in East Asia. When they joined the Triple Intervention in 1895, the Germans had their own agenda, planning to secure concessions in China, and their eyes soon turned to Qingdao. The German Asiatic squadron, in search of a suitable naval base and maritime harbor, had made extensive cruises along the Chinese coast and an official German commission had recommended the Jiaozhou Bay as the most desirable spot. Germany only needed an excuse or an occasion to achieve this cherished goal.

The excuse and the occasion soon appeared. When in 1897 two German missionaries were murdered in Shandong Province, the German Kaiser immediately responded by ordering an expeditionary force of four German men-of-war to the coast of Jiaozhou Bay and occupied the territory. In the face of imminent danger from German troops on Chinese territory, the imperial Court in Beijing was constrained to conclude the Convention of March 6, 1898, which forced China to lease Jiaozhou Bay to Germany for ninety-nine years. Qingdao, then known as Tsingtao, was the crucial port in this new German concession. Under the same Convention, Germany also obtained the concession to construct two railway lines in Shandong and to develop mining properties for a distance of 15 kilometers on each side of these railways. The Chinese, however, had responsibility and thus jurisdiction for the protection of the Qingdao–Jinan Railway. Two German companies, The Mining Company of Shandong and the Company for the Development of Mines and Industries, had their headquarters at Qingdao and exploited the coal, gold, lead, and mica mines in the district. The Germans also set up a German-Chinese silk factory and the Anglo-German Brewery, which produced the world-famous Tsingtao beer. Qingdao was linked to Tianjin, Shanghai, and other major cities by sea and rail and this made Qingdao both economically and strategically important. Shipping out of Qingdao in 1913 alone amounted to 930 vessels representing a total of 1,300,000 tons.

German colonies in Asia and the Pacific "were all nerve centres, presenting their impressions to the central brain at Berlin."[5] The Kaiser himself selected Qingdao as the most important among these nerve centers. As German Foreign Minister Bernhard von Bülow put it, Qingdao was a center from which Germany could wield "a decisive influence on the future of the Far East."[6] From the very beginning, Qingdao was designed as a military base to protect German interests in Asia, and especially East Asia. As far as the German Admiralty was concerned, in the ten years before the beginning of the Great War, Qingdao was "to serve as the major imperial naval base for operations that would be carried out against the European enemies in Far Eastern waters."[7]

[5] H. C. O'Neill, *The War in Africa and in the Far East* (London: Longmans, Green and Co., 1919), 12.
[6] O'Neill, *The War in Africa and in the Far East*, 16.
[7] Edwin P. Hoyt, *The Fall of Tsingtao* (London: A. Barker, 1975), 7.

The Germans clearly valued these Chinese concessions and invested in extensive development to make Qingdao a base for their Pacific squadron and a thriving commercial port. During the period from 1898 to 1914, the Germans spent not less than 162,480,000 marks on their concession. They built churches, schools, banks, a casino, and civil and military administrative buildings. Qingdao was home to a large number of foreigners and a beach resort in the summer heat. As a reflection of Qingdao's importance to Germany, it was the only German possession in the Pacific that had permanent defenses prior to 1913. At that time, Qingdao's population comprised 1,855 Germans and Austrians, 214 Americans, 327 Japanese, and about 52,000 Chinese, not counting the garrison of 2,300 Germans regularly stationed there.[8]

In early August 1914, to prepare for possible attacks by the British and Japanese, the Germans transported additional troops from Beijing and Tianjin to Qingdao. Interestingly enough, eighty-five men of the Austro-Hungarian regular troops in Beijing also joined the German troops in Qingdao. At the outbreak of hostilities, Germany had 3,710 soldiers, 1,424 reservists and volunteers, 150 native auxiliaries, and 681 sailors landed from the ships. The total defensive force was 5,965, including both Austro-German soldiers and reservists.[9] Germany even had a small air force of two planes, but one of them was lost in a crash that August. When the European war broke out, German control of Qingdao ensured immediate war in Asia.

CHINA'S DESTINY AND THE 1894–5 WAR

The 1895 defeat meant many things. If the war set the game in motion for Japan's involvement in the Great War and Germany's expanded interests in East Asia, it also sealed the fate of the Manchu dynasty and imperial China. It subjected parts of the country to direct foreign control, but its psychological impact was even greater. Han Chinese elites were forced to think seriously about their destiny and the value of their civilization; more importantly, it caused them to question their inherited identity. Liang Qichao, the formative thinker of the late Qing and early Republican period, wrote that the war awakened China from "the four thousand year great dream."[10] The influential translator of Western political philosophy, Yan Fu, wrote in 1895 that the impact of the Sino-Japanese War "will be so serious and significant that one might argue that China has not experienced an equivalent upheaval since the Qin dynasty," that is, since the unification of the country in 221 BCE. Yan was perhaps the first to use the phrase "national salvation" to awaken his countrymen to the seriousness of the situation.[11]

  [8] Japanese report on "Siege of Tsing-Tao," BA: WO 106/5517.
  [9] Japanese report on "Siege of Tsing-Tao," BA: WO 106/5517.
  [10] Liang Qichao, "Gai Ge Qi Yuan (The Origins of Reform)," in *Yinbing Shi Heji* (Beijing: Zhong hua shu ju, 1989), 113.
  [11] Wang Shi, ed., *Yan Fu Ji (Collections of Yan Fu's Writings)*, vol. 3 (Beijing: Zhong hua shu ju, 1986), 521.

The loss to Japan was a turning point and shared point of reference for Chinese perceptions of themselves and the world. Chinese elites, no matter what their attitude to their tradition and civilization, agreed that if China was not to perish, it would have to change. Thus, "change" became a buzzword whose synonym was first "reform" and then "revolution." With the 1911 Revolution, the venerable dynastic system disappeared and a republic was established on the model of France, with an army and bureaucracy on the model of Japan. When the Republic did not produce adequate change, elites demanded further major social and cultural trans-formations. The Great War and its effects in Asia provided the momentum and opportunity for China to redefine its relations with the world. Domestically, the clash of ideas, political theories, and the new prescription of national identity stimulated ideological, social, cultural, and intellectual creativity, and all these engendered a strong determination for further change.

New ideologies, explanations of history, and even reactions to developments in the Great War abounded and could be found in new print media across the country. The appearance of new political ideologies (nationalism rather than Confucianism; nation-state, instead of cultural definitions of collective life), the return to China of students trained in the West and in Japan, the activism of a new bourgeois class based on commercial wealth (rather than the old gentry and traditional mandarins based at least in theory on education), the emergence of a public sphere and modern print media, and, above all, the changing international system together all pushed China toward self-renewal and reinventing itself as a modern nation. At no other time in modern Chinese history has the mobilization of public opinion and its social and intellectual resources played such a crucial role in shaping China's political, cultural, and social directions. At no time previously had educated Chinese shown such enormous interest in international affairs or initiated a diplomacy aimed at renewing the state and preparing its entry onto the world stage. The Great War was the first major world event to engage the imagination of these new social and political elites, and it generated innovation and excitement. Just as in Japan after the Meiji Restoration, emerging worldviews and the destabilizing forces let loose by the war created a deep and irreversible ambition among the new elites to play a role in world affairs and to legitimize their domestic roles by success in that sphere.

Probably the key change after the 1895 war was the new power of public opinion. Prior to the Sino-Japanese War, there had been no independent political press in China, and indeed no "public" to read it. The war changed that, presenting new opportunities for the vigorous development of Chinese journalism. The rise of public opinion in politics started with the so-called public vehicle petition (*gongche shangshu*) organized by Kang Youwei. In April 1895, 8,000 provincial degree holders who had assembled in Beijing for the triennial national civil service examination learned that the Qing government had accepted the disastrous 1895 Treaty of Shimonoseki. Shocked, they mobilized to flood the Qing court with petitions demanding reforms, and further broke with tradition by organizing study societies and launching independent political newspapers that would introduce their voices into national politics. As Bao Tianxiao remembered it, after the

Sino-Japanese War, "Chinese nationalism had been aroused. The increasing attention to the national fate and nationalism helped shape Chinese attitudes toward
foreign affairs. Most educated people, who had never before discussed national
affairs, now began to ask: Why are others stronger than we are, and why are we
weaker?"[12] With expanded access to new information on national and foreign
affairs, many Chinese, even in the urban working class, began to demonstrate an
interest in foreign policy and eventually became what we can consider a true foreign
policy public. Their weapons of choice would be petitions, wall posters, public
demonstrations, boycotts, and strikes against foreign goods and companies. In
1900, there were virtually no national public demonstrations in support of the
Boxer Movement against Christians and foreign imperialists, but by 1905, there
were well-organized and sharply focused mass protests against American immigration laws. Although Yuan Shikai, as President of the Republic, was the target of
public denunciation for not standing up to the Twenty-one Demands of the
Japanese in 1915, his Ministry of Foreign Affairs in fact fought skillfully to represent China's needs using the new tools of international law and public opinion.[13]

Even given its weakness and chaos after Yuan's death in 1916, Chinese in the north
and south, in the government, and in the streets were determined to prevent Japan
from seizing Qingdao and further expanding its interest across Chinese territory.
The Chinese government and political elites had hoped to join the Great War as
soon as it broke out. In consequence, the war would become an important pivot
around which politics, diplomacy, foreign relations, and popular perceptions about
what it meant to be Chinese were worked out. If the war was a watershed in China's
self-reinvention and efforts to rise in the world, that legacy would also include
shaping Chinese perceptions of the world order and the West. The formal declaration of a Republic in February 1912 had meant that, rather than follow the
Japanese model into the modern world (constitutional monarchy on the German
model), the supporters of the new government had veered toward the other
newcomer to Asian politics, the United States. The Revolution forced the Chinese
to pay new attention to changes in the world system, and the Great War was the
first major event to engage the imagination of Chinese social and political elites.
Changes in the Chinese worldview and the destabilizing forces loosed by the war set
the stage for China to gain a foothold in world affairs, even though there seemed to
be little immediate impact in China itself. China, like Japan, expected to gain
substantial advantages from the war.

Following China's 1895 defeat, the great European empires and the United
States came to consider East Asia one of the last great arenas for imperial expansion.
Although the situation in China constituted informal, not formal, empire—in the
form of concessions, which were formal enough, though legally short of
sovereignty—the power scramble for property and resources, especially along the
China seaboard, had been seen by all European powers as an important colonial

---

[12] Bao Tianxiao, *Chuan yin lou hui yi lu* (Hong Kong: Da hua chu ban she, 1971), 145.
[13] Guanhua Wang, *In Search of Justice: The 1905–1906 Chinese Anti-American Boycott* (Cambridge,
MA: Harvard University Asia Center, distributed by Harvard University Press, 2001).

opportunity. And indeed, in the years after the Shimonoseki Treaty, Western commercial expansion there only intensified. As the American writer Brooks Adams pointed out in 1895, "Eastern Asia is the prize for which all the energetic nations are grasping."[14] On the eve of the war in 1914, the Powers largely controlled China's economic fate, and a durable European global hegemony seemed assured. It did not take much imagination to realize that the outbreak of general war in Europe was bound to have dramatic effects in the East. Japanese initiatives undertaken in 1914 constituted its first systematic entrance into this global game.

JAPAN'S ROAD TO THE GREAT WAR

Japan had long been determined to become an equal player in international politics and soon developed the ambition first to prevent any other power from dominating the Chinese mainland and Inner Asia, then to dominate China's domestic economy and control Chinese politics. But it was not yet able to fulfill its ambitions without allies, and so when the European war broke out in August 1914, many Japanese saw it as a great opportunity. Elder statesman Inoue Kaoru hailed the news as "divine aid in the new Taisho era for the development of the destiny of Japan."[15] The Cabinet of Okuma Shigenobu declared, "Japan must take the chance of a millennium" to "establish its rights and interests in Asia."[16] The biggest payoff for Japan would be to kick the Germans out of Asia altogether.

China at that point was engaged in the messy process of becoming a republic as part of the road to renewal and self-strengthening in the face of modern threats. Dominant factions in Japan were determined to make China a dependent before that transformation could be completed. Under the Anglo-Japanese alliance of 1902 (renewed in 1905 and again in 1911), Japan was not obliged to declare war on Germany in 1914. Britain initially did not want the Japanese involved in the war effort and was only interested in Japanese naval support against an attack on Hong Kong or Weihaiwei. From the British perspective, Japanese help was to be limited in scope and defined at the convenience of Great Britain. As early as August 3, the day before declaring war, British Foreign Secretary Edward Grey wrote to Sir Conyngham Greene, Britain's ambassador to Japan, that "at present moment, when war with Germany is a possibility, it might be well for you to warn Japanese Government that if hostilities spread to Far East, and an attack on Hong Kong or Wei-hai Wei were to take place, we should rely on their support."[17] The First Lord

[14] Cited in Akira Iriye, *Across the Pacific: An Inner History of American-East Asian Relations* (Chicago: Imprint Publications, 2005), 77.

[15] Frederick Dickinson, *War and National Reinvention: Japan in the Great War, 1914–1919* (Cambridge, MA: Harvard University Press, 1999), 35.

[16] Ikuhiko Hata, "Continental Expansion, 1905–1941," in John W. Hall, ed., *The Cambridge History of Japan* (Cambridge: Cambridge University Press, 1988), 6: 279.

[17] Edward Grey to Sir C. Greene, August 3, 1914, in BA: China: General Operation Telegrams, 1914: July 21 to September 25, ADM 137/11.

of the Admiralty, Winston Churchill, however, asked the Foreign Office to tell the Japanese government of his "warmest appreciation of the readiness of the Japanese government to help us." Churchill and others were concerned not to lose trade or influence in China and wanted to keep a restraining hand on Japan by agreeing to Japanese wishes. On August 5, Britain asked the Japanese to help protect their merchant vessels from German cruisers.[18]

None of the future Allies initially intended to invite Japan to join the war. Even the neutral Americans opposed Japanese intervention in Asia. The major concern for the European powers was that Japanese assistance might turn into full-blown involvement. Still, the risk had to be taken. As Grey stated in an August 6, 1914 instruction to Conyngham Greene in Tokyo: "As our warships will require some time to locate and destroy the German warships in Chinese waters, it is essential that the Japanese should hunt out and destroy the German armed merchant cruisers who are attacking our commerce now. If the Japanese Government would employ some of their warships in this way it would be of the very greatest assistance to us. It means, of course, an act of war against Germany, but we do not see how this is to be avoided."[19]

Japan had little at stake in the European war but was determined to squeeze itself into the conflict and did not give its British ally an option. As early as September 3, 1914, Ambassador Greene informed London that the Japanese government had no interest in sending military forces to Europe, with the following explanation: "It was not the province of forces recruited to the Japanese army as by obligatory service for defence of their own country to act as professional soldiers in European countries of which they had no knowledge and in which they took no interest."[20] Japan simply would not pick British chestnuts out of European fires, and despite the enthusiasm of French politicians such as Georges Clemenceau, the Japanese never sent troops to the Western Front. Japan's primary interest in the war was to expand in China and to that end it would inject itself into the war in its own way. This was why instead of providing the requested limited naval support, Japan suggested involvement on a larger scale than Grey had initially wanted. Japanese participation was to be based on the broad, perhaps even vague, grounds that they should be allowed to take such action as the development of events necessitated. Regardless of Britain's invitation, Japan would take action only to achieve its own goals. And if Britain declined to cooperate, the British worried that they not only "thereby placed the Japanese in sole possession of German concessions in China, but would forfeit the present warm sympathy of this country and impair value of the alliance."[21] In other words, no matter what Britain wanted Japan to do, Japan was determined to seize the moment to have a war with Germany.[22]

---

[18] Madeleine Chi, *China Diplomacy, 1914–1918* (Cambridge, MA: East Asian Research Center, distributed by Harvard University Press, 1970), 6.

[19] China: General Operation Telegrams, 1914: July 21 to September 25, BA: ADM 137/11.

[20] China: General Operation Telegrams, 1914: July 21 to September 25, BA: ADM 137/11.

[21] China: General Operation Telegrams, 1914: July 21 to September 25, BA: ADM 137/11.

[22] For details on this point, see J. Charles Schencking, "The Imperial Japanese Navy and the First World War: Unprecedented Opportunities and Harsh Realities," in Toshiro Minohara, Tze-Ki Hon,

Against this background, on August 6, 1914, two days after the British Declaration of War, the Japanese government informed Ambassador Greene that it was "favorable" to joining the war and would seek the emperor's approval immediately. It was clear that Japan had been preparing to attack Qingdao as it deliberated over its war policy. According to Greene, who then reported to London, "Owing to advanced stage of Japanese preparations," it might make sense for Britain to cooperate with Japan in a joint military action against the Germans in Qingdao. Greene added that it seemed likely Japan would make use of the present occasion to consolidate her footing in China, "and it appears to me therefore that it would be useful for future purposes that we should co-operate with her now either alone or with a French landing force if available, and above would seem to be the only possible way of doing so in the time still at our disposal."[23]

The Japanese foreign minister, Katō Takaaki, advised the Cabinet that involvement in the Asian end of the conflict promised great gain and low risk. Britain was likely to win and even if Britain lost, Germany could hurt Japan little. Katō hoped to mop up Germany's regional possessions, notably the leased naval base at Qingdao and the German North Pacific islands. He also envisaged supplementary advantages. The distraction of the European Powers meant Japan could profit from the chaos developing in China to consolidate its position on the Asian mainland. Further, Russia's pre-1914 military buildup had alarmed the Japanese leaders, and raising the level of Japanese belligerence could make getting rearmament through a recalcitrant legislature an easier project. In other words, Japan's participation can be explained by a combination of incentive, opportunity, and domestic politics.

The European war was also a national rallying point in Japanese domestic politics.[24] The death of the Meiji emperor in 1912 brought an era to an end and weakened the political regime. Japan lost its national purpose in the post-Meiji years, and its entry into the war would instill some sense of higher purpose in the Japanese people; it would allow them to return to "simplicity and purity" and redefine Japan as a nation. Joining the Great War thus helped Japan achieve three goals: revenging itself on Germany, expanding its interests in China, and rejuvenating its domestic politics. In 1912, elder statesman Marquis Inoue Kaoru had a variety of items on his wish list for the reign of the new Taishō Emperor. Among his priorities, and those of most Japanese policymakers by the autumn of 1914, was a systematic promotion of Japanese interests in China.

On August 8, four days after Britain joined the war, the Japanese government decided to declare war on Germany, though the official declaration was not announced for another week. This quick decision surprised even the elder statesman Yamagata Aritomo, since it had been orchestrated by Foreign Minister Katō, who guided it practically single-handedly through the Cabinet. Britain's initiative

and Evan Dawley, eds., *The Decade of the Great War: Japan and the Wider World in the 1910s* (Leiden; Boston: Brill, 2014), 83–106.

[23] China: General Operation Telegrams, 1914: July 21 to September 25, BA: ADM 137/11.

[24] For the best study on this issue, see Dickinson, *War and National Reinvention*; Dickinson, *World War I and the Triumph of a New Japan*.

provided a suitable occasion for intervention because of the importance the Japanese elder statesmen (the *Genrō*) attached to their alliance with the British, but these men had needed some convincing about the merits of belligerency. Yet had this occasion not succeeded, another most likely would have been found. Indeed, Japan entered the war with little hesitation following Britain's formal request for aid on August 7. Although Japanese insistence on doing more than Britain had requested made Edward Grey reluctant and suspicious, his hand was forced. The British government eventually decided to work with Japan and therefore took joint and combined action against Qingdao. As Grey told John Jordan, who was British minister to China on August 10, "Feeling in Japan, inflamed by memory of German intervention in 1895, cannot be restrained . . . Japan will be obliged to take action whether we co-operate or not."[25] Clearly, the Chinese and British both understood Japan's true intentions.

The Japanese government stated in the declaration of war that in consequence of aggressive action on the part of Germany, and in view of the fact that the general peace in the region of Eastern Asia was threatened, and also that her special interests were jeopardized, Great Britain had requested the support of Japan, and that the latter had acceded to this request. Simultaneously, the official announcement was made that the Japanese fleet had been fueled and was ready to put to sea. "Japan," said the Tokyo Foreign Office, "will take the necessary measures to discharge her obligations under the treaty with Great Britain."[26] On August 15, the Japanese delivered an ultimatum to Germany with the following preamble: "Considering it highly important and necessary in present situation to take measures to remove all causes of disturbance to the peace of the Far East, and to safeguard the general interests contemplated by agreement of alliance between Japan and Great Britain in order to secure a firm and enduring peace in Eastern Asia, the establishment of which is the ambitious aim of the said agreement, the Imperial Japanese Government sincerely believes it their duty to advise to Imperial German Government to carry out the following propositions."[27] Although Grey was not happy with the Japanese terms in the ultimatum, he thought it was "useless to criticize" at this time.[28]

Japan's official ultimatum to Germany in 1914 suspiciously resembled the "friendly advice" Germany had submitted to Japan during the Triple Intervention of 1895. Just as Germany had pressured Japan, Japan now "advised" Germany to withdraw her warships and hand over Qingdao. The similar wording clearly demonstrates the depth of Japanese bitterness about Germany's role in the intervention and establishes a direct link between the 1895 war and the Great War. Japan now demanded: (1) the withdrawal of all warships from the Far East, or failing this, their disarmament; and (2) the restoration to China through the intermediary of Japan, by September 15, the territory of Jiaozhou, unconditionally

[25] Edward Grey to J. Jordan (Peking), Foreign Office, August 10, 1914, BA: ADM 137/11.
[26] Greene to Grey, August 6, 1914, BA: ADM 137/11.
[27] Greene to Edward Grey, August 15, 1914, BA: ADM 137/11.
[28] Edward Grey to Greene, August 16, 1914, BA: ADM 137/11.

and without indemnity. The Germans were to provide their answer by the afternoon of August 23.[29] At the German refusal to comply, the Japanese launched an attack. As Frederick Dickinson points out, if the Europeans plunged into the war in defense of empire, Imperial Japan had now entered clearly anticipating not only the defense, but the formidable expansion of its imperial might.[30]

Indeed, the lengths to which members of the Entente and the Central Powers would go to pursue Japanese aid and support is astonishing and exemplifies, again, the global stakes of the conflict. The German ambassador to Japan, Count Graf von Rex, was so distressed by the prospect of Japan supporting the Entente that in an audience with Foreign Minister Katō, he broke the chair upon which he was sitting and almost tumbled to the floor. German and Austrian representatives in European capitals approached Japanese representatives several times during the first two years of the war over the possibility of working out a separate peace. The Germans were angry at the British for getting the Japanese into the war, since they thought the Great War was a European affair, to be fought between European nations. The German ambassador to the United States condemned the British for "seeking help from yellow men."[31]

According to the Japanese military authorities, by the terms of her alliance with Great Britain, Japan had engaged herself to maintain peace in the Far East. Not only was Qingdao calculated to serve as a naval base that would enable Germany to interfere with Britain commerce in the Pacific, but the existence of the port constituted to Japan herself a permanent direct threat.[32] So the Japanese focused on Qingdao. As they anticipated possible war with Germany, they started to withdraw Japanese ships and nationals who happened to be in Qingdao. They also prepared to mobilize and select the formations destined to be part of the Japanese expeditionary force to China. Most importantly, they collected information about Shandong and the fortress at Qingdao. In 1914, when the Germans had just settled in with expectations of enjoying the benefits Qingdao would bring militarily and economically, the war broke out. Qingdao would be the first major casualty of the war for Germany.

THE FIGHTING IN QINGDAO

Japan firmly took the lead in the Qingdao battle. It contributed larger forces than Britain—some 50,000 men, 12,000 horses, 102 heavy guns and howitzers, and 42 field and mountain guns. The British, including Indian soldiers, at Qingdao totaled about 1,200 men and 350 horses, with 300 Chinese auxiliaries. Besides the land troops, Japan had in place the following naval forces as well. Some

---

[29] Japanese report on "Siege of Tsing-Tao," BA: WO 106/5517.
[30] Dickinson, "Toward a Global Perspective of the Great War," 1154–83.
[31] John Morrow, *The Great War: An Imperial History* (London: Routledge, 2004), 36.
[32] Japanese report on "Siege of Tsing-Tao," BA: WO 106/5517.

of these took part in the Qingdao campaign directly, and some in a supporting capacity; they comprised three squadrons, the 1st, 2nd, and 4th: four dread-noughts, four battle cruisers, thirteen cruisers, 1st and 2nd class, nine coastguard ships, four gunboats, twenty-four destroyers, thirteen mine-sweepers, and some hospital and repair ships. Only two British warships joined the Qingdao battle. Greene worried in his telegram to London on August 9, it was possible that "public opinion at home might think it undignified for England to place all the risk involved in such an operation on the shoulders of her ally, and to take none herself," and suggested that British troops in Tianjin should also participate in the Qingdao battle. He further reported that Japan had demanded from Britain a "free hand, and no limited liability" if Japan officially joined the war.[33] The British government decided on August 22, 1914 that "owing to exigencies at home and in India, the British force to co-operate with the Japanese is to consist of one battalion of British infantry only." A battalion of the South Wales Borders and about half a battalion of the 36th Sikhs under Britain eventually joined the Qingdao battle. It also decided that these troops would be actually under the control of a Japanese commander.[34] These few British and Indian military forces arrived in Qingdao under the protection of Japanese warships. Britain hoped that since France and Russia were also at war with Germany, it would be necessary to inform their military and naval authorities as soon as the British and Japanese authorities had come to an agreement as to concerted action. The Japanese government much preferred that the French and Russians take no part in operations. Since neither Russia nor France had any troops stationed nearby and ready, they never did get involved in this battle. Interestingly though, French and British officials, in the face of Japan's military action, began discussions on the desirability of French and British naval cooperation in Qingdao. The French seemed to be worried that if France was not involved in military actions against Germany in China, its prestige across Asia would suffer.[35]

When the fighting commenced, the Germans had only 4,500 troops to defend Qingdao against the considerable Japanese military resources. Still, the Japanese were enormously cautious and prepared thoroughly. Their intelligence was careful and detailed. The Japanese knew all about the German concessions in Shandong, and their geographical situation and locations. One report explained, "River beds are generally wide and dry most times of the year; during the rains, however, they become dangerous torrents. In the interior of the concession there are several roads, made by the Germans, passable by motor-cars, but outside the German territory there are only tracks almost impassable in bad weather." The Japanese had long collected such detailed information clearly for possible military actions against the Germans so they would have accurate information for future infantry and moun-tain artillery movement. The report further claimed: "The Japanese know fairly exactly with what forces of the enemy they would have to deal, and what his

[33] China: General Operation Telegrams, July 21 to September 25, 1914, BA: ADM 137/11.
[34] FO to Sir C. Greene, August 22, 1914. China: General Operation Telegrams, July 21 to September 25, 1914, BA: ADM 137/11.
[35] Green to Grey, August 6, 1914, BA: ADM 137/11.

resources are. The information and the figures given further on in this report agree approximately with those already in the possession of the Japanese General Staff."

The Japanese had scouted every aspect of the German defenses. For instance, the third of the German military lines ran between five and six kilometers long, was four to five kilometers distant from the eastern edge of the town, and had been organized as the principal line of resistance. This line of heights had been strengthened in times of peace with a certain number of centers of resistance. The Japanese were also aware that there were permanent triangular earthworks with deep belts of barbed wire and concrete shelters for the garrison. The line was strengthened at the outbreak of hostilities by a particular number of trenches and redoubts designed to cover the intervals between the main emplacements. More barbed wire was erected and minefields were laid down in order to increase the effectiveness of the defense, according to a Japanese military report issued after the Qingdao battle. Such as it was, this line of defense was not without value but it was dominated by the opposing hills. The Japanese also had a tally of all the German weaponry and military personnel—they knew that the Germans had five gunboats at Qingdao at the outbreak of hostilities, in addition to a torpedo boat and a small Austrian cruiser.

On August 27, the Japanese Admiralty announced that it would officially blockade the German-leased territory in Shandong, launching the battle for Qingdao. The Japanese general staff drew up battle plans. The first contingent of Japanese troops, 20,000 strong, landed on Longkou, 150 miles north of Qingdao, on September 3. The Japanese forces thus had to cross the entire breadth of the peninsula to reach Qingdao. On their way they occupied Chinese cities and towns, seized the Chinese postal and telegraph offices, and subjected the populace to suffering and hardship, including the requisition of labor and supplies. The British force that acted in concert with the Japanese troops landed at Laoshan Bay, inside the German-leased territory, on September 23. On reaching Qingdao, the Japanese dug well-designed trenches and set up positions along the perimeter to surround the Germans. From the very beginning, the Japanese decided to mobilize large numbers of men rather than begin by bombardment. "Bombardment will not be hurried as Japanese do not wish to sacrifice lives and hope that garrison will not hold out to the last but surrender."[36]

Still, the Japanese were determined to make other inroads. On September 26, a contingent of 400 Japanese troops proceeded to the town of Weixian and occupied the railway station. On October 3, Japanese military forces compelled the withdrawal of Chinese troops from the vicinity of the railway; and three days later, on October 6, the Japanese moved to Jinan and occupied all three stations in the city, and thereby controlled the entire line of the railway from Qingdao to Jinan, despite the Chinese government's repeated protests. Japanese troops were distributed along the entire line and its employees were gradually replaced by Japanese subjects. The mining properties along the Railway were seized at the same time.

---

[36] Japanese report on "Siege of Tsing-Tao," BA: WO 106/5517.

On August 22, the Germans in Qingdao had received a telegram from the Kaiser that was looked upon as a death sentence by the German troops there: "God will protect you while you fight bravely. I trust in you."[37] The Kaiser ordered his governor in Qingdao to fight to the last man. But in the face of determined and overwhelming Japanese force, the Germans eventually ran out of ammunition. They defended Qingdao to their last artillery shell, but they did not continue fighting thereafter.

On November 7, 1914, the German commander, Alfred William Moritz Mayer-Weldeck, surrendered. A fortress that the Germans had expected to withstand a siege of at least six months had fallen in just six weeks. Thorough Japanese preparation and planning made it, in the words of a British postwar study, "one of the most scientific sieges in history."[38] Germany was thus defeated in China in the first year of the Great War, and according to British historian H. C. O'Neill, it "won no laurels in the East."[39] During the siege, about 200 Germans were killed. Japanese casualties included 422 killed, of whom 13 were officers, and 1,564 wounded, of whom 45 were officers. On November 11, Qingdao was transferred from German to Japanese control. On November 19, the British troops left for Hong Kong, and the Indian battalion soon followed on November 23. General Yamada was appointed Governor of Qingdao on November 26, and with this battle, the Japanese military effort in the Great War ended.[40]

Even more surprising than the boost to Japanese authority in China were the unexpected developments, as the European war largely freed Japanese action in Asia. As the Europeans exhausted each other in indecisive battles, Japan would become more important to both sides, giving Japan an even freer hand in China. Japan preferred to flirt with both belligerent parties. Accordingly, even though Japan was technically at war with Germany, it treated its German civilians well. As one American at the time observed:

> The Japanese have not disturbed any German residents . . . all are welcome to stay and continue their occupations as before—even though German editors are so very "continuing" in their way of writing that they publish most outrageous and hostile editorials daily. We wait in amazement to see how much longer Japanese magnanimity will ignore such a breach of common sense and press laws.[41]

The Qingdao battle was clearly transnational, with Germans, British, Japanese, Austro-Hungarians, Chinese, as well as Indians all involved. Chinese workers were requisitioned for the construction of defense works such as trenches in the intervals between the forts, obstacles, and advanced positions, and clearance of the field of fire.

[37] Wilson Leon Godshall, *Tsingtau Under Three Flags* (Shanghai: The Commercial Press, 1929), 146.
[38] Edmund Dane, *British Campaigns in Africa and the Pacific, 1914–1918* (London: Hodder and Stoughton, 1919), 206.
[39] O'Neill, *The War in Africa and in the Far East*, 21.
[40] Japanese Report on "Siege of Tsing-Tao," BA: WO 106/5517.
[41] Columbia Library: Carnegie Endowment for International Peace, correspondence 44, box 395: September 2, 1914, letter to James Brown Scott of the Endowment.

The Indian presence is important too, for it discloses the shared history of the war in Asia and deserves further study.

Indian troops (British India consists of present-day India, Pakistan, Bangladesh, and Burma) joined British and Japanese units, so they got a taste of fighting even before they traveled to Europe. One important question to study is the Indian soldiers' experience and mindset in China. In Europe, as I will explain later, Indians experienced racism and other culture shocks. What happened to them when they were in China? Did they feel proud of fighting against Germans on Asian territory? Did they experience the same level of racism in Asia as in Europe? What about their attitude towards fellow Asians such as the Chinese and Japanese? If they could help defeat the mighty Germans in Asia, did the Indians consider kicking the British out of India? Although it is beyond the capacity of this book to explore this issue, it is clear Indians played an important role on behalf of the British Empire in Asia, beginning at least with their participation in the invasions of China in the Opium Wars. A total of 18,000 troops, almost all Indian, and conspicuously well supplied, were sent to invade China in 1900–1 during the suppression of the Boxer Movement and the reprisals which followed.[42] In 1914, the Indian 36th Sikhs, with their full complement of prewar regulars, helped the Japanese army to besiege the Germans in Qingdao. Landing on the Yellow Sea coast to the south of Qingdao on October 23, the Sikhs completed the tiring thirty-mile march through typhoon rains and deep mud in good time. They then spent ten days in the water-logged Japanese front trenches, digging with their Sirhind tools, and remaining steady under shrapnel and high-explosive shellfire.[43]

Besides Qingdao, Japan also took German possessions in the northern Pacific; it occupied German islands north of the equator and ejected German forces from Micronesia in the South Pacific. The Japanese ejection of the German navy from the Marshall, Mariana, and Caroline Islands by September 1914 marked its emergence as not only a continental, but a Pacific empire.

Japanese ships played a key role in the mobilization of the British Empire between 1914 and 1918, when they conveyed Australian and New Zealand troops from the Pacific through the Indian Ocean to Aden on the Arabian Sea. Following attacks on Japanese merchant vessels in the Mediterranean, three Japanese destroyer divisions and one cruiser (thirteen ships in all) joined the Allied fight against German submarines in February 1917. Japan provided shipping, copper, munitions, and almost 1 billion yen in loans to its allies and provided desperately needed munitions (including 600,000 rifles to Russia). Where Japanese troops were not directly involved, substantial Japanese aid flowed. Several Japanese Red Cross units operated in Allied capitals throughout the war. According to one contemporary

---

[42] George Morton-Jack, *The Indian Army on the Western Front: India's Expeditionary Forces to France and Belgium in the First World War* (New York: Cambridge University Press, 2014), 130.

[43] Morton-Jack, *The Indian Army on the Western Front*, 211–12.

Western observer, "If this help had been denied, the collapse of Russia would have come long before it did." The human costs of the war in Japan were negligible; for most Japanese, life went on as usual.[44]

But after the fall of Qingdao, Allied requests for aid snowballed far beyond Japanese expectations. On November 6, 1914, Foreign Secretary Edward Grey urged Britain's ambassador to Tokyo to ask that a Japanese force "take part in the main operations of war in France, Belgium, and Germany in the same way as our Army is doing, and to fight alongside of our soldiers on the continent of Europe."[45] Soon, French newspapers reported informal French requests for 500,000 Japanese troops to join in operations on the Balkan Peninsula. Japan largely ignored the requests for deeper involvement. From Japan's perspective, this limited military support made sense in view of Japan's goal to expand its power base closer to home.

The most substantial Japanese military operation during the war was the 1918 expedition to Siberia.[46] The Russian Revolution of November 1917 and the conclusion of a separate peace with Germany the following March marked a serious strategic blow to the Entente. Not only did it mean the collapse of the Russian front, given the stated intention of the Bolsheviks to take Russia out of the war, but the future of the entire Russian Empire was thrown into question. Stretched to the limit on the Western Front, Britain and France turned to the United States to lead the effort to shore up friendly elements among the Russians. But the Entente still held high hopes for Japanese participation as well. At the very moment that the American Secretary of the Navy approached Japan's ambassador about the possibility of deploying Japanese battle cruisers to the Atlantic, Washington formally invited Japanese troops to join British, French, Italian, American, and Canadian forces in Siberia. If the scale of Japanese war aims had surprised Japan's allies in the first year of the war, the muscular Japanese response in the Siberian Expedition set off even greater alarm.

The collective Siberian intervention was supposed to include different purposes: securing Russia before the German defeat and engaging in an anti-Bolshevik campaign after the war was formally over.[47] After the formal American invitation, however, the Japanese Imperial Army immediately commandeered the agenda, violating every American expectation for the operation. It dispatched ten times the number of troops requested by Washington, entered Vladivostok and points along the Manchurian border, and seized all inhabited land along the

[44] Dickinson, *World War I and the Triumph of a New Japan*, 16.

[45] Dickinson, "Japanese Empire," in Gerwarth and Manela, eds., *Empires at War*, 206.

[46] Given the constant wrangling between Japan and her allies over the operation, historians have, not surprisingly, viewed the event as the most egregious example of autonomous Japanese action in the war.

[47] China was involved militarily in the Siberian intervention as well. Due to space and thematic limitation, this book has to leave the American, Chinese, and Japanese joint Siberian intervention out without detailed discussion.

Trans-Siberian Railway east of Chita. It even lent its support to White Russian rivals of the Entente's principal ally in western Siberia, Admiral A. V. Kolchak. Japanese forces would remain in Siberia until October 1922, over two years after the withdrawal of all other Allied forces in June 1920.

Given this record, and Japan's ignominious withdrawal in 1922 (to be discussed in Chapter 6), the Siberian Expedition did not, of course, loom large as a shining example of Japanese wartime cooperation. But when Prime Minister Hara Takeshi in January 1920 boasted of Japan's contribution to world peace, he referred not only to Japan's participation at the Paris Peace Conference, but to an entirely new account of Japanese wartime cooperation with allies across the globe that had catapulted Japan, for the first time, to the status of a world power. The Siberian Expedition nonetheless must be recognized as another example of the truly global reach of the war.

Doublespeak on the war abounded as all the players maneuvered for best advantage, but the British excelled in this arena. They had declared war on Germany in the name of protecting Belgian neutrality, but supported the Japanese violation of China's quickly declared neutrality. As their Imperial Army advanced across the peninsula from Longkou to Qingdao, the Japanese ignored steady and formal Chinese protests. The British professed not to see any violation.

Seeing that with the complete surrender of the Germans at Tsingtao, hostilities had terminated and both belligerents had abandoned military measures, the Chinese government requested the withdrawal of Japanese troops from the interior of Shandong to Qingdao, and the removal of special telegraph wires attached to Chinese telegraph poles. The Japanese government ignored these requests. China had no choice but to declare the special military zone there dissolved and thus revoke its previous declaration. It duly notified the British and Japanese ministers on January 7, 1915 of the act of revocation, to which the Japanese minister replied in a note of January 9, 1915. He stated, under instructions from his government, that the act of revocation was "improper, arbitrary, betraying want of confidence in international good faith and regardless of friendly relations," and that the Japanese government would not permit the movements and actions of the Japanese troops in Shandong to be in any way affected by the action of the Chinese government.

The Japanese quickly inserted themselves into the administration of the port. After the occupation of Qingdao and Jiaozhou Bay, Japan demanded the right to appoint nearly forty Japanese subjects to the staff of the Maritime Customs that China had established under the Sino-German agreement of April 17, 1899, as amended on December 1, 1905. The Chinese government did not feel justified in acceding to the proposal, reasoning that its acceptance might disorganize the customs administration, and that even when the Germans were in control, appointments to the Customs staff in Qingdao had always been made by China. While negotiations were still pending, General Kamio, under Japanese government instructions, took possession of the Customs offices and seized the documents and other property of the Chinese Customs. On October 1, 1917, the Japanese government established a civil administration at Qingdao which had broader jurisdiction than had been agreed to in the previous German lease. Public opinion in China, especially in Shandong, grew alarmed at the continued presence of Japanese troops along the Jiaozhou–Jinan railway, which extended Japanese control into the heart of Shandong. The establishment of a Japanese Bureau of Civil Administration aimed, in the view of the Chinese people, at the permanent occupation of that province. Even more striking were changes in the shipping trade of the port between 1914 and 1917. For 1913, the total tonnage of all vessels clearing from the port was 1,300,442, of which Japan's share was 222,693 tons; in 1917, it was 1,600,459, of which the Japanese share was 1,114,159 tons.[48] In 1916, the Japanese Dai Nippon Beer Company bought out British interests in the iconic jointly run Anglo-German Brewery, which had been idle since the war, and began to produce its Tsingtao brand beer with Japanese rather than German materials, an arrangement which lasted until 1945.[49]

Japan's actions made perfect sense from the Japanese perspective. As Ishii Kikujiro, known as friendly to the Anglo-Saxon powers, confided in his diary: "While foreign governments would not feel themselves endangered by calamity, epidemic, civil war or bolshevism in China, Japan could not exist without China and the Japanese people could not stand without the Chinese." This was why the Japanese often referred to an "Asian Monroe Doctrine." Just as the United States, for its own security, treated Latin America as its backyard, so Japan had to worry about China and neighbors such as Korea and Mongolia.[50] As the Europeans exhausted each other in battle, Japanese support (and its threatened withdrawal) became a key card that meant Japan would have a free hand in Asia.

Over the course of the Great War, the Japanese played a brilliant game that secured its rise as a world power at China's expense. For Japan, the biggest payoffs were kicking German interests out of Asia altogether and replacing Great Britain to establish itself as the dominant foreign power in China.

Interest in China, as mentioned earlier, motivated Japan's entry into the Great War. As early as August 26, 1914, three days after Japan declared war on Germany, the new minister to China, Eki Hioki, telegraphed Foreign Minister Katō that "the time was most opportune for the settlement of the China issue" because the Chinese were greatly concerned about Japanese military operations in Shandong and anxious not to offend Japan. But Katō's ambition in China was far greater, and he instructed Hioki to bide his time. What Katō wanted to achieve turned out to be the infamous "Twenty-one Demands."[51] Those demands formally presented to the Chinese government made its ambition crystal clear; far from marking a sudden act of aggression as is often remarked, the Twenty-one Demands negotiated with

---

[48] "The claim of China for direct restitution to herself of the leased territory of Kiao-Chow, the Tsingtao-Chinan railway and other German rights in respect of Shantung Province," BA: FO 608/210.

[49] Jeffrey W. Alexander, *Brewed in Japan: The Evolution of the Japanese Beer Industry* (Honolulu: University of Hawaii Press, 2013), 68.

[50] MacMillan, *Paris 1919*, 329.

[51] Noriko Kawamura, *Turbulence in the Pacific: Japanese-U.S. Relations During World War I* (Westport, CT: Praeger, 2000), 22.

Beijing between January and June 1915 signified, rather, Japan's coming of age in the scramble for power it had got a taste of in 1895. Without the Great War, Japan would not have had the opportunity to present those demands, and the Chinese would not have been able to launch their diplomatic and public opinion war in response.

2

The Great War in China and Japan, 1915–18

Europeans, says Christopher Clark, went to war in 1914 like "sleepwalkers"; China and Japan, however, entered the war wide awake, after long thought, careful planning, and strategic calculation.[1] And if, as we saw in Chapter 1, China was key to Japanese involvement, concern with Japan drove China to enter the war. A key to China's seemingly contradictory responses to the war is the alarm and consternation at the degradation of its international status following the Opium War and the Allied Eight Nation Invasion of 1900. This chapter examines the fear and ambition that drove policymakers on either side, how China and Japan used the Great War to forward their national objectives, and how the Great War shaped these nations for the rest of the century.

The China–Japan connection in the Great War is one of tragedy, irony, and contradiction. Japan and China shared a Confucian tradition but each turned the experience of Western imperialism to their own ends; they were archenemies who ended up on the same side; they were rivals who depended on and learned from each other; and each saw dealing with the other as the primary motivation for their war policies and postwar agendas. The Great War was a turning point in modern Chinese and Japanese history and created joint forces for transformative change in the national development of both.

CHINA'S WAR STRATEGIES AND JAPAN'S TWENTY-ONE DEMANDS

President Yuan Shikai proclaimed China's neutrality in a presidential mandate of August 6, 1914. Seeing an opportunity to forge a new international reputation and counter Japan's intention to seize Qingdao and expand its interests, the government and China's elites soon pushed to join the Great War. As Europe's "generation of 1914" went to war innocent of the bloody rites of passage to come, the new generation in China felt a sense of *weiji*—*wei* (danger) and *ji* (opportunity), or "crisis"—presented by the rupture of the international system. China recognized the danger of being dragged into the war. The belligerents all controlled

[1] Clark, *The Sleepwalkers.*

spheres of interest on Chinese soil, and their preoccupation in Europe might give Japan a free hand to bully China and thwart its development.

The war also presented China with opportunities, which drew new and old public figures of all persuasions into a debate on a common objective. The venerable reformer Liang Qichao counseled that if China exploited the situation properly, it could become a "completely qualified nation-state" and prepare for a rapid rise in the world.[2] Liang Shiyi, financier, Cabinet member, and President Yuan Shikai's shrewd confidante, also suggested as early as 1914 that China should join the war on the Allied side.[3] Liang told the president that Germany was not strong enough to win in the long term, so China should seize the opportunity to declare war. By doing so, Liang reasoned, China could recover Qingdao, win a seat at the postwar peace conference, and promote China's long-term national interests. Liang, known as "the Machiavelli of China,"[4] renewed his argument in 1915: "The Allied Powers will win absolutely. [That is why] we want to help them."[5] In a handwritten note dated November 1915, he insisted that the "time is right. We won't have a second chance."[6] As Chapter 6 will discuss in detail, a new generation of diplomats arose. Chief among them was V. K. Wellington Koo (Gu Weijun), then only in his twenties, who returned from the United States in 1912 with a PhD in international law from Columbia University. Yuan Shikai made Koo his English secretary, starting his career in Chinese diplomacy that lasted for many decades and through several changes of government.[7]

China's key reason to join the war was to counter Japan. In an early attempt to prevent war from spreading to China, the government had declared official neutrality.[8] China repeatedly pressed Britain about Japan's intentions regarding German-leased territory in China, to which Britain responded that China "need have no apprehension as to the results of any joint action which Great Britain and Japan might decide upon." China was advised to rely on Allied "assurance" that she would get Shandong back from Germany. In a long meeting with Wellington Koo on August 19, 1914, British Minister to China John Jordan again promised that Qingdao would be returned to China with no conditions.[9]

---

[2] Liang Qichao, "Ouzhan Zhongce (Some Preliminary Predictions about the European War)," in *Yinbing Shi Heji*, 4: 11–26; see also Ding Wenjiang, ed., *Liangrengong Xiansheng Nianpu (Life Chronology of Mr. Liang Qichao)* (Taipei: Shijie shuju, 1959), 439.

[3] Feng Gang et al., eds., *Minguo Liang Yansun Xiansheng Shiyi Nianpu (Life Chronology of Mr. Liang Shiyi)* (Taipei: Commercial Press, 1978), 1: 194–6.

[4] Michael Summerskill, *China on the Western Front* (London: Michael Summerskill, 1982), 30.

[5] Feng et al., eds., *Minguo Liang Yansun Xiansheng Shiyi Nianpu (Life Chronology of Mr. Liang Shiyi)*, 1: 271–2.

[6] See Feng et al., eds., *Minguo Liang Yansun Xiansheng Shiyi Nianpu (Life Chronology of Mr. Liang Shiyi)*, 1: 289; Su Wenzhuo, ed., *Liang Tan Yuying Ju Shi Suo Cang Shu Han Ying Cun* (Hong Kong: Su Wenzhuo, 1986), 208.

[7] Stephen G. Craft, *V.K. Wellington Koo and the Emergence of Modern China* (Lexington: University Press of Kentucky, 2003).

[8] The original declaration can be found in The Chinese Second Historical Archive, Nanjing, with the call number 1039(2)–53.

[9] Jordan, 1919 Annual Report to the British Foreign Office, FO 405/229, 9. See minutes of the meeting between Wellington Koo and Jordan on August 19, 1914, Zhong yang yanjiu yuan jindai shi

China maintained an expedient, watchful neutrality, which would last until August 1917, and was prepared to give it up the moment the opportunity rose. Modern-minded Chinese officials were especially enthusiastic. As the correspondent for *The Manchester Guardian* reported, "with a knowledge of foreign diplomacy, [they] took an immediate interest and combined to exhort the conservatives to action."[10] Zhang Guogan, an influential government official, suggested to then-Prime Minister Duan Qirui that the European war had such importance for China that the government should take the initiative and declare war on Germany. This might not only prevent Japan from grabbing the German concession on Qingdao in the short term, but would be a first step toward fuller participation in a future world system. Duan reassured Zhang that he was secretly preparing for this move.[11]

Japan's presentation of the Twenty-one Demands in early 1915 spurred Chinese determination to get involved in the Great War. With Qingdao's fall, the Japanese shifted their attention to Chinese internal affairs. On January 18, 1915, rather than making a public announcement or using the normal diplomatic channels, the Japanese minister to China met with Yuan privately to present a memo written on a few sheets of paper watermarked with battleships and machine guns. The document had five sections, with a total of twenty-one articles. The first section demanded that China cede all German interests in Shandong. The seven articles in the second section demanded that Japan be given full control of southern Manchuria and eastern Inner Mongolia. Section three provided that Japan was to assume full control of China's largest and most important mining concern, the Hanyeping Company. Section four stipulated that China could not cede or lease to a third power any harbor, bay, or island along the coast. But the most serious section was the fifth, which demanded that China appoint Japanese advisors in political, financial, and military affairs. The Japanese were also to take control of police departments in key places across China. These demands were so severe that George Morrison, the well-connected Australian correspondent, charged that they were "worse than many presented by a victor to his vanquished enemy."[12] The Japanese clearly meant to make China a vassal state while the major Powers were fighting for their own survival and would not have energy to spare for China or their own interests there.

Japan insisted that China keep the demands a secret and negotiate on its own, as Japan feared a repetition of the Triple Intervention of 1895. This was a defining moment for the new foreign policy public. While Wellington Koo and the Foreign Ministry skillfully managed backstage diplomacy, Liang Qichao and other public intellectuals launched a public relations campaign at home. Liang wrote a series of powerful articles warning Japan not to treat China like Korea, which Japan had

yanjiu suo, ed., *Zhong ri guanxi shi liao: Ouzhan yu Shandong wenti* (Taipei: Zhong yang yanjiu yuan jindai shi yanjiu suo, 1974), 1: 58–64.

[10] "China's Breach with Germany," *The Manchester Guardian*, May 23, 1917.

[11] Xu Tian (Zhang Guogan), "Dui De-Ao Canzhan (China's Declaration of War on Germany and Austria)," in *Jindaishi ziliao*, No. 2 (1954), 51.

[12] Cyril Pearl, *Morrison of Peking* (Sydney: Angus and Robertson, 1967), 307.

annexed in 1910. Inspired by Liang and other members of the elite, merchants and students in Shanghai, Beijing, Tianjin, Hangzhou, and cities across the country protested against the Japanese encroachment by holding rallies, writing to magazines and newspapers, and sending telegrams around the country. They demanded that the Yuan government reject the Japanese demands, and a swarm of associations and societies emerged to orchestrate the civil protests.[13] On March 18, 1915, about 40,000 people attended an anti-Twenty-one Demands rally in Shanghai. Japan's blatant bullying had confirmed for many Chinese that Japan posed a major threat. "Japan is a powerful enemy," wrote a young Mao Zedong in a letter to a friend on July 25, 1916; he predicted that China "could not survive without fighting in the next twenty years."[14] This broad-based response to the Twenty-one Demands in 1915 led to the mass protests of the May Fourth Movement of 1919.

While the appeal to public opinion on both the domestic and foreign policy fronts may not have produced a significant diplomatic result or real support from the Great Powers, the publicity at least compelled Japan to modify its demands and put the Japanese on the moral defensive. Chinese diplomats skillfully exploited the support gained through the public opinion campaign in their negotiations with the Japanese. British Minister to China John Jordan was impressed with Chinese negotiation skills during the roughly one hundred days and twenty-four sessions of official negotiations in connection with the Twenty-one Demands. He declared that if it was "merely a question of dialectical gymnastics, I should be inclined to back the Chinese."[15] The Chinese side did not give in until it faced a military showdown. As Jordan emphasized in his official report to the British Foreign Office, "the demands were forced through on the point of the bayonet, Japan having actually landed between 20,000 and 30,000 men in Manchuria and at Tsingtao."[16] Although the Chinese used everything at their disposal to deflect and delay, on May 7, 1915, the Japanese government delivered an ultimatum demanding a satisfactory reply within forty-eight hours. On May 25, 1915, China was constrained to sign among other things, a treaty ceding control of Shandong Province, accompanied by three sets of notes. The Chinese government felt forced to give their consent to maintain peace in the Far East, to spare the Chinese people unnecessary suffering, and to prevent the interests of friendly powers in China from being imperiled as they struggled at home. The Chinese felt confident that the final settlement of this question, and of other questions raised as a consequence of the Japanese demands, could be effected only at the peace conference that must follow the European conflict.

[13] The Chinese media's critical response to the Twenty-one Demands was so strong that Morrison advised the government to cool them down in order not to further damage Sino-Japanese relations; see Morrison to Cai Tinggan, March 13, 1915, in *Min Guo Dangan (Archival Materials of Republican China)* (Nanjing: No.3, 1988), 3.
[14] Mao to Xiao Zisheng, July 25, 1916, in Stuart R. Schram, ed., *Mao's Road to Power: Revolutionary Writings, 1912–1949* (Armonk, NY: M. E. Sharp, 1992), 1: 103.
[15] Jordan to Langley, March 22, 1915, BA: FO 350/13/31.
[16] Jordan Annual Report to Foreign Office, 1919, BA: FO 405/229, 9.

The Japanese used force on China but also used brilliant diplomacy to secure its rise as an Asian power. Japanese diplomats cut secret deals at China's expense that would keep them in a superior position at the war's end. Since no diplomatic support was forthcoming from other countries, Chinese officials kept a close eye on public opinion as they negotiated with Japan. Aware of the impact of foreign public opinion, members of the Chinese Foreign Ministry managed to leak the Japanese demands and secretly kept the Great Powers' representatives in Beijing fully informed about proceedings. Chinese diplomats abroad closely followed their host countries' media coverage of the Sino-Japanese negotiations.[17] On the domestic front, public elites such as Liang Qichao remained close to the policymaking process and kept the public informed, in addition to pressuring the Chinese government not simply to capitulate. Japan's demands presented the biggest challenge yet to China's survival and its desire to become a fully fledged nation-state.

The Twenty-one Demands focused Chinese of all types and persuasions on devising a feasible plan of action. Japan had provided China with a crisis of national identity by defeating it in 1895, but the 1915 demands aroused Chinese national consciousness and helped China identify its first specific goal in response to the First World War: a seat at the postwar peace conference.[18] Although China had early on expressed its intention to join the war, it was only after the Twenty-one Demands that sufficient momentum gathered for the government to act on its now almost irresistible desire to attend any postwar talks. As Liang Qichao argued, Japan's demands had made China's attendance an obvious necessity: Chinese diplomats must not compromise that ambition, since China would be "one of the main issues" at any postwar meetings. Liang reasoned that Japan would have a strong voice in those talks but asked why Japan had chosen to present its demands to China, and why now, rather than at the peace conference? The answer, he concluded, must be that Japan knew it might be difficult to get what it wanted from the other powers. Therefore, China's diplomats should not capitulate to the Twenty-one Demands but keep the postwar peace conference in mind.[19] When China did finally bow to Japan's ultimatum, the government decided to publish a tell-all document that explained how the negotiations had been conducted in order to maintain hope of eventually abrogating them.[20]

[17] Skimming the numerous reports from Chinese legations abroad during this negotiation period, one finds that many Chinese diplomats focused on foreign public opinion. For details, see Zhong yang yanjiu yuan jindai shi yanjiu suo, ed., *Zhong ri guanxi shi liao: ershiyi tiao jiaoshe (Documents on Sino-Japanese Relations Regarding the Twenty-one Demands Negotiations)*, 2 volumes (Taipei: Institute of Modern History, Academia Sinica, 1985).

[18] For an excellent article on this point, see Stephen G. Craft, "Angling for an Invitation to Paris: China's Entry into the First World War," *The International Historical Review*, 16:1 (1994), and "China and World War I," ch. 2 in Craft, *V.K. Wellington Koo*.

[19] Liang, "Zai Jing gao wai jiao dan ju" (Another Warning to the Foreign Policymaking Authorities), in *Yinbing Shi Heji*, 4: 108–9.

[20] For a complete declaration on the negotiations and China's attitude, see waijiaobu guan yu zhong ri jiao she shi mu xuan yan shu, May 13, 1915; and see Chen Daode, Zhang Minfu, and Rao Geping, eds., *Zhong Hua Min Guo Wai Jiao Shi Zhi Liao Xian Bian (1911–1919)*, (Bejing: Beijing daxue chu ban she, 1988) 206–14.

Many Chinese assumed that the right moment would come after the war, but the fate of Shandong was to be sealed well before then, thanks to secret treaties with the Allies. In early 1916, the British government had given assurances that it would stand by the Japanese.[21] On February 14, 1917, Britain officially told Japan that it "accedes with pleasure to the request of the Japanese government . . . [to] support Japan's claims in regard to the disposal of Germany's right in Shantung and possessions in islands north of the Equator on the occasion of a peace conference."[22] Japan made similar arrangements with France, Italy, and Russia.[23] By February 1917, Japan had "induced those powers, at a time when their fate hung in the balance, to recognize the position she had thus acquired and the reversion in her favour of German rights in Shantung."[24] Jordan explained to the Foreign Office that "with all our worldwide preoccupations at present . . . we cannot afford to antagonize the Japanese, and without antagonizing her [*sic*], we cannot get the principles for which we are fighting in Europe extended to the Far East."[25] The Chinese were, of course, kept in the dark about all these deals.

On January 18, 1915, the day Japan delivered the Twenty-one Demands, the Chinese Foreign Ministry sent a telegram to all Chinese ministers abroad. The telegram explained that the many crimes committed by Japan in China "could not be solved justly until our country attends the peace conference after the war." To prepare for its case at the postwar conference, the government set up a high-level research group on January 22, which included many influential officials from the Foreign Ministry,[26] including Foreign Minister Lu Zhengxiang,[27] Vice Minister Cao Rulin, and Counselor Wellington Koo.[28] The Foreign Ministry also decided to send a special envoy to visit Chinese diplomats abroad, coordinate their suggestions, and collect relevant documents. The envoy's mission also included holding secret consultations with the world's most distinguished international law experts.[29] In the fall, the American-educated Koo was appointed minister to the United States, where he could lobby in Washington and spread the Chinese point of view in the rest of the country.

Over the course of 1915, most Chinese intellectuals and other social elites endorsed the official goal of attending the peace conference. The foreign policy

[21] Grey Dispatch to Tokyo, February 4, 1916, BA: WO 106/34.

[22] Memorandum to the Japanese Ambassador, February 14, 1917, BA: FO 371/2950.

[23] The United States also signed a secret Lansing-Ishii Agreement with Japan in 1917. Regarding the French attitude toward the American China policy, see Quai d'Orsay, NS, Chine, 137: 122–4; see also Jordan to Langley, April, 16, 1916, BA: FO 350/15.

[24] Jordan Annual Report to Foreign Office, 1919, BA: FO 405/229/9.

[25] Jordan to Langley, August 28, 1918, BA: FO 350/16.

[26] Waijiaobu to all China's legations, January 18, 1915, Zhong yang yanjiu yuan jindai shi yanjiu suo, ed., *Zhong ri guanxi shi liao: Ouzhan yu Shandong wenti*, 2: 678–9.

[27] Lu replaced Sun Baoji on January 27, 1915 as foreign minister.

[28] Minute of Lu Group meeting on January 22, 1915, Chinese Second Historical Archives, 1039 (2)–377.

[29] Waijiaobu to all China's legations, January 18, 1915, Zhong yang yanjiu yuan jindai shi yanjiu suo, ed., *Zhong ri guanxi shi liao: Ouzhan yu Shandong wenti*, 2: 678–9. Waijiaobu to Minister Liu Shishun, January 21, 1915, Zhong yang yanjiu yuan jindai shi yanjiu suo, ed., *Zhong ri guanxi shi liao: Ouzhan yu Shandong wenti*, 2: 682–4.

elite wrote articles criticizing Japanese "hooligan behavior" but there was widespread agreement that China's best chance was to wait until after the war, when the ultimate success of Japan's invasion would depend on the results of the European conflict.[30] Both the government and the concerned public were determined to link China's fate to the postwar world order and international system, and to rely on the world community to win back what China had lost since the Opium War: its dignity, sovereignty, and prestige. The challenge was how to win a seat at the table. The Japanese foreign minister, Baron Katō, openly declared then that China was not qualified to take part in the peace conference because it was not a belligerent power.[31]

Many Chinese concluded that the surest way to the conference was to take part in the war. Indeed, in May 1915, after being forced to sign treaties associated with the Twenty-one Demands, the Chinese chief negotiator, Lu Zhengxiang, told President Yuan Shikai that only by joining the war could China hope to attend the postwar conference.[32] Even Cao Rulin, who was to be labeled a national traitor during the May Fourth Movement, suggested to Yuan in October 1915 that the best way to deal with Japan's ambitions in China was to enter the war on the side of the Allies. He argued that even if China could not send soldiers to Europe, it should still do everything it could to help the Allies, so as to be rewarded after the war.[33] Cao seemed so serious about this idea that, in his capacity as vice minister for foreign affairs, he asked the Chinese minister to Japan to inquire about Japan's possible response to China's entering the war.[34]

Not surprisingly, Japan strongly opposed China's formal entry into the war. As Jordan bluntly characterized the Japanese position, "It did not suit Japan to allow China to join the Entente. That is all. Japan's interest is to see the European war prolonged as much as possible and to keep China in a state which will facilitate the attainment of her own objects."[35] Japan unilaterally rejected China's bid to join the war in late 1915 when Britain, Russia, and France all seemed to support China's participation. As early as 1915, China also began working out a laborers-as-soldiers scheme designed to create a link with the Allied cause and to strengthen its case for claiming a role in the war when its official entry seemed uncertain. The Chinese vigorously promoted the idea of sending laborers to help the Allies. They called their plan *yigong daibing* ("laborers in the place of soldiers").[36] After President Yuan

[30] See Zhao Yun, "Ji zhong ri jiao she" (News on Sino–Japanese Negotiations); Jiang Sheng, "San ji zhou zhan zheng" (Comments on European War: Part 3); and Duan Liu, "Zhan zheng yu cai li" (War and Financial Power), all in *Jia yin zazhi*, 7 (July, 1915).

[31] *The Peking Gazette*, November 28, 1914.

[32] See Lu Zongxiang, "wo suo jin shou qian ding er shi yi tiao," in Chen Zhiqi, ed., *Zhong Hua Min Guo Wai Jiao Shi Liao Hui Bian*, vol. 1 (Taipei: Bo hai tan wen hua gong shi, 1996), 420.; Luo Guang, *Lu Zhengxiang Zhuan (Biography of Lu Zhengxian)* (Taipei: Shangwu yi shu guan, 1966), 105.

[33] Cao Rulin, *Yi Sheng Zhi Hui Yi (Memoir of Cao Rulin)* (Hong Kong: Chun Qiu chu ban she, 1966), 138.

[34] Guo Tingyi, ed., *Zhonghua Min Guo Shi Shi Ri Zhi* (Taipei: Zhong yang yan jiu yuan jin dai shi suo, 1979), 206.

[35] Jordan to Alston, February 1, 1916, BA: FO 350/15.

[36] Feng et al., eds., *Minguo Liang Yansun Xiansheng Shiyi Nianpu (Life Chronology of Mr. Liang Shiyi)*, 1: 310.

Shikai died in 1916, his successors feuded with each other but managed to provide 140,000 laborers, who worked on the Western Front during the war. Among all the foreign countries involved, China sent the largest number of workers to France and the Chinese stayed there longest. Even though Chinese participation had to come in a supporting role, it nonetheless represented a serious commitment.

CHINA'S "LABORERS-AS-SOLDIERS" STRATEGY

The Chinese government hoped to use its war policies to recover the sovereignty it had lost to Japan and the other powers. Although China was eager to send military forces to Europe after its official entry into the war, only France was interested in having Chinese troops join the fighting. Japan was strongly opposed, and Britain was not very excited at the prospect. With a dearth of transportation and funding, and lukewarm interest from the most belligerent nations, China failed to land soldiers in Europe. Instead, its largest contribution was sending workers to support the British and French war efforts.[37]

To strengthen their case, the Chinese vigorously promoted sending laborers to help the Allies. The program was the brainchild of Liang Shiyi, whose main initial target was Britain.[38] He first suggested that the Chinese send military laborers, not hired workers. If Britain had accepted this proposal, China would have been fighting on the Allied side in 1915. But Britain rejected the idea immediately and so Liang turned to France.

As the same time as the Chinese reeled under Japan's Twenty-one Demands, the French faced a manpower crisis: how were they to continue the deadly war while maintaining the home front? Following China's offer of help, the French immediately began planning how to get the Chinese to France, and eventually about 40,000 Chinese workers were recruited and transported. By 1916, Britain also clearly saw that its future was at stake, and British arrogance was partly replaced by desperation. Winston Churchill informed the House of Commons that "I would not even shrink from the word 'Chinese' for the purpose of carrying on the War."[39] British military authorities began to recruit Chinese in 1916 and over the next two years about 100,000 Chinese arrived in France in support of the British war effort. Many of the Chinese under British supervision would stay in France until 1920; they were the last of the British labor forces to leave France.[40] Most of the Chinese under the French stayed until 1922. In other words, among the foreign countries involved, China sent the largest number of workers and their workers stayed in France the longest.

[37] For details on China's laborers in Europe, see Xu Guoqi, *Strangers on the Western Front: Chinese Workers in the Great War* (Cambridge, MA: Harvard University Press, 2011).

[38] Feng et al., eds., *Minguo Liang Yansun Xiansheng Shiyi Nianpu (Life Chronology of Mr. Liang Shiyi)*, 1: 310.

[39] Parliamentary Debates, *House of Commons* (84) (July 10–31), 1379.

[40] "General Statement Regarding the YMCA Work for the Chinese in France," March 1919, YMCA Archives, box 204, folder: Chinese laborers in France reports, 1918–19.

The workers' main duties were to maintain the munitions supply lines, clean out and dig the trenches, and clear conquered territory. Trench warfare was a key feature of the Great War, and Asians played a crucial part by maintaining the war's infrastructures. The Chinese seemed to be especially expert at trench digging. One British officer testified that among the 100,000 men under him—English, Indians, and Chinese—the Chinese dug on an average 200 cubic feet per day, the Indians 160, and the Tommies 140. Another British officer reported: "In my company, I have found the Chinese labourers accomplish a greater amount of work per day in digging trenches than white labourers."[41] But besides digging trenches, some Chinese labor companies were also involved in more skilled work, such as dealing with the most advanced weapons during the war, the tanks.[42] The Chinese laborers were often praised for their efficiency and bravery. General Ferdinand Foch called the French-recruited Chinese "first-class workers who could be made into excellent soldiers, capable of exemplary bearing under modern artillery fire."[43]

During the war, everyone suffered, but the Chinese held up better under the cold of the French winter than did the Indians and Vietnamese. The Chinese rarely complained about the weather. Of Chinese tolerance of the cold, Captain A. McCormick observed, "One thing surprised me about them. I thought that they would have felt the cold more than we did, but seemingly not, for both when working and walking about, you would see them moving about stripped to the waist."[44]

Since the Chinese workers were part of their country's strategy for advancing its international status, other agencies besides the government became involved. Prominent among these was the Young Men's Christian Association (YMCA). During the war, many of China's best and brightest who had graduated from Western universities went to France to serve as YMCA secretaries. They had fallen under the spell of Woodrow Wilson's call for a new world order and the promise of a better world system from which China could benefit. They wanted to devote their knowledge, energy, and experience to help jumpstart that new world order. Future leaders such as Yan Yangchu, Jiang Tingfu, Cai Yuanpei, and Wang Jingwei, among others, through their work with the Chinese workers in Europe, became convinced that China could become a better nation through a different understanding and appreciation of their fellow citizens. Yet their worldview and understanding of China were very different from that of the laborers.

When Chinese laborers arrived in France, the YMCA took an active hand in shaping and influencing their lives. The YMCA secretaries helped their countrymen by writing letters, teaching them to read, helping them devise cultural entertainment for themselves, and giving them the means to better understand the world and Chinese affairs. Perhaps most importantly, they were determined to make the laborers into modern citizens. The experiences of these elite scholars and

[41] YMCA, *Young Men's Christian Association with the Chinese Labour Corps in France*, YMCA Archives, box 204, folder: Chinese laborers in France, 14.

[42] Controller of Labour War Diary, July 1918, BA: WO 95/83.

[43] General Foch's secret report to the Prime Minister, August 11, 1917, Vincennes, 16N 2450/ GQG/6498.

[44] Captain A. McCormick files, IWM 02/6/1, 207–8.

talented students helped them develop a new appreciation for the Chinese working class, spurred them to find solutions to Chinese problems, and changed their perceptions about China and its future. While the laborers learned from their own experiences and from the Chinese elites who worked with them, the Chinese laborers also taught their elite teachers. These workers would eventually become China's new citizens, and during their time in France they developed a new understanding and appreciation of their republic and its position in the world. The Chinese workers in France were mostly common villagers who knew little about China or the larger world when they were selected to go to Europe; still, these men directly and personally contributed to helping China transform its image at home and in the world. Their appearance in France served as a daily reminder to the world that the Chinese were actively involved in world affairs. Moreover, it was largely due to their work in Europe that Chinese diplomats managed to argue for fair treatment at the postwar peace conference. Their transnational roles reshaped China's national identity and bolstered its internationalization, which in turn helped shape the emerging global system. From their experience of wartime Europe and their work with the American, British, and French military, as well as fellow laborers from other countries, they developed historically unique perspectives on their world.[45]

Indian, Vietnamese, and Chinese workers in France often suffered racist and unfair treatment. Although China was no country's colony, the Chinese laborers are often wrongly included among the rolls of colonial workers. Historian John Horne wrote that Chinese workers employed by France in state arsenals (at least to 1917) "received much less than French workers, despite the equality of treatment stipulated in their contracts."[46] Frenchmen obviously disliked their women marrying Chinese. A police report from Le Havre, dated May 1917, noted that some Frenchmen were not happy to see Chinese workers there and rioted against them. The French were reported to be disappointed with the casualties their country had sustained. "It is frequently said (in the munitions factories), that if this continues, there will not be any men left in France; so why are we fighting? So that Chinese, Arabs, or Spaniards can marry our wives and daughters and share out the France for which we'll all, sooner or later, get ourselves killed at the front."[47]

An intriguing coda to these shared experiences was Chinese involvement in the postwar Allied Games, which the YMCA played a role in organizing: "These Games signalized to a vast number of soldiers of the various Armies of the Allies the end of the Great War and the beginning, in this unique love feast of diverse races and nationalities, of a greater and more hopeful peace than the world had yet known." The games had their origin in the Far Eastern Games organized by the YMCA among Chinese, Japanese, and Filipinos. YMCA officials thought that if a Chinese, a Japanese, and a Filipino could be induced to put aside their racial antipathies when

[45] For details on Chinese workers in the First World War, see Xu, *Strangers on the Western Front*.

[46] John Horne, *Labour at War: France and Britain, 1914–1918* (Oxford: Clarendon Press, 1991), 112.

[47] John Horne, "Immigrant Workers in France during World War I," *French Historical Studies*, 14:1 (1985), 8585.

they met on the field of sport, "men animated in advance by interest in and admiration for one another would be certain to find such a gathering pleasant and profitable in many ways."[48] The YMCA thus proposed a "military Olympics" to the American expeditionary forces with the slogan "Every Man in the Game." Since the Games were organized for military personnel, Chinese laborers seemed not to be qualified, and there were no Chinese military forces in Europe. Yet on January 9, 1919, American General John Pershing invited China to take part.[49] Chinese general Tang Zaili, head of the Chinese military mission in Europe, informed Pershing on January 20, 1919: "We are certainly appreciative of the splendid relation with you in the great common cause and as keenly preserve and strengthen this relationship as you do.... With anticipation of the great honor to attend on the field of sport in friendly competition, I hope that some of us shall be able to participate in these contests." Although China eventually did not send teams to take part, in May 1919 the Chinese contributed three trophies for General Pershing to present. As one Chinese official told Pershing, although China would be unable to enter teams, "I beg to assure you that we shall always be glad to do everything we can in cooperation with the American authorities towards making the Games a success."[50] Besides the Chinese, American President Wilson donated trophies, as did the French president and prime minister, and the king of Belgium, among others. China was represented on June 22, 1919, at the Games' dedication day, though the French were given the honor of heading the parade.[51] Once again, China had to march in the second ranks.

CHINA'S BROADER INVOLVEMENT

China's economy actually benefited from the war; although unlike Japan, it did not enjoy trade surpluses, its trade deficits declined noticeably. Besides sending its laborers to Europe, China also sent Britain large numbers of rifles that were moved secretly through Hong Kong. A Chinese person who claimed to be "prominent" and "in a position to know and appreciate the facts" wrote that during the war China was anxious to send troops to Europe, however, she did not do so because she did not have funds and ships, but instead supplied the Allies with enormous stores of war essentials in spite of her productivity being hampered by internal troubles and destruction caused by a great flood of the Yellow River. China built ships for the United States at her own yard, and some Chinese aviators flew over the enemy's lines, fought with enemy planes, and received medals from the French army.[52] The oldest and largest shipbuilding concern in China, the Jiangnan dock and engineering

---

[48] The Games Committee, *The Inter-Allied Games, Paris: 22nd June to 6th July, 1919* (n.p.: The Games Committee, n.d.), 11–14.

[49] Committee, *The Inter-Allied Games*, 36, 48.

[50] Committee, *The Inter-Allied Games*, 54.

[51] Committee, *The Inter-Allied Games*, 187.

[52] J. S. Tow, "China's Service to the Allied Cause," *The Economic World*, 17:6 (February 8, 1919), 184–5.

works at Shanghai, was placed at the disposal of the United States government in July 1918 for the construction of four 10,000-ton ocean steamers, the steel being shipped from the United States and all other materials being supplied in China. R. B. Mauchan, a Scottish engineer who was in charge of the dock's engineering work in China for fourteen years, declared:

> Building American ships in China will have a strong appeal for the young men of China. Knowing as they do the part shipping plays in winning this world war, they see a sentimental, as well as an economic, side to this venture. . . . Unlike many other undeveloped lands, China is intellectually awake. Shipbuilding is not a new venture, but has been carried on hundreds of years. Building American ships there, however, is new and novel. It has an appeal that strikes the Chinese mind with tremendous force at a time when all eyes are turned toward that country.[53]

Nor were the benefits only economic. The laborers that China sent to Europe would help shape both Western and Chinese political orders by serving as messengers between East and West, and have a lasting impact on China's national development because of their journey to the West and their new lives back home afterward. At a deeper level, the First World War left a lasting legacy by shaping Chinese perceptions of the world order and the West. Embittered at the injustice of the postwar peace conference, Chinese anger would be rekindled whenever their country was wronged by the Powers. The war and its aftermath, therefore, were pivotal in shaping modern Chinese historical consciousness and national mooring. China in the wake of the European war differed fundamentally from the China of 1914, to a great extent because of what happened during the war and at the Paris Peace Conference.

JAPAN'S GREAT WAR AND MODERN TRANSFORMATION

The costs of the war for Japan were negligible. Japan did not send military forces to Europe, and only seventy-five Japanese nurses traveled to France during the war. Nevertheless, the Great War played an incontrovertible role in modernizing Japan economically, diplomatically, and politically. As Frederick Dickinson has eloquently argued, for Japan, the Great War marked its "departure point from a primarily agricultural to an industrial state, and from a regional to a world power." The war also marked a decisive shift from nineteenth- to twentieth-century sensibilities. "Just as the intrusion of great power imperialism had prompted the original construction of modern Japan, the wartime destruction of a world civilization fashioned in Europe and diffused globally throughout the nineteenth century spurred an enormous Japanese effort in national reconstruction after 1919."[54]

---

[53] No Author, "Shipping and Shipbuilding in China," *The Economic World*, 17:2 (January 11, 1919), 46.
[54] Dickinson, *World War I and the Triumph of a New Japan*, 6–7.

Table 2.1. Japan's wartime foreign trade

	Exports		Imports	
	Annual averages*		Annual averages*	
	In yen, millions	Index (1910–14 = 100)	In yen, millions	Index (1910–14 = 100)
1910–14	593.1	100	662.3	100
1915–19	15,999	269.8	14,137	213.4
1920–4	18,104	305.3	24,257	366.2

Including Japan's trade with Japanese colonies. From W. G. Beasley, *Japanese Imperialism, 1894–1945* (Oxford: Clarendon Press, 1987), 125.

The economy benefited richly. The number of factories employing more than five workers rose from 31,000 in 1914 to 43,000 in 1919. During the war, for the first time since the end of the nineteenth century, Japan recorded significant trade surpluses. Exports grew from 591 million yen in 1914 to nearly 2 billion yen four years later, a three-fold increase, and this with a trade surplus of nearly 300 million yen.[55] In 1914, Japan's foreign trade was approximately equal in volume to China's. But then Japan took full advantage of opportunities presented by the war.

Table 2.1 clearly shows how the Japanese economy boomed. The boost in foreign trade thrust Japan's balance of payments into surplus for the first time in its history.[56] The net income from freight had been less than 40 million yen in 1914. By 1918, it was over 450 million yen. As for the commodity trade, average annual exports over the four war years were some 330 million yen larger than imports, while between 1911 and 1914 imports had exceeded exports by an annual average of 65 million yen. Overall industrial investment during the war multiplied seventeen times as enhanced profits were plowed back into new development. Total production output in Japan grew from 2,610 million yen to 10,212 million yen in 1918.[57]

Employment in industry increased accordingly. The industrial workforce nearly doubled between 1914 and 1919.[58] The war not only brought orders for Japanese manufacturers, but handicapped much of its prewar competition. Japan's merchant marine doubled in size as exports to Britain and the United States doubled, those to China quadrupled, and those to Russia sextupled. In 1918, Australian Premier William Morris [Billy] Hughes warned his British counterpart Arthur Balfour that the industrious Japanese were moving in everywhere. "We too must work in like fashion or retire like my ancestors from the fat plains to the lean and rugged hills." And it was not just the economic threat that worried the British; at sea, Japan was

[55] Iriye, *China and Japan in the Global Setting*, 23.
[56] Dickinson, *World War I and the Triumph of a New Japan*, 17.
[57] Kenneth D. Brown, "The Impact of the First World War on Japan," in Chris Wrigley, ed., *The First World War and the International Economy* (Cheltenham: Edward Elgar, 2000), 102–7.
[58] Iriye, *Japan and China in the Global Setting*, 22–3.

more powerful than it had been in 1914, and on land, it was extending its presence in China and moving into Russian Siberia.[59]

Fueled by incessant Allied requests for war assistance and material, and by new commercial opportunities opened by the withdrawal of European powers from the Asia-Pacific, the Japanese economy grew significantly faster than the international standard between 1913 and 1922. By 1920–4, manufactured goods comprised over 90 percent of Japanese exports. By 1925, Japan's overall population reached 60.74 million, number five in the world behind China, the US, Russia, and Germany. According to Dickinson, "Just as Perry's introduction of modern imperialism to Japan invited the creation of a modern nation-state, the First World War spurred the construction of what contemporaries referred to as the 'New Japan.'"[60]

As Dickinson brilliantly argued, historians of the twentieth century highlight deep structural changes that underlay a new world after the Great War. Japan's early twentieth-century enterprise in reconstruction, likewise, rested upon a striking structural transformation. While we acknowledge the dramatic wartime transition from a Eurocentric to an American-centric world, we might also recognize the gradual global shift of power east, represented by the rise of Imperial Japan. Japan's transition from an agrarian to industrial polity brought the most dramatic gains to Japan's regional presence. Japan's experience confirms that the extraordinary transformative power of the Great War lay less in its destructiveness than in the massive transnational subterranean processes it set off.[61]

The Great War also contributed to an overhaul of national foundations and set the stage for dramatic change after 1918. Rapid wartime industrial expansion spurred urban growth. The years from 1910 to 1920 were the most volatile decade of movement from agricultural to non-agricultural labor in Japan. The farming population dropped by two million during the war years, and Tokyo's population grew by 300,000, to 1.01 million between 1908 and 1920. "Ōsaka became Japan's industrial capital, with a population of 2 million by 1925—the sixth largest city in the world at the time." Postwar Japan saw the rise of a new urban middle class. Companies with over one hundred employees expanded from 46 to 53 percent between 1914 and 1922. "Between 1912 and 1926, per capita gross national product grew by 33 percent and per capita expenditures rose by 40 percent. Women made up an increasing proportion of the new urban middle class, comprising, in the early 1920s, 10 percent of the workforce in Tokyo's central business district, Marunouchi."[62]

This new economic prowess and the accompanying transformation of Japanese society supported the burgeoning of Japanese regional power. As Dickinson pointed out, by vanquishing German forces in China and German Micronesia, negotiating a comprehensive series of rights in China (the notorious Twenty-one Demands), and dispatching 50,000 troops to participate in an Allied intervention

[59] MacMillan, *Paris 1919*, 312.
[60] Dickinson, *World War I and the Triumph of a New Japan*, 6.
[61] For details on this, see Dickinson, *World War I and the Triumph of a New Japan*; Dickinson, "Toward a Global Perspective of the Great War."
[62] Dickinson, "Toward a Global Perspective of the Great War," 1168.

in Siberia, Japan expanded her political, military, and economic reach for the first time into Russia and the South Pacific. But added to the economic boom, these wartime gains highlight a dramatic increase in Japanese might relative to colonial powers that had dominated East Asian diplomacy since the mid-nineteenth century—Britain, France, Russia, and Germany. Diplomatically, Japanese power increased substantially, largely at the expense of China. While the conflagration would ultimately destroy four dynastic empires—Imperial Germany, the Austro-Hungarian Empire, Imperial Russia, and the Ottoman Empire—it brought nothing but opportunity for Imperial Japan. The Twenty-one Demands would consolidate Japan's long-held interests in Fujian Province and south Manchuria, and guarantee new areas of development in Germany's former concession in Shandong Province, Eastern Inner Mongolia adjacent to Russian Outer Mongolia, and Britain's long-time concession in Fujian Province. Great Power confirmation of these gains in 1916 (Russia) and 1917 (Britain, France, and Italy) meant that Japan had, in only three years' time and with minimal military effort, leaped from being only a minor player in the competition for influence in China to becoming the principal arbiter of developments on the Asian continent. It is no wonder that even Foreign Minister Katō's greatest domestic political rival, Field Marshal Yamagata Aritomo, expressed "great satisfaction" at the negotiation of these terms, which allowed Japan to keep its gains in China.[63]

These wartime shifts of power led to fundamental geopolitical changes for Japan as a new global presence. Japanese textiles now made their way to India as Imperial Navy destroyers steamed to the Mediterranean. But Japan's new clout could be seen most clearly in the degree to which belligerents from both sides scrambled for Japanese aid during the war. Their appeals ranged from Britain's initial August 1914 request that Japan join the war, to British and American requests for Japanese convoy aid, to French demands for Japanese troops in Europe, to German and Austrian overtures for a separate peace. The presence of Japanese representatives among the exalted assembly of delegates from the five victor nations at the Paris Peace Conference powerfully demonstrated Japan's arrival as a world power. As Prime Minister Hara Takashi proudly proclaimed at Paris, "As one of five great powers, the empire (Japan) contributed to the recovery of world peace. With this, the empire's status has gained all the more authority and her responsibility to the world has become increasingly weighty."[64]

The wartime transformation of the Japanese empire, state, and national economy thrust Japan to the forefront of a new twentieth-century world. Specialists on Europe have long noted the extraordinary political consequences of the 1914–18 years, in particular, the implosion of four key dynastic regimes. But Imperial Japan did not self-destruct in 1919. With its rapidly industrializing economy, urban middle class, and mass consumer culture, Japan underwent a political transformation equivalent to its earlier revolution of 1868. Just as the feudal dynasty gave way

---

[63] Dickinson, "Japanese Empire," in Gerwarth and Manela, eds., *Empires at War*, 203.
[64] Dickinson, "Toward a Global Perspective of the Great War," 1169.

to a modern monarchy in the mid-nineteenth century, political power moved from the nation's non-elected founders to political party cabinets in the 1920s.

According to Dickinson, a "global perspective on the First World War offers more than a roundup of the war's effects beyond Europe." While providing coverage of developments from the vantage point of 1914, not 1939, it pays attention to large processes that "cross not only borders but continents, even battle lines." The global view preserves "a sense of contingency about a subsequent catastrophe (the Second World War), whose scale of destruction commonly makes discussions of a slippery slope hard to resist." From the vantage point of modern Japan, the Great War was more than a global "moment"; it was "a major twentieth-century watershed." Like the arrival of Commodore Perry in 1853, the war raised fundamental questions about established and legitimated conceptions of "civilization." The effects of the Great War were global, not just because the conflict involved parties across the globe, but because its flames engulfed the heart of what peoples even far from the center of hostilities had believed to be the core of world civilization. "The task of reconstruction fell upon not just those in areas leveled by mortars." It "absorbed all who had had a substantial stake in European civilization," and from the statements of the Japanese during the war, it is clear how great a stake early twentieth-century Japan had in European civilization, which they took on its own terms as being universal, not merely European. "By the end of hostilities, many in Japan were convinced of the importance of a second national renovation (*ishin*)—a reconstruction of the nation on a par" with the original transformation of the traditional feudal polity to a nation-state. Like their nineteenth-century counterparts, "the architects of New Japan after 1918 loudly denounced the past, clamored for an 'opening' of Japan, and offered a buoyantly hopeful vision for the future. As in 1868, they sanctified the new nation-building enterprise with a striking proclamation by the emperor."[65]

Dickinson is correct to suggest that national reconstruction in interwar Japan "involved much more than lofty phrases and imperial proclamations." Like the original nation-building enterprise, it also derived from structural developments that transformed the foundations of the state. Just as latter nineteenth-century reforms rested upon a newly centralized system of prefectures and national system of taxation, education, conscription, communications, and transport, post-Versailles Japan was based in a newly industrialized, urbanized polity with an educated middle class and mass consumer culture. From these foundations, "the New Japan played a pivotal role in the decisive shift from nineteenth-century conceptions of civilization to a twentieth-century world, that is, from elite to mass politics," from national to increasingly multinational concerns, from unyielding faith in arms to arms control, from "brinksmanship to overtures for peace." Development of this formidable combination of new sensibilities was never consistent or complete, and still not enough to prevent a conflagration of even greater magnitude than the First World War.[66]

---

[65] Dickinson, "Toward a Global Perspective of the Great War," 1181–2.
[66] Dickinson, "Toward a Global Perspective of the Great War," 1182–3.

The Great War also had negative impacts for Japan. Although industry benefited enormously from the war, the great majority of Japanese saw their real spending power decline during the boom years of 1914–18. Given the widespread and well-publicized growth in national wealth during the war, citizens believed that rice should be readily available. When food costs rose faster than wages, the Japanese blamed both local officials and the Cabinet of Prime Minister Terauchi Masatake. The central government responded slowly to what journalists from 1917 began to refer to as the "rice price revolution."[67] In 1918, there was a series of mass demonstrations and armed clashes on a scale unprecedented in Japan's modern history. For eight weeks, from July 22 to October 4, rice riots swept from Hokkaido to Kyushu, in fishing villages and rural hamlets, in Tokyo streets, and even around coal pits.[68] The Japanese government worried that it might be facing something like the Russian Revolution and moved to suppress the unrest with decisive military force. To restore order, the soldiers turned their guns on the crowd, killing more than thirty civilians and wounding scores of others.[69]

In their scale and distribution, and in the massive mobilization of military and relief efforts necessary to suppress them, the 1918 rice riots were unprecedented. Reliable estimates indicate that protests occurred in 49 cities, 217 towns, and 231 villages. Estimates of the number of rioters range from a low of 700,000 to a high of 10 million. But whatever the precise figure may be, those who took to the streets represented diverse social backgrounds and a sizable portion of Japan's total population of about 56 million, a figure that takes on greater significance when we realize that most Japanese family members were not adults. More than 8,000 people were later prosecuted. The rice riots led to the breakdown of civil order, which played an important role in both the rise of Hara Takeshi, the first non-peer prime minister, and the beginning of cabinets routinely composed of party politicians. The political significance of the war, and the riots that followed, should not be overstressed however. The protests occurred in the context of worldwide campaigns for greater popular rights and earlier resistance movements within Japan. Still, the protests resulted in far more than the replacement of Terauchi by a commoner prime minister; the widespread civilian unrest engendered a host of long-lasting changes in central and local government policy. One major post-riot reform was the creation of permanent, systematized government measures for providing and distributing rice. Post-riot changes in colonial policy included ministerial orders that imports of sorghum from Manchuria to Korea be stepped up so this lower-quality grain could replace rice in the Korean diet and produce an exportable surplus for the home islands. Similarly, the colonial government in Taiwan encouraged the local consumption of sweet potato and extended its monopoly control over various agricultural products to ease the rice scarcity inside Japan.[70]

---

[67] Michael Lewis, *Rioters and Citizens: Mass Protest in Imperial Japan* (Berkeley: University of California Press, 1990), 1, 11.
[68] Lewis, *Rioters and Citizens*, 15.   [69] Lewis, *Rioters and Citizens*, xvii.
[70] Lewis, *Rioters and Citizens*, 16, 243, 246.

Chinese interest in the war developed out of a sense of victimization. Yet the very imperialist forces that had humiliated and oppressed China also served as inspiration. China sought to defeat Japanese imperialism by adopting the imperialists' motivation and ideology. The new ideology of nationalism that fueled China's revolution, internal renewal, and transformation was rooted in the Chinese desire to join the world—to become a modern nation-state, and a rich and powerful country. This same nationalism, however, suppressed the traditional values that had formerly marked Chinese civilization and undermined its unique character. In a sense, the dynamism of the era is reflected in its combination of political nationalism, cultural iconoclasm, and diplomatic internationalism in China's approach to world affairs. During the First World War, Chinese elites began to experiment with building a nation-state that jettisoned Chinese culture and tradition. They tried to redefine a national identity in terms that had nothing to do with China's own civilization and experience. The coexistence of liberalism and warlordism was a strange mix that made China seem a monster with two heads, each facing a different direction.[71] In fact, a dual policymaking process existed during this period: on one side were modern, outward-looking bureaucrats and social elites who tried hard to push China into the international system; and on the other were the warlords and ultra-conservatives who wished only to stop the clock, effectively mortgaging China's future for their own benefit. The tensions generated by this process created an acute dilemma that put in jeopardy the quest for a new national identity and made China's entry into the international system difficult and circuitous. If hostilities between China and Japan were a shared theme in both the First World War era and today, Chinese frustration about "What is China and who is Chinese?" is another important shared issue then and today.

The weakness of the Western Powers in Asia after the Great War left China and Japan each impaled on the horns of its own impossibility: only a Chinese government that already had the power to defend itself against Japan could earn enough legitimacy to mobilize (or coerce) the resources to do so; a government too weak to unify the country and mobilize those resources was too weak to defend the nation. Japan's impossibility was that it could neither find Chinese who would cooperate without being branded as traitors nor, in the long run, conquer China; the only Chinese leaders who could survive nationalist attacks on them for cooperating with Japan were those who had no need to cooperate because they were strong enough to defy Japan. A third impossibility was that after the Great War, the survival of a Japanese government depended on controlling China, or at least dominating it, and the survival of a Chinese government depended on frustrating that policy. These impossibilities could be dealt with only after the United States defeated Japan in 1945, the communist revolution unified China in 1949, and the United States, Japan, and a strong China came to terms with each other in the 1970s. Only then was the First World War in China and Japan partially resolved.

---

[71] For details on Chinese warlordism, see Arthur Waldron, "The Warlord: Twentieth-Century Chinese Understandings of Violence, Militarism, and Imperialism," *American Historical Review*, 96:4 (October, 1991), 1073–100.

PART II

EMPIRES AT WAR: THE GREAT WAR AND TRANSFORMATIONS IN THE NATIONAL DEVELOPMENT OF INDIA, KOREA, AND VIETNAM

3

India's Great War and National Awakening

Unlike China and Japan, which took the initiative in devising their Great War policies, India's involvement in the war came largely as a by-product of its inclusion in the British Empire, not as a decision made directly in India's interest. Indian nationalists were not in a position to make decisions on international relations, but this does not mean that they were passive. Many Indian elites chose to support the British war effort with the longer view that it would help them achieve their dream of eventual independence.

Indian involvement in the war under the British was important for at least two reasons. First, it expanded Indian relations with the outside world. In the past, the world at large had meant little to most Indians; they had rarely given much thought to international and military affairs. Their involvement in the war for the first time confronted them with a fuller realization of their relation to the rest of the British Empire and the world. Second, India's part in the war had a deep impact on its elites' thinking about their country and on the rise of Indian nationalism. In 1914, India was not considered a nation per se, instead it was an agglomeration of many races, castes, and creeds who tolerated one another but had little in common, except their domination by British rule. But the Great War opened a new world to the Indians and helped them realize their strength; moreover, they realized that this strength could be built on through their exposure to Western education and ideals. In other words, the war proved to be a road they shared with fellow Asians as well as Western peoples.

The British decision to seek Indian assistance "furnished a common cause for which all could work, irrespective of racial distinctions or beliefs"; it also gave the cause of nationalism in India "a decided fillip."[1] Distinguished historian of India Stanley Wolpert wrote that the war's impact on India "proved all-pervasive, transforming its economic balance, giving birth to massive new industries" and "stirring the waters of political change as they had never been roiled before. New aspirations were awakened, new pride; new constituencies arose, and along with them, a new consciousness of India's value to the survival of Britain's empire and an impatience to be free of imperial constraints."[2]

---

[1] Dewitt Mackenzie, *The Awakening of India* (London: Hodder and Stoughton, 1918), 18–21.
[2] Stanley Wolpert, *A New History of India* (New York: Oxford University Press, 2009), 310.

INDIA'S INDUCTION INTO THE GREAT WAR

It was Lord Hardinge, then viceroy of India, who signed a declaration of war by India against Germany and Austria.[3] At the beginning of this war between European peoples, Britain did not imagine it would need India's help.[4] But the British soon realized they would have to mobilize all their resources to prevail. As Herbert Asquith, the Liberal prime minister, put it to the House of Commons, "If we are entering into the struggle, let us now make sure that all the resources, not only of this United Kingdom, but of the vast Empire of which it's the centre, shall be thrown into the scale."[5] To secure Indian assistance, the British government paid lip service to the eventual transfer of political power. Asquith declared that in future, Indian questions were to be viewed from "a different angle of vision." He held out the promise of self-government as a reward for India's loyalty. Soon after, Lloyd George announced that the principle of self-determination was to be further extended "in tropical countries."[6]

In 1916, shortly after becoming prime minister, Lloyd George told the House of Commons that the time had come to formally consult with the Dominions and India about the best way to win the war. He intended, therefore, to create an Imperial War Cabinet. This was both a gesture and pragmatic. But did the British really mean it? The Dominions and India kept the British war effort going with their raw materials, their munitions, their loans, and above all with their manpower. The British believed the war might also help them keep India secure: "We have destroyed the menace to our Indian possessions."[7] But an internal threat was looming as nationalism began to take hold. That part the British got completely wrong. An expert on India and the First World War, Santanu Das, once pointed out that "The First World War thus catches the Indian psyche at a fragile spot between a continuing and somewhat strategic loyalty to the empire and strong nationalist aspirations." The 1919 Jallianwala Bagh massacre in Punjab, the very region that had contributed the highest number of troops, would crush the last vestiges of Indian hope that India's wartime contributions would change the relation between India and Britain.[8]

The Great War era coincided with a major national awakening among Indians. Both Indian elite society and the lives of the lower classes would be affected in its

---

[3] Lord Hardinge of Penshurst, *My Indian Years, 1910–1916: The Reminiscences of Lord Hardinge of Penshurst* (London: John Murray, 1948), 98.

[4] Britain indeed needed assistance from many different places. Even the Dalai Lama of Tibet offered a contingent of a thousand troops, while the innumerable lamas who owed him allegiance chanted prayers for a British victory at the behest of "The Lord of All the Beings in the Snowy Country." See H. H. Dodwell, ed., *The Cambridge History of India* (Delhi: S. Chand & Co., 1964), 6: 477.

[5] Morton-Jack, *The Indian Army on the Western Front*, 4.

[6] Shyam Narain Saxena, *Role of Indian Army in the First World War* (Delhi: Bhavan Prakashan, 1987), 5.

[7] George Riddell, *Lord Riddell's Intimate Diary of the Peace Conference and After, 1918–1923* (London: V. Gollancz, 1933), 42.

[8] Santanu Das, "Ardour and Anxiety: Politics and Literature on the Indian Home Front," in Heike Liebau, et al., eds., *The World in World Wars: Experiences, Perceptions and Perspectives from Africa and Asia* (Leiden: Brill, 2010), 367.

course, thus making it a point of no return in India's national development. Santanu Das has suggested that Indian political opinion was unanimous in its support for the war. Though the war was universally seen as a catastrophe for Europe, it was an opportunity for India. Some even came to call it "India's Opportunity." This situation closely parallels the Chinese sense of *weiji*, that the war brought both danger and opportunity. As P. S. Sivaswami, a member of the Indian executive council wrote, "[the Indian's] loyalty is not the merely instinctive loyalty of the Briton at home or the Colonial, but the outcome of gratitude for benefits conferred and of the conviction that the progress of India is indissolubly bound up with the integrity and solidarity of the British Empire."[9]

So Indian elites responded to the British call for help with enthusiasm. Bhupendranath Basu, a member of the Imperial Legislative Council, wrote in September 1914 that before the war, India was embroiled in domestic controversies: "Then came this great European war, sudden and swift: all doubt, all hesitation, all questions were swept away; there was but one feeling—to stand by England in the hour of danger. The great opportunity for India, in the highest sense, had come: she claimed to hold an equal position with other parts of the Empire—she wanted to prove her title." The Indians wanted to make sacrifices in the war "so that the old order of things may pass away and a new order be ushered in, based on mutual understanding and confidence and heralding an era brighter and happier than any in the past—the East and the West, India and England, marching onwards in comradeship, united in bonds forged on the field of battle and tempered in their common blood."[10] According to a leading Indian politician, S. P. Sinha, president of the Indian National Congress in 1915: "The question which, above all others, is engrossing our minds at the present moment is the War.... The War has given India an opportunity, as nothing else could have done, of demonstrating the courage, bravery and tenacity of her troops, even when pitted against the best organized armies of the world, and also the capacity of her sons of all classes, creeds and nationalities to rise as one people under the stimulus of an overpowering emotion."[11] In the face of such sacrifices, he expressed the hope that Britain would grant India self-government. He argued, "Towards this end the war is rapidly helping us onward. In the midst of carnage and massacre, there is being accomplished the destruction of much that is evil and there is the budding forth of much that will abide."[12] Some Indians went so far as to claim that "India is heart and soul with great Britain" in this war.[13]

The Indian National Congress was established in 1885 with putatively nationalist aims.[14] But until the outbreak of the Great War, it lacked both resources and a

---

[9] Das, "Ardour and Anxiety," 351–2.

[10] Bhupendranath Basu, *Why India is Heart and Soul with Great Britain* (London: Macmillan and Co., 1914), 8.

[11] S. P. Sinha, *The Future of India: Presidential Address to the Indian National Congress by Sir S. P. Sinha on the 27th December 1915* (London: Jas. Truscott & Son, 1916), 1, 2–3.

[12] Sinha, *The Future of India*, 44.

[13] Basu, *Why India is Heart and Soul with Great Britain*, 1.

[14] For an excellent study on the Indian National Congress during 1880 and 1915, see Gordon Johnson, *Provincial Politics and Indian Nationalism: Bombay and the Indian National Congress* (Cambridge: Cambridge University Press, 1973).

vision for achieving Indian national dreams. It did not challenge the legitimacy of the British rule, but instead focused on defending and protecting the rights of Indians within the British Empire. The outbreak of war changed all that. According to Jim Masselos, "By the end of the first decade of the twentieth century, the nationalist movement in India had undergone considerable change. Its techniques and objectives had broadened and there was a much greater participation of the elites in the Punjab, Bengal and Maharashtra than in the last two decades of the nineteenth century."[15] In December 1914, only a few months into the war, the Indian National Congress resolved to convey "to His Majesty the King-Emperor and the people of England its profound devotion to the Throne, its unswerving allegiance to the British connection, and its firm resolve to stand by the Empire at all hazards and at all costs."[16] It seems that nearly all prominent Indian politicians supported the military recruitment effort. One unexpected advocate of recruitment was in fact Mohandas K. Gandhi, then in his late forties and recently returned from twenty years in South Africa, where he had earned renown as a fighter for the equal rights of Indians as subjects of the British Crown. When the war started, Gandhi, whose arrival in London en route to India coincided with the outbreak of the war, decided "for the sake of the motherland and the Empire, to place his services at the disposal of the authorities," and took lead in organizing an ambulance unit from among Indian residents in England.[17] Once back in India, he offered to recruit soldiers for the British-Indian army. "I would like to do something," he once wrote to an official in the colonial government, "which Lord Chelmsford would consider to be real war work. I have an idea that, if I became your recruiting agent-in-chief, I might rain men on you."[18] But British officials did not take Gandhi's recruiting campaign seriously. Although Gandhi did not provide much active support, his enthusiasm for the British war effort was still clear.[19] More revealingly, when Annie Besant sought his support for the Home Rule Movement in India, Gandhi refused and told her "You are distrustful of the British; I am not, and I will not help in any agitation against them during the war."[20] Gandhi's attitude to the war and the British Empire indicated that he cherished the hope "that India would receive self-government at the end of the war if she whole-heartedly supported the British war effort."[21]

Gandhi was not alone. Bal Gangadhar Tilak was another who saw the war as an avenue to self-government. In 1917, Edwin Montagu recorded in his diary that Tilak was "at the moment probably the most powerful man in India."[22] Tilak, who was released from a Mandalay prison in June 1914 after serving a six-year sentence,

[15] Jim Masselos, *Indian Nationalism: An History* (New Delhi: Sterling Publishers, 1985), 137.

[16] B. R. Nanda, *Gokhale: The Indian Moderates and the British Raj* (Princeton, NJ: Princeton University Press, 1977), 446.

[17] Nanda, *Gokhale*, 446.

[18] B. R. Nanda, *Gandhi: Pan-Islamism, Imperialism, and Nationalism in India* (New Delhi: Oxford University Press, 2002), 163.

[19] Nanda, *Gandhi: Pan-Islamism, Imperialism, and Nationalism in India*, 163.

[20] B. R. Nanda, *Mahatma Gandhi: A Biography* (Boston: Beacon Press, 1958), 97.

[21] Nanda, *Mahatma Gandhi*, 105.

[22] Nanda, *Mahatma Gandhi*, 99.

cabled the king-emperor to assure his loyal support for the war.[23] Tilak's own paper, the *Mahratta*, published the following on October 4, 1914: "Indian hearts will be thrilled to know that Indian troops have landed in France."[24] Many nationalist leaders like him were vocal supporters of efforts to recruit Indians into the military, since they saw in it an opportunity to prove the value and loyalty of Indians to the empire and thus establish their right to equality as its citizens. When the war broke out, the Indian Home Rule movement became powerful. Annie Besant, who helped lead the movement, declared that "the price of India's loyalty is India's freedom." In 1916, she further declared to her followers that "We offer to God all that we have and keep nothing back. We give our name, we give our liberty. We give our lives, if need be, for the sake of Motherland and as God is just and as God is righteous, the sacrifice that we place before the Motherland's altar shall send up its flames to heaven and the answer it fire shall descend."[25]

To carry forward the Home Rule moment, Bal Gangadhar Tilak first established the Home Rule League in 1916. Tilak and Besant served as chief architects of the movement, which was launched during the war with a view to gaining substantial political concessions from the British government. Tilak publicly expressed, in February 1917, his great satisfaction at the intention of the government to enroll Indians in the Defense of India Force and urged the people to respond wholeheartedly to this call to the defense of motherland and empire. Their status, he said, would have to be made equal to "European British subjects in India" and it would therefore have to remain so after the war.[26]

How had the war affected the imagination of India's professional and middle classes and their national consciousness? According to Santanu Das, during the war years, "domestic politics became more 'national' than before." For example, Annie Besant, in her article "India's Loyalty and England's Duty," wrote, "When the war is over and we cannot doubt that the King-Emperor will, as reward for her [India's] glorious defence of the Empire, pin upon her breast the jeweled medal of Self-Government within the Empire. It will be, in a sense, a real Victoria Cross, for the great Empress would see in it the fulfilment of her promise in 1858, and the legend inscribed on it would be 'For Valour.'" Das also believes that "For many Indians, imperial war service became curiously a way of salvaging national and regional prestige." This kind of national awakening emerges poignantly from a series of poems published in *All about the War*. One of these poems was by A. Madhaviah:

> Sister! Brothers! Now's the hour
> That we prove our worth—
> Let who can, go fight and slay,
> . . .

---

[23] Wolpert, *A New History of India*, 302.

[24] Nanda, *Gokhale*, 447.

[25] U. N. Chakravorty, *Indian Nationalism and the First World War, 1914–18* (Calcutta: Progressive Publishers, 1997), 65–7.

[26] Erez Manela, *The Wilsonian Moment: Self-Determination and the International Origins of Anticolonial Nationalism* (New York: Oxford University Press, 2007), 82.

> Prove by all that's in our power,
> England's cause is ours.[27]

The war stimulated Indian commerce and industry, but it also made staggering demands on India's fragile economy. The virtual disappearance of European manufactured goods from Indian markets stimulated industrial growth in some sectors such as textiles, but Indians also paid a huge price, given the wartime inflation and economic and social dislocation. In India, wartime hardship "fostered a general mood of restlessness and anticipation, and this, combined with the tremendous contribution of men and materiel to the war effort, led many Indians to expect Britain to reward them at the end of the war. Already in 1916, one prominent moderate leader noted that the enormity of the war meant that the world was 'on the eve of a great reconstruction, and England and India will participate in that reconstruction.' The war, observed another leading politician, 'has put the clock . . . fifty years forward.' When it ended, Indians would surely be able to 'take their legitimate part in the administration of their own country.'"[28]

THE SITUATION IN EUROPE

At no time in Indian history had such massive numbers of Indians gone abroad, and even more significantly, they went to help their colonial masters fight a major war. When the Indian troops arrived in France in September 1914, "What an army!" reported the *New York World*. "Its 'native' contingent belongs to a civilization that was old when Germany was a forest, and early Britons stained their naked bodies blue."[29] General James Willcocks, commander of the Indian Corps, wrote in a letter to the viceroy, Lord Hardinge: "Our Indian soldiers serve for a very small remuneration; they were serving in a strange foreign land; they were the most patient soldiers in the world; they are doing what Asiatics have never been asked to do before."[30]

Life was certainly not easy for the Indian soldiers and laborers in France. On December 27, 1917, one Indian laborer wrote in a letter from France: "You enquire about the cold? I will tell plainly what the cold in France is like when I meet you. At present I can only say that the earth is white, the sky is white, the trees are white, the stones are white, the mud is white, the water is white, one's spittle freezes into a solid white lump."[31] While the weather was certainly a challenge, the widespread racism in Europe was even harder to bear.

Indians suffered badly from both racism and mistreatment under the British officers at the front. The soldiers were teased about not eating beef and other

[27] Das, "Ardour and Anxiety," 353–5.

[28] Manela, *The Wilsonian Moment*, 82.   [29] Wolpert, *A New History of India*, 302.

[30] DeWitt C. Ellinwood, *Between Two Worlds: A Rajput Officer in the Indian Army, 1905–21: Based on the Diary of Amar Singh of Jaipur* (Lanham, MD: Hamilton Books, 2005), 365.

[31] Letter 628, in David Omissi, *Indian Voices of the Great War: Soldiers' Letters, 1914–18* (New York: St. Martin's Press, 1999), 342.

customs. Attitudes about "Indian natural inferiority" were widespread among the British. Officers treated Indian workers with contempt and called them pejorative terms such as "niggers" and "golliwogs." The British rank and file were similarly inclined, and their contempt for the Indians was the least restrained. But the British infantryman tended to be "recruited from the UK's poorest areas and 65 percent of them had not reached the educational standard expected of British eleven year olds, leading one contemporary psychiatrist to describe them as 'wasters and half-wits.'" They were notorious for their ready violence against Indian civilians, "to keep the bleeding natives down," said one Welsh private.[32] Even the Germans piled on, with their propaganda machine attacking Britain for the use of its "colonial savages" in a white people's war.

As Indian historian Radhiha Singha's research shows, Lord Ampthill, advisor to the Directorate of Labour for the Indian Labour Corps (ILC) in France, worried that the unit's utility was compromised. At first, he was concerned by the "inferior physique and intelligence and exotic nature" of the men; he considered them "very engaging savages," with their friendly smiles, childish adornments, weird chants, and their unapologetic nudity. Ampthill complained about the French population's friendliness and kindness to the Indian laborers, but he also argued they had come to France inspired by a spirited desire to serve empire, not merely to earn a wage. Ampthill, who had served as Governor of Madras (1900–6) and briefly as pro tem viceroy in 1904, began to chafe at the fact that the ILC was being deployed by the War Office with a complete lack of political imagination, that it was overlooking the future of empire in India. He tried, without success, to get the men recategorized as sepoys (military personnel) rather than laborers, so they would feel they were serving in an honorable capacity, and the public would be reminded of India's continued presence in the European theater.

Ampthill also stressed that they had been heavily overtasked and badly needed some rest, as well as recognition for their work. He reported that the Indians in their letters home complained that they were treated "like animals. Nobody takes any notice of us [. . .] we get no credit for the work we do." Most Indian laborers did not intend to extend their contracts in early 1918 and just wanted to return home. But due to a shortage of transport and under ongoing pressure to extend their contracts, their repatriation was delayed. The men were not happy, and they showed it by occasional work stoppages. At least twelve instances of ILC companies going on strike were recorded between March and December 1918. The main plank of collective resistance, however, was their refusal to sign new contracts. By suggesting that they were now working only to oblige their officers, not because they were bound by contract, the men sought to bolster their demand to be returned home.[33]

[32] Morton-Jack, *The Indian Army on the Western Front*, 35.
[33] Radhika Singha, "The Recruiter's Eye on the Primitive: To France—and Back—in the Indian Labour Corps, 1917–1918," in James Kitchen, Alisa Miller, and Laura Rowe, eds., *Other Combatants, Other Fronts: Competing Histories of the First World War* (Newcastle upon Tyne: Cambridge Scholars, 2011), 215–16.

The arrival of Indian soldiers in England prompted efforts to constrain and control their mobility and sexuality, as well as those of white working-class women. Indeed, there had been many cases of romantic relations between Indian men and French women. Witnessing the romance between Indian soldiers and Western women, the British were worried about the "threat to white prestige," "European degeneracy and moral decay" implicit in the sexual mixing of the "colonizer's [female] body with that of the colonized." British authorities realized that the most dangerous aspect of this kind of interracial relationship was its being "detrimental to the prestige and spirit of European rule."[34] The government and army thus focused on controlling the Indians' access to white society. In the language of the times, authorities thought the Indians and working-class British women were highly sexed, which might lead to mutual attraction that would affront family and national values, and result in miscegenation, and ultimately, racial degeneration. To achieve the segregation of Indian men from white women, British female nurses were barred from attending to wounded Indian military personnel, with few exceptions. Indeed, their sexual relationships with white women spurred Indian thoughts about why at home and elsewhere they were treated as inferior to the white colonizers.[35] Authorities confined wounded Indian personnel to the hospital precincts on Britain's south coast, but controversy arose there over the employment of white female nurses. Authorities resolved the problem by limiting the nurses to supervisory positions and confining Indian forays to London to highly organized Cook's Tours. White dominion soldiers never faced such restrictions in any theater.[36]

The YMCA was permitted to organize recreation for Indian laborers and soldiers, as it did for the Chinese, provided it did not engage in proselytization. According to one official YMCA report of November 5, 1915, when the Indians arrived in France, the staff often found them terribly homesick, huddled in small groups trying to keep warm, and drearily discussing the strength of the enemy and news of the latest casualties at the front. Out of touch with home, and rarely able to send or receive letters, they were naturally depressed. To prevent them from visiting local prostitutes in Marseilles during the cold French winter, the YMCA provided a bioscope *tamasha* (a traditional theater) every night in the camps, where 400 to 600 soldiers gathered to warm themselves around stoves and enjoy pictures of cavalry maneuvers or travel scenes, and the buffooneries of the irrepressible Max Linder, whose French idea of humor seemed to satisfy their own. Like the Chinese laborers, the Indians were provided slide lectures twice a week on the war and other topics, and it was amazing to see how very little they knew about the things for which they were fighting or the geography of Europe; maps seemed new to many of them. Once, the YMCA set up a barber shop for the Indians, a move that disgusted the camp's British officer, who thought that British prestige would never recover. The YMCA offered regular French classes, and published French phrase books in Urdu,

[34] Singh, *The Testimonies of Indian Soldiers and the Two World Wars*, 81, 85.
[35] Singh, *The Testimonies of Indian Soldiers and the Two World Wars*, 83–4.
[36] Morrow, *The Great War: An Imperial History*, 107–8.

Gurmukhi, and Hindi, which were revised and reprinted by the Indian Soldiers' Fund. About 100,000 of these circulated, and it was amusing to hear a conversation between a Tommy and a "Jonny," as the British called the Gurkha, conducted in French. Indians were enthusiastic about French classes and an evening class could attract 400 men.[37]

The YMCA secretaries also helped the men write and read letters. The Indians were great correspondents. Scholar Claude Markovits suggests that in March 1915 they wrote between 10,000 and 20,000 letters a week, except when actually fighting or on the march.[38] When they were free, these laborers would crowd all day around the little hut where the Indian secretaries wrote their letters, and some of the YMCA staff marveled at their patience as they wrote in the bitter cold, hour after hour, and always came up smiling. With the Indians in France writing sometimes as many as 30,000 letters a month, one of the British censors eventually complained, "Your fellows have changed my job from a sinecure into a burden." These letters are of many kinds, but almost all avoided grumbling and the vast bulk were after one pattern: "I am well. Food and clothing very good. Weather somewhat cold." One YMCA report recorded two instances of Indian appreciation for the YMCA efforts that stand out vividly: "It is Christmas day, and the Sikhs have borrowed our shed for a solemn service of meditation and prayer. This finished they take up a collection, scores of coins of all sizes and countries, in aid of the work of the YMCA. Then follow sports." The second scene proceeded as follows: "The Sikhs are gathered in solemn consultation: 'What can we do to stop drunkenness and impurity in our midst? Let us invite the Sahib of the YMCA to address us!' "[39]

Activities such as direct observation of Western countries and writing letters helped Indians abroad reflect on who they were and what India was, and they developed new thinking about themselves and their homeland. According to Susan Vankoski, the Indian letters "reveal a genuine appreciation of French hospitality and warmth." One soldier wrote to a friend at home, "Tell the women to be brave like men. I am astonished to see the women of France, beautiful as they are, brace themselves up and show greater pluck even than men. They are even ready to arm themselves and take part in the fighting. My mother and wives ought to show courage like this." Another Indian decried what he thought the lack of universal education had done in India. He felt that France enjoyed an advantage in civilization because,

> The custom in this country is that when a child is five years old he is sent to school . . . These people appear to be superior to us solely because of education. Learning is a great benefit. Moreover the custom with us of having servants to do our menial work is profitless. These people themselves do their menial work with their

---

[37] IWM: K. 75345: Saunders, K.J., with the Indians in France: being an account of the work of the army YMCA of India with Indian expeditionary force A.

[38] Claude Markovits, "Indian Soldiers' Experiences in France during World War I," in Liebau et al., *The World in World Wars*, 36.

[39] IWM: K. 75345: Saunders, K.J, with the Indians in France: being an account of the work of the army YMCA OF India with Indian expeditionary force A.

own hands. They are not in the least ashamed of working. Our people are steeped to death in shame. If we would do all our work ourselves we would reap much benefit both for ourselves and also for our Sircar.

Compared to the charms of Europe, life in India was taking a beating in many soldiers' minds. Some, in their letters home, indicated that they would prefer to remain in Europe after the war. And indeed many eventually settled in Britain.[40] The Indians' observation of French society forced them to reflect their own. Finding that husbands and wives in France were more equal, one Sikh soldier wrote to his grandfather: "I know well that a woman in our country is of no more value than a pair of shoes and this is why the people of India are low in the scale. When I look at Europe, I bewail the lot of India. In Europe, everyone—man and woman, boy and girl—is educated. The men are at the war and the women are doing the work... You ought to educate your girls as well as your boys."[41]

By changing the thinking of Indians who went to Europe, the First World War accelerated political and social changes that might otherwise have taken generations. The mobilization of human resources and the sending of Indians to France either as soldiers or laborers had long-term significance for Indian national development. It helped create political fluidity. According to Indian historian Radhika Singha, as the Indian Army mobilized, caste and ethnic criteria for combatant service were relaxed and a much wider social and spatial vista was opened on recruitment into military work. It seems to Singha that one can discover a new historical aspiration at the resting place of one Indian in Europe:

> *Sukha Kalloo's epitaph*
> He left country, home and friends to save our
> King and Empire in the Great European War
>
> . . .
>
> By creed he was not Christian
> But this earthly life was sacrificed in the interests of others
> There is one God and Father of all who is
> For all and through all and in all.[42]

Singha writes that along India's frontier areas in particular, rendering or refusing war service in Europe left a permanent mark upon narratives of ethnic nationalism and the competing territorial claims based on them. For some in the ILC, war service provided the opportunity to travel to that metropolitan world with which they were negotiating at their own thresholds—but perceptions of home were also reframed in that endeavor. But she also looks beyond India's martial classes to explore the deepening colonial interest in the labor, military, and political potential of the empire's "primitive" subjects. During the Great War, when tribal labor was

---

[40] Susan Vankoski, "Letters Home, 1915-16: Punjabi Soldiers Reflect on War and Life in Europe and their Meanings for Home and Self," *International Journal of Punjab Studies*, 2:1 (1995), 43–63.

[41] Claude Markovits, "Indian Soldiers' Experiences in France During World War I," 45.

[42] Radhika Singha, "Front Lines and Status Lines: Sepoy and 'Menial' in the Great War 1916–1920," in Liebau et al., *The World in World Wars*, 55–106.

being sent overseas, the government of India felt it necessary to cast recruitment in a paternalist frame, but in fact, warfare was an ongoing reality for many communities on the Assam-Burma frontier, where militaristic border-making was a routine part of the colonial "civil administration." ILC recruitment therefore tapped into infrastructures and practices which had evolved from colonial border-making, and many Indians from those margins, who were categorized by colonial ethnography as belonging to a "rudimentary" stage of civilization, went to France, the center of Western civilization.[43] In other words, their war experiences, to a great extent, helped in shaping both Indian and Western civilizations.

Walter Lawrence of the Indian Civil Service could speak to the Indian troops in several of their own languages and was appointed in 1914 as a British special commissioner to monitor the wounded and sick in France and England. He wrote that through many hours of chatting with them, "I gained a new knowledge of the mentality of Indians, sitting with them and listening to their strange impressions of this wonderful new world into which they had tumbled."[44] According to Lawrence, while in Europe, the Indians were for the most part dejected and disappointed at circumstances which seemed to conspire against them. The Sikhs and the Gurkhas were soldiers of the desert and sun-parched mountains, men proud of their traditional powers, who found that Flanders was no place for them. "It was noticeable that the mountain men [of] Gurhwal and the Punjabi Mahomedans seemed to stand the novel conditions of static and mechanical fighting better than the more acclaimed Sikhs and Gurkhas." In Lawrence's close observation, the Indians came to Europe to fight but "They had the vaguest idea as to who these enemies were or what the war was about. With some reason it might have been thought that if it was a matter of gratitude, England rather than India should be grateful." But Lawrence also reported, "When the Indian troops left France, they found a more congenial terrain in Mesopotamia and Palestine; and in a campaign of rapid movement they won laurels and renown. I was sent to Syria in 1919, and found Indian troops happy, useful and efficient, in surroundings which seemed very familiar."[45]

Still, even in Europe the Indian soldiers were personally grateful for what kind treatment they received. "The French people welcomed the Indian forces because they knew that the Indians had shed blood for their cause," said one Sikh veteran. "The French had a great respect for us and kept us happy," recalled another. "They kept us in their own houses, so we learnt their language and ways of living. They presented . . . many things to each. . . . They were our best friends."[46] In one letter written from a Brighton hospital, "One gets such service as no one can get in his own house, not even a noble. One gets milk, meat, tea and all sorts of fruit, apples,

[43] Singha, "The Recruiter's Eye on the Primitive," 202.
[44] Walter Lawrence, *The India We Served* (Boston: Houghton Mifflin Company, 1929), 271.
[45] Lawrence, *The India We Served*, 271–3.
[46] Morton-Jack, *The Indian Army on the Western Front*, 293.

pears, and oranges, sweetmeats as much as excellent beds beyond description. These are no fables. This country compared with others is heaven."[47]

As with the Chinese, the Indians' direct contact with Westerners in Europe collectively broadened their perspective and generated new thinking about Eastern and Western civilizations. The Indians' important role in the war would contribute to their political awakening, new national thinking, and confidence.

INDIANS IN FRANCE AND THEIR CONTRIBUTIONS

Due to enormous Indian support for the British war effort, British politicians had to acknowledge India's contributions. Lord Hardinge, viceroy of India from 1910 to April 1916, once declared that since the war's outbreak, "all political controversies concerning India have been suspended by the educated and political classes with the object of not increasing the difficulties of the Government's task."[48] Hardinge later told *The New York Times* that "had India been as disloyal [to Britain] as the Germans would doubtless have liked it to be, our policy would have been tantamount to an evacuation of our Indian Empire, with the probability that we were condemning the few thousands of troops left behind, practically without artillery, and the whole white civilian population to being submerged under a tidal wave of revolt."[49] Even Britain's king issued a message to the princes and peoples of India on September 8, 1914. In it, he wrote that during the last few weeks, people of his empire "have moved with one mind and purpose to confront and overthrow an unparalleled assault upon the continuity of civilization and the peace of mankind."[50] He then expressed his appreciation for Indian devotion and loyalty: "Their one-voiced demand to be foremost in the conflict has touched my heart, and has inspired to the highest issues the love and devotion. . . . I find in this hour of trial a full harvest and a noble fulfillment of the assurance given by you that the destinies of Great Britain and India are indissolubly linked."[51]

Among Asians, only the Indians and Vietnamese were directly involved in the fighting in Europe.[52] Although India was treated as the lowest member of the British Empire, always noted as "the Dominions and India" in official documents, it in fact contributed the largest number of its men to the British war effort and more resources than any of the other colonies or dominions. With the British India Office and local governments mobilizing combatant and non-combatant labor, the

---

[47] Lawrence, *The India We Served*, 272.

[48] The London Correspondent of *The New York Times*, *Loyal India: An Interview with Lord Hardinge of Penshurst, Ex-Governor-General of India* (London: Sir Joseph Causton & Sons, 1916), 11.

[49] The London Correspondent of *The New York Times*, *Loyal India*, 5.

[50] Lord Sydenham of Combe, *India and the War* (London: Hodder and Stoughton, 1919), 39.

[51] Lord Sydenham of Combe, *India and the War*, 41.

[52] Thailand indeed sent volunteer forces to France, but they arrived too late to join the fighting. The Chinese offered to send military forces, but the Allied side was not very supportive and they did not arrive.

Indians "served as an enormous reservoir of men in the Allied cause."[53] Over the course of the war, 1,069 officers of the Indian Medical Corps, 1,200 nursing sisters, 2,142 assistant and sub-assistant surgeons, and 97 followers were sent to the various theaters.[54] About 1.2 million Indian men, 800,000 of them in combat roles, fought for the empire in France, Egypt, and Mesopotamia, and worked side by side with their colonial masters. The soldiers went to France first, then the laborers followed. In 1916, Britain turned to India for civilian labor resources, and the first group of 2,000 men left for France in May 1917.[55] In June 1917, another group of 6,370 also arrived in France. They were soon joined by about 20,000 new men.[56]

The 50,000 Indian laborers sent to France represented six different provinces. When it needed still more labor, the British authorities turned to recruiting Indian prisoners. Over the period from October 1916 to July 1919, some 16,000 Indian prisoners were sent to serve in the Jail Porter and Labour Corps in Mesopotamia. An additional 1,602 prisoners were recruited for miscellaneous services. The success of this practice convinced the general officer commanding Force D of the wisdom of maintaining contractual honesty with its labor units, including those recruited through "duration of war" agreements. "On various occasions," he pronounced, "When Asiatics viz. Egyptians, Chinamen and Indians have been kept under the stress of circumstances beyond their agreements, trouble has resulted."

The imperial quest for labor also yields new perspectives on the political transformations underway in the course of the Great War. The involvement of Indians in the war as soldiers and coolies elicited a complicated response from Indian elites. At one level, sections of the Indian intelligentsia had begun to characterize the use of penal provisions to enforce labor contracts as "unsuited to modern conditions" and to lay the blame for such laws on "foreign" capital. Yet even as they called for labor to be granted juridical equality, they also demanded a "nationalization" of the labor market through stringent restrictions on the emigration of unskilled labor. Coolies had to be protected against their own "poverty and ignorance," but this was also a quality said to compromise India's prestige among British colonies and to encourage civic discrimination against respectable Indian settlers. Another issue was preserving labor for India's own economic development. Yet when Indian elites reconstructed "India's Contribution to the Great War," they probably had their own reasons for letting the figure of the coolie blur into that of the soldier. As a result of their war effort, Indian elites could base their fitness for citizenship on the services of a much more impressive number of fighters, instead of coolies.[57]

[53] Ellinwood, *Between Two Worlds*, 358.

[54] Saxena, *Role of Indian Army in the First World War*, 116–17.

[55] John Starling and Ivor Lee, *No Labour, No Battle: Military Labour during the First World War* (Stroud: Spellmount, 2009), 258.

[56] Starling and Lee, *No Labour, No Battle*, 25.

[57] Radhika Singha, "Finding Labor from India for the War in Iraq: The Jail Porter and Labor Corps, 1916–1920," *Comparative Studies in Society and History*, 49:2 (2007), 1–34.

Indians not only sent the largest number of human resources to France, they also shouldered many other sacrifices at home. As the war drew on, the empire put an ever-increasing burden on India's economic resources. Indians paid the cost of maintaining their troops overseas, including providing uniforms and equipment. The direct cash contribution to the war was officially put at £146.2 million, and indirect support in money and material was enormous as well.[58] India sent, for instance, 172,815 animals and 3,691,836 tons of stores and supplies. In addition, like Vietnam and China, India raised a substantial sum of money by selling war bonds, and this was turned over to the British government.[59] The war not only drew heavily on India's human, financial, and material resources, it also brought to India heavy taxes and war loans, as well as high-handed policies with special courts and detentions and restrictions on civil rights. Of course, Indians also benefited from the war economically. A sort of reversal in economic relations between Britain and India helped make India more fiscally autonomous from the metropole and also helped Indian capitalists reap and enjoy certain benefits of increased production and profit during the war.

"These levies of Indians," Maurice Barres remarked when Indian troops arrived in France in September 1914, "make up one of the overwhelming surprises in this War of Nations." Indeed, one early official report by the British commented: "Few could have foreseen that Indian troops were destined to stand one day in the cause of liberty, side by side with soldiers of Britain, the Dominions, and the Allies in three continents, to fight the Hun and the Turk to standstill, and to take their part in upholding the British Empire."

Barres further wondered, "But what do these Indians think, Sihks and Gurkhas alike?" "What conception of this war have they formed? What is it, and what are they fighting for?"[60] On October 10, 1914, James Willcocks' "Order of the Day No. 1" to the Indian Corps shows the kind of sentiments the British hoped were guiding the troops' thoughts. It deserves to be quoted at length, since it reveals a crucial link between rising Indian nationalism and the British imperial mindset:

> On the eve of going into the field to join our British comrades, who have covered themselves with glory in this Great War, it is our firm resolve to prove ourselves worthy of the honour which has been conferred on us as representatives of the Army of India. In a few days we shall be fighting as has never been our good fortune to fight before, and against enemies who have a long history. But is their history as long as yours? You are the descendants of men who have been mighty rulers and Great Warriors for many centuries. You will never forget this. You will recall the glories of your race. Hindu and Mahomedan will be fighting side by side with British soldiers and our gallant French Allies. You will be helping to make history. You will be the first Indian soldiers of the King-Emperor who will have the honour of showing in Europe that the sons of India

[58] Saxena, *Role of Indian Army in the First World War*, 122.

[59] Dewitt C. Ellinwood and S. D. Pradhan, eds., *India and World War 1* (New Delhi: Manohar, 1978), 143.

[60] For details on this, see No Author, *Our Indian Army: A Record of the Peace Contingent's Visit to England*, (London: Issued for the India Office by Adams bros. & Shardlow Ltd., 1920); see also Morton-Jack, *The Indian Army on the Western Front*, 299.

have lost none of their ancient martial instincts and are worthy of the confidence reposed in them. In battle you will remember that your religions enjoin on you that to give your life doing your duty is your highest reward. The eyes of your co-religionists and your fellow-countrymen are on you.... You will fight for your King-Emperor and your faith, so that history will record the doings of India's sons and your children will proudly tell of the deeds of their fathers.[61]

Indian troops fought in France and Belgium, at Gallipoli, in Salonika, Palestine, Egypt and the Soudan, Mesopotamia and the Red Sea littoral, Somaliland, Cameroon, East Africa, Persia, the trans-Caspia, and in North China. India in all provided seven overseas expeditionary forces for the British war effort. The combatant units in France alone comprised 85,000 troops under 1,500 British officers, directly supported by 26,000 Indian non-combatants.[62]

Questions about Indian military worthiness arose as soon as India was brought into the war. Some British writers or officers considered Indian soldiers without their white officers "like sheep without a shepherd."[63] Lloyd George doubted the Indians would ever be able to manage on their own. He had never visited India and knew very little about it but, in the offhand way of his time, he considered Indians, along with other brown-skinned peoples, to be inferior.[64] A British officer commented that as a matter of racial fact, the Indians were among the dregs of the Western Front's fighting material. They were "not, of course, as good or nearly as good as British troops. How could they be?"[65] By 1916, it had already become acutely difficult to recruit Indians for the war, in response to which the government of India observed that frontier expeditions at home were usually of short duration and their casualties insignificant, but in the present war, conditions at the front were reported to be "abnormally hard, and losses, due both to sickness and casualties in action, extremely heavy."[66]

One hundred years on, debates about Indian contributions to the war still abound. The authoritative *Oxford History of the British Empire* dismisses the Indian units as "failures."[67] Scholar David Omissi has characterized the overall Indian contribution as "poor."[68] And Pradeep Barua has written how "Indian unit after unit broke and fled the horror of the trenches."[69] Greenhurt reminds us, however, that "the First World War was the first fully industrialized war, whereas the Indian

---

[61] Morton-Jack, *The Indian Army on the Western Front*, 299.

[62] Morton-Jack, *The Indian Army on the Western Front*, 1.

[63] Morton-Jack, *The Indian Army on the Western Front*, 17.

[64] John Grigg, *The Young Lloyd George* (Berkeley: University of California Press, 1974), 296–7.

[65] Morton-Jack, *The Indian Army on the Western Front*, 17.

[66] For detailed information on Indian casualties, see Table 4: War Office, "Statistical Abstract of Information Regarding the Armies at Home and Abroad, 1914–1920" (London: War Office, 1920), 786.

[67] J. M. Brown and W. M. Roger Louis, eds., *Oxford History of the British Empire* (Oxford: Oxford University Press, 1999), 4: 122.

[68] David Omissi, *The Sepoy and the Raj: The Indian Army, 1860–1940* (London: Macmillan, 1994), 13–38.

[69] Pradeep Barua, *Gentlemen of the Raj: The Indian Army Officer Corps, 1817–1949* (Westport, CT: Praeger, 2003), 14–16.

soldier was the product of a pre-industrial culture [and] an illiterate peasant."[70] Kaushik Roy describes the Indian military presence in France from 1914 to 1915 as "marginal."[71] According to Morton-Jack, the growing criticism of the Indian battalions was "that they were removed from the Western front in late 1915 because they were too weak to remain."[72]

It is beyond the scope of this book to evaluate these accounts of the Indians' military performance, but I would like to draw attention to countervailing stories. Indian troops entered the war early and engaged in direct fighting in Ypres from October 23 to November 5, 1914. From mid-November 1914 to February 1918, the Indian infantry's fighting duties were mainly defensive. For the seven weeks leading up to Christmas 1914, the Indian Corps held a sector at the southern end of the British Expeditionary Force line, by the village of Neuve Chapelle. When British efforts were failing in 1914, there was great praise for the Indian troops' decisive entry into the war. "That the Indian expeditionary Force arrived is in the nick of time," Lord Curzon declared. "That it helped to save the cause both of the Allies and of civilization, after the sanguinary tumult of the opening weeks of the War has been openly acknowledged by the highest in the land, from the Sovereign downwards. I recall that it was emphatically stated to me by Lord French himself."[73] The Indian cavalry fought from winter 1914 to spring 1916, when it was disbanded. On New Year's Eve 1915, *The Manchester Guardian* carried an official announcement entitled "The Withdrawal of the Indians—Facts about Their Service in France." It reported, "They have left France with a record of which they may well be proud. . . . The truth is [they] did as well as could have been reasonably expected, [and] they proved themselves to be first-line troops in the fullest meaning of the term." Willcocks was confident in 1917 that "my splendid Indian soldiers need have no fear of the verdict which the historians will record."[74] Of course, Indian troops did sometimes flee and they were defeated. But as Morton-Jack wrote, "Indians fled not because they were Indian, but for the same reason as European or African troops: They were human. The Indians naturally do not like shellfire and trench fighting," wrote Willcocks, "Who does?"[75]

It is true that Indian forces were moved out of the Western Front. Some suggested that causalities, declining morale, and doubts about the wisdom of using non-white troops in Europe led to the permanent withdrawal of the Indians by the end of 1915. But as Morton-Jack pointed out recently, "The Indian Corps' departure from the Western front was because it was required to fight elsewhere, and not because it was deemed inadequate to fight on where it was."[76] Although they went through many setbacks, hardships, and difficulties, the Indians did fight

[70] Cited in Morton-Jack, *The Indian Army on the Western Front*, 16.
[71] Kaushik Roy, "The Army in India in Mesopotamia from 1916 to 1918: Tactics, Technology and Logistics Reconsidered," in Ian F. W. Beckett, ed., *1917: Beyond the Western Front* (Boston: Brill, 2009), 132.
[72] Morton-Jack, *The Indian Army on the Western Front*, 18.
[73] Morton-Jack, *The Indian Army on the Western Front*, 19–20.
[74] Morton-Jack, *The Indian Army on the Western Front*, 12.
[75] Morton-Jack, *The Indian Army on the Western Front*, 186.
[76] Morton-Jack, *The Indian Army on the Western Front*, 170.

heroically. According to Morton-Jack, "First Ypres was in fact the battle in which the Home Army came to depend on the Army of India not to fail. The Indian Corps may not have 'saved' the BEF all by itself, but it was a vital link in a chain of reinforcement without which the BEF, and the Allies, would have suffered a disastrous defeat."[77] On the last day of October 1914, Khudadad Khan of the Indian Corps was the first Indian to be awarded the Victoria Cross, a decoration that honored the soldier who performed "some signal act of valour or devotion to their country." When all of his fellows were killed on a Belgium battlefield, he fought on as calmly as if he were doing his routine job.[78] Jamadar Mir Dost received the Victoria Cross for his bravery and ability on April 26, 1915, when he led his platoon during an attack and afterwards gathered remaining soldiers of the regiment and kept them under his command until a retreat was ordered. He was said to have "displayed remarkable courage in helping to carry eight British and Indian officers into safety, whilst exposed to very heavy fire."[79] A British officer's diary entry of October 25, 1914 shows how tough-minded the Indian soldier could be in horrifying conditions: "Regiment in trenches up till midnight— very shaken. . . . I saw a sepoy sitting on a dead German & eating food his ration tin resting on the dead man's back. Dead everywhere."[80] The British commander of the 18th (Indian) Division reported that though it was one of the later formations of the war, "Its short life has been full of active work and interesting experiences."[81]

Indian forces entered Mesopotamia in the autumn of 1914. This expedition was launched from India by the Indian Army, and its operations were controlled by the government of India. Though control was taken over by the British War Office early in 1916, India had recruited, equipped, and supplied the great army that would so highly distinguish itself.

According to one source, 302,199 men were deployed to Mesopotamia, of whom 15,652 were killed and 31,187 wounded. India sent 104,419 men to Egypt, where 3,513 were killed and 8,001 wounded. As mentioned previously, in France, India had 86,382 men fighting on the Western Front and 4,844 were killed, with 16,297 wounded. Of the 34,511 men sent to East Africa, 2,460 were killed and 1,886 wounded. Of the 24,451 men sent to the Persian Gulf, 368 were killed and 210 wounded, and among the 17,573 Indian troops in Aden, 455 men were killed and 566 wounded. In Gallipoli and Salonika, of the 9,717 Indian fighters, 1,618 died and 3,669 were wounded. Altogether, 579,252 Indian troops fought in different theaters during the war, of whom 29,010 were killed and 61,916 were wounded.[82] Another source suggests that Indian forces in the various theaters

---

[77] Morton-Jack, *The Indian Army on the Western Front*, 148.

[78] Asghar Ali, *Our Heroes of the Great War* (Bombay: *The Times* Press, 1922), 18–34.

[79] Ali, *Our Heroes of the Great War*, 47.

[80] War diary of Capt. J. W. Barnett, IWM: 90/37/1.

[81] IWM: An account of the operations of the 18th (Indian) division in Mesopotamia, December 1917 to December 1918, by major-General H.D. Fanshawe (London: St. Martin's Press), n.p.

[82] Roy, "The Army in India in Mesopotamia from 1916 to 1918," 158.

suffered 53,486 dead from all causes.[83] Among Indian ranks, the total figure for casualties was 106,600, or well over half the combatant strength of the prewar Army.[84]

We also have to keep in mind the Indian laborers in the war zones of Europe and the Middle East. British authorities started to recruit Indians, as they did the Chinese, for France in 1916, with the first groups arrived in spring 1917. The Indian non-combatants who directly supported Indian fighters in France belonged largely to Indian Army administrative units. Some worked in animal transport, including mule trains, and others in field hospitals. One of their officers would later write, "We of the Headquarters Mule Transport recognized that our part was but a modest one, but we were prepared to play it to the full, and to do all in our humble power to further the good cause."[85] The ILC was praised for its work during the German offensive of March 1918, in particular, for its steadiness during the chaos of the retreat, and the loss of life under shelling. The men behaved impressively when forced to leave camp at a moment's notice. Their withdrawal was carried out with "admirable steadiness"—there was no panic, although some among them had to endure shell fire, bombardment by airplanes, and machine gun fire day and night. Whenever called upon, they halted to assist and even turned back to help load stores onto trains, trucks, and wagons. "One Company assisted the wounded with a hospital train and performed this work—for which they had no training—in such a manner as to win high praise from the Medical Officers."[86] Indian laborers stayed in France until the end of 1918; 1,500 of them died in service there.[87]

Given all the different perspectives and standards, it is perhaps impossible to come to a consensus about the Indians' war contribution. Still, James Willcocks, the commander of Indian troops in Europe, assured his readers in *Blackwood's Magazine* in 1917 that:

> the Indian soldiers are due a great debt of gratitude by the people of [Britain], because at a time when our own countrymen were fighting against enormous odds and performing deeds of deathless glory, the Indian Corps was able to step in and fill a gap, and thus to help roll ball the billows thundering against that thin but still un-shattered granite wall. No claim is made for them except that they arrived in the very nick of time and took their place in the sadly reduced battle line, thus relieving the strain which was becoming nigh intolerable for our own brave men.[88]

In 1919, Indian troops were invited to take part in the great peace celebration in London. The Indian inclusion in the procession, according to one official report, was "a fitting crown to their achievements."[89] Although the Indians did not arrive on time for the main event, they did a victory march of their own through London,

---

[83] Ellinwood, *India and the World War 1*, 145.
[84] No Author, *Our Indian Army*.
[85] Morton-Jack, *The Indian Army on the Western Front*, 6.
[86] Starling and Lee, *No Labour, No Battle*, 260.
[87] Starling and Lee, *No Labour, No Battle*, 260–3.
[88] Morton-Jack, *The Indian Army on the Western Front*, 148.
[89] No Author, *Our Indian Army*.

and the British king reviewed them at Buckingham Palace.[90] F. E. Smith, the secretary of state at the India Office, said of India's soldiers at opening of the Indian Army Memorial at Neuve Chapelle in 1927: "They had accepted a duty. They discharged it. More cannot be said; more need not be said."[91] The official British verdict on the Indian troops was set in stone at that memorial: "To the honour of the Army of India which fought in France and Belgium, 1914–1918, and in perpetual remembrance of those whose names are here recorded and who have no known grave."[92] In New Delhi, there is also a national monument to the soldiers killed in the First World War called the India Gate. This memorial was dedicated in 1921 "to the dead of the Indian armies who fell honoured in France and Flanders, Mesopotamia and Persia, East Africa, Gallipoli and elsewhere in the Near and the Far East, and in sacred memory also of those whose names are recorded and who fell in India or the North-West Frontier and during the Third Afghan War."[93] As James Willcocks reported to Buckingham Palace shortly before he left the Indian Corps: "The truth is that the Indians have done well, beyond all expectations; they have stood a long test which indelibly stamps them as worthy of their Sovereign's uniform. . . . They have freely given their lives, health, and most cherished ideas for England. Can man do more?"[94] This statement might well serve as our judgment of the Indians' role in the war.

Regardless of the disagreements over India's involvement in the war, the war without a doubt had a substantial impact on India itself. Returned soldiers and laborers brought with them new confidence and a sharpened political and social consciousness. As a consequence of the war, a new feeling of a social equality and yearning for political freedom not only took hold in the minds of urbanites, but percolated out to the villages where most of the soldiers and laborers had been recruited. Those men brought home the ideas and energy that would help drive social and political change.

THE GREAT WAR AND INDIAN NATIONALISM

The reissue of the *Cambridge History of India* by the Delhi publisher S. Chand declared in 1964: "To estimate what the war did for India is a problem that may perplex the wisest, since the issue is still unknown."[95] More than fifty years later, we may still not be able to write with great certainty about the war's complete impact

---

[90] No Author, *Our Indian Army.*
[91] Morton-Jack, *The Indian Army on the Western Front*, 301.
[92] Saxena, *Role of Indian Army in the First World War*, 133.
[93] Santanu Das, "The Indian Sepoy in Europe, 1914–1918: Images, Letters, Literature," in Helmut Bley and Anorthe Kremers, eds., *The World During the First World War* (Essen: Klartext, 2014), 169–70.
[94] Morton-Jack, *The Indian Army on the Western Front*, 305.
[95] Dodwell, ed., *The Cambridge History of India*, 6: 476. (Professor Gordon Johnson alerted me to the following: volume 6 of the *Cambridge History of India* was published in 1932. In the early 1960s, the Press allowed S. Chand in Delhi to do a photographic reprint of the old *Cambridge History of India*, and that publisher decided to add a piece by R. R. Sethi, which is what I am quoting. But according to Gordon Johnson, Sethi's piece did not have any Cambridge authority behind it.)

on Indian society. But we are sure about one thing—the war clearly motivated Indians politically. Even British authorities realized the serious implications of the war for Britain and for India. In *The Times History of the War in 1914* there runs the following commentary:

> The more they [Indians] learned of the goodness of our Western civilization and the higher, especially, we raised the standard of the native Indian Army, the stronger became the pressure upon us from below, seeking some outlet for the high ambitions which we ourselves had awakened. Looking only at the military side of the question, no one conversant with the facts could fail to see that the time was at hand when we could no longer deny to a force of British subjects, with the glorious record and splendid efficiency of our native Indian troops, the right to stand shoulder to shoulder with their British comrades in defence of the Empire, wherever it might be assailed.[96]

The war thus opened Indians' eyes to the outside world and allowed them to dream and have high expectations at a time when world politics were changing and their "mother country" was embroiled in a major war. As mentioned earlier, when the king-emperor asked for help, India's educated class responded enthusiastically. Santanu Das has suggested a certain level of political calculation in their responses, since they saw in the war opportunity. Ahmed Iqbal, a famous poet, seems to reflect what was on the minds of Indian elites then with the lines:

> The world will witness when from my heart
> Springs the storm of expression;
> My silence conceals
> The seed of aspiration.[97]

Nearly all prominent Indian politicians supported the British war recruitment effort, and many linked support for the war with their right to equal status as citizens of the British Empire. They hoped that Britain would reward Indians with a greater voice in their own government once the war had concluded. Thus, the war awakened their national consciousness and nationalism.

Up until 1914, Indian politics remained, as Jawarharlal Nehru later wrote, "very dull."[98] But when the war broke out, Indian National Congress president Babu Bhupendra Nath Basu declared, "Now is our time; we must throw away our lethargy; let us bind our loin cloth and heed forward to our goal and that goal is not unworthy of our highest aspirations. . . . We are beginning to feel the strength and growing solidarity of the people of India; India has realized that she must be a vital and equal part of the Empire and she has worthily seized her great opportunity."[99] The goal he was referring to was, of course, self-government. Another influential Indian politician, S. P. Sinha, also urged Indians to pursue that goal: "The only satisfactory form of self-government to which India aspires cannot be anything short of

---

[96] *The Times*, The Times *History of the War, 1914* (London: *The Times*, 1914), 153.
[97] Mackenzie, *The Awakening of India*, 159.
[98] Manela, *The Wilsonian Moment*, 81.
[99] Saxena, *Role of Indian Army in the First World War*, 6.

what President Lincoln so pithily described as 'government of the people, for the people, and by the people'"[100] But Mahatma Gandhi took a go-slow approach, cautioning that "it was more becoming and far-sighted not to press our demands while the war lasted."[101]

The British government clearly realized the dangers of Indian nationalism taking hold after the war and treated every Indian as a potential nationalist or revolutionary. During the war, the British intelligence boss for India, Sir Charles Cleveland, issued secret instructions to immigration officers at all Indian ports: "Every Indian returning from America or Canada," he warned, "whether labourer, artisan or student, must be regarded as a probable active revolutionary, or at any rate as a sympathizer with the revolutionary party."[102] Because Britain had sought Indian assistance and so many Indians responded and took part in the deadly fighting among the Western Powers, it was only natural that they would ask for their own rights and become nationalists. One 1919 commentary argued:

> Indian soldiers shed their blood on three different continents in the company of their European brethren, and India made a valuable contribution to the successful prosecution of the struggle in a variety of other ways. How, under these circumstances, could India not feel, as England and France feel, that the political, social, and economic institutions and methods of the people must be improved in order that their progress should be rapid and healthy? They would naturally aspire to become, intellectually, physically, socially and politically what people in other nations are and would like to be in the near future. There is an awakening throughout the land; the national consciousness has been quickened. The very political and social controversies of the last four years are an indication of the new life which has been poured into the Indian nation. People want self-government conceded to them. They want social elevation and equality.[103]

Their war service offered Indians a way to salvage national prestige. As Timothy C. Winegard writes, "The First World War was, more so than its 1939–45 counterpart, the decisive chapter of the twentieth century for the Dominions. It forever altered the configuration of the empire and, through momentous Dominion participation, hastened the realization of full nationhood, both legally and culturally."[104] For Captain Amar Singh of the Indian Army, his service in the Great War was an opportunity to fulfill his duty and "to express his sense of honor and nationhood." He was gratified that Indian troops would fight alongside European troops. He expected that India would gain in stature as a result, a view of the war that was common among knowledgeable Indians.[105]

[100] Sinha, *The Future of India*, 7.

[101] Santanu Das, "Indians at Home, Mesopotamia and France," in Santanu Das, ed., *Race, Empire and First World War Writing* (Cambridge: Cambridge University Press, 2011), 73.

[102] Peter Hopkirk, *On Secret Service East of Constantinople: The Plot to Bring Down the British Empire* (London: John Murray, 1994), 67.

[103] Vaman Govind Kale, *India's War Finance and Post-war Problems* (Poona: The Aryabhushan Press, 1919), 151.

[104] Timothy C. Winegard, *Indigenous Peoples of the British Dominions and the First World War* (New York: Cambridge University Press, 2011), 11.

[105] Ellinwood, *Between Two Worlds*, 356.

Their war experience gave Indians fresh confidence and political awareness. One Indian elite commented, "The war has changed us very much. It has changed the angle of vision in India as well [as] in England."[106] And as one veteran pointed out, "When we saw various peoples and got their views, we started protesting against the inequalities and disparities which the British had created between the white and the black."[107] Indian officer Amar Singh told his fellow officers that "This is the first time we Indians have had the honour to fight Europeans on their own soil and must play up to the Government that has brought us up to this level."[108] Reflecting in October 1915, Singh wrote in his diary, "They [the soldiers] must see it through whatever happens. It is on them that the honour of India rests. India will get tremendous concessions after the war which she would not have gained otherwise—at least not for several years to come."[109] In November 1914, he wrote in his diary: "Ever since my coming to France I have been admiring and studying the avenues these people have in their towns as well in the country seats."[110] In June 1915, he wrote that "I have been awfully impressed with the forests and avenues and often think what I could do in this line in my own place [back in India.]"[111]

During the war, a handful of revolutionaries attempted to organize violent anti-British uprisings in Bengal and the Punjab, but they failed to excite significant popular support. Their efforts were, moreover, easily thwarted by the security forces, which were aided by the wartime measures of the 1915 Defence of India Act that gave the British extraordinary powers of arrest and trial. By one estimate, forty-six revolutionaries were tried and executed under the provisions of the act in the war years, and another sixty-four received life sentences. In February 1915, Muslim soldiers of the Indian 5th Light Infantry, stationed in Singapore, also rebelled against their British officers. The British asked for Japanese help to suppress the rebellion. Later, the British would complain that the Japanese had arrived too late and done nothing, while Indians strongly criticized the Japanese for helping Western Powers to suppress fellow Asian nationalists.[112] The Home Rule League that Tilak established in 1916 had branches across the country that could help mobilize the Indian masses around the goal of self-government. Annie Besant, though not a native Indian, served in 1917 as the Indian National Congress (INC) president, and sometimes collaborated and sometimes competed with Tilak as she also set out to enlist grassroots support for home rule. But up to 1919, even as the demand for home rule was intensifying, the goal of most home rulers remained

---

[106] Ellinwood, *India and World War 1*, 22.

[107] Das, "Indians at Home, Mesopotamia and France," in Das, *Race, Empire and First World War Writing*, 84.

[108] Ellinwood, *Between Two Worlds*, 370.

[109] Ellinwood, *Between Two Worlds*, 392.

[110] Ellinwood, *Between Two Worlds*, 403.

[111] Ellinwood, *Between Two Worlds*, 404.

[112] For details on the mutiny, see R. W. E. Harris and Harry Miller, *Singapore Mutiny* (Singapore: Oxford University Press, 1984); see also Harumi Goto-Shibata, "Internationalism and Nationalism: Anti-Western Sentiments in Japanese Foreign Policy Debates, 1918–22," in Naoko Shimazu, ed., *Nationalisms in Japan* (London: Routledge, 2006), 70.

reforms within the imperial system—Indian self-government within the empire—rather than challenging the legitimacy of empire itself.

If the war ignited Indian national consciousness, British lip service paid to greater Indian rights and Allied propaganda declarations during the war further fed India's nationalist dream: "The cause of right, liberty and democracy was never so emphatically and persistently proclaimed as during the recent world-war and the expressions used by the statesmen of Allied nations to explain their aims have become household words in India."[113] In light of the growing activism for home rule, London grew increasingly concerned with preserving the stability of British rule. To ensure the continued loyalty of INC moderates and defuse the demands of extremists, the British Cabinet decided that it would be prudent to declare Britain's intention to allow Indians a greater measure of self-government after the war. In August 1917, the Secretary of State for India, Edwin Montagu, officially announced a government policy to promote "the increasing association of Indians in every branch of administration and the gradual development of self-governing institutions with a view to the progressive realisation of responsible government in India as an integral part of the British Empire."[114] The 1917 British Declaration for India was a direct response to Indian national awakening. Critics might call this high-sounding declaration an empty promise, and all the war and Indian sacrifice actually brought to India was a high rate of inflation, currency devaluation, and increased taxation. Still, the declaration was a positive step in the long term. It was the beginning of new relationship with Britain and was made possible by India's ready contributions and involvement in the war. By promising India a certain level of self-rule, the 1917 declaration can be viewed as the first major step on the long journey to independence; this remains true no matter how small the step and how half-hearted the British. Still, though it promised more than Britain ever had before, it fell short of the basic right of self-determination, which was destined to become a central tenet of the postwar international order. Clearly, London used this document to regain the initiative in Indian politics and it seemed to have the desired effect during the war.

The Montagu Declaration, as it came to be known, was initially well received by many of the INC moderates. In the summer of 1918, when the British government published a report that laid out its plans for implementing the promises of the Montagu Declaration, it became clear that Indian expectations now went far beyond the gradual reforms proposed. By now, INC leaders and the nationalist press frequently raised the call for "the immediate grant of self-determination to India," and they condemned the British report as "inadequate, unsatisfactory, and disappointing." In a pamphlet criticizing the reform proposals, INC leader Pandit Madan Mohan Malaviya noted that since the war had been fought "for the rights of small nations to control their own destinies, Britain could not now deny the people of India those same rights. What was now needed was the introduction of a

---

[113] Kale, *India's War Finance and Post-war Problems*, 150.
[114] Ellinwood, *India and World War 1*, 21–2.

substantial measure of responsible government in India, which would mark a clear recognition of her higher status and also of the principle of self-determination."[115]

According to another report issued after the war, "The year 1919 opened full of promise for India.... But as the year proceeded, the picture changed. The disastrous monsoon of 1918 began to produce its full effects in continued scarcity and steadily rising prices. The still unsatisfied political aspirations of the educated classes, combined with the economic hardships borne by the poor, produced an atmosphere dangerous to the public peace."[116] Rapid inflation, the collapse of India's export trade, and revelations of how British military incompetence had wasted the lives of Indian soldiers in Mesopotamia disillusioned even those Indians who had thought that at least British rule provided good government. But most damaging was the discovery that the British did not want to keep promises they had made in 1917. Sir J. P. Hewett noted that one might "regret" that the 1917 plan was made "when the preoccupations of the war were engaging everyone's interest; and that no discussion took place, whether outside or inside the Houses of Parliament." But the plan was a pledge by Parliament to the people of India. "It must be honoured by every Englishman."[117] But when the war was over, under the India Act of 1919, the British government decided to retain key powers and offered little to Indian politicians. Adding insult to injury, London passed the Rowlatt Act in March 1919, which attempted to make many of the high-handed wartime policies permanent in the postwar period. The response of India's politically conscious class was reflected in a letter written by C. F. Andrews to Tagore in May 1919: "I find that every Indian I meet is saying: 'take away the d—d reforms. We don't want them and we won't have them. Answer us this: are we to be treated as serfs with no human rights at all?'"[118] Tagore naturally was furious. He wrote on May 30, 1919 that "The universal agony of indignation roused in the hearts of the people has been ignored by our rulers—possible congratulating themselves for imparting what they imagine as a salutary lesson ... The time has come when badges of honour make our shame glaring in the incongruous context of humiliation." Tagore thereupon resigned the knighthood that had been conferred upon him after he won the Nobel Prize in Literature in 1913.[119]

Stanley Wolpert pointed out that "if war had raised too many hopes too high, its aftermath crushed them too brutally. By 1919 India's era of late-Victorian liberal cooperation and Edwardian politesse was forever ended."[120] Unfortunately, armistice brought to India not peace or freedom or autonomy, but the sword of continued repression. "The aftermath of World War One brought such widespread disillusionment to India that Congress abandoned its policy of cooperation with the

---

[115] Manela, *The Wilsonian Moment*, 91.
[116] L. F. Rushbrook Williams, *India in 1919: A Report Prepared for Presentation to Parliament in Accordance with the Requirements of the 26th Section of the Government of India Act* (Calcutta: Superintendent Government Printing, India, 1920), iii.
[117] Sir J. P. Hewett, *The Indian Reform Proposals* (London: Indo-British Association, 1918), 1.
[118] Nanda, *Gandhi: Pan-Islamism, Imperialism, and Nationalism in India*, 186.
[119] Wolpert, *A New History of India*, 314.   [120] Wolpert, *A New History of India*, 314.

British Raj to follow Gandhi's revolutionary call for nonviolent noncooperation."[121] Once they realized the British would not grant them self-government, Indian nationalists changed course. After the Great War, as discontent against British rule became widespread, the country was ripe for national unrest.[122] Muslims were incensed over the caliphate, workers staged strikes, and peasants protested about their rents. The government of India then made matters worse by introducing legislation to increase its own powers. The INC, a pillar of the empire until 1914, had become its most determined enemy once the war was over. The spring of 1919 was thus a "crucial watershed, in which the national movement swung decisively toward the goal of terminating British rule in India."[123]

During this transformation of the nationalist movement, Mohandas K. Gandhi became one of its towering figures. During the war, Gandhi had arrived in India from South Africa with the tools of political organization and civil disobedience, which he had perfected, to transform the largely middle-class INC into a formidable mass movement. He became more and more disillusioned with the British government after 1919. He concluded that it "is immoral, unjust and arrogant beyond description. It defends one lie with other lies. It does most things under the threat of force. If the people tolerate all these things and do nothing, they will never progress."[124] In addition to the man-made calamity of the war, the influenza epidemic of 1918–19 claimed 21.5 million victims globally, most of them in Asia, and particularly in India, where 12.5 million people died.[125] Gandhi used its devastation as an example of Britain's moral unfitness to rule India. Gandhi "shifted in 1919 from a position of firm if critical support for Indian membership in the British Empire to one of determined opposition to it."[126] Winston Churchill considered Mohandas K. Gandhi a "seditious fakir."[127]

Historian A. Rumbold called the period between the outbreak of the Great War and 1922, when Gandhi's campaign of non-cooperation came to an end with his arrest, a watershed in the history of British power in India.[128] Gandhi initially was invested in leading India gently toward a share of its own government. But in March and April 1919, huge demonstrations and public meetings took place in India's major cities. On April 6, Gandhi called for a general strike across the country. Although he urged his followers to refrain from violence, there were sporadic outbreaks of looting and rioting. The British, especially those on the ground, started to panic. Was there, one local English-language newspaper asked, some malevolent and highly dangerous organization which is at work below the surface? Were the disturbances caused by the Bolsheviks? Infiltrators from Egypt?

[121] Wolpert, *A New History of India*, 315.
[122] Saroj Sharma, *Indian Elite and Nationalism: A Study of Indo-English fiction* (Jaipur: Rawat Publications, 1997), 75.
[123] Manela, *The Wilsonian Moment*, 175.
[124] Masselos, *Indian Nationalism*, 163.
[125] Morrow, *The Great War: An Imperial History*, 285.
[126] Manela, *The Wilsonian Moment*, 9.   [127] Masselos, *Indian Nationalism*, 151.
[128] For details, see Algernon Rumbold, *Watershed in India, 1914–1922* (London: Athlone Press, 1979).

Or perhaps a worldwide Muslim conspiracy? After all, in 1914, the population of
Muslims in British India was about 57 million. Indian Muslims considered the war
between Turkey and the Balkan states as a war between Islam and Christianity, and
largely sided with Turkey. The question of the loyalty of Indian Muslims to Britain
came to the fore at the outbreak of the First World War, especially when Turkey
joined the war against Britain.[129] The worst trouble came in the Punjab, where, on
April 13, at Amritsar, a panicked British officer ordered his troops to fire point-
blank into a large crowd, killing about 400 demonstrators. In the manner of the
Amritsar Massacre, sporadic violence by Indians, particularly in Delhi and the
Punjab, elicited extreme violence from the British, with a tally of at least 1,200
Indians killed and 3,600 wounded.[130] The British violence galvanized even moderate public opinion and accelerated the transformation of the INC from a gentlemen's debating club into a mass-based political party, with Gandhi emerging as its
leader.[131] Indians became increasingly hostile to British rule and their calls for
home rule only intensified. Prior to the massacres, Gandhi had hoped to cooperate
with the British on working out constitutional reforms, but he changed his mind
and decided to turn to non-cooperation. The British sent him to jail to serve a six-
year sentence.

According to Harvard historian Erez Manela, the Wilsonian moment also played
an important role in the development of Indian nationalism. Indian nationalists
launched concerted efforts to enlist the support of world opinion, especially
American opinion, on behalf of their cause. Besant's arrest for circulating copies
of Wilson's war address helped their efforts, since it raised a furor among American
theosophists, who launched a public campaign for her release and denounced
Britain's "jailor's regime" in India. Indian revolutionaries who advocated violent
action to liberate India from British rule also hoped that Wilson's international
leadership would aid their cause. Manela suggests that the usefulness of Wilson's
rhetoric for Indians was reflected in the response of Lala Lajpat Rai, the Swadeshi
movement leader, to the Montagu Declaration. Welcoming Great Britain's willingness to move India toward self-government, he nonetheless rejected its claim
that the British government alone possessed the right to determine the nature and
pace of political progress in India. The new principles of justice recently introduced
in the international arena with the declaration of President Wilson that "people
must be free to determine their own form of government" rendered such claims
untenable. As Manela points out, Lajpat Rai, like many nationalist leaders across
the colonial world at the time, saw the Indian nationalist movement as part of a
broader struggle against imperialism. When Woodrow Wilson emerged as an
eloquent spokesman for projections of a postwar transformation of international
relations, Lajpat Rai was thrilled. Soon after Wilson's Fourteen Points address, he

[129] For details on Indian Muslims and the Great War, see Yuvaraj Deva Prasad, *The Indian Muslims
and World War I: A Phase of Disillusionment with British Rule, 1914–1918* (New Delhi: Janaki
Prakashan, 1985).

[130] Morrow, *The Great War: An Imperial History*, 313.

[131] Pankaj Mishra, *From the Ruins of Empire: The Intellectuals Who Remade Asia* (New York: Farrar,
Straus and Giroux, 2012), 202.

wrote in *Young India* that "one begins to wish that the whole world could be constituted into a single republic, with President Wilson as its head." The president's address was "bound to help all the subject peoples of the world in their fight for the right of self-determination" and so constituted a great step toward real democracy in international affairs; it was an educational and political tool whose value was "simply incalculable." The following month, after Wilson declared that the war "had its roots in the disregard of the rights of small nations and of nationalities which lacked the union and force" to determine their political lives, Lajpat Rai cabled the president personally to thank him for his words. They were bound, he said, to constitute "a new charter of [the] world's freedom" and "thrill the millions of the world's subject races." Wilson had "put the whole thing in a nutshell," and the future of the world depended on the willingness of the Great Powers to implement his principles. No matter what the Indian nationalists guessed were Wilson's real intentions, Manela suggests that "Indian home-rule campaigners incorporated his principles into their rhetorical arsenal as they redefined their own goals and adjusted their expectations and demands to keep pace with the transformation they perceived in the international arena."[132]

According to Manela, Indians, like other colonial nationalists, held up US colonial rule in the Philippines at the time not as a blemish on the American record, but as a model, which the British would do well to follow. Shortly after the armistice, Lajpat Rai wrote to Wilson that India should be granted "at least such progressive measures of Home Rule as the present administration has established in the Philippines." If the United States could prepare the uncivilized Filipinos for self-government in less than twenty years, went the refrain in the nationalist press, how could the British claim that an ancient civilization such as India was unfit for it after a century and a half of British rule? Surely, such a claim reflected most poorly on the British themselves.[133]

Like the East Asians, Indians were excited about Wilsonian New World Order ideas and looked forward to the postwar peace conference. But Wilson and his so-called moment proved a major disappointment. Indians would have to wait until the end of another world war for their dreams of national self-determination and independence to come true.

THE INDIANS COME TO PARIS

When the INC convened in December 1918 for its annual session, "in view of the pronouncements of President Wilson, Mr. Lloyd George, and other British statesmen, that to ensure the future peace of the world, the principle of Self-Determination should be applied to all progressive nations," it adopted a resolution that called for the application of the principles of self-determination to India and demanded that India be recognized by the Powers as "one of the progressive nations

[132] Manela, *The Wilsonian Moment*, 90.   [133] Manela, *The Wilsonian Moment*, 92–3.

to whom the principle of self-determination should be applied."[134] The Congress further urged that elected delegates represent India at the peace conference. Other organizations involved in the home rule movement, such as Annie Besant's All-India Home Rule League, congratulated the British sovereign on the Allied victory but demanded as "absolutely essential" the immediate implementation of home rule in India.

The Indians anticipated that the American president would be a key advocate for the values he had announced in his Fourteen Points speech. One man wrote the following to Wilson: "Honoured Sir, the aching heart of India cries out to you, whom we believe to be an instrument of God in the reconstruction of the world."[135] Nobel laureate Rabindranath Tagore admired Wilson and even intended to dedicate his 1917 book, *Nationalism*, to him.[136] In the preface to a collection of the president's wartime addresses published in India, the prominent liberal politician and intellectual V. S. Srinivas Sastri wrote, "Imagination fails to picture the wild delirium of joy with which he [Woodrow Wilson] would have been welcomed in Asiatic capitals. It would have been as though one of the great teachers of humanity, Christ or Buddha, had come back to his home."[137] From early in the war, Indian nationalists, already mobilizing in the cause of home rule, had recognized the importance of the Wilsonian rhetoric to their campaign. They appropriated it to redefine the goals of their movement and made concerted efforts to take advantage of new opportunities and forums that emerged in the international arena to advance those goals. When the armistice came, Lajpat Rai sent congratulatory telegrams to President Wilson and to the British government, the texts of which he reproduced in his journal, *Young India*. Rai expressed the hope that a "grant of autonomy to India and other countries under the rule of the Allies" would follow immediately. In the issue of January 1919, he published yet another appeal that he had sent directly to Wilson, in which he "succinctly laid out his hopes that the president would take up the role of liberator of colonial peoples at the peace table." "Your deep historical learning," he wrote, "equips you most fully to understand India's problem," and "your moral outlook, the farthest and noblest of our generation, assures us of your sympathy; your position, the most commanding in the world to-day, gives you the power, as you have the right, to protect all who suffer under alien and undemocratic rule."[138]

Indian nationalists had begun to view the United States and its president as potential allies in their struggle for home rule as early as the spring of 1917, after Wilson announced that the United States would declare war on Germany in the name of democracy, popular government, and the "rights and liberties of small nations." Wilson's "noble and moving utterance" received full and favorable coverage in India's leading nationalist dailies. In addition to providing a detailed

[134] Manela, *The Wilsonian Moment*, 96.   [135] Manela, *The Wilsonian Moment*, 78.
[136] Manela, *The Wilsonian Moment*, 92.
[137] Erez Manela, "Imaging Woodrow Wilson in Asia: Dreams of East-West Harmony and the Revolt against Empire in 1919," *American Historical Review*, 111: 5 (December 2006), 1327.
[138] Manela, *The Wilsonian Moment*, 93.

summary of its contents and extensive verbatim excerpts, the dailies told Indian readers that crowds outside the US Capitol building in Washington had cheered frantically as the president entered and left, and inside the chamber members of Congress, even the few "supposed Pacifists," greeted his words with deafening cheers. The speech, one paper reported, was also hailed abroad as "a new declaration of rights" and "a new gospel in the governance of mankind." Perhaps the most intriguing comment described the president's address as a "fitting sequel to the Russian Revolution," since both events were "bound to have the most profound influence in the destinies of nations." The revolution in question was the one that took place in March 1917, not the Bolshevik Revolution, which lay more than six months in the future. Wilson's principles and democratic revolution in Russia both represented the advance of the same progressive spirit in world politics.

Given India's contribution to the war and the British Empire, it was natural that the Indians looked forward to their representation at the peace conference. But there were challenges. With the war over, no decision had been reached as to whether India would be allowed to attend the postwar peace conference on its own account. India had been included in the Imperial War Cabinet along with the self-governing Dominions thanks to its participation in the war. But its participation in the peace conference seemed to be a low priority compared to that of other dominion members. This did not sit well with the growing ranks of nationalists.[139]

Indian politician S. P. Sinha would argue that India should not be differentiated from the Dominions in the matter of representation in the League of Nations:

> If Great Britain adopts a firm attitude with regard to India's claim to representation, I cannot think that President Wilson or any of the representatives of the other Great Powers will force a decision which would create grave difficulties within the British Empire. They cannot but be aware of the great part played by India in the war and when it is pointed out that the League of Nations is intended to be a permanent institution from which it is not desirable to exclude a country with India's past traditions and glorious civilization . . . [140]

The Indian nationalists clearly became disillusioned with the League of Nations, whose structure was established to protect European imperial interests rather than national self-determination. True, India gained membership in the League of Nations. Yet, as with the Paris Peace Conference delegation, the Indian representatives to the League of Nations were chosen by the government of India and often supported the official stance of the British Raj, not the interests of Indian nationalists.[141] India's nationalists argued that in proportion to the population and the country's contributions toward winning the war, India fully deserved at least three representatives at the peace conference. Some suggested that their representatives

---

[139] Hugh Purcell, *The Maharaja of Bikaner* (London: Haus, 2010), x.

[140] Memo from S. P. Sinha, January 22, 1919, BA: FO 608/241.

[141] There were arguments that Indian inclusion in the League of Nations was a ploy by Britain to gain more power. See D. N. Verma, *India and the League of Nations* (Patna: Bharati Bhawan, 1968), and Vangala Shiva Ram and Brij Mohan Sharma, *India and the League of Nations* (Lucknow: Upper India Publishing House, 1932).

should not be nominees of the government, but should be elected by the INC. The INC proceeded to nominate B. G. Tilak, who had served two sentences for sedition, the last from 1908 to 1914, Gandhi, and the Muslim leader Syed Hasan Imam. But Montagu rejected the idea of allowing the INC's delegates to represent India, and in his letter to Lord Chelmsford reported, "We have refused passports and nothing has been done."[142]

Despite the urgings of various Indian groups, the colonial government would not appoint any of the new nationalist leaders. Eventually, India was allowed two representatives, led by Edwin Montagu, the Secretary of State for India, who would be in charge of the delegation. The two carefully chosen Indians were loyalists to the empire: Satyendra P. Sinha, a distinguished judge, and Ganga Singh, maharaja of Bikaner, who ruled a small state in north-west India and represented the nominally autonomous princely states. This delegation could participate, the Powers agreed, in deliberations that touched upon Indian interests. Sinha, who represented British India proper, was a veteran imperial administrator who would soon become the first native Indian to rise to the peerage, and the first to serve as Undersecretary of State for India in the British Cabinet. A prominent member of the INC, Sinha even served as its president in the 1915 session. By 1919, however, the movement had so changed with the rise of the home rule leagues and the return of Tilak's extremists that Sinha's support for India's imperial connection now marginalized him. In Paris, Montagu warned his colleagues repeatedly of the risks of alienating a large group of Indians who had been notably loyal to the British. But his warnings and prickly personality merely produced irritation. Lloyd George wrote to him: "In fact throughout the Conference your attitude has often struck me as being not so much that of a member of the British Cabinet, but of a successor on the throne of Aurangzeb!"[143]

In his March 13, 1919 memorandum to the British imperial delegation to the peace conference, Montagu claimed, "If India has a right to be considered a participant in the Peace Conference as a Power with limited interests, its interests are nowhere so conspicuous" as in the solution of Mesopotamian questions. In short, the British government in India argued that Mesopotamia should be taken away from Turkey and become part of India, coming, in other words, under British control. The British officials in the India Office tried, unsuccessfully, to put in claims for Indian mandates over Mesopotamia and German East Africa. Indian Muslims made up a quarter of British India's population and hoped that after the war the sultan of the Ottoman Empire would be allowed to stay in Istanbul with some sort of authority over Muslim holy places throughout the Middle East. This proposal clearly had nothing to do with the Indian national cause, but rather stated the British position in a fight with other Powers for control of the Middle East. However, France did not support the idea and eventually it was dropped.

Interestingly, British India also had an opinion on the general question of Japanese policy in China: "It is very desirable, from the Indian point of view,

[142] Purcell, *The Maharaja of Bikaner*, 86.   [143] MacMillan, *Paris 1919*, 403.

that Japan should not be permitted to establish herself, politically or commercially, in the two Chinese provinces of Szechuan and Yunnan, which border on Tibet and the Indian Empire. If, in return for compensation elsewhere, Japan could be induced formally to recognize that these two provinces and Tibet itself lie outside her sphere of influence, it would be a great advantage." The British also concerned themselves with the fate of another nearby region that would become South East Asia: "The possibility has been suggested that France, exhausted by the war and faced with new and exacting responsibilities in other directions, may find herself unable to maintain her position—already none too strong—in Indo-China, and may seek for some means of relieving herself of the burden."[144] These, too, lay far from the interests of India's political class.

In a memorandum on the British Empire and the League of Nations prepared in March 1919, the well-known author of "Studies in Colonial Nationalism" and a recognized authority on the constitutional relations of different parts of the empire, Richard Jebb, wrote:

> Putting aside the sentiment of the past, it might seem the more natural course for the Dominions to ally themselves with the United States, with which they share the vital policy of excluding Asiatic settlement from their territories. Conversely, India might then seem destined to go with China and Japan, supporting their effort to obtain admission for Asiatic emigrants to the high-wage countries of the new world. And since the ancient tribal idea, or "ethnological basis," of political organization has been revived in the war, it might be argued that in the natural order of things this Asiatic group ought to arise, harmoniously confronting in the League an American-Australasian group and two or three European groups, Latin, Teuton and Slav.

But Jebb also argued that, despite recent developments, this "racialism" was really out of date, whether as a basis for the formation of states or the Leagues of Nations. "In that view the inter-racial character of the existing Britannic Commonwealth is in itself a good reason for trying to perpetuate it."[145]

Interestingly, the minutes of the British Empire delegation meeting held the evening before the April 28 plenary conference relate that in the course of discussing the Japanese proposal for racial equality, Lord Sinha, the Indian delegate, said if it were raised "he would be obliged to come forward in the Plenary Session in support of the Japanese position."[146]

The Muslim League, established in 1906 as a counterweight to the Hindu-dominated INC, also welcomed the proposal to establish a League of Nations for deciding international questions. "The rights of the non-White races," it added, should receive equal consideration at the hands of the League of Nations "as those of the White races." This Muslim demand for racial equality reflected not only concern for the international rights of India, but also echoed rising indignation among Indian Muslims about the rumors that the victorious European powers intended to dismantle the Ottoman Empire and dethrone

---

[144] Indian Desiderata for Peace Settlement, BA: FO 608/211.
[145] Richard Jebb Memo, BA: FO 608/241.   [146] Purcell, *The Maharaja of Bikaner*, 101.

the sultan in Istanbul, whom many of them saw as the symbolic head of the Islamic world.

The Indians petitioned the Powers at the peace conference to recognize India as a nation. "We have done so in the dawn of peace; why not in the guardianship of peace?"[147] But it seemed to be an impossible quest. Like the Chinese, Indian nationalists and members of various societies and organizations flooded Paris and the peace conference with telegrams appealing for India's self-determination. For instance, Madras Mahajana Sabsa wrote to the president of the Paris Peace Conference on February 16, 1919, arguing that India should be represented in the League of Nations, on a basis equal to that of the self-governing Dominions. He demanded that the Conference recognize India's right to fully responsible government. Many of these telegrams demanded, prayed, or appealed for India to be granted self-determination or at least home rule. But the British government simply collected these telegrams and refused to circulate them to the other delegations. Still, over the course of the peace conference, Indian nationalists actively promoted India's self-determination. Mrs. Besant's Theosophist group set up shop in Stockholm and stayed in contact with the Indian Committee in Germany, with Lenin's Executive Committee for India, and with other commit-tees working in Central Asia and China. Mrs. Besant's group worked vigorously to get home rule for India discussed at the peace conference. Tilak even directly appealed to President Wilson, but received only a dismissive reply which suggested that the question of self-determination for India would be taken up in due time by the proper authorities.

Indians were bound to be disappointed, since Britain was unlikely to give up India or any of its colonial possessions. Britain, it seemed, would be in a false position if she insisted on self-determination for other people's colonies, but refused to surrender any of her own, nevertheless, that is the position the British took up and stuck to. As British senior diplomat Sir Eyre Crowe declared to another senior British diplomat, Harold Nicolson, "'Nonsense, my dear Nicolson,' said Crowe, sacrificing the whole of British liberal idealism without a second thought, 'you are not being clear-headed. You think that you are being logical and sincere. You are not. Would you apply self-determination to India, Egypt, Malta, and Gibraltar? If you are *not* prepared to go as far as this, then you have no right to claim that you are logical. If you *are* prepared to go as far as this, then you had better return at once to London.'"[148] At the Paris Peace Conference, Montagu threatened to resign as Secretary of State for India and sent Lloyd George a sharp letter to denounce his attitudes toward India. Colonel House advised against his resignation for the reason that he had a chance to do a "great work for India." According to House, Montagu was "one of the few Englishmen I know who wants to give India a responsible government as fast as she is ready for it."[149]

---

[147] Letter to Cecil, January 23, 1919, BA: FO 608/241.   [148] MacMillan, *Paris 1919*, 49.
[149] "The Diary of Colonel House, April 5, 1919," in Arthur Stanley Link, ed., *The Papers of Woodrow Wilson* (Princeton, NJ: Princeton University Press, 1981), 57: 35.

The factors that shaped the proceedings of the peace conference were many and complicated, and there was simply no way for people in Asia to even guess at all the dynamics. The Indians, Chinese, Vietnamese, and Koreans might believe that world leaders such as Wilson, Lloyd George, and Clemenceau could be the saviors of their respective national dreams, but they had no idea of the personal politics at work. For example, Wilson considered Lloyd George "as slippery as an eel," while Lloyd George thought Wilson unscrupulous and bigoted. Wilson believed Clemenceau belonged among the "mad men" of history.[150]

There was grave concern about the effect that US influence would have on the future of British rule in India. It would be very difficult for the British, Montagu had noted even before the armistice, not to "fall in line" with the US program at the war's end, given Wilson's preponderant power. "We have been so long accustomed to dictate to the world ... our position," he wrote, that it was "rather galling now that we find ourselves playing second fiddle to the autocratic ruler of the United States." Montagu was equally unhappy with the INC. He wrote to the viceroy that there was no longer, as there had been before the war, a division between moderates and extremists. Now, there were only "Extremists and super-Extremists," since both factions wanted to move much further, and much faster, toward self-government than the British were willing to concede. Chelmsford, who was more conservative than Montagu and unenthused even about mild reforms, was quick to agree that the session in Delhi was an unqualified triumph for the most extreme elements in the Congress.

Indian confidence in and trust of Wilson was equally misguided. According to David Miller, legal advisor to the American delegation, the Indians' use of the term "self-governing" was unfortunate since Wilson would never challenge the British about India, which the British government had treated according to her own colonial program.[151] Americans even had mixed feelings about whether India should be allowed to join the League of Nations. According to Miller:

> For myself, I have great admiration for India's performance. The spirit which she has shown is fine. Nevertheless, the impression of the whole world is that she is not self-governed, that the greater part is governed by the laws of Westminster, and the lesser part is governed by princes whose power is recognized and supported by the British government, within certain limits. Therefore, even though it may be hard to exclude India [from the League of Nations], still we ought to recognize that all governments derive their just powers from the consent of the governed.[152]

The major issue of how to deal with America's own colony, the Philippines, also played its part in shaping the American approach. As Miller confessed:

> The difficulty in my mind is that if India is admitted on any principle that principle would probably extend to the Philippine Islands. Under the definition which I have

---

[150] Morrow, *The Great War: An Imperial History*, 288.
[151] David Miller, *My Diary at the Conference of Paris, with Documents* (New York: Printed for the author by the Appeal Printing Company, 1924), 1: 164–5.
[152] Miller, *My Diary at the Conference of Paris*, 1: 165.

proposed, the Philippines would be excluded. This seems right to me. For though it is the intention of the United States to grant them political freedom at the earliest practicable date, and since they are now satisfied with the stage at which they have arrived, still I think it would be unwise to admit them at present.[153]

So much for Indian fantasies about the American Philippine model. Only with strong mixed feelings and reservations did Wilson eventually allow India to join the League of Nations.[154] Edwin Montagu and Ganga Singh signed the Treaty of Versailles on behalf of India. In his letter to Lord Chelmsford, Montagu pondered the changes made in the constitution of the British Empire and concluded:

It would seem to me that we are riding two constitutional horses. From the back of the first we proclaim the unity of the Empire... From the back of the other horse we proclaim that the British Empire should be represented by something like fourteen representatives to everybody else's five on certain matters; ... As regards India, I would only make this observation. Ex-Pro-Consuls and others are holding up their hands with horror at any substantial efforts towards self-government, and at the same time we have gone—shall I say lightly?—into a series of decisions which put India so far as international affairs are concerned on a basis wholly inconsistent with the position of a subordinate country.[155]

As a colonialist, Montagu clearly did not share the Indians' national dream, but his judgment certainly reflected how India had been transformed in the short period of the war. With all the lip service paid by the British government to the idea of self-rule, with all their sacrifices and contributions in support of the British war effort, and all their aspirations to self-determination, the Indians, in the end, achieved little at the peace conference. The reissue of the *Cambridge History of India* by the Delhi publisher S. Chand might be right to argue that "the closing scenes of the world war brought to India, despite all her sacrifices in the cause of victory, not peace, but a sword."[156] India's admission to the League of Nations and her representation on the governing body of the International Labour Office fell far short of Indian expectations.[157] The demands of the nationalists went nowhere. Britain reneged on its promise of self-rule and resumed repressive policies after the war. No wonder there was a general feeling of disappointment. The future Chinese communist leader, Mao Zedong, observed in 1919 that at the Paris Peace Conference India had "earned itself a clown wearing a flaming red turban as representative" to the Paris peace conference and "the demands of the Indian people have not been granted," despite the fact that India had risked "its own life to help Britain" during the war.[158]

[153] Miller, *My Diary at the Conference of Paris*, 1: 165–6.
[154] Miller, *My Diary at the Conference of Paris*, 1: 167.
[155] Purcell, *The Maharaja of Bikaner*, x.
[156] Dodwell, *The Cambridge History of India* (please note that this quote was from India's version in 1964), 6: 488.
[157] Saxena, *Role of Indian Army in the First World War*, 140–1.
[158] Schram, *Mao's Road to Power*, 1: 33.

It is high time to think about the war and India from the broad perspective of shared history. From any perspective, the war and its aftermath changed Indian perceptions of themselves, the British Empire, and the world. The fact that the British depended on India for over a million soldiers and significant wartime resources clearly proves its importance to the empire. While the war and Indian contributions raised Indian hopes and expectations for greater political autonomy, Indian soldiers returning home from the war told horror stories about the violence of the "civilized" powers of Europe, which damaged the British reputation and the foundations of its civilizing mission. The Jallianwala Bagh massacre in 1919, in which the British army, under the direction of General Reginald Dyer, opened fire on an unarmed crowd of Indian men, women, and children, permanently tarnished the image of benevolent colonial rule and ushered in a new era of discontent across India, a story that will be examined in detail in Chapter 8.

4

Colonial Vietnam and the War

If China and Japan were destined to get involved in the Great War as early as 1895, the Vietnamese were dragged into the orbit of European hostilities even earlier—in 1885, when Indochina became a French colony. Indochina contributed both human and material resources to the French war effort. As with the other Asian peoples drawn into the war, Vietnamese experiences in the First World War marked a turning point in their history. For many, the journey to France meant more than answering the call of their colonial master, it was also an eye-opening learning experience, as they had the opportunity to observe and interact with Westerners in their European homeland. It allowed them to compare and contrast the French with others and rethink their own national identity and position in the world. The future Vietnamese leader Ho Chi-minh went to Paris in 1919 to lobby for his country's independence, and what happened to him there had a significant impact on the Vietnamese search for a national identity and the future development of Indochina.

VIETNAMESE SOCIETY AND THE GREAT WAR

Vietnam was known as Indochina during the First World War period, and the Vietnamese were then called either Indochinese or Annamites. As the name implies, this society was influenced by both China and India, and became "the locus of competition" between Asia's two great civilizations.[1] India and China had historically dominated the region's religions, philosophies, art, and political organization for over 2,000 years. The Vietnamese traced their cultural past over the centuries-long period of Chinese rule, which at the same time inspired their determination to assert their independence. After many years under China's control, Vietnam then lost its traditional name and its unity as France colonized it in the late nineteenth century. Vietnamese history is thus the story of a long struggle for national identity. The dominant characteristic of the Vietnamese is, according to one scholar, the "spirit of resistance."[2] Two millennia of struggle against the political and cultural domination of China, the historian William Duiker points out, "had created in

---

[1] Stanley Karnow, *Vietnam: A History* (New York: Penguin Books, 1997), 110.
[2] Gary R. Hess, *Vietnam and the United States: Origins and Legacy of War* (Boston: Twayne Publishers, 1990), 1.

Vietnam a distinctly 'national' ethnic spirit, more self-conscious, and more passionate than that found virtually anywhere in Southeast Asia."[3]

When France turned Vietnam into its colony, the French changed and influenced Vietnamese politics, society, and economics in far-reaching ways. The French language was introduced and written Vietnamese was Romanized instead of using Chinese characters. Albert Sarraut, the Governor-General of Indochina during 1911–14 and 1916–19, acknowledged that "It was frequently repeated that until 1914, the colonies were, for most of our compatriots, no more than a terrain favorable to the development of our military glory, to the enterprises of adventure seekers, to the generous experiences of our civilizing genius." The economic and political value of Indochina was largely disregarded. Colonies were widely viewed as the expensive fantasy of a large nation. Georges Clemenceau, the famous "Tiger" who would lead France during the First World War, but was at that stage a left-wing radical, cursed imperialism as a policy that enriched capitalists and wasted funds that should be spent on domestic social programs.[4]

This view still persisted on the eve of the war. Some in France suggested and seriously played with the idea of making a deal with Germany in which they would exchange Indochina for Alsace-Lorraine.[5] This kind of talk of course ended when the Great War broke out, and France and Germany were once again engaged in hostilities. Only when many Vietnamese came to aid the French war effort with material sources from Indochina did the French population suddenly appreciate the value of their colony.[6] Then it became a resource. As Sarraut observed during the war, "Indochina is, in all views, the most important, the most developed, and the most prosperous of our colonies."[7]

When the Great War broke out, France indeed turned to its colonies for support. The French government rallied to mobilize both human and material resources in Vietnam, and although Indochina had a wealth of resources, the colonial government had difficulties organizing them at first. As Sarraut noted:

> We will surely never know what difficulties the colonial governments encountered during the war to respond to the pressing needs of the Motherland, in men, in resources, in money. The patriotic fervor couldn't compensate all the shortcomings of sudden improvisations, lacking efficient prewar preparations. Men? We had men everywhere, but we lacked the means to inventory them, to examine them, and above all to group them and route them towards points of concentration. It was necessary, in many cases, to impose on the indigenous people long, tiring, and oftentimes useless displacements. Routes and means of transport were insufficient.[8]

---

[3] William Duiker, *The Rise of Nationalism in Vietnam, 1900–1941* (Ithaca: Cornell University Press, 1976), 16.

[4] Karnow, *Vietnam: A History*, 95.

[5] Philippe M. F. Peycam, *The Birth of Vietnamese Political Journalism: Saigon, 1916–1930* (New York: Columbia University Press, 2012), 38.

[6] Albert Sarraut, *La Mise en valeur des Colonies Françaises* (Paris: Payot, 1923), 37–8.

[7] Sarraut, *La Mise en valeur des Colonies Françaises*, 463.

[8] Sarraut, *La Mise en valeur des Colonies Françaises*, 57–8.

Despite initial difficulties, Indochina in fact contributed enormously to the French war effort. According to Sarraut, military recruitment there started in 1915 with 3,000 men; in 1916, 36,000 Indochinese went to France; in 1917, the number was 9,922, for a total of 48,922 Vietnamese joining the French military. These soldiers served in several different combat units: two were stationed in France, two in Macedonia, and one in Djibouti.[9] French recruitment of Indochinese laborers also started in 1915 with 4,631 men; in 1916, 26,098 laborers went to France; in 1917, 11,719 Vietnamese laborers arrived in France; in 1918, 5,806 Indochinese arrived in France; and in 1919, 727 Indochinese still managed to be brought to France for the French postwar reconstruction effort. Therefore, a total of 48,981 Indochinese laborers served in France during the war.[10] There is also evidence that Vietnamese women went to France to serve there. A few volunteered to work in health services or at factories "by the side of our French sisters." There were even reports of female Indochinese in the workers' camps.[11]

The Vietnamese who went to France during the war included soldiers and reservists recalled for active duty, as well as workers. On December 17, 1915, the colonial government launched its campaign to recruit men, and this appeal for volunteers was reinforced by a royal edict of January 20, 1916, which offered the men a bonus of 200 francs after they passed a medical examination and were inducted into the army. It promised them a salary and their families a monthly allowance. About 40,000 soldiers, workers, and seamen volunteered between October 1916 and July 1917.[12] Soldiers already in service had contracts specifying that once their period of active duty had expired, they were to remain at the army's disposal for thirty-eight years. Volunteers signed contracts to serve in the army during the war plus six months after the signing of the armistice.[13] The key reason most men enlisted to serve in France was to escape poverty and earn money to sustain their families. Most of the Vietnamese who went to France were poor and illiterate peasants from Tonkin and north Annam.[14] For volunteering, they received a bonus and advance pay before they left for Europe. The volunteers for combat received the same wage, pension, and monthly allowance as the professional soldiers and reservists. However, their package of bonuses was different. Of their 200 franc bonus, 50 francs was paid when a volunteer signed his contract and the other 150 francs when he departed for France. He also received 0.40 francs for each day he stayed in the recruiting center and training camps, and throughout his service during the war. Skilled workers and clerical staff were all to receive a 40 franc bonus. Unskilled workers received only 25 francs as a bonus for volunteering. The base pay of all workers was the same, namely 0.75 francs per day. However, there was a substantial difference in the supplementary pay they would

    [9] Kimloan Vu-Hill, *Coolies into Rebels: Impact of World War I on French Indochina* (Paris: Les Indes savantes, 2011), 44.
    [10] Sarraut, *La Mise en valeur des Colonies Françaises*, 42.
    [11] Kimloan Vu-Hill, "Sacrifice, Sex, Race: Vietnamese Experiences in the First World War," in Das, *Race, Empire and First World War Writing*, 55.
    [12] Vu-Hill, *Coolies into Rebels*, 40.   [13] Vu-Hill, *Coolies into Rebels*, 41.
    [14] Vu-Hill, *Coolies into Rebels*, 32.

receive: 0.25–0.75 francs per day for unskilled workers; 2.75–3.50 francs per day for skilled workers. Base pay would increase as they gained seniority.[15]

Although the recruitment was largely peaceful and voluntary, at the beginning there was resentment in some of the villages in Tonkin and violent resistance in the southern provinces of Cochin China. Most of that resistance was led by members of religious sects and secret societies.[16] The overwhelming majority of recruits who went to France were volunteers. As in the case of the Chinese laborers, admission to service required passing a medical examination. "They were motivated by the terms offered by the government, by dreams of the adventure, by economic crises in Indochina, and by the desire to escape from poverty."[17] These workers were employed in France in industries working for the state, and then, progressively, they worked for railroad networks and in the liberated regions. As the war dragged on, its reliance on its Asian colony only became greater.[18]

Besides committing its human resources, Indochina made other sacrifices for the French war effort. By the end of 1916 alone, it had loaned France more than 60 million francs as well as goods valued at approximately 30 million francs. Another figure puts the French government's wartime loans from its colony at over 167 million francs between 1915 and 1920, and the sale of the war bonds in Indochina reached 13,816,117 francs. Indochina lent France more than 367 million of the 600 million francs borrowed from all its colonies in Asia and Africa. Thirty percent of that amount came from native Vietnamese individuals. According to Albert Sarraut, Indochina's total cash contribution between 1915 and 1920 amounted to 382,150,437 francs; donations by individuals amounted to 14,835,803 francs. The Vietnamese sent cash donations of 10 million francs just to aid war victims and contributed 11,477,346 francs to the 1915 military campaign.[19] War aid also included raw materials such as coal, rubber, and minerals; dry goods such as rice, tea, tobacco; fabrics such as cotton and khaki; and clothing. Over the course of the war, Indochina supplied France with 335,882 tons of rice, corn, alcohol, beans, tobacco, cotton, rubber, copra, timber, cooking oil, and lard. As with colonial India, Indochina had to ensure the wages, pensions, and family benefits for the men who had been mobilized, as well as pay the expenses of the Indochinese military hospital. The latter added up to 4,040,000 francs sent to France in 1917 and 1918.[20] Once the war was over, Indochina also helped to pay for the reconstruction of five cities that had been destroyed—Carency, Origny-en-Thiérache, Hauvigne, Chauvignon, and Laffaux.

While the French benefited enormously from the Vietnamese contributions, it is fair to say that Indochina also benefited to the extent that its exports increased: in

[15] Vu-Hill, *Coolies into Rebels*, 42.

[16] Hue-Tam Ho Tai, *Radicalism and the Origins of the Vietnamese Revolution* (Cambridge, MA: Harvard University Press, 1992), 30–1.

[17] Vu-Hill, *Coolies into Rebels*, 10.

[18] Peycam, *The Birth of Vietnamese Political Journalism*, 60.

[19] Vu-Hill, *Coolies into Rebels*, 37–8.

[20] Pierre Brocheux, *Ho Chi Minh: A Biography*, trans. Chaire Duiker (New York: Cambridge University Press, 2007), 19.

the first year of the war, exports grew by 9,270,816 francs, while exports from France to Indochina decreased by 5,090,092 francs.[21] As Kimloan Vu-Hill argued, the First World War changed the nature of the relationship between France and its colony. From being a debtor, Indochina became a creditor. The Vietnamese loans to France meant that it could maintain its economy and feed its people during the war.[22]

However, the most important legacy of the war was its effect on colonial society: it changed the mindset of the Vietnamese, awakened their sense of nationalism, and fed their personal growth with experiences of Europe and contact with men from other civilizations. The war in Europe also damaged the French reputation in Indochina. As Albert Sarraut wrote, "The dreadful holocaust of our dead, the still-dark image of our richest provinces devastated, the procession of pains from which we will suffer for a long time to come, all these sorrows, in moments where our effort of will tries to divert the oppressive anguish, underlining, through the effect of contrast, one of the consoling consequences of the ordeal that we have endured: the Great War had the clear advantage of revealing the colonies to the French public."[23] According to Philippe M. F. Peycam, "In the early twentieth century, Western pretensions of unchallengeable supremacy suffered a number of palpable blows: the Japanese victory over Russia in 1905, the butchery of World War I among European nations, the 1917 Soviet Revolution in Russia, and, in the Asian French colony, the persistence of opposition to colonial rule at both popular and elite levels." For several years, the French did not do well in the war and this drove them to something close to concessions. "When the fate of France itself hung in the balance in Europe and when a less assured colonial state was trying to hold on to its position by conceding to the Vietnamese population limited, shared responsibility. The purpose was to obtain native support for the war effort and, beyond it, for the supposedly mutually beneficial project offered by French republican colonialism."[24] This latter phenomenon arose against the background of major sociocultural transformations, most acutely experienced in the main urban centers of Saigon and Hanoi. Opposition crystallized into a historical moment in the midst of the First World War: "Arising from the aspirations of urban, Western-educated Vietnamese, this pursuit adopted original forms of activism, using newspapers as a distinct political force that flourished within the constraints of the colonial legal framework."[25] As France and its empire became engulfed in the war, the colonial port city of Saigon found itself developing into a "space of possibilities." "Within its boundaries, a complex process of imposed acculturation and social interactions led to new expressions of Vietnamese consciousness on both an individual and a collective level."[26]

[21] Vu-Hill, *Coolies into Rebels*, 38.
[22] Vu-Hill, *Coolies into Rebels*, 50.
[23] Sarraut, *La Mise en valeur des Colonies Françaises*, 37.
[24] Peycam, *The Birth of Vietnamese Political Journalism*, 3–4.
[25] Peycam, *The Birth of Vietnamese Political Journalism*, 6.
[26] Peycam, *The Birth of Vietnamese Political Journalism*, 13.

The French colonial government itself contributed to the dramatic social changes in Indochina with its policy adjustments. When Sarraut returned in 1917 to serve his second term as governor-general, he introduced a well-publicized program of "Franco-Vietnamese collaboration" to mobilize Vietnamese support for the ongoing war in Europe. This was a subtle policy aimed at building a concrete partnership with Vietnamese elites. The governor-general decided to allow individual Vietnamese regarded as loyal to France to participate in what he considered the most critical arena of political action: public expression in the press and in publishing. Between 1916 and 1919, a series of Vietnamese-run newspapers aimed at a Vietnamese audience emerged in the public landscape of colonial Indochina. This surge in the number of Vietnamese-run publications was the most tangible expression of Sarraut's political strategy toward the established Vietnamese elite.[27] So long as the war in Europe went on, government control over political activity and self-imposed restraint on the part of the emerging Vietnamese intellectual activists remained the rule, "depriving the colonial press and sections of the colonial administration of any excuse to call for the suspension of the experiment."[28]

Ho Chi-minh realized that the reforms of colonial institutions proposed by Albert Sarraut, who was appointed Minister of Colonies by the government of Prime Minister Aristide Briand in 1921, were weak and limited, that they would have no effect on the living conditions of the Vietnamese people, and that colonized peoples would continue to live in scorn and humiliation. This situation would not change as long as the colonial regime and all French personnel in the colonies continued to dominate local peoples. Shortly after the war, in 1919, as Albert Sarraut left his post as governor-general, he promised the Vietnamese some participation in the affairs of their country, but not political freedom. This led Ho to not only denounce the colonial system, but also to criticize Sarraut.[29] Sarraut commented after the war that his so-called cooperation policy in Vietnam had not produced positive results. He wrote, "Less generous perhaps than other nations in the verbal liberalism of the constitutions granted, we compensated for the parsimony of our colonial franchise by sincere feeling." What he meant here was that the French sincerity of feeling for the Vietnamese was proved by the fact that the Vietnamese enjoyed fewer rights than the natives of other colonial countries.[30] In February 1919, when the news of Sarraut's expected return to France in May was received, Vietnamese journalists began a bold move to create an autonomous Vietnamese public politics, with newspapers as their main instrument of nationalist expression.[31] Thus, the First World War provided the Vietnamese with "an unexpected opportunity to test France's ability to live up to the vaunted self-representations of invincibility" Sarraut had promoted.[32] The activities of Vietnamese journalists and newspapers surely helped cultivate the nationalist

---

[27] Peycam, *The Birth of Vietnamese Political Journalism*, 62.
[28] Peycam, *The Birth of Vietnamese Political Journalism*, 66.
[29] Brocheux, *Ho Chi Minh*, 19.
[30] Joseph Buttinger, *Vietnam: A Political History* (New York: Praeger, 1968), 143–4.
[31] Peycam, *The Birth of Vietnamese Political Journalism*, 67.
[32] Peycam, *The Birth of Vietnamese Political Journalism*, 59.

dream. Although colonial control may explain the limited effect of Vietnamese efforts at political reform, "events that occurred during and immediately after World War I wrought a real transformation of Vietnam's political elite and educational system, which in turn brought into the open further schisms in the Reform Movement."[33] I will turn to this point in some detail later in this chapter.

Therefore, the outbreak of the Great War provided Indochina with momentum for change and transformation. When the war had just broken out, Ho Chi-minh, an unknown person at the time, wrote to one of his friends and mentors: "Gunfire rings out through the air and corpses cover the ground. The five Great Powers are engaged in battle. Nine countries are at war.... I think that in the next three or four months the destiny of Asia will change dramatically. Too bad for those who are fighting and struggling. We just have to remain calm." Realizing the opportunity the war present-ed, Ho concluded that he should go France immediately to take the pulse of the larger world and to better understand the role his country might play.[34] He might have anticipated that the conflict would lead to the eventual collapse of the French colonial system.[35] Even though at the time Ho was engaged in undistinguished work, he worried about the fate of his country. In a poem composed in 1914, he wrote:

> In confronting the skies and the waters,
> Under the impulse of will that makes a hero
> One must fight for one's compatriots.[36]

The Chinese Revolution in 1911 and societal transformations in China further contributed to the Vietnamese political awakening. Against the background of the fighting in Europe and ongoing changes in Asia, many Vietnamese turned to political activities. These developments together should be seen to "constitute a new historical moment for Vietnam and the beginning of a new historical trajec-tory."[37] The first expression of a modern national consciousness was the movement led by Phan Boi Chau during the first two decades of the twentieth century. That movement aimed to create Vietnamese discontent with the kind of modernity that was being forced upon their country. Chau and his followers knew that a new era was dawning and found inspiration in the example of Japan, which had embraced Western ways with its Meiji Restoration and transformed itself into a strong independent state. But Chau's movement failed and he had to flee, first to Japan and then to China.[38] Interestingly, Chau's organization invited the young Ho Chi-minh to study in Japan and join his nationalist movement. But Ho declined because he distrusted reliance on the Japanese, a situation he allegedly described as "driving the tiger out the front door while welcoming the wolf in through the back."[39] Instead, he was determined to visit France and observe Western civilization, as did many elite Chinese.

[33] Tai, *Radicalism and the Origins of the Vietnamese Revolution*, 30–1.
[34] Brocheux, *Ho Chi Minh*, 12.
[35] William Duiker, *Ho Chi Minh* (New York: Hyperion, 2000), 51.
[36] Duiker, *Ho Chi Minh*, 53.   [37] Peycam, *The Birth of Vietnamese Political Journalism*, 60.
[38] Hess, *Vietnam and the United States*, 10–11.
[39] Hess, *Vietnam and the United States*, 14.

Still, the failure of Chau's movement did not stop others from trying to rebel against French rule during the war, when the French military presence in Vietnam was not great. The first and most striking incident took place on February 14, 1916, with an attack on a Saigon prison by a few hundred armed insurgents who were trying to free their fellow fighters. Two months later, an elaborate attempt to overthrow the French was carried out in the royal capital of Hue. That effort was also defeated. In August 1917, a military-led insurgency broke out and the French were not able to suppress it until January 1918.[40]

As they pursued national independence, some Vietnamese even turned to the Chinese. Prince Cuong De actively cultivated Chinese support and friendship. At one point, he received word that the Chinese minister of war, Duan Qirui, might back Vietnamese anti-French operations in China. When Cuong De met with Duan in the summer of 1914, he was led to believe that Duan was interested in striking at the French, since the French were the weakest imperialists in China. Even President Yuan Shikai made vague promises of sending a large sum of money to support Cuong De's nationalist activities. With the outbreak of war in Europe, Duan spoke of hitting the French in China while they were preoccupied in Europe. But as the Japanese threat mounted in China, the Chinese became more concerned with that fight, and the Vietnamese realized the Chinese could not keep their promises.[41] Nevertheless, many Vietnamese anticolonial insurgents lived in China and published articles in Chinese newspapers to rally their fellow nationalists. Interestingly, the French government suspected that the Japanese were behind some of the anti-French activities in Chinese territory and elsewhere, and pursued diplomatic discussions with them. Ultimately, they worked out a mutually acceptable arrangement whereby the French would provide information on Korean nationalists in their Shanghai settlement if the Japanese would keep Cuong De under surveillance, prevent him from going to another country, and perhaps forward periodic accounts of his activities.[42] These connections between the Vietnamese, Chinese, and Japanese in the Great War period thus hinged on matters of nationalism and shaking loose from—or keeping at arm's length—the colonial Europeans.

The Vietnamese failures to overthrow colonial rule by force, the subsequent wave of repression by the French colonial government, and the increased prospect of France's victory in Europe led a growing number of educated Vietnamese to conclude that new rules should be devised to guide their role in colonial politics. A different path of action was needed, one that took advantage of the European war. This was exactly the strategy adopted by Ho Chi-minh. As they thought through the most effective forms of political action, some Vietnamese nationalists had compared their cause to that of the Koreans. But Ho Chi-minh and his fellows quickly concluded that Indochina could not follow the model put forward by the Korean March First Movement. Ho and others believed that the Vietnamese faced

[40] Peycam, *The Birth of Vietnamese Political Journalism*, 61.
[41] David G. Marr, *Vietnamese Anticolonialism, 1885–1925* (Berkley: University of California Press, 1971), 236–7.
[42] Marr, *Vietnamese Anticolonialism*, 237–8.

different challenges and difficulties compared to their Korean counterparts, since French domination had deeply and solidly rooted itself in Indochina and seemed to be impossible to overthrow from within. It was difficult to mobilize popular Vietnamese support for nationwide protests due to their political passivity. Indochina's nationalists agreed that as a first step toward emancipation they should aim at obtaining all rights related to freedom of education and speech in order to enlighten the Vietnamese population.[43] Ho Chi-minh later explained the idea this way: the objective of the French administration was always different from that of the Japanese in Korea. The Japanese wanted to Japanize the Koreans entirely. But it seemed to Ho that:

> France, contrarily, desires to perpetuate the inequality between the Annamites and the French; it wants, in profiting from the work of Annamites, to indefinitely continue to drain of all sorts of products of which Indochina has so much and to prevent the Annamites from creating for themselves an independent economy. All of the taxes as well as the restrictive measures and the regime of public instruction were inspired by these considerations. In creating obstacles to civilization and to the progress of the Annamite race, the French are assured of their ability to indefinitely keep them on the margins of world civilization and to force them to submit to their perpetually renewed demands. During these past few years, the conditions of existence in Indochina have become more deplorable than they have ever been.[44]

Thus, Ho would launch his independence movement in Paris by appealing for international support.

THE VIETNAMESE IN FRANCE

During the Great War, the French exploited the human resources of their colonial empire, using them as "human fodder," as Ho Chi-minh called them. The French government claimed that it had brought civilization to its colonies and in return was now owed a "blood tax."[45] Ho resented this use of the Vietnamese. In his famous 1925 treatise, he wrote:

> Before 1914, they were nothing but dirty Negroes and dirty Annamites, good for no more than pulling rickshaws and receiving baton blows from our administrators. The fresh and joyous war declared, they became the "dear children" and "brave friends" of our fatherly and caring administrators[. . .]. They (the *indigénes*) were suddenly promoted to the highest rank of "defenders of law and liberty." This honor, however, cost them dearly, for to defend this right and this freedom, of which they themselves

[43] Thu Trang-Gaspard, *Ho Chí Minh à Paris (1917–1923)* (Paris: Editions L'Harmattan, 1992), 67–9.

[44] Trang-Gaspard, *Ho Chí Minh à Paris*, 70.

[45] Michael Goebel, "Fighting and Working in the Metropole: The Nationalizing Effects of the First World War throughout the French Empire, 1916–1930," in Bley and Kremers, *The World During the First World War*, 101.

are deprived, they had to abruptly leave their rice fields or their sheep, their children and their wives, to come across the ocean to rot on the battlefield of Europe . . .

They perished in the poetic desert of the Balkans, wondering whether the mother country intended to install herself as a favourite in the Turk's harem: why else should they have been sent here to be hacked up? Others, on the banks of the Marne or in the mud of Champagne, were heroically getting slaughtered so that the commanders' laurels might be sprinkled with their blood, and the field marshals' batons carved from their bones.[46]

After the war, "once the cannons had been satisfied with black or yellow flesh," the clock was turned back again: "Our leaders' declarations of love were silenced by their enchantment and Negroes and Annamites automatically turned [back] into people of a 'dirty race.'"[47]

While serving in France, about 4,000 to 5,000 Vietnamese worked as drivers to transport men and supplies at and near the front.[48] During the battle of the Somme, Indochinese drivers remained at the wheel for thirty-six hours straight without displaying any more fatigue than did their French counterparts. Richard Fogarty suggests that Indochinese drivers were easier on the machinery than their French colleagues and the upkeep of trucks driven by the former cost less than a quarter of that for vehicles driven by French soldiers. They also drove safely, successfully avoiding fatal accidents. The Vietnamese civilians gained a reputation for "intelligence, calmness, skill, and aptitude for precise tasks."[49] Some of the soldiers also received high praise. Recalling one Vietnamese company's perform-ance in a fight, their battalion commander later wrote, "The soldiers have shown that they are excellent combatants who have remarkable courage and are capable of taking the place of French soldiers in the front lines." Vietnamese soldiers were justly proud of their performance in the battlefields. One declared, "We partici-pated in the battle on par with the French. Many of us died and many were wounded."[50] Most did not go home until mid-1919. In 1920, about 4,000 workers and soldiers remained in France; many of them had taken jobs there.[51] By the end of the war, 1,548 Vietnamese workers had died and 1,797 Vietnamese soldiers had lost their lives in Europe.

Their voyage to France brought much suffering, as did the transport of the Chinese and Indians. Seasickness, disease, poor conditions, and bad food were major complaints. Some workers had to sleep with livestock en route. After arriving in France, new challenges and hardships faced them. Many Asian workers were treated badly and had only tattered clothes. Long hours and short rations were common for the Indochinese workers. One complained: "There has been no rest, not even a Sunday off. If we were tired, we just took the liberty to rest. However, for

[46] Mishra, *From the Ruins of Empire*, 193–4.
[47] Goebel, "Fighting and Working in the Metropole," 109–10.
[48] Sarraut, *La Mise en valeur des Colonies Françaises*, 43.
[49] Richard Standish Fogarty, *Race and War in France: Colonial Subjects in the French Army, 1914–1918* (Baltimore: Johns Hopkins University Press, 2008), 65–6.
[50] Vu-Hill, *Coolies into Rebels*, 85.   [51] Vu-Hill, *Coolies into Rebels*, 119.

each day we were absent without permission, we were thrown in jail for fifteen days and [the colonial government in Indochina] cut off the monthly allowance to our families." Because of the hard work, the same man reported: "I am a young man, but I feel so old. I hope I will live to return to my family."[52] Another laborer reported that the only food he had had for two weeks was "one loaf of bread."[53] A corporal named Duong declared, "Life in the trenches is unbearable." One Sergeant Phung complained that he had to stand guard in a trench for "eight days without taking off his shoes and without a change of clothing." In winter, life was even more miserable, since the men were not used to the cold.[54] The Vietnamese, like Indians, suffered terribly during the cold French winters. "It was so cold," one wrote, "that my saliva froze immediately after I spit it on the ground." Another wrote, "The chill of winter pierces my heart."[55] Such was their suffering that some Vietnamese soldiers were sent to warmer places to fight.

Besides the hard work, lack of food, and cold winters, the lack of interpreters created additional problems for the Vietnamese. Most of the workers could not speak French and their employers could not communicate with them in Vietnamese, and each group of two to three hundred workers had but one interpreter. As a result, poor communication and cultural misunderstandings between the men and their employers were not uncommon. The Vietnamese were criticized for certain habits or customs—for instance, blackening their teeth because they thought black teeth made them attractive. "A dog hath his teeth white, so [the Vietnamese] will blacken theirs." Not surprisingly, this practice aroused public curiosity and made them a target of ridicule by the French, which sometimes led to confrontations. French ignorance of Vietnamese cultural practices and beliefs also generated protest. In Toulouse, long hair became an issue between the Vietnamese and their superiors. Vietnamese men and women liked to let their hair grow long. "The Vietnamese loved their hair as much as their heads." And so cutting their hair "was not so much a sign of repressed sexuality or castration as it was a sacrifice of the self." Thus, "when their hair was cut or taken away, they experienced pain." And by custom it was lucky (or unlucky) to have a haircut during certain periods, such as the traditional New Year celebration. But long hair became a health concern for the French regional health services, with reports that it carried lice. On February 7, 1917, one French lieutenant ordered a subordinate to cut the hair of more than 200 Vietnamese workers. When they realized that their hair was to be cut, they protested by rolling on the ground, crying, and lamenting their loss. Afterward, they all gathered in a courtyard and decided not to work that afternoon.[56]

[52] Vu-Hill, *Coolies into Rebels*, 77.

[53] Vu-Hill, "Sacrifice, Sex, Race," in Das, *Race, Empire and First World War Writing*, 58.

[54] Vu-Hill, *Coolies into Rebels*, 73.

[55] K. Hill, "Strangers in a Foreign Land: Vietnamese Soldiers and Workers in France during World War 1," in Nhung Tuyet Tran and Anthony Reid, eds., *Viet Nam: Borderless Histories* (Madison, WI: University of Wisconsin Press, 2005), 261.

[56] Vu-Hill, *Coolies into Rebels*, 105–6.

The Vietnamese also suffered racism in Europe, even though they had come to support the British or French war efforts. Among nineteenth-century British, the widespread assumption was that "Asians and Africans were children, to be firmly dealt with for their own good."[57] The official code "forbade any hint of sentimental sympathy with colonial or subject peoples. Sternness in dealings with the heathen became a virtue never to be compromised; they were children to be judged, ruled, and directed. And yet mixed with this arrogant belief in racial domination one often finds elements of incredible ignorance concerning, say, Oriental or African customs and cultures."[58] Due to racial stereotypes, Frenchmen thought the Vietnamese were not physically strong enough to do a solid day's work like their white counterparts. General Joffre maintained that the Indochinese "do not possess the physical qualities of vigor and endurance necessary to be employed usefully in European warfare."[59] The Vietnamese were clearly not happy with the mistreatment and racism. One Indochinese commented: "We held our heads high in indignation; our tongues uttered trains of words, speaking only of retaliation."[60] The Vietnamese learned from French workers to fight for their rights by protests and strikes.

For relief during periods of boredom, some Vietnamese gambled. Card games were an especially popular pastime among the Vietnamese in France. But gambling also led to disputes and violence, since some men lost substantial sums. Sergeant Luong, for example, lost all his money and was forced to ask his family in Indochina for money in order to survive.[61] But most Vietnamese behaved responsibly and deposited their money in savings banks, sending some to their families and investing some in treasury bonds. By early 1918, 36,715 workers had deposited 271,887 francs, remitted 5,261,026 francs to their families, and purchased treasury bonds worth 411,030 francs. Unfortunately for the recruits and their families, inflation and currency depreciation devalued the considerable sums they had saved. The franc/piaster conversion rate in their contracts was 2.50 francs for each piaster. But during the war, the franc depreciated steadily to 4 francs for each piaster. In 1916, for every 50 francs they sent home, their families in Indochina received sixty sapeques (copper coins). By 1917, however, the rate had fallen to only 37.5 sapeques.[62] Nevertheless, these earnings and savings improved some Vietnamese lives financially back home and contributed, if only in small ways, to the country's economic development.

To dissuade the Vietnamese from gambling or committing crimes, the French authorities developed a few recreational and educational programs. In Marseille,

---

[57] V. G. Kiernan, *The Lords of Human Kind: Black Man, Yellow Man, and White Man in an Age of Empire* (New York: Columbia University Press, 1986), 153.

[58] Nicholas Griffin, *Use of Chinese Labour by the British Army, 1916–1920: The "Raw Importation," its Scope and problems* (PhD thesis, University of Oklahoma, 1973), 14.

[59] Fogarty, *Race and War in France*, 45.

[60] Vu-Hill, "Sacrifice, Sex, Race," in Das, *Race, Empire and First World War Writing*, 54.

[61] Vu-Hill, *Coolies into Rebels*, 101.

[62] Vu-Hill, *Coolies into Rebels*, 102.

every evening after 6.00 p.m. workers dressed in khaki uniforms and English-style tunics flocked to the *Cercle Indochinois* (Indochinese Club) to relax, write letters home, and socialize with fellow Vietnamese. The club provided magazines, newspapers, and tea free of charge. The club was founded in January 1916 by a committee to assist Indochinese workers, with support from the French Ministry of War, the Governor-General of Indochina, and a number of organizations. The *Alliance Française*, founded by Albert Sarraut in 1915, provided social services and organized cultural activities for the Vietnamese workers and soldiers in France. Members of the *Alliance* also offered free French lessons.[63] The Vietnamese seemed enthusiastic about the opportunity to learn French while in Europe. One cavalry corporal named Le Van Nghiep was so proud of placing second out of sixty candidates in the exam for the elementary certificate in French that he wrote to a friend in Hanoi and asked him to publish an article about his success, along with his picture, in the local paper. The letter, unfortunately, ended up on the desk of a French censor, who sniffed that this Vietnamese had carried his language studies "rather far" and his "modesty is fading."[64] Nonetheless, by the war's end, about 25,000 men had learned to read and write French through this program.[65]

Despite of all the problems, challenges, and racism, living and working in Europe side by side with the French and other peoples provided the Vietnamese a unique opportunity to observe, to learn, and to understand different cultures and civilizations. Some had opportunities to interact with American soldiers when they came to each other's assistance during battles. The personal letters of Vietnamese soldiers reveal their impressions. One wrote that the American army was "the strongest and the most powerful among the allies." Another wrote that the Americans were "fierce fighters." The third even made the shocking suggestion that the French were not so tough and rather, "the presence of the Americans on the battlefield restored the confidence of the Vietnamese."[66] Many Chinese and Vietnamese had daily contact. Despite language difficulties, the Chinese and Vietnamese got along well and at times developed close bonds. Whenever the Chinese got into fights with Africans, with whom the Chinese seemed to have ongoing difficulties, the Vietnamese joined in against the Africans. The French government did not want the Vietnamese to be infected by Chinese ideas of patriotism and nationalism and tried hard to keep them separate.[67]

French people were the ruling class in Vietnam and the social gap between them and the Vietnamese was huge. But in France, Vietnamese workers and soldiers had opportunities to date, have sex with, and even marry Frenchwomen. One soldier wrote, "On Sundays we go strolling with [French] women, as we would do in Indochina, with our own women at home."[68] The Franco-Vietnamese relations

---

[63] Hill, "Strangers in a Foreign Land," in Tran and Reid, eds., *Viet Nam: Borderless Histories*, 270.
[64] Fogarty, *Race and War in France*, 153.   [65] Vu-Hill, *Coolies into Rebels*, 100.
[66] Hill, "Strangers in a Foreign Land," in Tran and Reid, eds., *Viet Nam: Borderless Histories*, 263.
[67] Chen Sanjing, Lu Fangshang, and Yang Cuihua, eds., *Ouzhan Huagong shiliao (Archival Sources about Chinese Laborers during the First World War)* (Taipei: Zhongyang yanjiuyuan jindai shi yanjiusuo, 1997), 380–1.
[68] Fogarty, *Race and War in France*, 202.

in France were the opposite of those in the colonial setting, where French men had relationships with Vietnamese women. Interestingly, despite French racism, it seems that both the Vietnamese and Chinese were popular with Frenchwomen. They often sought them out because they had money and were kind. Love and intimacy led to marriages. Despite the French government's effort to deter French women from having relationships with, or marrying, Vietnamese men, by 1918, there were 250 French-Indochinese couples who were legally married in France. Another 1,363 couples lived together without the approval of the French authorities or parental consent.[69] The interpreter Pham Van Khuong received several letters from his fiancée, Ninon, in Toulouse, who professed her love and her desire to go to Indochina with him after the war. However, he also received letters from another young Frenchwoman, who reproached him bitterly for having earlier promised marriage to her, only to admit later that he already had a wife back home. Some of these men worked themselves into the good graces of solidly respectable families. Another interpreter, Dinh Van Giah, expressed a desire to marry a nurse at the hospital where he worked, but he already had a wife and family in Tonkin, and his new French beloved was the daughter of an officer in the French army. Some wanted to use their marriages to Frenchwomen to gain French citizenship and economic security. "I plan to obtain naturalization by marrying a Frenchwoman, which will permit me to set myself up in a job [here] later," Corporal Trong wrote home to his parents in August 1917.[70] After the war, of the 2,900 Vietnamese soldiers and workers who remained in France, most of them had French wives.[71]

Besides dating French women, the Vietnamese frequently sent home images of French women, sometimes in the nude. A sergeant major named Ho sent his brother in Indochina letters he had received from Frenchwomen, telling him to save them as "sacred things" that the sergeant could, upon his return, show to European colonial masters who did not believe his stories and who might mock him for his pretensions to relations with white women.[72] Some Vietnamese boasted of their French concubines or mistresses. To impress his male buddies at home, one man sent a picture showing himself lying in bed, with his French "concubine" caressing him.[73] Many Frenchmen became angry because the Vietnamese workers did not have to fight and dared to get involved romantically with Frenchwomen.[74] The French authorities were also concerned about the photographs sent home showing the Vietnamese in the company of white women. The French believed these proofs of interracial contact were damaging to their "prestige in the Far East," so the French censors confiscated any such images they could find. In August 1817, one Vietnamese letter-writer observed that officials had forbidden sending nude French women's images home because "the French fear ridicule." Censors

[69] Vu-Hill, *Coolies into Rebels*, 111.   [70] Fogarty, *Race and War in France*, 208.
[71] Hill, "Strangers in a Foreign Land," in Tran and Reid, eds., *Viet Nam: Borderless Histories*, 281.
[72] Fogarty, *Race and War in France*, 222.
[73] Vu-Hill, "Sacrifice, Sex, Race," in Das, *Race, Empire and First World War Writing*, 59.
[74] Vu-Hill, *Coolies into Rebels*, 103.

were quite candid about the consequences for public order and French rule in the colonies: examples of the "deplorable attitude" many Indochinese had acquired during their stay in France would lead the population of Indochina to think the French lived in a state of "shameful debauchery."[75] This possibility worried French authorities deeply and they sometimes used drastic measures to stop the Vietnamese from dating Frenchwomen. One man was imprisoned for fifteen days for "daring to fall in love with a French girl."[76]

The French authorities were right to be concerned, since for the Vietnamese, breaking through the old social boundaries symbolized their coming of age and fed their national awakening. They could challenge the colonial order and political taboos established by the French in Vietnam.[77] According to one scholar, "The likely effect of such interracial relationships on the status of Frenchwomen in the colonies was apparent.... These women were supposed to be pillars of the community there, embodying French ideas about civilization and domesticity, and defining the boundaries that separated colonizers from colonized." For some of them, despite their status as colonial subjects living in France, they were no different from Frenchmen living in Indochina: marrying local women, and frequenting local brothels and cabarets. Many characterized their sexual relations with Frenchwomen as political activities. They wrote back home that France was now paying for the sins of its sons, who had built the colonial empire and had often taken native women as concubines. Sex with Frenchwomen was "like a revenge on the European, the Frenchman who down there causes old Indochina to blush and incites jealousy." One soldier wrote, "In our country, the women of this race are very difficult to approach, but us being here, two francs is enough for us to have fun with them." Another wrote to a friend also in France that "like many others, you can say that you have more than served France; you are defending her and you are repopulating her" with the children of mixed races.[78] The Vietnamese experience in France made them feel no longer inferior to the French, and they began to question and resent French dominance in Vietnam.[79] Such attitudes among men, many of whom would eventually return to their homes, "presented a significant potential threat to the colonial order."[80]

Given all this, the French decision to bring large numbers of Vietnamese to France probably had the largest influence and impact on Vietnamese society. According to Kimloan Vu-Hill, "World War I marked a new chapter in the history of colonial Viet Nam. It removed the barriers that prevented Vietnamese labor from entering France en-masse" and thus marked "a new phase in the history of French Indochina, in which people in France and the colonies were brought together to fight for a common cause." The largely poor peasants' journey to France transformed them from ignorant, illiterate peasants to men with experience of the

---

[75] Fogarty, *Race and War in France*, 220–2.   [76] Fogarty, *Race and War in France*, 214.

[77] Vu-Hill, "Sacrifice, Sex, Race," in Das, *Race, Empire and First World War Writing*, 60.

[78] Fogarty, *Race and War in France*, 202–12.

[79] Hill, "Strangers in a Foreign Land," in Tran and Reid, eds., *Viet Nam: Borderless Histories*, 281.

[80] Fogarty, *Race and War in France*, 209–10.

wider world and with new skills, knowledge, and ideas. "This transformation would have significant consequences, not only for their individual lives but also for Indochina and France, although those consequences were not necessarily what the men themselves, or the government of Indochina and France, had hoped for."[81] Some scholars have observed that the war in Europe gave the Vietnamese "firsthand experience of French politics and worker militancy; they had also seen that France and the French were not invincible in war or immune from political and social difficulties." For these men, "the myth of French superiority had been shattered and they were no longer content to accept French rule of their homeland."[82]

The Vietnamese who went to France "were transformed, and in many cases radicalized, in varying degrees by their experiences." From poor and ignorant subjects of the French colonial empire, they became professional soldiers and workers, and more confident and politically conscious subjects. They no longer felt inferior to the French or their native leaders. French authorities feared that these men would return to Indochina with new ideas and be less "submissive" to "their traditional discipline." They instructed the colonial government in June 1918 to interrogate and maintain close surveillance on returning soldiers.[83] To the degree that the First World War raised their financial and social status, when the soldiers and workers returned home, they would become an important force in shaping Vietnamese society and politics. Indeed, a number of workers who returned from France became directly involved in organizing, leading, and agitating in the labor movement of the 1920s. Ton Duc Thang, a sailor in the French fleet during the First World War and later a president of the Democratic Republic of Vietnam, used his knowledge of organized labor to found the first Association of Workers of the Saigon Arsenal. Nguyen Trong Nghi, a worker in a French factory, became an agitator and leader of workers' demonstrations in Nam Dinh in the late 1920s.

But their experience of the war itself was often devastating. One soldier said the war was "frightening and brought only ruin." He warned others to resist being recruited: "My friend! It is better that you do not come here. I would advise you to come here in peacetime. But it is wartime. Stay there."[84] Many veterans, moreover, felt betrayed both by their own society and by France and its failure to look after them. These disillusioned and embittered veterans formed a large class of men "who were receptive to the arguments of those who changed the status quo— namely, the communist party—and took their anger to the streets. . . . By recruiting men from Indochina, France had inadvertently set in train events that would eventually contribute to the loss of its Indochinese colonies."[85] In the course of war, the Vietnamese gained first-hand knowledge of French military organization, strategy, and fighting power, with which they were not impressed. Their experiences surely transformed their worldviews: "One thing is certain; they were not the

[81] Vu-Hill, *Coolies into Rebels*, 50–1.   [82] Vu-Hill, *Coolies into Rebels*, 10.
[83] Fogarty, *Race and War in France*, 220–5.   [84] Vu-Hill, *Coolies into Rebels*, 86.
[85] Vu-Hill, "Sacrifice, Sex, Race," in Das, *Race, Empire and First World War Writing*, 64–5.

same men who had left for Europe on large ships. Moreover, they no longer viewed the French as superior."[86]

Ho Chi-minh became a popular figure among his compatriots in France during the war years, and political tracts under his name were distributed among them advocating independence for Indochina.[87]

HO CHI-MINH AND THE PARIS PEACE CONFERENCE

Among all the Vietnamese who were in France during the war, none was more important in transforming Vietnam than Ho Chi-minh. By end of the Great War, Ho had concluded that:

> France has never put into practice, in the administration of Indochina, the principles of liberty and humanity that are dear to it. In politics, she [France] has practiced despotism; in public instruction, obscurantism; in economic and financial matters, she has only exhausted Indochina to enrich herself; finally, she has put such restrictions to the freedom of thought and speech that Annamite aspirations to independence had difficulty emerging.

Ho believed that this was the time for the Vietnamese to pursue definitive autonomy and perhaps eventual independence. By the end of the war, approximately 50,000 Vietnamese remained in France. While most worked in factories, a few hundred had come to study; because of the highly politicized atmosphere within the intellectual community in France, such students were ripe for political agitation.[88]

Historians are still not certain about the exact date Ho Chi-minh settled in France. According to diverse foreign and Vietnamese authors, he might have arrived in Paris at the end of 1917.[89] The problem was that Ho worked on ships and might have entered and left France several times. He is known to have visited the United States and Britain with the ships he worked on. According to a generally accepted source, Ho left Vietnam in 1911 at age twenty-one as a chef's assistant on a ship bound for France. When he arrived in Marseilles in September 1911, he applied to the Ministry of Colonies for admittance to a government school that trained bureaucrats to serve in France's overseas possessions. "I am eager to learn and hope to serve France among my compatriots," he wrote.[90] He spent some time in London and in late 1917 (some say 1919) crossed the English Channel and settled in Paris. Ho was involved in political debates and activities from the start. At one point, he tried to join the French army, but did not succeed. Ho Chi-minh clearly meant to become influential among the Vietnamese in France.[91]

[86] Vu-Hill, *Coolies into Rebels*, 91.
[87] Vu-Hill, "Sacrifice, Sex, Race," in Das, *Race, Empire and First World War Writing*, 62–5.
[88] Duiker, *Ho Chi Minh*, 56.   [89] For details, see Thu, *Hồ Chí Minh à Paris*.
[90] Karnow, *Vietnam: A History*, 131.   [91] Vu-Hill, *Coolies into Rebels*, 68.

Ho Chi-minh made a living in Paris by selling Vietnamese food or Chinese calligraphy; sometimes, he even made money as a forger of Chinese antiquities. A French police dossier suggests that he also worked at enlarging and retouching photographs—"a keepsake of your relatives and friends," read his business card. He advertised in *La Vie Ouvrière* (*The Working Life*): "You who desire to have a living keepsake of those close to you, have your photographs retouched by Nguyen Ai Quoc. Beautiful portraits and frames for 45 francs." According to many detailed descriptions of Ho's activities from the French secret police reports compiled after he had attracted attention for his political activities, Ho was very skilled with his hands. He had, for example, found a way to slip candles into lamp glasses, which provided him with lighting for a penny without being indisposed by petrol fumes. Ho definitely knew the Chinese language and taught Chinese to his Vietnamese compatriots. At that time, most Vietnamese thought that learned Vietnamese should write and read Chinese, and only secondarily Vietnamese. Ho might also have spoken a bit of English, but his French skills were questionable, at least in his early years in France.

Although a poor man at the bottom of French society, Ho was a motivated and devoted political activist. The French police, who kept dossiers on foreigners, described Ho in a slightly literary tone: "General appearance somewhat arched and awkward, his mouth constantly half-open in a rather ingenuous smile."[92] Shortly after his 1917 arrival in France, Ho cultivated close relations with two famous veteran Vietnamese nationalists: Phan Van Truong, and especially Phan Chau Trinh. Both Phans were subject to the attentive vigilance of the French authorities. Phan Van Truong was a lawyer who had lived in France for over ten years and spoke and wrote French well. Phan Chau Trinh was a friend of Ho Chi-minh's father—the two men belonged to the same scholar class in 1901—and it is logical that a warm, confident friendship between the scholar and the son of his colleague should develop. Both senior nationalists helped and supported the young Ho by introducing him to their circles. Through them, Ho soon came to know many people, including future French Communist Party members such as Charles Longuet, Marcel Cachin, Paul Vaillant-Couturier, and Jacques Duclos.

Ho's time in France of course coincided with the arrival of large numbers of Vietnamese to support France's war effort, and he soon founded a Vietnamese network, the Association of Annamite Patriots. Ho Chi-minh, aka Nguyen Ai Quoc, as a Vietnamese nationalist, actively lobbied for the Vietnamese national cause from the beginning of the peace conference. Ho also worked as a journalist and wrote in *L'Humanité*, founded the anticolonial newspaper *Le Paria*, and arranged funding to undertake conference tours across France and the African colonies. He attended all the Comintern Congresses. According to his secret police dossier, each time he spoke, he berated the delegates of the Third International about how little they worried about the fate of peoples oppressed by the injustice of the colonial system. At that time, the International Proletariat was still in its

---

[92] Karnow, *Vietnam: A History*, 131.

infancy, and the leaders of the French left were still nationalists and sectarians. Ho sometimes grew furious with them. He left a stormy interview with the Head of Overseas Affairs of the Communist Party, Jacques Doriot, who directed him to "tone it down." He approached diverse political personalities and succeeded in interesting a number of deputies in his cause.

For all of his activity in the early years, Ho seems not to have become well known. He did not gain prominence for his political ideas or attract attention to his nationalist movement or himself as Nguyen Ai Quoc. Few paid attention to that name besides the police. "You must know this man?" said Arnoux to Albert Sarraut, Minister of the Colonies, who responded to Arnoux with the following: "I'm telling you that this Nguyen Ai Quoc doesn't exist. It's only a *pseudonym for Phan Chau Trinh*."[93] But Ho, in September 1919, had actually had an audience with Albert Sarraut, then recently returned from Indochina![94]

As a sort of personal protection, Ho had used various names in his adult life. When he left Vietnam in 1911, he seems to have been called Nguyen Tat Thanh. When in France, one of his new pseudonyms was Nguyen O Phap ("Nguyen who hates the French"). But during the Paris Peace Conference, the name Nguyen Ai Quoc was the one that finally became known. We don't know when Ho started to use the name for himself or whether in the beginning he chose it for the invisible groups of Vietnamese nationalists in France, since Nguyen Ai Quoc literally means "Nguyen who loves his country." But he definitely used that name by 1919, if not earlier, since that was his signature on a Vietnamese declaration related to the peace conference. The first known published appearance of the name appears in the June 18, 1919 issue of *L'Humanité*, over a piece that commented on the eight demands made by the "Annamite People."

The story of Ho at the Paris Peace Conference runs like this. In cooperation with other Vietnamese in Paris, Ho prepared a petition for Vietnamese autonomy that was presented to the conference. That petition was made by a "Group of Annamite Patriots in France," although no evidence exists concerning the founding of this group.[95] The petition was clearly influenced and motivated by Wilson's ideas, but it was not at all politically radical. It did not ask for independence, but rather for autonomy, equal rights, and political freedoms. It called for the following:

1. General amnesty for all native political prisoners;
2. Reform of Indochinese justice by granting the natives the same judicial guarantees as Europeans;
3. Freedom of the press and opinion;
4. Freedom of association;
5. Freedom of emigration and foreign travel;

---

[93] For more information on the name, see Thu Trang, *Những hoạt động của Phan Chu Trinh tại Pháp* (Paris: Sudestasie, 1983), 9–56.
[94] Quinn-Judge, *Ho Chi Minh:* The Missing Years, 11.
[95] Tai, *Radicalism and the Origins of the Vietnamese Revolution*, 69.

6. Freedom of instruction and the creation in all provinces of technical and professional schools for indigenous people;

7. Replacement of rule by decree with the rule of law;

8. Election of a permanent Vietnamese delegation to the French parliament, to keep it informed of the wishes of indigenous people.

It is important to keep in mind that although the name Nguyen Ai Quoc was later associated with Ho Chi-minh, claims that the petition was prepared by Ho alone or that the name Nguyen Ai Quoc pointed only to Ho are questionable. There were indications that the document was influenced or prepared in large part by the two Vietnamese nationalists Phan Van Truong and Phan Chau Trinh; the translation was certainly done by Phan Van Truong, who had the necessary legal French to prepare the document. Ho's French was not simply good enough for him to have done that work. And it is plausible that "Nguyen Ai Quoc" was chosen to represent all of them, including the future Ho, to protect them from the French police. We can also suggest that because Ho was not well known at the time, it would have been easier for him to take such open action.[96]

In a short time, however, the name Nguyen Ai Quoc became associated specifically with Ho Chi-minh. Ho's audacious actions on behalf of his country in 1919 earned him fame as a Vietnamese patriot. The secretive and enigmatic signatory, Nguyen the Patriot, gave him a large audience and, at the same time, a reputation as an audacious and clever person; this aroused both interest and suspicion. Whatever its original designation, the emergence of the name Nguyen Ai Quoc reflected collective changes in Vietnamese society and its people during the First World War era. It clearly pointed to Vietnamese nationalist dreams and was a cry for independence. That the name eventually became associated with Ho contributed to the mythical status of the future Vietnamese communist leader, but it is not proof of Ho's authorship of the petition.

For India, Korea, and Vietnam—all colonies—Wilson's national self-determination ideas were very attractive. They were all understandably excited at the prospects of the postwar peace. However, like the claims of the Indians and the Chinese, the Vietnamese petition to the conference principals did not succeed and in fact was ignored. It was considered "too obscure" to receive an answer from Wilson or Clemenceau, although Colonel Edward House, a member of American delegation and a Wilson confidante, sent a polite note to Ho on June 19 that acknowledged having got it.[97] The British delegation's review of the Annamite claims concluded with "this is exclusively a matter for the French Govt. and it does not seem necessary even to acknowledge receipt."[98]

The European war had widened the political horizons of many Vietnamese, who, in spite of government control over information, realized that their situation largely depended on what happened on the world stage. "This realization led to the

---

[96] For more information on the name, see Thu, *Những hoạt động của Phan Chu Trinh tại Pháp*, 9–56.

[97] MacMillan, *Paris 1919*, 59.   [98] "Claims of the Annamites," BA: FO 608/209.

hope that, in recognition of their wartime loyalty, French authorities would grant them an institutional framework that would provide the new political avenues they sought."[99] But the French considered Ho's petition a "libel" and did not undertake discussion of any political changes in Vietnam.[100] Vietnamese trust in Wilson was bound to fail, too. From his prominence and prestige at the Paris Peace Conference of 1919, Wilson hesitated to recognize new nations, especially those outside Europe. As had happened in the Philippines earlier, he applied the principle of national self-determination only with great caution. He would not undermine British rule in Ireland, Egypt, and India, or French rule in Indochina. Wilson recognized only new nations that emerged from the collapse of the Russian, German, Austro-Hungarian, and Ottoman empires. He applied the principle of national self-determination only to the defeated empires. Even there, he was hesitant to recognize new governments until he was certain they possessed the historical qualities of nationality that he understood from the American experience. As Birdsall asserts, "The alliance of reactionary nationalisms in Europe and America undermined Wilson's position from the start."[101]

Nevertheless, the Vietnamese petition had clearly been influenced by Wilsonian ideals. Interestingly, this was not the last time Ho Chi-minh would follow the American lead. The Vietnamese Declaration of Independence, issued after the Second World War in 1945, was "[t]he most clearly patterned" on the American Declaration of Independence.[102] Ho later described his failure in 1919 in an article entitled "The Anti-French Resistance," dated between 1921 and 1926. Ho wrote: "While waiting for the realization of the principle of nationalities through the effective recognition of the sacred right of the peoples to self-determination," the people of the former Empire of Annam, now French Indochina, "proposed to the governments of the Entente in general and French government in particular certain demands... When the Great War ended, the Vietnamese people like other peoples were deceived by Wilson's 'generous' declarations on the right of peoples to self-determination. A group of Vietnamese, which included myself, sent the following demands to the French Parliament and to all delegations to the Versailles Conference." Ho also pointed out that he and his fellow nationalists, to echo Wilsonian internationalism, "added a tribute to the peoples and to feelings of humanity." However, after a time of waiting and study, "We realized that the 'Wilson doctrine' was but a big fraud."[103]

If Ho failed to achieve his nationalist goals at Paris, his political career took a big leap, from being nobody to being widely known. Although the petition was ignored, Ho himself caused consternation in official circles in Paris. On June 23, 1919, the President of France wrote to Albert Sarraut that he had received a copy of the petition and asked Sarraut to look into the matter and ascertain the identity of

---

[99] Peycam, *The Birth of Vietnamese Political Journalism*, 61.

[100] Quinn-Judge, *Ho Chi Minh: The Missing Years*, 13.

[101] Paul Birdsall, *Versailles Twenty Years After* (New York: Reynal & Hitchcock, 1941), 11.

[102] David Armitage, *The Declaration of Independence: A Global History* (Harvard University Press, 2008), 134.

[103] Ho Chi Minh and Walden F. Bello. *Down with Colonialism* (New York: Verso, 2007), 5–6.

the author.[104] As soon as "Demands of the Annamite People in Eight Points" appeared, Nguyen Ai Quoc became the object of diligent investigation by French police. As mentioned earlier, the Vietnamese nationalist movement had a clearly international flavor. Ho's political activities had him working closely with European communists, Chinese, and Koreans, who were fighting against the Japanese colonial regime.[105] Although he failed to get the attention of Clemenceau, Lloyd George, and Wilson, Ho was taken quite seriously by fellow Asians. He seems to have developed friendships with Chinese student activists like Zhou Enlai and Deng Xiaoping, who were in France then as well. These friendships would come in handy when he later launched revolution in Vietnam. Ho is also said to have introduced some of the better French speakers among the Chinese into the French Communist Party, including the two sons of Chen Duxiu.[106] Given his familiarity with Chinese history and culture, it is not surprising that Ho often used the figure of the Chinese sage to sell his idea of equality between Asians and Westerners.[107]

Ho also paid close attention to Korean affairs and received and read issues of *Korea Review*, a monthly journal devoted to the "Cause of Political and Religious Freedom for Korea." Edited in Philadelphia by Korean students, the journal largely focused on Korea's history and Japanese cruelty, and proposed a declaration of independence for the Republic of Korea. Many of Ho's political ideas in 1919 came from his contact with the Korean nationalists in the United States and Paris, and Ho borrowed heavily from the Korean independence movement, according to reports by the French police agent "Jean" who followed Ho around Paris pretending to be his friend. He maintained close contact with the Korean representative to the Paris Peace Conference, Kimm Kyusik (Chapter 5 will discuss Korea and the peace conference in detail). Kimm actually recommended Ho to the Chinese media, and Ho's first major media interviews were conducted with a Chinese newspaper in Tianjin called *Yishibao*. The same newspaper had published several articles by the nationalist Cuong De, and the tone and message of these articles were identical, and similar to that of the 1919 Vietnamese petition. More interestingly, copies of these articles were found on the walls of the Chinese workers' barracks in Marseille in June 1919. Ho obviously understood the value of this Chinese newspaper and once told the police agent "Jean" that he had an arrangement with the Korean delegation to send copies of his writings for publication in the Tianjin paper. According to Sophie Quinn-Judge, "There seems to have been a degree of coordination between what was happening in Paris and the Phan Boi Chau-Cuong De circle in China."[108] In March 1919, Cuong De and a few students independently sent telegrams to the general secretariat of the Paris Peace Conference, to President Wilson, and to the French government, calling for an autonomous Indochina.[109]

---

[104] Duiker, *Ho Chi Minh*, 60.
[105] Brocheux, *Ho Chi Minh: A Biography*, 14.
[106] Quinn-Judge, *Ho Chi Minh: The Missing Years*, 36.
[107] Quinn-Judge, *Ho Chi Minh: The Missing Years*, 18.
[108] Quinn-Judge, *Ho Chi Minh: The Missing Years*, 19.
[109] Marr, *Vietnamese Anticolonialism*, 237–8.

Ho's interviews with the Chinese reporter have several points of interest. It mentions that "Nguyen Ai Quoc" had exchanged ideas with the Korean nationalists when he made a trip to America, supposedly sometime in 1913. The Chinese newspaper reported that Ho's Chinese was good enough that he was able to carry on written correspondence. When asked "With what goal have you come to France?" Ho replied that he aimed to "reclaim the liberties from which we must benefit." Regarding what steps the Vietnamese needed to take to achieve independence, Ho replied, "Outside of some steps taken with members of [the French] Parliament, I have searched a little everywhere to group together sympathies. Among others the socialist party proved to be dissatisfied with the methods of the Government and has voluntarily given us its support. There in France is our only hope. As for our action in other countries, it's [in America] that we have had the most success. Everywhere else, we have only encountered difficulties." By "success in America," he might mean President Wilson's pronouncements on national self-determination. Regarding the question of Vietnamese independence, the interviews suggested it was "so important" "for the peace of the nations of the Far East." Ho mentioned he knew enough about the Korean nationalist movement to realize the Vietnamese situation was very different and that the Vietnamese should avoid large-scale protests against the French.[110] Besides the long interview articles with Ho, *Yishibao* dedicated much space to publishing articles on the question of Indochina's independence.

Although the world had started to pay attention to Ho during and after the Paris Peace Conference, he became frustrated about where to go politically for Vietnam. In the early 1920s in Paris, a French acquaintance recalled later: "He seemed to be mocking the world, and also mocking himself."[111] In early January 1920, he complained that Indochina was unknown among other nations. "We need to make a lot of noise in order to become known," he told the agent Jean, "Korea is now well-known to all nations, because the Koreans have raised their voices."[112] He turned to writing articles about Indochina for *Populaire* and so, "attracting the attention of some leaders in the French Socialist Party, entered politics."[113] In his "Speech at the Tours Congress," a socialists conference in December 1920, Ho informed the audience that he would like to "protest against the abhorrent crimes committed [by France] in my native land." He also made an impassioned plea, "In the name of all mankind, in the name of all Socialists, right wing or left wing, we appeal to you, comrades. Save us!"[114] In his 1921 article "Indochina," he wrote, "The wind from working-class Russia, revolutionary China, or militant India" has helped the Indochinese to be clear-headed and "cured them of intoxication." "The Indochinese are making tremendous progress, and occasion permitting, will show themselves to be worthy of their masters."[115] He tried to raise the cause of Vietnamese freedom at a meeting critical of the peace settlement in Asia, at which

---

[110] Quinn-Judge, *Ho Chi Minh: The Missing Years*, 18–19.
[111] Karnow, *Vietnam: A History*, 109.
[112] Quinn-Judge, *Ho Chi Minh: The Missing Years*, 28–9.
[113] Charles L. Mee, Jr, *The End of Order: Versailles, 1919* (New York: Dutton, 1980), 106.
[114] Ho Chi Minh, *Down With Colonialism*, 1–2.
[115] Ho Chi Minh, *Down With Colonialism*, 3–4.

the socialist Deputy Marius Moutet spoke, along with Professor Felicien Challaye and representatives of the Korean and Chinese communities. A large number of Chinese were at the meeting.[116] But he soon became disillusioned by the French socialist party because the socialists showed little interest in colonial issues.

In his tireless pursuit of the anticolonial struggle, Ho moved toward more radical positions, finally taking up the communist revolutionary stance proposed by the Russian Bolsheviks. According to the French historian Pierre Brocheux, "The turning point in this evolution came around 1920."[117] According to Hue-Tam Ho Tai, a Harvard historian, in late 1920 Ho became a founding member of the French Communist Party and saw communism as the means to save his country from colonial rule.[118] After his deep disappointment with Wilsonian ideals and promises of a more equal postwar world order, Ho Chi-minh would later claim he had concluded that "The liberation of the proletariat is the necessary condition for national liberation. Both these liberations can only come from communism and world revolution."[119] Ho had found in the ideology of Lenin and the communist international the "path to our liberation."[120] In his article "Indochina," he wrote: "The tyranny of capitalism has prepared the ground: the only thing for socialism to do is to sow the seeds of emancipation."[121] Ho Chi-minh officially joined the Communist Party in 1921. To a great extent, Ho's turn to communism is more motivated by national independence and nationalism than communist objective. As Ho would later explain, "It was patriotism and not Communism that originally inspired me."[122] But in 1923, he traveled to Moscow, which he called "the home of the revolution," and became a follower of Bolshevism.[123] A year later, Ho went as a Comintern agent to China, where his energies were devoted to organizing Vietnamese opposition to French rule.[124] Vietnamese history was once again intertwined with that of China. Ho's shift to communism paralleled the Chinese path. The Chinese case will be discussed in detail in Chapter 6.

As Ho was becoming a communist and seeking a solution to the question of Vietnamese nationalism in an international setting, the large numbers of Vietnamese soldiers and workers who had served in the war were charting their own courses. Those who returned home began organizing, leading, and agitating in the 1920s labor movement. Ton Duc Thang, a sailor in the French fleet during the First World War and later the President of the Democratic Republic of Vietnam, used his knowledge of organized labor to found the first Association of Workers of the Saigon Arsenal in 1920. Nguyen Trong Nghi, a worker in a French factory during the war, was an agitator and leader of worker's demonstrations in Nam Dinh in the late 1920s.

[116] Quinn-Judge, *Ho Chi Minh: The Missing Years*, 29.
[117] Brocheux, *Ho Chi Minh: A Biography*, 13.
[118] Tai, *Radicalism and the Origins of the Vietnamese Revolution*, 69.
[119] Ho Chi Minh, *Down With Colonialism*, 5–6.
[120] Hess, *Vietnam and the United States*, 15.
[121] Ho Chi Minh, *Down With Colonialism*, 3–4.
[122] Karnow, *Vietnam: A History*, 134.
[123] Quinn-Judge, *Ho Chi Minh: The Missing Years*, 13.
[124] Hess, *Vietnam and the United States*, 15.

"The 1921 reform of the village political system in Tonkin and the emergence of a modern organized labor movement in the late 1920s were direct consequences of the war on French colonialism in Indochina." Those Vietnamese who remained in France formed the earliest "Indochinese colonies in France."[125] Vietnamese communities emerged in cities throughout France in the 1920s, and the Vietnamese diaspora there formed a significant political block. In the decades between the two world wars, a number of them engaged in political struggle to liberate Indochina. Kimloan Vu-Hill is right when she suggests, "Without World War I, the path to revolution and to national independence would have taken a different direction."[126] The First World War indeed marked a turning point in the history of French Indochina and Vietnamese national development.

125 Vu-Hill, *Coolies into Rebels*, 10–12.
126 Vu-Hill, *Coolies into Rebels*, 9.

5

Koreans

From the March First Movement
to the Paris Peace Conference

Unlike India, Japan, Vietnam, or China, the First World War had little direct impact on the population of the Korean peninsula. Koreans did not get involved in the war, nor were they much interested in it.[1] Nonetheless, the war marks a major turning point in Korean history because it gave rise to the Wilsonian ideals and promises of a new world order that would be worked out at the postwar peace conference. According to Henry Chung, who was deeply involved in the Korean independence movement, "The world war had no small influence on the growing nationalism of Korea. The war aims enunciated by statesmen of Allied nations that 'no people should be forced under a sovereignty under which it does not wish to live' strengthened the fighting spirit of the Korean people."[2] When Korean nationalists learned of President Woodrow Wilson's Fourteen Points address and his subsequent declarations in January 1918, they were, like the Chinese and Indians, excited at the prospect of a new international order and its implications for the future of Korea. Many Korean nationalists recognized "the Wilsonian moment" as

[1] There were some Koreans, especially the educated, who had access to the news and were keenly observing the Great War and speculating on the future of international affairs after the First World War broke out. They naturally hoped the war might result in some development favorable to the Korean national cause. As Chong-sik Lee pointed out, early in 1915, a number of Korean nationalist leaders in China and Manchuria organized themselves into the Korean Revolutionary Corps, and they believed the First World War would soon end with Germany's victory. Since Japan had aided the Allies and offended the Chinese through the Twenty-one Demands, the Koreans reasoned that Germany and China would join to attack Japan. Korea then could take the side of Germany and China, provide some assistance in the war, and be able to obtain independence when Japan was defeated. Some Korean students in Japan also hoped in 1916 that "If China and Japan open fire against each other, Britain and Russian will be too busy to do anything in the Far East because of their involvement in Europe. Since the United States has great sympathy toward China, she may assist China. A small island nation like Japan could not counter China." One Korean nationalist student in Japan by name of Pak I-gyu even declared that "The result of a war between China and Japan is obvious. We must [on this occasion] obtain the influence of the United States through the Christian church. If we declare the revival of Korea, there must be some reaction from the United States and China. We hope for the earliest breakup of diplomatic relations between Japan and China." See Chong-sik Lee, *The Politics of Korean Nationalism* (Berkeley: University of California Press, 1963), 101–2.

[2] Henry Chung, *The Case of Korea: A Collection of Evidence on the Japanese Domination of Korea, and on the Development of the Korean Independence Movement* (New York: Fleming H. Revell Company, 1921), 191–2.

an unprecedented opportunity for Korea and decided to take quick action to make the most of it.

In the Japanese Empire, of which Korea was a part, the war years were a period of relative prosperity. But just as Japanese leaders planned to use the war to expand Japan's power in Asia and raise its standing in world affairs, Korean nationalists hoped it could help them throw off Japanese rule and create an independent Korea that would be an equal member in the expanding community of nations. Korean connections to the war and postwar peace conference were, of course, strongly linked through the Americans, the Chinese, and the Japanese. To protect themselves as they worked to overcome Japanese colonial rule, many Korean nationalists lived in China and launched their independence campaign there. Their March 1, 1919 declaration of independence was written with a style that was closer to classical Chinese. The Korean journey to the rallying cry for independence they made at the postwar peace conference is a shared history in the clearest sense, since it involved not only Koreans, but Chinese and Americans too, in the project to end Japanese colonial rule in Korea.

KOREA UNDER JAPANESE CONTROL AND THE RISE OF KOREAN NATIONALISM

Like China and Japan, the Korean peninsula for centuries had been largely isolated from the rest of the world. Korea had been a tributary nation under China, but in the late nineteenth century, Japan became determined to pull the "hermit kingdom" into its orbit. After defeating China in 1895 and Russia in 1905, Japan succeeded in making Korea a colony in 1910. Japan's decisive victory in 1895 put an end to centuries of Chinese suzerainty, and with China no longer a significant factor, the rising Russo-Japanese competition over Korea became a central feature of Japanese politics for the next decade. In 1905, Japan's surprise victory over Russia cemented its power in Korea and increased its sway in China. In the resulting Portsmouth Treaty, named after the Maine naval shipyard in which it was signed in September 1905, with US President Theodore Roosevelt acting as mediator, the Russians effectively recognized Korea as a Japanese protectorate. Among the key provisions of the treaty were Russia's acknowledgment that Japan possessed paramount political, military, and economic interests in Korea, and Russia's pledge not to hinder Japan from taking whatever actions it deemed necessary for the "guidance, protection, and control" of the Korean government. Many saw Japan's victory over Russia as a challenge to Europe's claim to a superior civilization, a claim that underlay the imperial order in international affairs. The sense of an "awakening East" the Japanese victory produced "helped spur challenges to the legitimacy of empire and its embedded assumptions of Western superiority." The Swadeshi movement in India and the constitutional movement in China all occurred within a few years of 1905. But the Japanese victory, though it undermined the legitimating claims of Western imperialism, offered "no new levers" that could help colonial nationalists challenge imperialism in practice. As Erez Manela eloquently argues, "Efforts to adopt the Japanese model in order to construct stronger, wealthier, more 'modern' societies, while potentially attractive, were long-term projects. And Japan itself—as an actual state rather than as a model—showed little interest in using its growing international clout to challenge the logic of the existing order. On the contrary, it strove to join it as an imperial power itself."[3]

Just as the Chinese defeat in 1895 brought nationalism into sharper focus among its political elite, Koreans had also become increasingly conscious of the importance of the new ideology to their collective future. In 1896, a group of Western-educated Korean intellectuals and professionals established the Independence Club, the first Korean organization actively to embrace and espouse a recognizably modern nationalism. Motivated by Chinese efforts at reform and deep concern for Korea's international status and national fate, club members advocated political and economic reforms along Western liberal lines in order to strengthen Korea against further encroachment and launch it on the path to modernity. The Independence Club leveled strong criticisms against the government and even transformed itself as a sort of citizens' assembly. It published journals and organized political activities to broadcast its political ideas. Its publications "served as a vehicle for its views and in particular for the views of the new intelligentsia and their western liberal ideas, and in this way it played a major role in advancing public awareness and understanding."[4]

The club's activities were aimed at three principal goals. First of all, to safeguard the nation's independence in the face of external aggression, it urged that Korea should adopt an independent and neutral foreign policy. Second, the club initiated a popular rights movement as a way to invite wider participation in the political process. Setting forth ideological grounds such as the right of the individual to the security of his person and property, the rights of free speech and assembly, the full equality of all people, and the doctrine of the sovereignty of the people, the club argued for the right of the governed to participate in their governing. "For the first time in Korea, then, the Independence Club in effect had launched a movement for political democracy." Third, the club promoted a self-strengthening movement. The principal points in this program were to establish schools in each village that would provide a new-style education, to build textile and paper mills and ironworks to advance the country's commercialization and industrialization, and to ensure the nation's security by developing a modern national defense capacity.[5]

The club's founder, Philip Jaisohn, instilled Western, and especially American, political ideas such as popular sovereignty into his club's political movement. Another prominent club member was Syngman Rhee, who would become the first President of the Republic of South Korea, ruling from 1948 to 1960. Rhee, born in 1875 to a family of scholar-officials, studied the Confucian classics before entering an American missionary school in 1894. To help promote the program of the Independence Club, Jaisohn founded a Korean-English newspaper, *Tongnip*

[3] Manela, *The Wilsonian Moment*, 122–3
[4] Ki-Baik Lee, *A New History of Korea*, trans. Edward W. Wagner with Edward J. Shultz (Cambridge, MA: Published for the Harvard-Yenching Institute by Harvard University Press, 1984), 304.
[5] Lee, *A New History of Korea*, 304.

Sinmun (*The Independent*). In the period between 1896 and 1898, the club and its paper advocated modernization, citing both Japan and the United States as models for Korean development. Conservatives in the court, who feared that reforms would undermine their power, strongly opposed the club and its agenda, and soon banned it and its paper. Jaisohn went into exile in the United States after the club's failure, where he became a naturalized US citizen. Rhee was arrested and imprisoned for six years, during which time he converted to Christianity. The Independence Club episode was similar in many respects to the contemporaneous "Hundred Days" reforms in China. That movement, led by Kang Youwei and Liang Qichao and conducted under the name of Emperor Guangxu, also advocated modernization and was suppressed in 1898 by court conservatives. The Korean government, in late 1898, ordered that the club be dissolved and arrested many of its leaders. After the demise of the Independence Club, intellectuals formed many other political and social organizations, which contributed greatly to raising the political and social consciousness of educated Koreans, especially in urban areas. While Korean rulers were prepared to rely on the support of foreign powers to preserve their kingdom's territorial integrity, this new intellectual class committed itself to securing their nation's independence and freedom.[6]

Once Japan had turned Korea into a protectorate, the Korean people faced increasingly repressive Japanese rule, and this fed into increased nationalist consciousness and activities. Korean groups in the United States tried to forestall the protectorate through diplomatic action, and expatriate organizations based in Hawaii collaborated to send emissaries to petition American President Theodore Roosevelt to find some means to preserve an "autonomous government" in Korea. Roosevelt gave the two emissaries—Syngman Rhee, recently released from prison, and P. K. Yoon (Yun Pyonggu), a Protestant minister—a hearing in New York City, but told them that he could do little to help them. In fact, the American government had signed a secret agreement and cut a deal with Japan. Japanese Prime Minister Katsura Taro and US Secretary of War William Howard Taft signed the Taft–Katsura Memorandum on July 29, 1905. This memorandum said the United States would not interfere with Japan's occupation of Korea, and Japan would not interfere with America's occupation of the Philippines. This was a direct betrayal of a treaty with Korea signed in 1882, in which the United States promised to recognize Korean sovereignty, but more importantly, it set a pattern for decision making at the 1919 peace conference. But the Koreans could not know of the deal, since the full text of the memorandum did not become public until 1922.[7]

The years after 1905 saw the rapid spread of nationalist consciousness and activities in Korea. Armed groups engaged Japanese forces in guerrilla warfare in the countryside, while in the cities, patriotic societies were established and then

---

[6] Lee, *A New History of Korea*, 302; see also Lee, *The Politics of Korean Nationalism*, 125–6.

[7] For the US and other countries' treaties with Korea and Korean pleas, see "Appendix No. 2: Korea—What the Conferee Nations Have Said and Pledged" and "Appendix No. 3: Brief for Korea," in No Author, *Korea's Appeal to the Conference on Limitation of Armament* (Washington, DC: Government Printing Office, 1922), 12–16, 17–44.

disbanded by the Japanese in quick succession. This period also saw a sharp rise in the activity and success of Protestant missionaries in Korea, most of them from the United States. Although the missionaries were careful not to offend the Japanese authorities by showing open support for Korean nationalism, an increasing number of Korean Christians became prominent in nationalist activities as new ideas about progress, modernity, and nationhood spread among the growing ranks of intellectuals and professionals. Korean Buddhists and adherents of Chondogyo, or "heavenly way," as the Tonghak sect was then known, were also prominent in nationalist organizations and activities. A modern discourse of Korean national identity, which had begun to emerge in the 1890s, borrowing from Western models, continued to expand and develop in those years. Korean intellectuals studied Korean language and mythology, as well as world history, in their quest to develop ideas on the nature and significance of the nation. They often concluded, as was typical among emerging national movements in Europe and elsewhere, that the Korean nation had arisen in the mists of antiquity and possessed a well-defined and homogeneous ethnic character.

The Korea Preservation Society formed in 1904. After Korea became a Japanese colony, and staging an overt independence movement had become impossible, many nationalist activists fled to the safety of overseas havens such as China and the United States. Korean exiles in Shanghai maintained a covert relationship with the Chinese government. Korean nationalists continued their appeal to international opinion in resistance to Japanese rule. In 1907, as the Second International Peace Conference was convening at the Hague (the first conference had occurred in 1899), the Korean Emperor Kojong secretly sent envoys to ask for the restoration of Korean independence. The envoys were admitted to the conference through the good offices of the Russian representative, who, naturally enough, was more than happy to use them to embarrass Japan in an international forum. The envoys claimed that the Japanese–Korean Protectorate Treaty of 1905 was void since Korea had signed it under duress and asked that the Powers intervene to restore Korean sovereignty. The Korean representatives failed to sway the diplomats at the Hague meeting, and they were quickly ejected from the conference under Japanese pressure. The chief Korean envoy, devastated by this failure, committed ritual suicide. Still, the episode was a great embarrassment to the Japanese authorities in Korea, and when Kojong's role in it was discovered, he was forced to abdicate. Far from advancing Korean independence, the Hague affair caused the Japanese to tighten their grip and set the stage for full annexation of the peninsula by Japan in August 1910.

Korean historiography often characterizes the period of direct military rule that lasted from 1910 to 1919 as the "Dark Period." This largely coincided with the Great War era. Under heavy Japanese repression, "religious organizations remained one of the sole venues for organized activities, and the influence of the Protestant churches continued to grow."[8] The Japanese authorities, adopting a policy that

---

[8] Carter J. Eckert, Ki-Baik Lee, Young Ick Lew, Michael Robinson, and Edward W. Wagner, *Korea, Old and New: A History* (Cambridge, MA: Harvard University Press, 1990), 260.

called for the complete assimilation of Koreans into the Japanese nation, suppressed all political and cultural activities. Koreans had no freedom of speech and not a single newspaper was allowed to be published with a Korean voice and interest. The Japanese were determined to wipe out Korean resistance. In the 1910–19 period, the Japanese choked off Korean publications by simply issuing "no permits for Korean language newspapers outside the governor-general's Korean newspaper, *The Daily News*."[9] No assembly was permitted for political discussion; no attempt was made to institute a system of self-government or to encourage the Koreans to believe they had the right to manage their own affairs.[10] When comparing their fate with that of the Indians, Korean nationalists complained: "In India the people are at least allowed to formulate their complaints through their own Press. In Korea this privilege of criticism of rulers is denied."[11] The Korean press, hitherto relatively free, came under heavy censorship, and all nationalist organizations were outlawed. In an interview reported in the Japanese papers, the Japanese civil administrator of Korea himself had admitted that racial discrimination existed in Korea. "There were certain more or less justifiable grievances which had irritated the Koreans, though he denied that they were responsible for the prevailing unrest, which he believed was due to sentimental reasons connected with the words self-determination or independence."[12] Under Japanese control, Korean nationalists complained:

> Even our rights of religious conscience and economic enterprise are all tied and bound with the merciless cord of tight restrictions . . . In public affairs there is such discrimination between Koreans and Japanese, based on a Japanese assumption of racial superiority, that Koreans are not allowed to receive the same education that Japanese do. This policy will reduce Koreans to permanent slavery and destroy the Korean race. The Japanese are attempting to eradicate Korean history by substituting a false history written by Japanese. With the exception of a few minor officials, the Japanese occupy or completely control all organs of government, communication and transportation. Japan will not permit Koreans to obtain the knowledge or experience necessary for self-government.[13]

The discovery in 1911 of a plot to assassinate the Japanese governor-general, General Terauchi Masatake, led to dozens of arrests, including most of the nationalist leaders still in Korea.

With a complete ban in place on nationalist activities, many activists left the country, spurring the growth of patriotic organizations in Korean expatriate communities in Russia, China, Japan, and the United States. Japan, ironically, became a

---

[9] Michael Robinson, "Colonial Publication Policy and the Korean Nationalist Movement," in Hyung-Gu Lynn, ed., *Critical Readings on the Colonial Period of Korea 1910–1945* (Leiden: Brill, 2013), 1: 150.

[10] No Author, "The Nervousness about Korea," *The Japan Chronicle*, February 19, 1919.

[11] No Author, *The Independence Movement in Korea: A Record of Some of the Events of the Spring of 1919* (Kobe: Printed and published at the office of *The Japan Chronicle*, 1919), 11.

[12] No Author, *The Independence Movement in Korea*, 19–20.

[13] Frank P. Baldwin, *The March First Movement: Korean Challenge and Japanese Response* (PhD thesis, Columbia University, 1969), 43.

major incubator for Korean national sentiments in this period, since Korean students, encouraged to attend Japanese universities as part of the assimilation policy, gained access to literature promoting liberal ideas and criticizing Japanese rule that the military authorities had banned from Korea itself. One of the most important expatriate organizations emerged in 1909, when two existing groups merged to form the Korean National Association (KNA), under the leadership of An Changho. An, a tireless organizer and a major figure among Korean activists abroad, had been educated by missionaries and immigrated to the United States in 1902, settling in California but traveling extensively to expatriate Korean communities in Hawaii, Mexico, and China. Syngman Rhee, who had remained in the United States following his failed mission to Theodore Roosevelt, pursued graduate studies at Harvard and then at Princeton. He also began to play a leading role in the KNA after 1912. Kimm Kyusik (aka Kiusic Kimm or Chin Chung Won) organized the Mutual Assistance Society in 1912 in Shanghai and formed ties with Chinese revolutionaries, while people like Syngman Rhee founded the KNA in Hawaii in 1909 and proceeded to conduct his international activities from a base in America.

When an international socialist congress was convened in Stockholm in 1917, Korean independence activists in exile in China were dispatched to present a demand for the independence of Korea. Korean representatives also attended the World Conference of Small Nations held in New York that same year, and appealed to world opinion to support Korea's nationhood.[14] The armed struggle of independence forces outside Korea, the diplomatic maneuvers of patriots who had taken refuge in foreign lands, and the energetic work within Korea of the clandestine organizations and educational bodies, according to Korean historian Ki-Baik Lee:

> all . . . sustained the will of the Korean people to oppose Japan and strengthened their spirit of resistance. All over Korea, then, popular disturbances broke out one after the other. Under the harsh colonial rule of imperial Japan the nationalistic spirit of resistance had grown and spread to all segments of Korean society and had almost reached the point of explosion. The Korean people were only awaiting an opportune moment to arise, when the turn of international events brought on the inevitable eruption.[15]

The presence of so many Korean patriots abroad mattered because, among other things, during the war years they had easy access to information that the Japanese censors worked hard to prevent from circulating in Korea itself. Though the KNA had begun to promote the cause of Korean independence among the American public even before the war in Europe began, Korean activists in the United States recognized early on the usefulness of Wilson's rhetoric to their cause. They took the lead in preparing the Korean claim for self-determination that they would present before world opinion. Syngman Rhee had written a book in 1904 at the age of twenty-nine when he was in prison (1899–1904). His book was later published in

[14] Lee, *A New History of Korea*, 339.   [15] Lee, *A New History of Korea*, 340.

1910 in Los Angeles.[16] Rhee's book immediately became a bible for Koreans fighting for the restoration of sovereignty and independence.[17] Rhee in this book called upon all Koreans to strive for these goals. Rhee thought that Koreans had unique chances with the shake-up of the imperial order brought about by the Great War. Rhee and many others claimed that the Wilsonian ideals were definitely applicable to the Korean independence case. On a personal level, Rhee had received his doctoral degree at Princeton and knew Wilson; he had received his diploma from Wilson himself. As Frank Baldwin put it, "Thus Rhee could hope for a unique affinity and sympathy for Korea's cause."[18]

Like other anticolonial activists, Korean hopes for Wilson's support were based on long-standing views of the United States as an exemplar of modern civilization and the Power most sympathetic toward the colonials' aspirations for independence. Moreover, such perceptions of the United States were more common and more deeply entrenched than among other colonial peoples due to the impact of Protestant missions in Korea and the prominence of expatriate activists who studied and lived in the United States. Like many educated Egyptians, Indians, and Chinese, they considered the United States wealthy and powerful enough not to depend on colonial exploitation, and Wilson's rhetoric seemed to confirm this impression. Even after the Japanese annexed Korea with US acquiescence, Korean nationalists, encouraged by resident American diplomats and missionaries, continued to believe that the United States supported their independence. Wilson's declarations on the establishment of new universal principles for international relations, they thought, would apply to Korea as well. Eager to seize the opportunity, Koreans moved to frame their demands for independence in the new Wilsonian language, with the intention of presenting them before the president himself in Paris.

Shortly after the armistice, a group of Korean activists wrote to Wilson to persuade him that his wartime rhetoric applied to Korea. In a letter to Wilson on November 25, 1918, Rhee and others wrote that:

> We, the common people of Korea, with a passion for self-government and political independence, come to you knowing that your Excellency is an arbiter of justice and a champion of equal rights for all peoples, strong or weak, with the hope that your Excellency may exert your good offices in helping us get our share of justice at this significant time when the particular purposes of individual states are about to give way to the common will of mankind.

The letter went on to point out that although Koreans had not been officially associated with the Allies in the war, "thousands of our countrymen fought as volunteers for the Allied cause on the Russian front for the first two years of the war. And our people in America proportionately contributed to the cause of democracy, both in men and money." It also argued that Americans had a moral obligation to aid

---

[16] It was republished in 2001 as Syngman Rhee, *The Spirit of Independence: A Primer of Korean Modernization and Reform*, trans., annot., and intro. Han-Kyo Kim (Honolulu: University of Hawaii Press, 2001).

[17] Rhee, *The Spirit of Independence*, xii.

[18] Baldwin, *The March First Movement*, 16.

the Koreans in their aspirations for self-determination, since "the United States cannot afford, for the safety of its own interests," to tolerate Japanese aggression in the Far East, and the world cannot be made "safe for democracy" so long as 20,000,000 "liberty-loving Koreans are forced to live under an alien yoke."[19] The Korean nationalists repeated the same lines in their multiple communications with the American government, and believed that Wilson had "said very truly that all homogeneous nations that have a separate and distinct language, civilization and culture ought to be allowed independence." When Wilson declared his Fourteen Points in January 1918, grounded in the idea of national self-determination, many Koreans living abroad were led to believe that Japanese rule over their country was drawing to a close and thus started to campaign actively for independence.[20] Wilson, of course, had never defined the prerequisites of nationhood in such a detailed fashion in his wartime rhetoric. But the authors of the Korean petition read into his advocacy for self-determination the characteristics that they and other nationalists commonly considered as defining national identity—ethnicity, language, cultural tradition, and history—and sought to make the case that Korea met the standard. While this approach implied that not all claimants deserved satisfaction if they did not meet the criteria, other petitioners did not recognize such fine distinctions. One group of Koreans residing in New York City, for example, treated Korean nationhood as self-evident and simply asked that the postwar settlement grant Korea the same rights promised to small nations. The United States and its allies have "endorsed the grand principle of self-determination of weaker and smaller nations, so nobly advocated by President Wilson," and Korea, like other small nations, had the right "to regulate her national life according to her own standards and ideas." The United States, therefore, should work to secure for Korea the right of self-determination. While Dae-yeol Ku points out that Wilson's wartime speeches seemed to be full of promise for Korean nationalists,[21] Baldwin also suggests that Koreans expected that Wilson would support their cause in Paris.[22] The widespread and intense antipathy against Japanese colonialism, along with the encouragement of Wilson's declarations, raised Korean hopes. And when Wilson announced that he would personally attend the postwar peace conference, the Korean pleas to Wilson increased in number and intensity. Wilson's secretary, Ray Baker, wrote:

> Here are the burning words from a Korean delegation under a date of November 20 [1918], interpreting his words according to their desires: The war just finished has decided once for all the contest between democracy and autocracy, and President Wilson has said very truly that all homogeneous nations that have a separate and

[19] Syngman Rhee, *The Syngman Rhee Correspondence in English, 1904–1948*, ed. Young Ice Lew, Young Seob Oh, Steve G. Jenks, and Andrew D. Calhoun (Seoul: Institute for Modern Korean Studies, Yonsei University, 2009), 1: 57.

[20] No Author, *Korea's Appeal to the Conference on Limitation of Armament*, 3–16.

[21] Dae-yeol Ku, *Korea Under Colonialism: The March First Movement and Anglo-Japanese Relations* (Seoul: The Royal Asiatic Society Korea Branch, 1985), 37–45.

[22] Baldwin, *The March First Movement*, 21–6.

distinct language, civilization and culture ought to be allowed independence.... Under Japanese control Korea as a nation is doomed to extinction. Therefore, we, the undersigned citizens of Korea, hereby appeal to the people and the Government of the civilized world to take up the cause of Korea against Japan.[23]

Koreans in China and Japan often discussed the war, self-determination, and the prospects for Korean independence. They also paid close attention to the wartime developments in the international arena. An important watershed came in the summer of 1918, when news reached them of Wilson's Independence Day address. In it, he had said explicitly for the first time that his principles would apply not only to the peoples actually engaged in the war, but to "many others also, who suffer under the mastery but cannot act; peoples of many races and in every part of the world." Korean students in Japan understood this reference as a direct assault on Japanese rule of the peninsula and decided that it was time for them to act. Chang Toksu, a student leader in Japan, traveled to Shanghai that summer and, together with Yo Unhyong, the principal of a Korean school in Shanghai, founded the New Korea Youth Association (NKYA) and began to plan their campaign.

When Charles R. Crane, Wilson's friend, confidant, and advisor arrived in Shanghai in November 1918, Yo Unhyong, who attended a reception in Crane's honor, was "inspired by Crane's speech on the principle of self-determination." He approached the American after his speech and, he later testified, had an exchange with Crane that encouraged him to believe that the principle of self-determination would be applied to Korea at the peace conference. Excited, Yo and his colleagues quickly drafted a petition calling for Korean independence and gave a copy to Crane to deliver to Wilson personally. A second copy was handed to Thomas Millard, the publisher of the popular English-language Shanghai magazine *Millard's Review*, who was leaving for Washington and then Paris, with the request that he deliver it personally to the American delegation.[24] To make sure the petition carried some weight, these Koreans decided to use the name "New Korea Youth Party," which they coined just for this purpose. The petition included the following plea:

> Koreans are struggling with all their hearts, minds and bodies for independence, justice and peace. We are crying out to the conscience of the world, especially to the Americans who uphold the grand principles of President Wilson that a nation should be ruled in accordance with the consent of the governed. As long as Japan practices cruel policies the world peace which we so much desire can never be realized. In conclusion we declare that we are not conquered, but merely cheated and destroyed by the Japanese falsehood. This same falsehood and their imperialism are going to ruin all Asia, not letting the admirable ideas of President Wilson of peace and democracy get a foothold.... Korea must be redeemed. Democracy must exist in Asia. Now, you Americans once guaranteed, in the first treaty between Korea and the United States of America some thirty years ago, the independence of Korea. Therefore we appeal to you to help us secure this same independence.[25]

---

[23] Baldwin, *The March First Movement*, 23.   [24] Baldwin, *The March First Movement*, 35.
[25] Baldwin, *The March First Movement*, 36.

As the Koreans in China were busy taking advantage of the "Wilsonian moment," the Korean community in the United States, including Hawaii, moved quickly too. That group might have been small, numbering only about 6,000 at the time, but they were well educated, politically active, and well organized, and their role in the Korean response to Wilson's declarations was therefore disproportionately large. This was also true for the small groups of educated Koreans in Shanghai and Tokyo, each no more than seven or eight hundred strong, which played, as we will see, an important role in the nationalist movement. In December 1918, the KNA published an open letter to Korean residents in the United States and Mexico, calling for unity in the fight for national independence. A "unity meeting" was convened in San Francisco and resolved that, in light of Wilson's vision for the postwar settlement, expatriate Koreans in the West should submit a petition to the peace conference assembly and make an appeal to the United States and to Wilson himself to recognize Korean independence. The meeting elected Syngman Rhee, Min Chanho (an ordained Methodist minister), and the twenty-nine-year-old Henry Chung (Chong Hangyong) to take on this task.

Chung's story is especially compelling. Like Rhee, he was born into a scholarly family and trained in classical Chinese texts and Confucian classics. Under the influence of stories about the wonders of the West that he heard from a local teacher who had returned from the United States, he cut off his traditional topknot at fourteen and decided to emigrate, on his own, to the New World. He arrived on the West Coast and soon after accepted the invitation from a sympathetic American couple in small-town Nebraska to come and live with them. Though there were few other Koreans living in the area, Chung did well in his studies, graduating from his Nebraska high school as valedictorian. He later studied at Northwestern University and received a PhD from the American University in Washington, DC. Even in Nebraska, he had already become involved with the Korean national cause; like many Korean and other colonial nationalists at the time, Chung's opposition to colonialism was rooted in a worldview that was both liberal and cosmopolitan, part of a broader vision of bringing progress and modernity, as he saw them, to his land of origin and integrating within a progressive international order.

THE MARCH FIRST MOVEMENT

According to Dae-yeol Ku, news of the Wilsonian ideals "has been generally regarded as the starting point of the March First Movement."[26] While nationalists abroad worked to promote Korean independence, many Koreans at home received information about the outside world through their exiled compatriots and had come to contemplate the same possibility. Korean exiles living in Shanghai headquartered in the French concession to stay outside the reach of the Japanese police. They sent news and the texts of Wilson's addresses to nationalists inside Korea

---

[26] Ku, *Korea Under Colonialism*, 37.

"through a network of couriers who crossed the border from China on foot." One young schoolteacher who was active in the nationalist underground remembered the excitement she felt when a message came from Shanghai with the following: "President Wilson of the United States has proclaimed a fourteen point program for world peace. One of those points is the self-determination of peoples. You must make the most of this situation. Your voice must be heard. President Wilson will certainly help you."[27] Though the term "self-determination" was actually nowhere to be found among the Fourteen Points, as Manela pointed out, this technicality mattered little at the time, since the term "Fourteen Points" quickly came to stand for the sum total of Wilson's vision as it was perceived by Koreans and others. By year's end, with news of the international situation trickling in through such clandestine contacts, as well as through Westerners living in Korea, "anticipation that the doctrine of self-determination would drive relief to Korea had become increasingly widespread, especially among the young and the educated."[28] The American consul general in Seoul reported in January 1919 on the new mood among Koreans:

> There can be no doubt that the present general movement throughout the world looking towards the self-determination of peoples, and particularly of the subject races, has produced its effects on the thought of the people in this country. At the outset of the war there was a strong undercurrent among the Koreans of hostility to the Allies, a feeling that arose from a not unnatural antagonism to Japan, one of the Allies. As the war progressed, however, and the ultimate aims of the Allies were carefully and fully stated, those Koreans who are accustomed to look beyond immediate conditions in their own country and to view affairs here in light of world conditions began to see that they might also be affected in no adverse manner by the victory of the Allies.[29]

It is important to keep in mind that the idea of Korean independence was declared first by a group of Korean students before March 1, 1919. As the delegates assembled in Paris and the peace conference opened over the winter, Korean students in Tokyo, who organized as the Korean Youth Independence Association, decided they must do something dramatic to bring Korean claims to the attention of the world. They decided to issue a "declaration of independence" in the name of Koreans everywhere. Yi Kwangsu, a young novelist who would become a pioneer of modern Korean literature, was asked to draft the declaration. Yi himself believed that independence required the gradual evolution of Korean national character and confessed privately that he was unsure whether Korean society was actually ready for independence, but he concluded that Koreans could not pass up the opportunity that Wilson's presence at the peace conference offered. The declaration was prepared in Korean, Japanese, and English, and the students dispatched copies to Wilson, Clemenceau, and Lloyd George in Paris, to politicians, scholars, and newspapers in Japan, and even to the Governor-General of Korea. On February 8, the document was read with much fanfare before a large crowd at the Tokyo YMCA. In the name of "the twenty million Korean people," it declared "before

[27] Manela, *The Wilsonian Moment*, 130–1.   [28] Manela, *The Wilsonian Moment*, 131.
[29] Baldwin, *The March First Movement*, 252–3.

those nations of the world which have secured victory for Freedom and Justice, the realization of our independence." Soon after, the Japanese police broke up the meeting, arresting twenty-seven of those present.

Since the colonial authorities had outlawed all political groups in Korea, religious organizations would play an important role in nationalist activities. Religious leaders, who had a broad following among the populace, could help mobilize Koreans against colonial rule, and activists therefore worked to convince them that they must follow the lead of the Tokyo students and launch a campaign for independence on the peninsula itself. Both Christian and Buddhist leaders were prominent in the independence movement, as was the leadership of Chondogyo. Upon learning of the students' declaration in Tokyo, Son Pyong-hui, the Chondogyo supreme leader, is reported to have said: "At a time when young students are carrying out this kind of righteous action, we cannot just sit and watch." At the same time, the Shanghai group dispatched Sonu Hyok, a Protestant Christian, to Korea to help convince Christian leaders to hold peaceful demonstrations in Paris to support the Korean cause. Such demonstrations, they said, would show the world that the Korean population, despite Japanese propaganda to the contrary, was unhappy under Japanese rule and was rallying to the cause of independence. Since religious organizations provided the only umbrella under which organized activities could take place, and as the influence of the Protestant churches continued to grow, religious leaders assumed leadership roles in the independent movement at home. No wonder the central figures who signed the Korean Declaration of Independence in the name of all Koreans were the thirty-three men led by Son Pyong-hui for Chondogyo believers, Yi Sung-hun for the Christian groups, and Han Yong-un for the Buddhists.

These Koreans waited for an opportunity to bring their national dream to their whole society and the wider world. Externally, with the wide public excitement over the doctrine of the self-determination, Koreans were persuaded that at last the world was ready to bring an end to the "age of force" and usher in an "age of justice."[30] Internally, the unexpected death of the former Emperor Kojong on January 22, 1919, whom the Japanese had deposed in 1907 in the wake of the failed Korean mission to Hague, provided the perfect excuse for Koreans to mobilize around the call for self determination. Since mourning activities fell inside the domain of religious activity, the religious leaders and Korean activists immediately decided to use the funeral rites of the former king for political action. This event turned out to be largest mass protest in Korean history and a turning point in the Korean independence movement under Japanese colonial rule. To a great degree, the uprising was truly a mass movement without visible leadership, brought about by circumstances in Korea. A lead article titled "The Nervousness about Korea," published in *The Japan Chronicle* on February 19, 1919, stated: "It is not surprising that the death of the former Emperor of Korea should have aroused feelings of regret in the minds of the Koreans for their vanished independence."[31]

[30] Lee, *A New History of Korea*, 340–1.
[31] No Author, "The Nervousness about Korea," *The Japan Chronicle*, February 19, 1919.

As the news of Kojong's death got out, rumors quickly spread that the Japanese had poisoned the former emperor because of his opposition to their rule. Since Japanese censorship prevented the circulation of more reliable news, the spread of rumors in Korean society became a major source of information and gradually fueled the uprising. Japanese censorship in Korea was so strict and severe that during the First World War the Japanese censors tried to keep a damper on any language touching on self-determination and banned the showing of a foreign film on the grounds that it included images of President Wilson. But Koreans found out about Wilson and his ideas by stealth and by rumor. The United States and President Wilson himself were rumored to support the Korean demands and the president was to come to Korea by airplane to assist; there were also rumors that scores of United States battleships had been dispatched to Korea and that American troops had already landed at Inchon. Another rumor claimed that the peace conference had recognized Korean independence, and one widespread story described that shortly before Wilson left for Paris, he was approached by a Korean who asked him if Korea would be discussed at the peace conference. The president replied that if the Koreans remained quiescent, they would not be heard, but if they protested, they would get a hearing. One American missionary in Pyongyang reported that, with Wilson's advocacy of self-determination being well known among educated Koreans, they believed that they had to act immediately. The peace conference would hear and rectify "every political 'sore' and difficulty throughout the whole world." After it adjourned, no further adjustments would be possible.

As the preparations for the royal funeral procession began, the Japanese military authorities felt compelled to relax restrictions. With the death of the former emperor providing an excellent excuse for Koreans to assemble and travel, as many as 200,000 Korean people streamed from the provinces to Seoul to pay their respects to the departed monarch. As people gathered, nationalist leaders debated whether they should petition the Japanese for independence or simply declare it unilaterally. They finally decided on the latter course. They would draft a declaration of independence and hold non-violent demonstrations across the country to show the world their desire for self-determination. They would also present petitions to the representatives of foreign powers in Tokyo and send a letter to President Wilson asking for his support. To evade the Japanese censors, the petitions addressed to Wilson and the peace conference delegations were to be smuggled across the border to Manchuria and sent by the Chinese postal system to Shanghai and thence to Paris. The date of the proclamation was set for March 1, to take advantage of the crowds gathered in Seoul for the imperial funeral proceedings that day. That morning, a group of thirty-three eminent civic and religious leaders—Christians, Chondogyo, and Buddhists—gathered in a Seoul restaurant to sign and proclaim Korea's Declaration of Independence.

The text of the declaration of March 1, 1919, drafted by a twenty-nine-year-old scholar-publisher, Choe Namson (1890–1957), was read publicly in Seoul's Pagoda Park. The declaration, which adopted Wilsonian language to assert Korea's right to liberty and equality within the world of nations, launched a broad popular movement against Japanese rule. The declaration gives us a clear sense of Korean thinking about colonial rule and their future expectations:

> We herewith proclaim the independence of Korea and the liberty of the Korean people. We tell it to the world in witness of the equality of all nations and we pass it on to our posterity as their inherent right.... A new era wakes before our eyes, the old world of force is gone, and the new world of righteousness and truth is here. Out of the experience and travail of the old world arises this light in life's affairs.... [There followed three points:] 1. This work of ours is in behalf of truth, religion and life, undertaken at the request of our people, in order to make known their desire for liberty. Let no violence be done to anyone. 2. Let those who follow us, every man, all the time, every hour, show forth with gladness this same mind. 3. Let all things be done decently and in order, so that our behavior to the very end may be honorable and upright.[32]

To emphasize the peaceful nature of their movement, they sent a copy of the declaration to the Japanese governor-general and notified the colonial police of their intention to stage non-violent protests. As soon as they finished proclaiming the declaration of independence, the thirty-three signers themselves informed the Japanese authorities of their action and so were immediately arrested. It was their plan that the independence movement they had launched would be carried forward by the students and then by the entire people. That same day at 2.00 p.m., according to a witness report, "a violent demonstration of Koreans took place in Seoul, being participated in by several thousand persons, comprising students, male and female, laborers and other classes. Troops, as well as a large police force, were called out to pacify the mob, who did not disperse until nightfall."[33]

Korean students, like their Chinese counterparts during the May Fourth Movement, soon took a leading role in the March First Movement. In fact, the same morning of the declaration in Pagoda Park, a group of students had prepared their own manifesto, also calling for Korean independence. They posted it along the main streets of the capital. This manifesto, whose authors remain obscure, was clearly not the work of the religious leaders who had signed the declaration of independence, but was most likely prepared and circulated by students who had learned of the plan to issue the declaration and wanted to show their support for it. But its style was very different from the official declaration, far sharper and more confrontational. Still, its message was similar: a new age of self-determination had come in world affairs, and Koreans must have their independence. Reflecting on the rumors that had been circulating since the emperor's death, the student manifesto blamed the Japanese for poisoning him in order to subvert the efforts of Korean nationalists to make their case in the international arena. Their declaration claimed that "As we advocated national independence to the Paris Peace

---

[32] For the complete text of the Declaration of Independence, see Chung, *The Case of Korea*, 199–203.
[33] No Author, *The Independence Movement in Korea*, 3.

Conference, the cunning Japanese produced a certificate saying, 'The Korean People are happy with Japanese rule and do not wish to be separate from the Japanese,' in order to cover the eyes and ears of the world." When the Japanese submitted this statement to the emperor for the affixation of his royal seal, the student manifesto speculated, he had refused to sign it and the Japanese therefore decided to assassinate him. The student manifesto then concluded with a rousing call to action that placed Korean aspirations squarely within the context of recent international developments:

> Since the American President proclaimed the Fourteen Points, the voice of national self-determination has swept the world, and twelve nations, including Poland, Ireland, and Czechoslovakia, have obtained independence. How could we, the people of the great Korean nation, miss this opportunity? Our compatriots abroad are utilizing this opportunity to appeal for the recovery of national sovereignty... Now is the great opportunity to reform the world and recover us the ruined nation. If the entire nation rises in unity, we may recover our lost national rights and save the already ruined nation.[34]

With copies of the student manifesto posted in the streets and the "official" declaration of independence being read aloud in the heart of downtown Seoul to a large cheering crowd shouting "Long live Korean independence!" March 1, 1919 marks the beginning of the long journey to Korean independence. One young participant recalled learning of the movement at his school on the morning of March 1, and going immediately to the student gathering place. He heard a student representative address his fellows with the following: "Today we Koreans will declare our independence. Our representatives have gone to the Paris Peace Conference. To show our desire for independence to the world we must shout 'manse' [long life] for Korean Independence." Over the following months, more than a million people (some sources even suggested over two million) got involved in the movement across the peninsula. The demonstrations for independence involved Koreans of every province, religion, education, age, and occupation. Store owners closed their shops and workers went on strike in show of support.

The sustained protest initiated on March 1 has become known in Korean history as the March First Movement. It was sustained by local religious organizations and educational bodies, in contrast to the independence movement overseas, which had been carried on by a variety of Korean activist exiles. Several provisional governments were soon established both inside and outside Korea in the immediate wake of the March First Movement. To take advantage of the moment, in the week of April 16–23, representatives from every province in Korea met secretly in Seoul and organized a provisional government. A constitution was drafted and Rhee was elected President of the Republic of Korea. At about the same time, exiled Korean patriots in Siberia and in Shanghai held similar meetings and established separate provisional governments. The provisional government in Shanghai later gained

[34] Lee, *The Politics of Korean Nationalism*, 110–12.

recognition by the Chinese Nationalist government. A Korean Liberation Army was created later in China to fight for Korean independence.

The provisional government in Shanghai and its self-declared officials included both men who were already active overseas and others who had gone into exile in the aftermath of the March First Movement. The provisional governments justified their creation as based on the Korean Declaration of Independence and reflective of the power the Korean people had manifested in the March First Movement. Both the widespread independence movement and the establishment of the republic demonstrated that the political consciousness of the Korean people had already reached a new stage.[35] The movement shattered Japan's ruthless colonial rule and greatly bolstered the Korean people's struggle for independence, as it increased the world's awareness of their aspirations for liberation.

The activists for Korean independence perceived their most important audience to be not the Japanese authorities, but the world leaders gathered at the Paris Peace Conference. Korean nationalists, in their recounting the history of Japanese injustice in Korea, "drew heavily on Wilsonian imagery" as they associated themselves "with the worldwide movement for reform," which was "the central force of our age and a just movement for the right of all peoples to determine their own existence." This offered Koreans an opportunity to recover their country and "move with a new current of world thought," with "the conscience of mankind" on their side. Modern Korea dates its national consciousness from the protests against the Japanese in 1919. It provided the main impetus for the struggle for freedom carried on by the whole of the Korean people and was intended to be a peaceful movement. In retrospect, the March First Movement has been seen as "the greatest mass movement of the Korean people in all their history" and of a piece with its time. The slogan "Long live Korean independence" was similar to that of the May Fourth Movement in China.[36]

According to Erez Manela, the March First Movement was an unprecedented manifestation of Korean nationalism as a mass phenomenon, no longer limited to intellectual elites.[37] It signaled the beginning of modern nationalism in Korea. Like the Chinese May Fourth Movement, the March First Movement might not be considered a success, since it did not achieve its goal of gaining international recognition for Korean independence, nor even the more modest goal of raising the question of Korea officially at the postwar peace conference negotiations. Still, as Manela points out, "even if it failed in its proclaimed objectives, the movement played a pivotal role in the history of Korean nationalism. In the immediate term, it prompted the replacement of the harsh military rule of 1910–1919 with the more accommodating 'cultural policy' of the 1920s. More broadly, it changed the character and scope of the Korean nationalist movement, mobilizing Koreans against Japanese rule." In other words, as in the Chinese case, "March First transformed the Korean national movement and helped to shape its subsequent

[35] Lee, *A New History of Korea*, 344–5.   [36] Lee, *A New History of Korea*, 341–2.
[37] Manela, *The Wilsonian Moment*, 119.

identity and development;" indeed, it served as a crucial step in Korean national development.[38]

The March First Movement in Korea provided a much-needed boost for Rhee and other Korean nationalists. In the First Korean Congress, which took place in Philadelphia, Rhee prepared and introduced a draft resolution known as the "Appeal to America," which was adopted by the delegates on April 14, 1919. It reads:

> We, the Koreans in [the First Korean] Congress, assembled in Philadelphia, April 14–16, 1919, representing eighteen million people of our race who are now suffering untold miseries and barbarous treatment by the Japanese military authorities in Korea, hereby appeal to the great and generous American people. . . . We appeal to you for support and sympathy because we know you love justice; you also fought for liberty and democracy, and you stand for Christianity and humanity. Our cause is a just one before the laws of God and man. Our aim is freedom from militaristic autocracy; our object is democracy for Asia; our hope is universal Christianity. Therefore we feel that our appeal merits your consideration. . . . We further ask you, the great American public, to give us your moral and material help so that our brethren in Korea will know that your sympathy is with them and that you are truly the champions of liberty and international justice.[39]

The congress concluded with the delegates marching to Independence Hall in Philadelphia on the afternoon of April 16, and Rhee's reading of the March First Declaration of Independence. There they gave three cheers of "Long live the Republic of Korea!" and "Long live America!"[40]

The Japanese were stunned by the enormity of the movement, in which over a million Koreans participated directly in more than 1,500 separate gatherings, in all but seven of the country's 218 county administrations.[41] Members of the Japanese Diet wanted to know why such serious Korean protests could not be "nipped in the bud" by the Japanese colonial government, why the authorities did not know that such demonstrations were about to happen, and why they seemed to have no knowledge of the sentiments of the Korean people.[42] Of course, as some in Japan pointed out then, since "no paper which touches on politics is allowed to be printed in Korea, it is very difficult to ascertain what is going on in that country, and why there should be so much unrest."[43] Caught off guard, the Japanese colonial government's response to the protests was quick and brutal. Japanese military forces crushed the demonstrations, arresting some 46,968 demonstrators, killing 7,509, and injuring 15,961, while over 700 houses were destroyed or burned, along with 47 churches and 2 schools. In the most cruel acts of suppression, like that at

[38] Manela, *The Wilsonian Moment*, 213.

[39] No Author, *Korea's Appeal to the Conference on Limitation of Armament*, 3–16.

[40] Young Ick Yu, *The Making of the First Korean President: Syngman Rhee's Quest for Independence, 1875–1948* (Honolulu: University of Hawaii Press, 2014), 97.

[41] Lee, *A New History of Korea*, 344.

[42] No Author, *The Independence Movement in Korea*, 6.

[43] No Author, *The Independence Movement in Korea*, 11.

the village of Cheam-ni near Suwon, twenty-nine people were herded into a church which was then set ablaze to burn them alive.[44] But such brutal suppression only intensified the collective Korean hatred of the Japanese and made the Koreans more determined to get rid of Japanese rule. As the following section will discuss in detail, the March First Movement embarrassed Japan across the world. It badly shamed the Japanese, who had claimed that their rule was benevolent and supported by Koreans. Japanese, propaganda often claimed that the Korean people had willingly submitted to Japanese colonial rule. Now the Koreans used their demonstrations to inform the world to the contrary. With the widespread protests, Japan was forced to change its policy in Korea, at least nominally, from the brutal rule to so-called "enlightened administration." "But all this simply represented a different approach to the pursuit of the very same objects as before," as Lee argues. "Japan's professed 'enlightened administration' was no more than a superficial and deceptive moderation of its earlier policy of forceful repression, carried out under pressure of world opinion. There was no basic change, therefore, in Japan's colonial policy."[45]

Dae-yeol Ku is right in arguing that "The March First Movement stands out as the largest scale Korean national resistance movement of the entire colonial period. It was also extremely important in terms of the contemporaneous international relations of Korean peninsula."[46] The March First Movement clearly belongs to a history shared among Asians, since it not only damaged Japanese rule in Korea, but just as importantly, it exerted a decisive influence on the Vietnamese nationalists and on the Chinese May Fourth Movement, which will be discussed in detail in Chapter 6. Like the March First Movement, the May Fourth Movement was a turning point in the formation of modern China. Students at Peking University formed an association to save the nation and published the *Guomin* (*Citizens*) monthly. Its April 1919 edition contained special features on the Korean independence movement. They included the text of the March First Declaration of Independence and five commentaries on the Korean independence movement. *Guomin* reported that when a Korean farmer waving the national flag got his hand chopped off by the Japanese, he grabbed it with the other hand and kept shouting, "Hurrah for independence!" Chinese intellectuals at the time publicly acknowledged that the May Fourth Movement was influenced by the March First Movement. Among those who praised the Korean struggle for independence were Chen Duxiu and Fu Sinian, both towering figures in China then, and Mao Zedong, the future Chinese communist leader. Chen Duxiu was especially impressed with the March First Movement. He wrote: "This Korean independence movement is great, earnest, and heroic. . . . We hope Koreans' independent thought will keep growing and trust one day Korean people will realize their glorious independence."[47] It was reported

[44] Lee, *A New History of Korea*, 344.   [45] Lee, *A New History of Korea*, 346–7.

[46] Ku Dae-yeol, "Korean International Relations in the Colonial Period," in Lynn, *Critical Readings on the Colonial Period of Korea*, 1: 197.

[47] Chen Duxiu, "Chaoxian Duli Yundong zhi ganxiang" ("Thoughts on the Korean Independent Movement"), *Meizhou Pinlun*, March 23, 1919.

that some Koreans in China had presented a memorial to Chinese President Xu Shichang in thanks for his support of the Korean cause. The memorialist, who called himself the representative of 20,000,000 Koreans, emphasized the close relations between China and Korea since ancient times, and asked President Xu to use his good offices to press the Korean cause on behalf of the Korean people, who have no delegates of their own at Paris.[48]

The March First Movement also had a great impact on the "Satyagraha," or non-violent resistance, launched by the INC on April 5, 1919. This Indian independence movement embraced the non-violence principle of the Korean religious leaders. The fact that Rabindranath Tagore wrote the poem "Lamp Bearer of the East" on the tenth anniversary of the March First Movement, and Jawaharlal Nehru praised it in the book "Glimpses of World History," which he wrote in prison for his daughter, both demonstrate the deep influence of the Korean independence movement on Indians.

Even in the Philippines, then a US colony, university students in Manila launched an independence movement in June 1919, citing the example of the March First Movement. The Philippines invoked the idea of the League of Nations in the push for their country's self-determination and a postcolonial order more generally. As Emily S. Rosenberg observes in her article "World War I, Wilsonianism, and Challenges to U.S. Empire," one Philippine journal, *Revista Filipina*, at the time championed not only Philippine independence, but independence for Korea as well. Its articles argued that granting independence to the Philippines would put pressure on Japan to do likewise in Korea. "We hope the Allied conference will not fail to weigh the Korean contention, as well as all such other similar contentions, in their true merits, and thus remove all possible stumbling blocks on the road to a true and efficient League of Nations. There is no national opportunity for greatness as ample and as tremendous as that spelled by self-determination, for the full enjoyment and expansion of which the Allies have so happily and liberally dedicated the best of their efforts."[49] A Korean scholar has pointed out that "If the day comes when world history is written in such a truthful way as 'Glimpses of World History' authored by Nehru, then the March First Movement should be reassessed as the first beacon that lighted the hope for freedom for three-fourths of mankind."[50]

Of course, the March First Movement itself was shaped by outside forces, such as Wilsonian ideals and values from China and elsewhere. Its famous Declaration of Independence had a strong Chinese flavor, not only in the sense that it was written in classical Chinese, but more so because it reflected China's own reality and the broader Asian reality. Most clearly, the Koreans directly linked their nationalist dream with the Chinese national fate by arguing that Japanese action "to bind by force twenty millions

[48] No Author, *The Independence Movement in Korea*, 18.

[49] Emily S. Rosenberg, "World War I, Wilsonianism, and Challenges to U.S. Empire," *Diplomatic History*, 38:4 (2014), 861.

[50] Shin Yong-ha, "Why Did Mao, Nehru and Tagore Applaud the March First Movement?" *Chosun Ilbo*, February 27, 2009.

of resentful Koreans will mean not only loss of peace forever for this part of the Far East," but would also increase the ever-growing suspicions of "the four hundred millions of China"—upon whom depended the peace of Asia. The Declaration of Independence further stated that "Today Korean independence will mean not only daily life and happiness for us, but also it would mean Japan's departure from an evil way and exaltation to the place of true protector of the East, so that China too, even in her dreams, would put all fear of Japan aside. This thought comes from no minor resentment, but from a large hope for the future."[51] Clearly, the Koreans and Chinese shared their mutual hatred of Japanese aggression and colonial rule.

THE PARIS PEACE CONFERENCE AND KOREA

Not every Korean had such high expectations of the Great War's aftermath. Yun Chi-Ho, for instance, believed the Korean nationalists were foolish for placing their hopes in Wilsonian ideals.[52] Pak Yong-man was another who disagreed with Syngman Rhee's approach, though Pak, like Rhee, was a devoted fighter for Korean independence. In April, after the outbreak of the March First Movement, Pak was appointed Minister of Foreign Affairs by the Korean provisional governments in Shanghai and Seoul. But he refused to serve in those governments under the premier/chief executive Syngman Rhee. Instead, Pak went to Beijing to launch his own independence movement. Arriving there in late May 1919, he organized the Society to Promote the Unification of Military Organizations. He also initiated a campaign on March 3, 1919 to denounce Rhee's petition to Wilson asking that Korea be placed under the mandate system of the League of Nations. He later played an active role in the national representative conference in Shanghai in January 1923, as a leader of the so-called Creation Faction, which aimed at destroying the Shanghai provisional government in favor of an entirely new provisional government. Pak was assassinated under mysterious circumstances in Beijing in 1928.[53]

Still, like their fellow Asians, most Korean nationalists were excited at the prospects of the Paris Peace Conference and were ready to place their faith in a new postwar world order. But they also remembered the treaty Korea signed with the US in 1882, in which the American government recognized Korean sovereignty and promised to exercise the "good offices" of the United States if it became the target of aggression by another nation. The Korean nationalist Henry Chung sent a letter to the US Senate on December 10, 1918, appealing for its support of Korean independence. The letter stated that Japanese occupation of Korea led to calamity culturally, religiously, and politically: "We, the common people of Korea, with a passion for self-government and political independence, come to the Senate of

[51] "Claims of Korea at the Peace Conference," BA: FO 608/211.
[52] See his December 19, 1918 diary entry: Yun Chi-Ho, *Yun Chi-Ho Diary*, vol. 7 (n.p.: n.d.).
[53] Yu, *The Making of the First Korean President*, 87–8.

the United States, knowing that this august body stands for justice and a 'square deal' for all peoples, strong or weak, with the hope that the United States Senate may exert its good offices in helping us secure our share of justice at this time, when the destiny of subject nationalities is about to be decided at the Peace Conference."[54] By 1919, Korean nationalists thought the time had arrived for the Americans to deliver on that promise. They sensed that history was on their side and they were eager to seize the moment. Certainly, the American doctrine of self-determination was at the root of Korean demonstrations for independence, so far as overseas Koreans were concerned. "Korean nationalists in the United States, Shanghai and Japan became active as a result of the war-time speeches of the President; and even Koreans in Peking, Chientao, and Russian Siberia launched similar movements, though their activities were not well publicized."[55] Soon after the armistice was signed, a joint meeting of the central congress of the KNA and the North American regional congress of the KNA, both headquartered in San Francisco, elected Syngman Rhee, Min Chanho, and Chong Han-gyong (Henry Chung) as their unofficial delegates to Paris. Henry Chung, in an interview given in April 1919, explained:

> So complete is Japanese domination over Corea, that it is practically impossible for the people to forcibly overthrow their Government. The only hope I believe is at the Peace Conference, and particularly in President Wilson and the representatives of Great Britain. Corea would be satisfied if she were made an international charge, because such nations as the United States and Great Britain recognize the principles of democratic Government and would insure justice to the country now oppressed under the heel of Japan.[56]

Korean communities elsewhere were also engaged in the movement, with many different organizations and groups preparing to send their own delegates to Paris. Korean expatriates in Shanghai met in January 1919, organized the NKYA, and decided to send a representative, Kimm Kyusik, to the peace conference. Kimm Kyusik was a young Korean Christian who was fluent in English. He was an orphan who had been raised by a well-known American missionary, Horace G. Underwood, and later traveled to the United States to attend Roanoke College in Virginia and Princeton University. He returned to teach at several Christian schools in Korea, but left for China in 1913 to escape Japanese rule. Besides sending a member to the peace conference, the NKYA also sent representatives to Korea, Japan, Manchuria, Siberia, and other areas to explore ways to develop specific independence activities.

Syngman Rhee, Min Chanho, Henry Chung, and representatives of the KNA set out for Washington in December 1918 to apply for passports and prepare for the trip to Paris. In a message addressed to President Wilson, they informed him of their appointment to the peace conference as representatives of the 1.5 million expatriate Koreans living in America, Hawaii, Mexico, China, and Russia, and attached a memorandum, which they intended to present to the peace conference

[54] Rhee, *The Syngman Rhee Correspondence in English*, 4: 129–30.
[55] Ku, *Korea Under Colonialism*, 293.   [56] Ku, *Korea Under Colonialism*, 39.

upon arrival in Paris. The text told the story of the Japanese conquest of Korea and the subsequent suppression of the local economy, culture, and religion, including, the document emphasized, Christianity. They expected Wilson "will show his friendly feelings towards the Korean people by consenting to our request as set forth" in the memorials and petitions.[57] In a petition dated February 16, 1919, Rhee asked the president to take steps at the peace conference to call for Korean independence.

Besides preparing to send representatives to Paris, the Koreans were also busy submitting petitions and memorials to Wilson and other world politicians. Many petitions at the time cited Wilson's own words back to him, assuring Wilson that the Korean independence movement met the standard of "well-defined national aspirations" laid out in his February 11, 1918 address. Since Koreans were an ethnically and linguistically distinct people and had a long history of civilization, they should have the opportunity to "choose the government under which they wish to live." The signatories to Korean petitions often claimed that they represented their countrymen both at home and abroad.[58]

Koreans in New York organized themselves into the New York Association. When they met on November 30, 1918, they passed a resolution to present their grievances to President Wilson, the members of the House and Senate foreign relations committees, and the US delegates to the peace conference. It stated: "Through the President and the Congress of the United States the Korean people venture to apply to all the civilized nations of the world to consider their cause, and secure for them the same rights of self-determination and of free political existence which has [*sic*] been promised to the other small nations of the world by the government of the United States and the Entente Allies in accordance with the declaration of their war aims."[59] A Shanghai-based Korean group, called the Korean Independence Committee, also presented a petition to the American minister in Peking.[60]

Although Rhee had known Wilson when both were at Princeton, where he was a regular guest at the informal social gatherings at the Wilson home, he was unable to turn this relationship to his cause. Wilson seemed both to like and admire him and he introduced him to strangers on occasion as "the future redeemer of Korean independence."[61] During the First World War, Rhee was busy running the Korean Christian Institute in Honolulu but also followed the war closely, especially Wilson, whom Rhee called his "intimate friend," and his new world order.[62] The American government actually stood in the way. Rhee was not even able to secure a meeting with Wilson, despite several attempts from Rhee's side. On February 25, 1919, the White House informed Rhee that "it is not possible to arrange an appointment for you with the President." On March 3, 1919, the White House again informed

[57] Baldwin, *The March First Movement*, 128–9.
[58] Yu, *The Making of the First Korean President*, 313–15.
[59] Baldwin, *The March First Movement*, 44–5.   [60] Ku, *Korea Under Colonialism*, 40.
[61] Yu, *The Making of the First Korean President*, 33.
[62] Yu, *The Making of the First Korean President*, 89.

Rhee that it was impossible for him to see Wilson.[63] In his March 4 note to the president's secretary, Joseph Tumulty, Rhee wrote "It is certainly a disappointment to us that the President cannot spare even a few minutes of his time for a cause so dear to the entire Korean race."[64] Moreover, when Rhee and his group went to the State Department for their "permits of departure" for Paris, they were refused on the grounds that Korean annexation was not a matter arising out of the Great War and therefore, presentation of the Korean case in Paris could bring no success and cause nothing but difficulties.[65] Secretary of State Robert Lansing reportedly stated that Korean representation at the Paris Peace Conference would be "unfortunate at this time" and instructed the State Department to deny the Koreans permission to participate. The Koreans considered this denial "a great disappointment."[66]

Rhee did manage to secure a meeting with Assistant Secretary of State Frank Polk on February 26, 1919, and asked him for a travel permit. On February 28, 1919, Rhee again wrote a letter to Polk and another letter to Joseph Tumulty asking for travel permit.[67] Polk promised to get back to Rhee after checking with Secretary of State Robert Lansing. But Polk rejected the request after being told by his boss, "It will be considered unfortunate for the Koreans to come to Paris at the time."[68]

With Rhee and other Koreans in the US refused travel permits, the sole representative for the Koreans in Paris was Kimm Kyusik, a delegate from Shanghai. But getting to Paris presented a challenge for Kimm as well. The Japanese authorities naturally would not provide him with travel documents. And all berths on ships bound to France were booked until March 1919. The Chinese in the end were able to provide the crucial assistance. They not only gave him a Chinese passport, but more importantly, they invited him to travel to Paris with the Chinese delegation. Kimm thus left for Paris in January 1919 with Chinese travel documents and under a Chinese name in order to evade the Japanese police.[69] Once in France, Kimm took up residence in a small house near the city with five Chinese.

As the sole Korean representative, Kimm Kyusik worked hard. He made several attempts to gain the sympathy of the American delegates, with no clear success. When at Paris, Kimm submitted a long memorandum to the peace conference in April 1919. In the memorandum, Kimm wrote that "Korea is the key to the question in the Far East. There will never be lasting peace in Asia until justice has been done to a cruelly oppressed people and a hearing given to their desperate appeal." The memorandum requested the following: "The Korean people beg your Conference to appoint, if necessary, a commission to hear our case and to ultimately allow us a

[63] Rhee, *The Syngman Rhee Correspondence in English*, 2: 204, 2: 207.
[64] Rhee, *The Syngman Rhee Correspondence in English*, 1: 75.
[65] Ku, *Korea Under Colonialism*, 38–9.
[66] Rhee, *The Syngman Rhee Correspondence in English*, 4: 149–50.
[67] Rhee, *The Syngman Rhee Correspondence in English*, 1: 71, 1: 72–3.
[68] Yu, *The Making of the First Korean President*, 91.
[69] Baldwin, *The March First Movement*, 36.

voice in your august council."[70] Later, Kimm also sent individual appeals to Lloyd George, Wilson, and others to ask them to support Korean nationalist aspirations.[71]

On May 10, he sent Wilson, Lloyd George, and Clemenceau copies of Korean petitions and a statement to the conference assembly. The statement set "forth a series of facts and views in support of our claim for the reconstitution of Korea as an independent state." It argued that Japan's annexation of Korea was illegal and contrary to Wilson's Fourteen Points, and should be declared null and void. Korea should be recognized as an independent state. The petitions and statement were presented in the name and on behalf of the provisional republican government of Korea and the 18,700,000 Koreans living in Korea and elsewhere.[72] On May 24, Kimm submitted a statement to the peace conference assembly from Syngman Rhee, the newly elected president of the provisional government, asking the conference to recognize the provisional government and grant its representative, Kimm, the opportunity to speak for Korea.[73] As late as June, Kimm still tried to present Korea's case. In his appeal to Clemenceau on June 11, 1919, Kimm wrote:

> We earnestly solicit the august Conference not to overlook the plea of the Korean people and nation for liberation. We ask the Conference to recognize our just claim for the right of self-determination, to exert its good offices in helping to solve this very grave Far Eastern problem, and to aid us to establish the true and right relation with Japan and the Japanese people. Thus may the East be enabled to join the West in peaceful progress and free development and establish really harmonious international relations. We petition your Conference to appoint a commission, if necessary, to hear our case.[74]

In his letter to S. K. Hornbeck on June 14, 1919, Kimm wrote: "We should like very much to have an interview with President Wilson, Colonel House, and Secretary Lansing even in an unofficial way, if possible, and have an opportunity to personally present certain facts concerning the grave situation in Korea."[75]

While not able to go to Paris himself, Rhee, in the capacity of president of the provisional government, sent at least five official communications to President Wilson in Paris and two to the US State Department between April 30 and June 28, 1919. He also sent communications to the heads of France, Britain, Italy, China, and Japan, as well as to the chairman of the conference, Clemenceau, during the same period. In his letter to Chinese delegate Wang Zhengting, Rhee wrote that "I have read with great interest what you and your fellow delegates are doing, for your country at the Peace Conference." This rarely quoted letter is worth quoting at length here, since it clearly reveals the shared expectations, hope, and experience, as well as the shared mutual hatred toward the Japanese, of the Koreans and Chinese. In the

[70] Rhee, *The Syngman Rhee Correspondence in English*, 4: 159–60.
[71] Rhee, *The Syngman Rhee Correspondence in English*, 4: 176–7, 190–1.
[72] "The claim of the Korean people and nation for liberation from Japan and for the reconstitution of Korea as an independent state, petition, Paris, April, 1919," BA: FO 608/211.
[73] Link, ed., *The Papers of Woodrow Wilson*, 59: 473–5.
[74] Rhee, *The Syngman Rhee Correspondence in English*, 4: 222.
[75] Rhee, *The Syngman Rhee Correspondence in English*, 4: 226.

letter, Rhee congratulated Wang and his fellow Chinese "most heartily on the firm and patriotic stand you are taking for the justice and welfare of the Far East." He also sincerely hoped that "in spite of all the obstacles and hindrances that are placed before your path, you will continue your firm stand and maintain the principle, which your delegation has so far shown and advocated." He told Wang that "This sentiment and wish is not only my personal, but that of all my countrymen in America and elsewhere." Rhee clearly told Wang that "we have common cause and common enemy in aggressive and imperialistic Japan. She has already destroyed the identity of my country and she is now trying to do the same in your nation. Therefore, we, the Koreans, in a humble way, wish to express our sympathy and offer our moral support to you in your noble struggle in outwitting the cunning and grasping islanders who are taking part at the same Peace table with you." Since Koreans were not able to present their case officially before the peace conference, Rhee hoped the Chinese would "sympathize with us."[76]

Besides his appeal to their shared feeling and sympathy with the Chinese, Rhee put greater hope on Wilson. The following was sent to Wilson on June 14: "Mr. President: I have the honor to inform you, that on April 23, 1919, Korea took [its] place, with other Republics of the world, and became a completely organized, self-governed, democratic State."[77] All of his communications sought support for Korean independence and gave notification of the creation of his government. To Rhee's great disappointment, the peace conference did not take up any discussion of Korea, and no government recognized his government. In Paris, Kimm made one final plea, on June 11, 1919, to Wilson, Lloyd George, and Clemenceau for a hearing on Korea, but it again went unanswered.[78]

But even as the Koreans moved to seize the moment in Paris by launching mass protests in March of 1919, Wilson's own fortunes at the conference were beginning to wane. The Koreans did not realize that the Powers, the US included, had decided beforehand to table the Korea issue and not receive any Koreans in Paris. On March 25, 1919, Stanley Hornbeck sent a memo, with an appeal from the Korean group in Shanghai to Joseph Grew, the secretary of the commission, asking that the Korean delegate be heard at the conference. The memo noted that a Korean representative had arrived in Paris and ended with the recommendation "that the Commissioners consider whether it may be possible to hear the Korean representative or to receive a statement from him." Grew sent the memo to E. T. Williams, who returned it with the following comment: "Since you refer this to me, I can only say that in view of the fact that the U.S. has recognized the annexation of Korea, the representative ought not be received."[79] The British government adopted the same policy. As one senior British official in Paris wrote, "No member of the Korean Delegation, so far as I know, has as yet called here; but I presume that as the Conference does not

[76] Rhee to Wang, March 11, 1919. Rhee, *The Syngman Rhee Correspondence in English*, 1: 77–8.
[77] Yu, *The Making of the First Korean President*, 104.
[78] Rhee, *The Syngman Rhee Correspondence in English*, 4: 221–2.
[79] Baldwin, *The March First Movement*, 144–5.

recognize the existence of this delegation and in view of Japanese susceptibility it would be better if Mr. Kimm calls that he should not be received." This position was seconded by another British official.[80]

As Kimm desperately sought a hearing at the conference, reports of the brutal Japanese suppression of the demonstrations across Korea reached Paris. These, in addition to Chinese complaints, further damaged the Japanese reputation and image. The reports from Korea reached Paris through both the media and diplomats. The British ambassador to Japan sent many secret communiqués to London, such as the following:

> Reports of atrocities committed by Japanese gendarmerie and military in Corea continued to reach me. I have repeatedly brought them to notice of vice minister for Foreign Affairs who told me a few days ago that he is 'disgusted' at what was happening, adding that Governor-General has sent in his resignation. Public in Japan knows little about atrocities as vernacular press has apparently been requested to publish as little as possible and do not seem interested or affected, I venture to point out that military machine which is now about to be given a mandate from League of Nations for Government of North Pacific Islands is same as is now acting in above manner in Corea.

Greene asked London, "Would it be possible to draw attention of Japanese delegates at Paris to unfavourable impression which is being created by reports of manner in which Corea is being administered?"[81] But British Foreign Minister Balfour responded, "I am of opinion that it would be undesirable to raise the question of Korea with the Japanese Delegates here and that any remonstrance on the subject of the alleged atrocities by Japanese gendarmeries and soldiers in Corea should be made to the Japanese Embassy in London and to the Japanese Government in Tokio."[82]

An American diplomat who visited Korea reported that so brutal was the Japanese suppression that in one village only six out of forty houses were intact. Inhabitants stated that their men had been massacred by Japanese soldiers in revenge for the independence "demonstrations" elsewhere. Surviving villagers were in a state of piteous destitution. On being asked what had happened, the villagers said that the day before, the soldiers had suddenly appeared, collected all the male Christian inhabitants in church, and then started mutilating them, completing their work with sword and bayonet. The number killed was estimated at about thirty. The church and village were subsequently set on fire. The American diplomat personally saw two charred bodies. The American concluded that the crimes were certainly committed by Japanese military authorities to terrorize people and that they had deliberately ordered the burning of churches.

The British ambassador meanwhile held several discussions with Japanese officials and warned that the barbaric crimes against the Koreans would be denounced

---

[80] "Claims of Korea at the Peace Conference," BA: FO 608/211.
[81] Greene to London, May 30, 1919, BA: FO 608/211.
[82] Balfour to Curzon, June 17, 1919, BA: FO 608/211.

by the civilized world. This would hurt Japan's prestige and negatively affect Japanese diplomacy at the peace conference. The Japanese vice minister for foreign affairs protested that accounts of the Japanese atrocities in the press and elsewhere were exaggerated. He tried to defend the Japanese actions in Korea by countering with the hostility Western Powers showed to the racial equality proposal Japan had presented at the peace conference. Greene took the opportunity to ask him how he expected the world to recognize Japanese claims in this direction when atrocities such as those in Korea were being committed. Greene also emphasized that the American, British, and French governments all had reliable and independent reports confirming the atrocities, and the fact remained that the Japanese military in Korea seemed to outrival Germans in the Great War in their brutality. Greene pointed to the "impossibility of recognizing Japanese claims regarding racial equality in view of such atrocities" in Korea.[83]

Using "very frank and unequivocal terms," Lord Curzon himself informed the Japanese ambassador in London in July 1919 that:

> I knew from my own journeys in Korea that its people were backward and rather stupid, but I knew also that they were simple and patriotic people. It seemed to me that they had been treated in a manner which was not justified by any behavior on their part, and which it would be difficult for anyone who was acquainted with even an outline of the facts not to condemn. In the ferment of new ideas created by the war, the Koreans had held meetings and demonstrations on behalf of their own independence; but there was no evidence that these had been seditious in character or accompanied by violence; on the contrary, the Koreans were the most peaceable of people. On the other hand, I had seen a mass of evidence testifying to the extreme ferocity with which the Japanese gendarmerie and military forces had dealt with these movements. Our consul-general in Seoul had officially reported that the acts of brutal savagery committed by the Japanese soldiery in terrorizing the people could only be paralleled by the acts of the Germans in Belgium.

Curzon said he had in front of him "pages of evidence describing the most barbarous and revolting atrocities, the publication of which would produce a sensation in the civilized world and would redound to the discredit of the Japanese Government." He continued, "The persecution of the Koreans has assumed an anti-Christian form, and deeply affected all foreign nations whose subjects were either resident or interested in that country. So undeniable were the facts of the case as I had put them before the Ambassador that they had been admitted in a public speech by Viscount Kato himself in Japan; nor indeed did I imagine for a moment that his Excellency would contest a word of what I had said." Curzon further related:

> It seemed to me a great mistake that the Japanese, in their administrations of Korea, so entirely ignored the natives of the country they were endeavouring to rule. The share allowed to the Koreans in the administration of their own country was constantly diminishing, while the number of Japanese officials went up by leaps and bounds; the

---

[83] "Japanese Atrocities in Corea [Korea]," BA: FO 608/211.

Japanese military element was always in the foreground, and ready at the slightest provocation to show its strength. Of the thirteen provincial Governors in Korea, only four were now Koreans. It was the same with the prefects. I knew of a case in which an efficient and popular Korean prefect had been removed to make room for a Japanese, who was reported to have been a second-class clerk in the water works in the capital. Even the Korean headmen of wards and villages were now being replaced by Japanese. The Japanese language was being forced everywhere on the Koreans, and the Japanese officials made no effort to understand or speak the language of the country. So intent were the Japanese upon thrusting their own language on the Koreans that no University was allowed in Korea at which any foreign language could be taught. Further, on the excuse of developing the waste and uncultivated lands of Korea, Japanese farmers were being imported, and Korean farmers were being turned out of their farms in Southern Korea by thousands to make place for the Japanese newcomers. In the railway station of Seoul, large crowds of such dispossessed people could be seen any day, emigrating to Manchuria. These were facts, all of them resting on undisputed authority, which I ventured to place before the Ambassador.[84]

London could use these reports about the repression, horrifying crimes, and all the back-door protests across Korea to shame and humiliate the Japanese, but the British and Americans would not give the Koreans a hearing. It is true that at least in early February 1919, Colonel House inquired about Korea through his aides. Colonel House's assistant and interpreter, Colonel Stephen Bonsal, met with Kimm in person. Bonsal was clearly sympathetic to the Koreans and not happy to see that "Japan, the great law- and treaty-breaker in the Far East, sits in the Council of the Great Powers and is not even to be interrogated as to her recent conduct." However, although Colonel House might have understood the Koreans' desire for independence, he asked Bonsal to inform Kimm that the Korean case simply would not be considered at the conference. As Bonsal wrote in his diary, "as a matter of protocol neither Mr. Kimm nor his distressful country have any standing at the Great Assizes, nor will they have a look in at the Conference."[85] On August 9, 1919, Kimm finally left for America to work with Syngman Rhee on a propaganda campaign, since he could make no headway in Paris.[86] It has to be pointed out that Kimm's efforts were not fruitless. When in Paris, Kimm established the Bureau of Korea Information to transmit news about the uprisings in Korea and to propagate the Korean cause. The Bureau sent news items to newspapers in France and published pamphlets for general distribution. As Lee Chong-sik wrote, "Obstructed in his attempts to influence the official delegates, Kimm found, nevertheless, a significant number of foreign sympathizers on the periphery of the conference."[87] Rhee traveled to Shanghai in late 1920 and stayed until May 1921, when he returned to Hawaii. Naturally, the Korean nationalists were badly disappointed by Wilson's reneging on the ideals he had once trumpeted and the lopsided

---

[84] Earl Curzon to Mr. Alston, Foreign Office, July 22, 1919, BA: FO 608/211.

[85] Stephen Bonsal, *Suitors and Suppliants: The Little Nations at Versailles* (New York: Prentice-Hall, 1946), 220–5.

[86] Baldwin, *The March First Movement*, 148; Ku, *Korea Under Colonialism*, 93–4.

[87] Lee, *The Politics of Korean Nationalism*, 141.

shape of the postwar world order. In Korea, as in China, there was growing disillusionment with the West after the war, especially with the realization that the principle of self-determination would not be extended to Asia. But Korean nationalists continued to fight for their cause. The establishment of the League of Nations held out some hope for their future. Korean students in Japan wrote: "Now the League of Nations is being formed and no nation will any longer dare to use military methods for territorial expansion." If their demands were not granted, the Koreans threatened, "We declare eternal war against Japan and disavow any responsibility for the ensuing tragedy."[88] Disappointed though they might be, Rhee and his many followers still tried to use international means to seek Korean independence. They did not miss any opportunity to appeal for their cause. Korea's petition to the Conference on the Limitation of Armaments, dated December 1, 1921, which was signed by Syngman Rhee, Henry Chung, and others, reads as follows: "The United States should assist China, as she is doing. She is hearing China's cry for justice. . . . For the same reason she should assist Korea." The document contends that Korea "differs from China today only in that the processes of foreign intrusion have fully accomplished in Korea what are still in progress in China. Confronted with their menace, Korea vainly invokes the Covenant for her protection. Her 'appeal to the national honor' was made in vain, for it went unheeded." Koreans further linked their case with that of the Chinese by saying that "If the observance of this pledge be now essential to the preservation of China, it is more essential for the restoration of Korea, which presents in concrete form the fruit of every policy which threatens China's economic or political integrity. The processes involving China are those which submerged Korea. They are identical in origin, in purpose, and in result. They cannot be thwarted in China if they are to be disregarded in Korea."[89]

But the Koreans and the Chinese shared additional aspects of this moment's history. After the Paris Peace Conference, Koreans in the United States launched a public relations campaign that spotlighted Japanese untrustworthiness with regard to the Shandong issue, a major point of contention between the Japanese and Chinese. In his letter to Kimm, Young L. Park wrote on October 1, 1919 that "China is a weakest country but a nearest friend of us today."[90] As Chapter 6 will discuss in detail, the American Congress used Shandong to kill the Treaty of Versailles and refused to join the League of Nations. As one scholar has pointed out, this was perhaps a costly victory for the Koreans, since Korea's best chance for regaining its independence lay with the League of Nations, which "might have responded to an American move for a change in Korea."[91] The Chinese not only helped Kimm make his way to Paris, but they were broadly sympathetic to the cause of Korean independence. By helping the Koreans, the Chinese certainly hoped to embarrass Japan. Moreover, many Chinese leaders at the time openly appealed to world opinion on Korea's

[88] Baldwin, *The March First Movement*, 43.
[89] No Author, *Korea's Appeal to the Conference on Limitation of Armament*, 3–11.
[90] Rhee, *The Syngman Rhee Correspondence in English*, 4: 435.
[91] Baldwin, *The March First Movement*, 154.

behalf, including Sun Yat-sen, who told US diplomats that the peace conference should take up the question of Korean independence. Mao Zedong lamented the failure of India and Korea at Paris. "Korea bewails the loss of its independence; so many of its people have died, and so much of its land has been devastated, but it was simply ignored by the Peace Conference." Mao thus concluded that "So much for national self-determination! I think it's really shameless!"[92] Unfortunately, with China locked in its own deadly fight against the Japanese, it could do little for Korea at the peace conference. As Kimm Kyusik told the media in late May 1919, "There is no question that the Chinese delegates have been sympathetic. However China itself is in quite a difficult situation and is not very influential."[93] Like the Koreans, the Chinese would also lose their case at Paris.

[92] Schram, *Mao's Road to Power*, 1: 337.
[93] Shi Yuanhua, *Hanguo duli yundong yu zhongguo guanxi lunji (Collected papers on the Korean Independent Movement and its Relationship with Chin)* (Beijing: Minzu chubanshe, 2009), 1: 6.

PART III

THE CHINESE AND JAPANESE ROLES: HIGH EXPECTATIONS AND GRAVE DISAPPOINTMENTS

6

China and Japan at Paris
Old Rivalries in a New World

Newborn nationalist elites across Asia saw hope. Proud Europe had destroyed itself and Woodrow Wilson had called for a democratic new world system of open agreements, self-determination, and free trade. Yet the Paris Peace Conference left Japan, China, and the colonial people of Asia slighted and disillusioned—open to calls for radical action. Japanese diplomats and the Japanese public alike had expected the talks to legitimate Japan's Asian hegemony and to ratify recent gains in China. More importantly, the Japanese aspired to be finally respected and accepted into the club of Western Powers. Chinese diplomats rallied their meager resources but were ignored in their efforts to recover what had been taken from China by their "robber neighbor," as widely read intellectual Liang Qichao called Japan.[1] Self-determination for Vietnam, Korea, and South East Asia was not even considered, and Japan's proposal for racial equality was summarily dismissed.

Japanese ambition, Chinese resistance, and Western obstinacy at the conference created public outrage in China and Japan that locked their countries into self-fulfilling prophecies of mutual conflict. The conference created unresolved challenges for the emerging world system as well as paving the way for Hitler's Germany, militarist Japan, and ultimately, Mao's China. Left undecided was whether Japan was to lead Asia or dominate it.

JAPAN'S OBJECTIVES

The Japanese delegation reflected Japan's half-century rise from isolation and poverty to affluence, dignity, and power. The delegation was headed by Marquis Kinmochi Saionji, in his seventieth year and in poor health, and the veteran statesman, Baron Nobuaki Makino, former Minister for Foreign Affairs in the Yamamoto Cabinet of 1913. The British ambassador to Japan, who knew Makino well, characterized him as "not brilliant."[2] The Taishō Emperor, who had been brain-damaged as a child but was nonetheless heir to the successes of the canny Meiji emperor, also appointed Utemi Chinda, ambassador to Britain, Keishiro

---

[1] Joseph Richmond Levenson, *Liang Qichao and the Mind of Modern China* (Berkeley: University of California Press, 1970), 189.
[2] British Embassy, Tokyo to London, December 2, 1918, BA: FO 608/211.

Matsui, ambassador to France, and Hikokichi Ijuin, ambassador to Italy, as plenipotentiary members of the delegation. Besides these substantial representatives of the aristocratic elite, the delegation included men from business, education, the military, and other backgrounds. Some criticized the delegation's make-up. Former Minister of Justice and respected politician Yukio Ozaki sniped that Marquis Saionji "might be an authority on cooking, but he seemed to have no definite ideas with regard to the welfare of his country." Ozaki doubted that the delegation was up to the challenges ahead. How was this motley group to press such issues as international racial discrimination or Japan's claims to islands in the South Seas? Here was Japan's challenge, he said: "It is as though a man with a drawn sword in his hand knocked at the door of another. Who would open to him?"[3]

The Japanese press weighed in. Public opinion was a growing force as Japan moved to a system of party politics in which governments could be overthrown on issues of popular interest. Party-sponsored newspapers and journals rallied their followers and set the terms of debate. The *Asahi Shimbun* claimed that the public expected Japan to take over German possessions in China and across the Pacific Ocean. Above all, the delegation must persuade the conference to address racial discrimination, which, if not curbed, would menace the future peace of the world. Newspapers headlined the new wave of anti-Japanese feeling in the West and the increasing American racial restrictions on immigration. They sharply recalled the 1905 San Francisco School Board decision to segregate Asian children. "Fairness and equality," the editor declared confidently, "must be secured for the coloured races who form sixty-two per cent of the whole of mankind."[4] But Japan's concerns were focused. The *Nihon Oyobi Nihonjin*, a popular Tokyo monthly, noted that "Japan's interests concerned questions relating to Asia."[5] The December 1918 issue of *Ajia Jiron* laid out Japan's objectives: recognition by the Powers of Japan's services in connection with peace in the Far East and the war generally; recognition of Japan's special position in China and Siberia; German recognition of Japan's special rights in Qingdao and privileges with regard to the Shandong Railway; the Powers' abandoning racial prejudice and pledging to give Japanese and Chinese equality of privilege with the white man; and reform of the Powers' oppression in Asiatic countries to remove the causes of native discontent.[6]

Not all Japanese put racial discrimination among their top issues. As Viscount Takaaki Katō pointed out: "The questions to be discussed and agreed upon at the sittings of the Peace Conference are of extreme complexity." Japan's most important goal was to be handed Shandong officially.[7] As the British ambassador to Japan observed, "Formation of League of Nations is generally approved in principle. Abolition of race discrimination as a condition of Japan's adherence is however put forward outside official circles as principal Japanese plank at Peace Conference."[8]

[3] British Embassy, Tokyo to London, March 21, 1919, BA: FO 608/211.
[4] Cited in *The Japan Times*, January 15, 1919.
[5] "Japanese Views about Peace," *The Japan Chronicle*, October 27, 1918.
[6] British Embassy, Tokyo to London, December 28, 1918, BA: FO 608/211.
[7] British Embassy, Tokyo, January 13, 1919, BA: FO 608/211.
[8] British Embassy, Tokyo, December 2, 1918, BA: FO 608/211.

One article in *Nichi Nichi* argued that the peace conference had made plain that "Japan is the leader of the Far East." Specific territorial concerns followed after: The "question of Siberia is closely connected with that of China" since "the Powers will not be in a position to control Siberia after the war." In an article in *Taiyo* of November 1918, Kiroku Hayashi, a professor at Keio University and author of books on European diplomacy and on the Russian Empire, made the following suggestions: in regard to such general questions as the making of peace and the conclusion of an armistice affecting the European front, "Japan must leave it principally to others to speak; but in regard to Far Eastern questions Japan has a leading voice and must be the chief authority in this decision."

The British embassy summarized this information for Foreign Minister Balfour on November 12, 1918, reporting that "the Japanese Press has been greatly occupied during the last few weeks with the question of Japan's claims at the forthcoming Peace Conference." The embassy's report characterized the attitude of the press as follows:

1. Questions in Europe were not the concern of Japan.

2. Qingdao must not be returned to Germans but the question of its future disposal must be settled directly between China and Japan.

3. If Great Britain retains the South Sea Islands south of the equator, Japan would certainly want to retain those to the north.

4. Japan would have something to say as regards the settlement in Eastern Siberia.

5. The question of discrimination against the Japanese in America, Canada, and Australia would appear likely to be brought up at the Conference as arising out of the proposal for a League of Nations.[9]

Clearly, the major focus for the Japanese at the peace conference was to receive Shandong and legalize its interests in China.[10] To work toward its objectives, Japan had turned to the secret treaties it signed with Britain, France, and others; to firm up their control of Shandong, the Japanese had found many ways to pressure the Chinese and other foreign governments. China was not only a divided nation politically, but its Peking regime, as late as 1918, signed a treaty with Japan to receive financial support. As the British minister to China, John Jordan, reported to his government on February 5, 1919, the Chinese strongman Duan Qirui was negotiating an agreement that would supply him with 20,000,000 dollars worth of military equipment.[11] By intervening in Chinese domestic politics, Japan was determined to keep China weak so that Japanese interests in China would be preserved. The Japanese military authorities even tried to control the Chinese armies and

[9] British Embassy, Tokyo to Balfour, November 12, 1918, BA: FO 608/211.
[10] For details on Japan's basic objectives at Paris, see Morinosuke Kajimaand Kajima Heiwa Kenkyujo, *The Diplomacy of Japan, 1894–1922* (Tokyo: Kajima Institute of International Peace, 1980), 3: 343–53; K. K. Kawakami, *Japan and World Peace* (New York: Macmillan, 1919).
[11] Jordan to London, February 5, 1919, BA: FO 608/211.

their munitions supply and stop all construction of trunk railways from Europe built with European or American capital. One British official in the Foreign Office commented that he saw:

practically no limit to the aims and ambitions of the military party in Japan. That party might possibly allege the fear of Europe obtaining domination over China and eventually over Japan as a justification of their policy of aggression in China, but since the defeat of Russia in 1905 and more especially since the collapse of that Power in the Great War the excuse can no longer hold water. Speaking generally I believe that the Japanese General staff supported by the chauvinist parties aim at securing Japan's hegemony of the Far East and the conversion of China into a Japanese protectorate.[12]

Given this focus on Shandong and other Japanese interests in Asia, the Japanese delegation was usually "silent, unemotional, but watchful; rising with power only when their own interests were affected." Such was Colonel House's description of Japan's delegates throughout the Peace Conference.[13] Although they were quiet, they did make active contact with Colonel House, who was President Wilson's confidant and trusted advisor. The Japanese analyzed the American delegation and put House down as a friend. House described his own function as that of "troubleshooter."[14]

Lloyd George, Wilson, and Clemenceau in particular stereotyped the Japanese, and treated them with scant courtesy. At the Paris Peace Conference, Wilson confided to David Miller, who was the legal advisor to the American delegation, that he "did not trust Japanese."[15] Makino and Chinda sat in the Council of Ten but, according to some observers, they were so polite that it was not clear that they understood "what subjects were being discussed."[16] On one occasion, there was a tied vote, and the chairman turned to the Japanese delegate for the deciding vote, inquiring, "Do you vote with the French and the Americans, or with the British and the Italians?" According to one witness, "The inscrutable little yellow man sucked in his breath and responded simply, 'Yes.'"[17] At another session of the Council of Four, a Japanese delegate made a remark. Clemenceau understood English, but not Japanese-English, so he turned and in a loud stage whisper asked, "Qu'est-ce qu'il dit, le petit?" (What's the little fellow saying?).[18] When it was decided to expedite business by dissolving the Council of Ten and setting up the Council of Four, Japan was not included. The Japanese delegation did complain to Clemenceau about its exclusion from the Big Four meetings and was not given an opportunity to participate in the conference as often as they would like.[19]

But the Japanese could defend their interests and position forcefully. As American historian Thomas Bailey put it, "If the Japanese sat like brown Buddhas when non-Asiatic interests were involved, they left no doubt as to where they stood

[12] R. Macleay, handwritten memo, June 17, 1919, BA: FO 608/211.
[13] Birdsall, *Versailles Twenty Years After*, 83.   [14] Birdsall, *Versailles Twenty Years After*, 91.
[15] Link, ed., *The Papers of Woodrow Wilson*, 54: 370.
[16] Charles L. Mee, *The End of Order: Versailles 1919* (New York: Dutton, 1980), 50.
[17] Thomas Andrew Bailey, *Woodrow Wilson and the Lost Peace* (New York: Macmillan, 1944), 272.
[18] Bailey, *Woodrow Wilson and the Lost Peace*, 173.
[19] Link, ed., *The Papers of Woodrow Wilson*, 59: 528.

when their own interests were affected." Keeping generally quiet, he added, "They spoke with all the more authority when they finally broke their silence. And they did so with directness, clarity, and pertinacity."[20] The Japanese came to Paris with three demands: first, a formal recognition of the principle of racial equality; second, title to the German islands of the North Pacific; and third, acquisition of Germany's economic and other rights in the Chinese province of Shandong. They were determined to get them all, and if not all, Shandong would be an absolute necessity. Makino laid out these claims on January 27, 1919, declaring that the Japanese government "feels justified" in receiving its demands from the Powers.[21]

But would Japan succeed in getting Shandong? The Japanese had to face substantial criticisms at the conference. After all, Japan had not sent any military forces to Europe to fight the Germans. Clemenceau clearly thought that Japan had not done enough and told his fellow peacemakers in January 1919: "Who can say that in the war she played a part that can be compared for instance to that of France? Japan defended its interests in the Far East, but when she was requested to intervene in Europe, everyone knows what the answer of Japan was."[22] Britain obviously agreed. Earl Curzon had once pointed out to the Japanese ambassador in London that during the war "Japan had pursued a policy which aimed at securing commercial and political supremacy in China by many forms of pressure, and particularly by a series of loans in return for valuable concessions." It seemed clear that "the object of Japan for many years, and especially during the war, had been, if not to reduce China to complete dependence, at any rate to acquire a hold over her resources which would make Japan her practical master in the future." Curzon informed the Japanese that he was aware agreements had been concluded between China and Japan, by which the latter justified her actions in Paris, and for which she had secured the assent of the Allied Powers. But:

> viewing the circumstances in which these agreements had been concluded, and the fact that China had not been in a position to defend herself, I could not regard them as possessing any great validity. Others of the Allies had been hampered by treaties or conventions concluded in the earlier stages of the war, under conditions entirely different from those that now prevailed.... It was unwise of Japan to insist upon the technical rights secured to her by her agreements with China in respect of Shantung. I was aware that a declaration of her intention had been made ... to the other Allied Powers in Paris; but this declaration, which was to a large extent a justification of the action taken by the Powers, had never been published to the world.[23]

The Japanese also faced mistrust from the Americans. When the Japanese government learned that Wilson's Fourteen Points were to be the basis of the peace settlement, it worried that the principle of self-determination posed a serious problem for the disposal of the German colonies, especially German interests in

---

[20] Bailey, *Woodrow Wilson and the Lost Peace*, 272.
[21] Department of State, *FRUS: The Paris Peace Conference, 1919*, 3:738–757.
[22] MacMillan, *Paris 1919*, 315.
[23] Earl Curzon to Mr. Alston (No. 125), Foreign Office, July 18, 1919, BA: FO 608/211.

China.[24] Japanese leaders were also genuinely concerned about the possibility that the racial prejudice of the Western Powers might jeopardize Japan's position in the League of Nations; they were resolved to prevent such a possibility.[25] The Japanese were alarmed by the hostility among Americans. The sympathy of Americans for the Chinese people contrasted sharply with their distrust of the Japanese, especially after the war had strengthened Japan's position among the nations. Breckinridge Long, the Third Assistant Secretary of State with special responsibility for Far Eastern affairs before and during the Paris Peace Conference, told an interviewer that from 1917 onward, suspicion of Japan was a constant factor in American thinking. Robert Lansing, who was a member of the American delegation at Paris and Secretary of State, became convinced that Japan had to be checked in its intentions for China. He compared Japan to Germany.[26] The Japanese issue in particular presented a challenge to Wilson's new world order.

Early in the conference, Wilson flatly announced that he would not recognize the major Powers' secret understandings with Japan. Nonetheless, the secret treaties which Japan concluded with Britain, France, and others proved to be powerful weapons. They guaranteed permanent possession of Shandong and the German Pacific islands as early as 1917, and secured for Britain the German islands south of the equator, in exchange for Japan providing anti-submarine reinforcements for Mediterranean waters. At the April 22, 1919 meeting which dealt with the Shandong case, Clemenceau pointedly told Wilson that "This morning I reread our treaty with Japan: it binds us toward her, as well as Great Britain. I want to warn you about it."[27] The Japanese had faithfully carried out their end of the bargain, and the British and French were honor-bound to observe theirs. But more than honor was involved, for if the British had indeed repudiated their agreement at that late date, they could have lost their claim to islands in the Pacific that New Zealand and Australia were demanding. Wilson simply could not win against the collective efforts of Japan, Britain, and France. To make matters worse for Wilson, Japan had also concluded secret treaties in 1915 and 1918 with the Chinese regarding Shandong.

Given all their preparatory maneuvering, the Japanese were reasonably confident that their claims would eventually be satisfied.[28] Still, to make their position absolutely clear, on April 24, 1919, they threatened not to sign the peace treaty and withdraw from the proceedings unless they were granted Shandong. According to Colonel Stephen Bonsal, who was an assistant to and interpreter for Colonel House in Paris, the Japanese sense of timing was exquisite. Italy had left the conference due to Italian failure to receive Fiume, so "should the Rising Sun Empire withdraw, our World Congress, or whatever it is, could dwindle to the proportions of a rump parliament."[29] To make sure its points were heeded, on April 30, 1919, Japan again

[24] Kawamura, *Turbulence in the Pacific*, 139–40.
[25] Kawamura, *Turbulence in the Pacific*, 141.
[26] MacMillan, *Paris 1919*, 330.   [27] Link, ed., *The Papers of Woodrow Wilson*, 57: 599.
[28] For recent studies on Japan and the First World War, see Dickinson, *War and National Reinvention*; Kawamura, *Turbulence in The Pacific*.
[29] Bonsal, *Suitors and Suppliants*, 237.

threatened to withdraw from the conference and the League of Nations if its demands regarding China were not satisfied.

The Japanese threats were put very clearly to Wilson and the others.[30] Convinced that they were not a bluff, Wilson chose to compromise. This, he hoped, would provide an "outlet to permit the Japanese to save their face and let the League of Nations decide the matter later." As he put it to Lloyd George and Clemenceau, he believed "It is necessary to do everything to assure that she [Japan] joins the League of Nations." He was afraid that if Japan boycotted the new international body "she would do all that she could want to do in the Far East." According to Kawamura, "The Shandong compromise, therefore, was a means to keep the influence of Wilsonian idealism alive in East Asia." Wilson said, "I am above all concerned not to create a chasm between the East and the West."[31] Thus, with the exception of the racial equality proposal, which will be discussed in detail in Chapter 7, Japan seemed to get what it wanted. When the world's nations gathered to formalize the peace treaty and create a League of Nations, Japan was accorded the status of one of the Great Powers, alongside the United States, Great Britain, France, and Italy, each with two representatives.

Wilson's dilemma was this: if he gave Shandong to Japan, China might not vote for the League; if he gave Shandong to China, Japan would not vote for the League. As American Secretary of State Robert Lansing observed, Wilson held "the formation of the League in accordance with the provisions of the Covenant to be superior to every other consideration and that to accomplish this object almost any sacrifice would be justifiable."[32] British senior diplomat Harold Nicolson thought Wilson's behavior was "pathetic" in his "palpable surrender" over Shandong to Japan. Wilson himself recognized that "I shall be accused of violating my own principles."[33] Nevertheless, on April 30, the United States, Britain, and France decided to allow Japan to retain the former German interests in China, including Shandong. Despite the efforts and the brilliant performance of the Chinese delegation, to be described later in this chapter, Japan's voice proved to be the more powerful. In the announcement he later drew up for the press, Wilson described the settlement as being "as satisfactory as could be got out of the tangle of treaties in which China herself was involved."[34]

Clearly, Wilson was not happy with his decision. On the evening of April 30, 1919, after the Shandong decision, Wilson told his personal secretary Ray Stannard Baker that it was the best that "could be had out of a dirty past." "The only hope was to keep the world together, get the League of Nations with Japan in it, and then try to secure justice for the Chinese, not as regarding Japan alone, but England, France, and Russia, all of whom had concessions in China. If Japan went home

[30] MacMillan, *Paris 1919*, 337–8.   [31] Kawamura, *Turbulence in the Pacific*, 147–8.

[32] Robert Lansing, *The Peace Negotiations: A Personal Narrative* (Boston: Houghton Mifflin Company, 1921), 245. For a recent study on Lansing and the Shandong issue, see Stephen G. Graft, "John Bassett Moore, Robert Lansing and the Shandong Question," *Pacific Historical Review*, 66:2 (May 1997).

[33] Harold Nicolson, *Peacemaking, 1919* (Boston: Houghton Mifflin Company, 1933), 146–7.

[34] MacMillan, *Paris 1919*, 338.

there was danger of a Japanese-Russian-German alliance and a return to the old 'Balance of Power' system in the world." Wilson told Baker quite frankly that with Italy already out of the peace conference, the defection of Japan might well break up the conference and destroy the League of Nations. He asked him to explain to the Chinese how sorry he was that he could not do more for them, but he had to grant Japan's wishes in order to save the League.[35] According to Kawamura, Wilson's absolute faith in the universality of his ideals, and his unyielding determination to turn his vision of a new world order into a reality, prevented him from understanding what was driving an emerging non-Western country like Japan to expand at the expense of weaker neighbors. Japanese leaders, who took advantage of the European war to expand Japan's foothold in East Asia, considered Wilsonian opposition to Japanese claims as just another attempt by Western Powers to block the growth of an Asian regional power. Forgetting the blemishes in their conduct in China and Korea, the Japanese experienced President Wilson's interference in Sino-Japanese negotiations over Shandong as a humiliation and considered his failure to support the principle of racial equality unjust. The Japanese viewed Wilsonian internationalism "simply as hypocritical rhetoric that hindered the advancement of their country."[36]

Wilson did not want to sacrifice China, but he eventually did so to save his own cherished plans. As Wilson later claimed, he agreed to give Shandong to Japan in the peace treaty only after he was convinced that "Japan would bolt the conference and decline to sign the treaty" if it did not get Shandong.[37] However, members of the American delegation to the peace conference disagreed with Wilson on the Shandong issue. In Lansing's judgment, the Japanese case was so flagrantly contrary to international law, justice, the principle of self-determination, and common sense that he thought the Japanese should be allowed to leave Paris. But he recognized that the Japanese would not leave because they needed the international recognition that participation in the conference conferred. But it seemed inconceivable that Wilson should agree to hand a piece of China to Japan. Robert Lansing and Henry White thus supported Tasker Bliss—all members of American delegation—when he criticized Wilson by saying it was wrong to sacrifice China: "It can't be right to do wrong even to make peace. Peace is desirable, but there are things dearer than peace—justice and freedom. . . . If we support Japan's claim, we abandon the democracy of China to the domination of the Prussianized militarism of Japan."[38] Paul Reinsch, the American minister to China, even resigned to protest Wilson's compromise.[39] Wilson's Shandong betrayal certainly gave point to Clemenceau's biting remark that Wilson "talked like Jesus Christ but acted like Lloyd

[35] Birdsall, *Versailles Twenty Years After*, 114.   [36] Kawamura, *Turbulence in the Pacific*, 148.
[37] Link, ed., *The Papers of Woodrow Wilson*, 61: 593.
[38] T. H. Bliss to Wilson, April 29, 1919, *The Papers of Bliss*, Folder 247/W. Wilson/April 1919, Library of Congress, Manuscript Division; see also Wensi Jin, *China at the Paris Peace Conference in 1919* (Jamaica, NY: St. John's University Press, 1961), 26.
[39] See Link, ed., *The Papers of Woodrow Wilson*, 61: 631–4; Paul S. Reinsch, *An American Diplomat in China* (Garden City: Doubleday, Page & Company, 1922), 364–82.

George." Important diplomats and politicians, such as Harold Nicolson, all condemned the Shandong settlement as "the worst surrender of all."[40]

Japan's successes and China's failure at Paris contributed to Wilson's eventual defeat at home. In the US Senate, the most damaging criticisms, as the key Wilson opponent Henry Cabot Lodge had hoped, came from pro-China senators. The betrayal of Shandong not only led to critiques of Wilson, but raised the related question of whether the American delegation had been unanimous on the issue, with the implicit question of whether the president had behaved dictatorially and ignored informed counsel. Robert Lansing expressed the opinion that Wilson "could have secured justice for China without the alleged surrendering of Shantung to Japan."[41] In his denunciation of the Treaty of Versailles, Lodge's sixth reservation specifically named the "scandal of Shantung." It declared that the US withheld its assent to the articles of the treaty countenancing this arrangement and reserved full liberty of action in any controversy arising out of them.[42] As one insider revealed, when the American Senate was debating about the peace treaty, the Shandong issue was "the main theme. Especially in view of reported Japanese atrocities in Corea sentiment is strongly hostile."[43] The betrayal of Shandong thus became the shared history of China, Japan, the US, and, to a certain extent, Korea.

CHINESE OBJECTIVES

The Chinese had been preparing for the postwar peace conference since they received the Twenty-one Demands from Japan in 1915. Given all China's misfortune and mishaps in connection with its attempts at engagement in the First World War, it is perhaps surprising that the Chinese people were genuinely jubilant when the fighting ended with the Allies' victory. When the news reached China, the government in Beijing immediately declared a three-day national holiday, to commence upon the armistice. Excitement mounted once they learned that Woodrow Wilson would personally attend the gathering with his blueprint for the new world order. While not every Chinese citizen believed in Wilson, feelings ran high at the dramatic conclusion of the war. Chinese students in Beijing gathered at the American Legation, where they chanted "Long live President Wilson!" Some of them had memorized and could easily recite his speech on the Fourteen Points. Chen Duxiu, Dean of the School of Letters at Peking University, a leading figure in the New Cultural Movement, and later a co-founder of the Chinese Communist Party, was then so convinced of Wilson's sincerity and noble objectives that he called Wilson "the best good man in the world."[44] Chen believed the end of the

---

[40] Bailey, *Woodrow Wilson and the Lost Peace*, 282.

[41] Thomas A. Bailey, *Woodrow Wilson and the Great Betrayal* (New York: The Macmillan Company, 1945), 83.

[42] Bailey, *Woodrow Wilson and the Great Betrayal*, 161–2.

[43] Link, ed., *The Papers of Woodrow Wilson*, 61: 618.

[44] Chen Duxiu, *Duxiu Wencun (Surviving Writings of Chen Duxiu)* (Hefei: Anhui renmin chu ban she, 1987), 388.

First World War was a turning point in human history. "Might is no longer reliable, justice and reason can no longer be denied," he wrote.[45]

Many leading Chinese figures believed that Wilson had become China's best hope; he was the world leader of "spiritual democracy."[46] Even Li Dazhao, the other founder of the Chinese Communist Party, wrote that Wilson was "famous for his deep love of world peace," and that he had "single-handedly shouldered the future" of a fair world.[47] Cai Yuanpei, the president of Beijing University, declared that the Allies' victory symbolized the end of an age of "darkness" and the coming of an age of openness in the world.[48] Liang Qichao also lauded the Allied victory as representing the "progress of the new age," since the war had been fought for "the purpose of securing permanent peace for the world."[49] Jiang Tingfu attested that during the First World War, he had "believed in every word which President Wilson uttered."[50] An American YMCA official in China wrote back to the office in the US on December 31, 1918 that "President Wilson's clear expression of sympathy and friendship to smaller nations touched the heart of the Chinese people in such a way as to almost seem pathetic."[51] Eugene Barnett, also a member of the YMCA in China, wrote:

It is marvelous to see the almost reverential regard in which President Wilson is held in China at the present time. A volume of his speeches printed in English and Chinese by the commercial press has been the year's "best seller." The first question asked one by a stranger casually met is one's name and the second question is as to one's country. When one replies nowadays that his "humble country is America," it is almost invariably the signal for a panegyric on "Wilson—statesman, humanitarian, the outstanding figure in the world today." In schoolboys' speeches and in sermons alike Wilson is quoted as though he were a modern Confucius. It is wonderful how Wilson's principles and his courageous advocacy of them have caught the imagination of the Chinese people.[52]

During the three-day holiday declared at the war's end, 60,000 people, many of them nationalist students and their teachers, turned out for Peking's victory parade. To popular rejoicing, a monument called the Von Ketteler Memorial in Peking—a symbol of national humiliation for many Chinese, put up by the Kaiser's government to commemorate a German diplomat who had been killed during the Boxer

[45] Chen Duxiu, "Fa Kan Ci (Preface for a New Magazine)," *Mei zhou ping lun (Weekly Review)* 1:1 (1918).

[46] Fu Sinian and Luo Jialun, eds., *Xin Chao (New Tide)*, 1:5 (1919).

[47] Li Dazhao, "Wei erxun yu ping he" ("Wilson and Peace"), in Li Dazhao, *Li Dazhao Wen Ji (Collections of Li Dazhao Writings)* (Beijing: Ren min chu ban she, 1984), 1: 285.

[48] Tang Zhengchan, *Cai Yuanpei Zhuan (Biography of Cai Yuanpei)* (Shanghai: Shanghai ren min chu ban she, 1985), 159.

[49] *Dongfang zazhi*, 16:2 (February 1919).

[50] Min-Chien T. Z. Tyau, *China Awakened* (New York: Macmillan, 1922), 268.

[51] China correspondence and reports, November–December 1918, YMCA Archives, box 153, folder: China correspondence and reports, November 1918–October 1919.

[52] From Eugene Barnett from Hankow, April 30, 1919, YMCA Archives, box 153, folder: China correspondence and reports, April–May 1919.

Rebellion two decades earlier—was dismantled. It was relocated to a park in the capital and renamed the Monument of the Right over Might.[53] Wilson himself seemed to be willing to be a Chinese friend and told Koo, who was then Chinese minister to Washington, on November 26, 1918 that "the ideals of China and the United States were along the same lines and said he would gladly do his best to support China at the peace conference."[54]

The high expectations for Wilson and the peace conference brought many of China's best-trained and brightest minds to Paris either as official members of the delegation or as semi-private or private citizens. The sixty members of the Chinese delegation included diplomats from the generation who maintained continuity in the Foreign Ministry from the late Qing dynasty through, in some cases, to the 1950s. Lu Zhengxiang (Lou Tseng-Tsiang), C. T. Wang (Wang Zhengting), Wellington Koo, Alfred Sze (Shi Zhaoji), and Wei Chenzu were the plenipotentiaries of the delegation. Except for Lu Zhengxiang, foreign minister at the time, and Wang Zhengting, who represented the breakaway southern government in Canton and was stationed in the United States when he chosen to join the conference delegation, the others were high-ranking diplomats stationed in European countries or the United States.[55] The Chinese minister to Japan had not been commissioned to attend, which indicates that China chose to focus on the West and simply not deal with Japan at the conference. The head of the Chinese delegation, Lu Zhengxiang, had the new sort of learning that China needed if it was to survive. He had spent many of the years before the Great War in one European capital or another and married a Belgian woman. Besides Lu, four other members of the delegation were educated in the West and understood both Chinese and world affairs well. Wellington Koo's participation was especially critical due to his thorough preparation for the conference and diplomatic skills. Koo, born into a rich merchant's family, had both Chinese classical training and a Western education at St. John's University in Shanghai before going to the United States to take a doctoral degree in international law at Columbia University.[56] In 1912, immediately after finishing his PhD program, he was summoned back to China to serve as English-language secretary to President Yuan Shikai. Soon he was working for the Foreign Ministry, and there he commenced his brilliant career as a professional diplomat.[57] In 1915, he was the youngest diplomat of his rank in Washington, representing his country at

---

[53] Von Ketteler was a German minister to China killed during the Boxer Uprising. As compensation for his murder, the Chinese government was compelled to erect a three-arch stone *pailou* (gateway) bearing inscriptions of official apology in Chinese, German, and Latin in the center of the capital, across the entire width of the main street. This was done in the summer of 1901 and the gateway became a landmark, an everyday reminder of Chinese humiliation and helplessness in the face of the Powers.

[54] Link, ed., *The Papers of Woodrow Wilson*, 57: 633.

[55] Wei was minister to Belgium, while Shi was minister to Great Britain and a Cornell graduate. Wang graduated from Yale University.

[56] His dissertation, entitled "The Status of Aliens in China," was written under the direction of John Bassett Moore, a leading expert in international law and diplomacy.

[57] Koo had not finished his dissertation when he left for China. His dissertation committee wrote the conclusion for him and got it published as No. 126 of Studies in History, Economics and Public Law by Columbia University.

only twenty-seven years of age. President Wilson was deeply impressed and remarked that Koo spoke English in the way the famous British writer Thomas Macaulay wrote it.[58] Along with the formal delegation, influential social elites also traveled to Paris in private or semi-official capacities. They included Liang Qichao and his comrades, who left for Paris "dreaming of bringing about justice and humaneness through diplomacy, and believing that the peace conference would really mean an overhaul of unjust international relations and establish a solid foundation for everlasting peace."[59] Among the others who came to Paris to witness the historical event and push China's cause were Wang Jingwei and Li Shizeng, who had come to France early in the century to become anarchists and then became cultural ambassadors before returning to China to join Sun Yat-sen's revolution; Ye Gongchuo, a close associate of Liang Shiyi and a high-ranking official in both the Peking government and later the Nationalist government; and Chen Youren, a Trinidad-born lawyer and close follower of Sun Yat-sen.[60]

China had earned a seat at the peace conference with its official declaration of war against Germany and the large number of Chinese laborers in Europe. On August 14, 1917, when the government was finally allowed to join the war officially, the Allied and Associated Powers at Peking promised that they would "do all that rests with them to insure that China shall enjoy in her international relations the position and the regard due to a great country." Based on this assurance and Wilson's high-sounding ideals, the Chinese hoped to get five seats at the conference, like the other major Powers. But that did not happen. Instead, China was treated as a third-rank nation with only two seats, though Japan had five. Lu Zhengxiang wrote on January 14, 1919 to seek "utmost consideration" for China's appeal for the five seats, "which is due to her as a great country." But the major Powers did not budge, and so the Chinese tasted their first bitter pill.[61]

The most optimistic among the Chinese delegation anticipated that after the war every nation would be entitled to a free existence and an opportunity of free development: "We feel ourselves justified, on the eve of the opening of the peace conference, to bring to the knowledge of the civilized world the aspirations of the Chinese people."[62] Territorial integrity was certainly a part of those aspirations. Responding to the widespread expectations among their fellow countrymen, Chinese diplomats took every possible step to push for the recovery of their lost territories, especially the immediate return of Shandong. The Chinese went to Paris with one set of demands and another set of readjustments, in the form of desiderata that included both long-term objectives and short-term goals:

---

[58] Bonsal, *Suitors and Suppliants*, 288.
[59] Liang Qichao, "Ou You Xin Yin lu" ("Recollections of My Journey in Europe), in Liang *Yin Bing Shi He Ji*, 23: 38.
[60] For Ye Gongchuo's trip to Europe, see Xia'an hui gao nian pu bian yin hui, ed., *Ye Xia'an Xianshen Nianpu* (Shanghai: Xia'an hui gao nian pu bian yin hui, 1946), 63–9.
[61] Lu Zhengxiang memo, January 14, 1919, BA: FO 608/211.
[62] Chinese Manifesto Relating to the Chinese Aspirations at the Final Settlement of the War, BA: FO 608/211.

1. Territorial integrity, or restoration to China of the foreign concessions and leased territories.

2. Restoration of national sovereignty, or the abolition of restrictions imposed upon China by the Protocol of 1901; in particular, the withdrawal of foreign troops and abolition of foreign consular jurisdictions.

3. Economic freedom, or the exercise of complete tariff autonomy.[63]

These requests represented long-term objectives under which the Chinese hoped to achieve the revision of all treaties granting privileges under the most-favored nation clause, but they also wanted remission of the Boxer Indemnity. Their immediate goals included the termination of old treaties with Germany and Austria-Hungary in consequence of China's participation in the war and the retrocession of Shandong. The Powers simply refused to consider China's long-term objectives, claiming that they were not directly related to the war.

But Shandong *was* directly related to the war. In the beginning, the delegates pressed on the point with high hopes. On January 28, 1919, Wellington Koo presented China's case. He argued that China had every right to ask for the direct restitution of Shandong: China had reserved its right of sovereignty even after Germany took control of the area; the people in Shandong were homogeneously Chinese and met every requirement of the principle of nationality; Shandong was an integral part of Chinese territory; its inhabitants were "entirely Chinese in race, language and religion"; and the German-leased territory was "the cradle of Chinese civilization, the birthplace of Confucius and Mencius, and a Holy Land for the Chinese." As to the agreements China had signed with Japan during the war, Koo argued that they had been signed only under Japanese threat and only as a temporary expedient. Those treaties were a "corollary to the Twenty-one Demands" and the Chinese considered them merely temporary arrangements because they dealt primarily with questions which had arisen from the war; therefore, they could not be satisfactorily settled except at the final peace conference. Furthermore, China's Declaration of War on Germany "expressly abrogates the Lease Convention with consequent reversion of leasehold rights; anyhow the Convention expressly denies Germany right of transfer to a third Power." Because China had declared war on the side of the Allies, any arrangements concluded between itself and Germany had been abrogated.[64] In other words, with China's entry into the war, Germany had forfeited its leasehold and as such, no longer possessed any rights in Shandong to surrender to another power. The Chinese therefore considered their declaration of war on Germany to be an automatic cancellation of the Sino-Japanese Treaty of 1915 with respect to Shandong.

---

[63] Department of State, *Papers Relating to the Foreign Relations of the United States: The Paris Peace Conference, 1919* (Washington, DC: US Government Printing Office, 1942), 2: 492, 509–11.

[64] For an official report on that meeting, see Secretary's Notes of a Conversation held in M. Pichon's room at the Quai d'Orsay, Paris, January 28, 1919, Department of State, *FRUS: The Paris Peace Conference, 1919*, 3: 749–57.

China further maintained that morally, Japan had no right to keep Shandong under established principles of international law regarding the termination of treaties and agreements: namely, when a treaty or agreement was concluded under threat of force, that treaty or agreement was voidable. Thus, China demanded the nullification of the Sino-Japanese Treaty of 1915 on three grounds: it was made under duress and threat; it impaired China's independence; and it was a menace to the future peace of the world. The Chinese delegation pointed out that this treaty had been concluded in direct contradiction of the principle of "open covenants." If the League of Nations was not to be built on sand, all secret agreements of whatever kind must meet their proper fate. To support its arguments and demonstrate its sincere trust in open diplomacy, the Chinese delegation distributed at the conference copies of the secret treaties and agreements it had been force to sign with Japan, along with its written demand for the direct return of Shandong from Germany.[65] From the Chinese perspective, "By restoring it [Shandong] to China, together with the railway and other rights, the Peace Conference would be not only redressing a wrong which had been wantonly committed by Germany, but also serving the common interests of all nations in the Far East." "Moreover, the fact that China, participating in the glorious victory of the Allies and Associates, received direct from Germany the restitution of Tsingtao and other rights of Shantung, will comport to her national dignity and serve to illustrate further the principle of right and justice for which the Allies and Associates have fought the common enemy." Koo also informed the conference that Shandong's direct restitution was "simpler and less likely to cause complications" and "essential to durable peace in Far East." If the peace conference allowed Shandong to fall under foreign control, that decision would leave a "dagger pointed at the heart of China."

Koo's arguments were powerful enough to make the Japanese nervous. Since Japan's focus at the conference was to keep what it had gained in China during the war, the Japanese delegation saw China's arguments as "a venture to captivate the world by her tongue and pen."[66] British minister John Jordan reported from Peking: "It is no exaggeration to say that the feeling of the Chinese over the Shantung question has been aroused in a manner that is not to be mistaken. It permeates all classes."[67] Koo's powerful and eloquent presentations won him both admiration and support. American Secretary of State Robert Lansing, who was also

[65] See Lu Zhengxiang to Waijiaobu, January 27, 30, February 5, 1919, in Zhongguo she hui ke xue yuan, Jin dai shi yan jiu suo, Jin dai shi zi liao bian ji shi, and Tianjin shi li shi bo wu guan, *Mi Ji Lu Cun (Collections of Secret Documents)* (Beijing: Zhongguo she hui ke xue chu ban she, 1984), 72–8; see also Chinese Delegation to the Peace Conference, "The Claim of China for Direct Restitution to Herself of the Leased Territory of Kiaochow, the Tsingtao-Chinan Railway and Other German Rights in Respect of Shantung Province," Paris, February 1919, in Manuscript Division, Library of Congress: Woodrow Wilson Papers (hereafter cited as Wilson Papers), Ser. 6: Peace Conference Documents, 6F/China/reel 461.

[66] *The New York Times*, February 2, 1919.

[67] Jordan to Curzon, May 10, 1919, in Kenneth Bourne, ed., *British Documents on Foreign Affairs: Reports and Papers from the Foreign Office Confidential Print*, vol. 23: *China, January 1919–December 1920* (Frederick, MD: University Publications of America, 1994), 63.

a member of the American delegation, thought that Koo had simply overwhelmed the Japanese. Clemenceau, who was, as a rule, not given to praise and quite cynical, described Koo as "a young Chinese cat, Parisian of speech and dress, absorbed in the pleasure of patting and pawing the mouse, even if this was reserved for the Japanese."[68]

But if they were thwarted in their diplomatic goals, the Chinese in Paris nonetheless succeeded in making substantial contributions to the League of Nations and the cause of national self-determination.[69] China had perhaps the strongest faith in the League's underlying vision. At home and overseas, the Chinese had formed societies to study the issue and support that cause. On January 25, when a resolution for the creation of a commission on the subject was under discussion, China's chief delegate, Lu Zhengxiang, declared that China supported the establishment of the League of Nations "wholeheartedly."[70] Wellington Koo also told the conference assembly that "just as no people have been more eager to see the formation of a League of Nations than the people of China, so no people are more gratified than we are to note the distinct step of progress made by the commission of the League of Nations."[71]

Strong belief in the League motivated the Chinese to take an active role in its creation and to make it work in China's interest. Koo, as a member of the original committee of fifteen who drafted a covenant for the League, contributed considerably. For example, Koo made a suggestion about Article 15 that one American legal advisor called "very interesting." Wilson's original paragraph reads, "If the difference between the Body of Delegates be a question which by international law is solely within the domestic legislative jurisdiction of one of the parties, it shall so report, and shall make no recommendation as to its settlement." Koo proposed adding the following language: "unless a recommendation is desired by the party within whose exclusive jurisdiction the question lies." The drafting committee accepted the amendment. David Miller, who was the legal advisor to American delegation to the peace conference, understood Koo's proposal to be a natural Chinese reaction to past foreign interference with Chinese internal affairs.[72] An American amendment to Article 10, which reads "Nothing in this Covenant shall be deemed to affect the validity of international engagements such as treaties of arbitration or regional understandings like the Monroe Doctrine for securing the maintenance of peace," caused Koo to protest. "I do not wish to be understood as opposing the introduction of this amendment. I approve of it in principle, but I should like to suggest that the Monroe Doctrine should be named specifically and alone in this

---

[68] MacMillan, *Paris 1919*, 331.

[69] For the most recent study on China and the League of Nations, see Tang Qihua, *Beijing Zheng Fu Yu Guo Ji Lian Meng, 1919–1928 (The Beijing Government and the League of Nations)* (Taipei: Dong da tu shu gong si, 1998); Zhang Li, *Guo Ji He Zuo Zai Zhongguo: Guo Ji Lian Meng Jiao Se De Kao Cha, 1919–1946 (China's international cooperation)* (Taipei: Zhong Yang Yan Jiu Yuan Jin Dai Shi Yan Jiu Suo Zhuan Kan, 1999).

[70] Department of State, *FRUS: The Paris Peace Conference, 1919*, 1: 186.

[71] Wellington Koo et al., *China and the League of Nations* (London: G. Allen & Unwin Ltd., 1919), 3–5.

[72] David Hunter Miller, *The Drafting of the Covenant* (New York: G. P. Putnam's Sons, 1928), 1: 331–2.

article and not made one of a class of 'regional understandings.'" Koo, of course, did not want Japan to use the amendment as a precedent for a similar Japanese doctrine, and therefore wanted to cut the words "regional understandings" or at least "regional."[73] Koo persisted in trying to convince the Americans of the necessity of changing this wording, but did not succeed.[74] Although the amendment was finally adopted as originally drafted, Koo's suggestion did receive favorable consideration in discussions of Article 20, which again included the words "or understandings." There was again some discussion of the Monroe Doctrine, and it was agreed that it would be impossible to put in a reservation for that doctrine without a similar reservation for an as-yet-unformulated Asiatic doctrine of the Japanese. In the end, the idea was not approved.[75] Clearly, China was not only interested in the League of Nations, it also contributed to turning the League of Nations into a reality. As early as March 24, 1919, when Wilson met with Koo, Liang Qichao, and Carson Chang in Paris, he personally acknowledged that China was "taking a part in its [the League of Nations'] formation."[76]

Many other Chinese besides Koo shared their ideas with the Americans and occasionally inserted suggestions into American proposals. Members of the American delegation were friendly and helpful to the Chinese, and the two sides cooperated informally in many ways. Americans provided much valuable advice to the Chinese delegates, especially when they engaged in their battle to revise the peace treaty once the major Powers awarded Shandong to Japan.[77] According to Ray Stannard Baker, who was Wilson's personal secretary, the Chinese delegate Wei Chenzu "blew into our offices as breezily every day or so as any American and was on familiar terms with everyone." Even before the conference started, Koo contacted David Miller and told him that he would like to consult with Miller informally from time to time in advance of formal communications between the two governments. Miller informed him that this would be "entirely agreeable."[78] Many Chinese proposals were discussed with the Americans informally before they were submitted. For example, on January 22, 1919, Wang Zhengting had lunch with Americans such as Miller and James T. Shotwell, a Columbia University history professor and director of research at the Carnegie Endowment for International Peace, to discuss his proposal for dealing with China's past treaties with Germany and Austria. Shotwell suggested that Wang add an item claiming restitution to China for the looting of Peking in 1900. This suggestion eventually resulted in Article 131 of the Treaty of Versailles, which restored to China the astronomical instruments used by the Jesuits at the Qing dynasty court.[79] Miller also suggested that China "might properly present her whole case rather than

[73] Miller, *The Drafting of the Covenant*, 1: 442–50.

[74] Miller, *The Drafting of the Covenant*, 1: 453.

[75] Miller, *My Diary at the Conference of Paris*, 1: 187–8.

[76] Link, ed., *The Papers of Woodrow Wilson*, 57: 635.

[77] For this point, see Gu Wijun, *Gu weijun huiyilu (Wellington Koo Memoir)*, Vol. 1 (Beijing: Zhonghua shu ju, 1983), 200.

[78] Miller, *My Diary at the Conference of Paris*, 1: 60.

[79] James T. Shotwell, *At the Paris Peace Conference* (New York: Macmillan, 1937), 136–9.

simply the part of it which related to Germany and Austria as the matter was bound up with her relations with Japan and the Allies in the West."[80]

China's key goals flew in the face of Japanese objectives. The recovery of Shandong, which the Japanese saw as the "artery" pumping Japanese power into the Asian mainland, was simply impossible, given the Japanese determination to become an imperial power. The upshot of this failure would soon play out across China and have serious consequences for developments during the rest of the twentieth century.

Still, China's failure at Paris did not mean total defeat. For the first time, Chinese voices gripped the world's attention, and the world finally got a sense of what China was enduring. Yes, China failed to recover Shandong, but thanks to its opposition to the treaty, Japan was soon forced to return the territory at the Washington Conference of 1921–2. More importantly, by refusing to sign the Treaty of Versailles, China managed to negotiate the first equal treaty signed with a major Power since the Opium War. On May 20, 1921, Germany and China signed an accord that promised their relations "must rest on the principles of perfect equality and absolute reciprocity in accordance with the rules of the general law of nations." Germany "agrees to the abrogation of consular jurisdiction in China, relinquishes in favor of China all the rights that the German government possesses."[81] With this treaty, China arguably scored a diplomatic success. China and Germany, both deeply disappointed with the Treaty of Versailles and the shape of the new world order, were determined to turn a new page in their relations after 1921. To a great extent, this explains why Germany enjoyed good relations with China throughout the 1920s and 1930s. The Sino-German Treaty was not an isolated event, but reflected a new Chinese stance in its international relations. In the wake of the peace conference, China's broader interactions with other nations consistently pursued the recovery of national sovereignty and the status of an equal and active member of the family of nations. China used the Great War as a springboard for national renewal. The major Powers' decision to satisfy Japan also sparked the May Fourth Movement, a key turning point in modern China's national development, as we will now see.

CHINESE DISILLUSIONMENT WITH THE WEST AND THE MAY FOURTH MOVEMENT

The Chinese delegation deliberated over whether to sign the peace treaty. On May 14, 1919, Lu Zhengxiang wrote to President Xu Shichang for instructions. In his telegram, Lu admitted, "I signed the 1915 treaty [with Japan]. If I have any conscience, I will not sign this new treaty.... With public opinion in China now tremendously aroused, I am very reluctant to sign for fear of future criticism."[82]

---

[80] Miller, *My Diary at the Conference of Paris*, diary entry of January 22, 1919, 1:88.
[81] The Carnegie Endowment for International Peace, ed., *Shantung: Treaties and Agreements* (Washington, DC: The Carnegie Endowment for International Peace, 1921), 116–17.
[82] Luo Guang, *Lu Zhengxiang Zhuan (Biography of Lu Zhengxian)*, 113.

Lu laid out a clear connection between China's war aims and postwar policy and its relations with Japan. Wellington Koo even told Colonel House on May 9, 1919 that he might not sign the peace treaty, which was so unfair to China. "If he signed it," Koo informed the American, "It would be my death sentence," since he knew the Chinese would not accept the treaty.[83] Given all that had happened to them—their plea for the direct return of Shandong having fallen on deaf ears, their proposal for a revision about China's reservation on the peace treaty having been summarily rejected, their request for lodging a reservation being turned down, and now their plea to make a declaration being brusquely disregarded—the Chinese felt that "the Peace Conference has denied to the Chinese Delegates the privilege of making any suggestions." Thus, there was no alternative but to refuse to sign a treaty that some of them considered China's "death warrant."[84]

It had never occurred to the Powers that a weak China might dare to stand up to them. Balfour for one had not reckoned on China being the only country to refuse the treaty. He wrote to Jordan, "I sincerely hope that [the] Chinese government will not do anything foolish and likely to alienate sympathies of the Allies such as refusing to sign the treaty."[85] He could not have known that the Chinese delegation had determined not to sign the treaty unless some sort of reservation was allowed. According to Koo, "There was no doubt consensus of opinion among the delegates that without a reservation we should not sign." On June 28, all members of the Chinese delegation having so decided, they absented themselves from the signing ceremony. Koo remembered the day as more than merely sad: "It was a memorable day for me and for the whole delegation and for China. China's absence must have been a surprise if not a shock to the Conference, to the diplomatic world in France, and to the entire world beyond."[86] In his official memorandum to the conference, Koo observed, "China is now at a parting of the ways. She has come to the West for justice. If she should fail to get it, the people would perhaps attribute its failure not so much to Japan's insistence on her own claims as to the attitude of the West which declined to lend a helping hand to China merely because some of its leading Powers had privately pledged to support Japan."[87] By refusing to compromise on the Shandong issue and by its refusal to sign the Treaty of Versailles, China had succeeded in forcing the world to take notice of its situation and set the stage for the favorable resolution of the Shandong problem at the Washington Conference in 1921–2. From this perspective, Koo later wrote that China's refusal to sign the Treaty of Versailles was an extremely important step in its national and diplomatic development.[88] Even Wilson understood the enormous implication of the Chinese

[83] Bonsal, *Suitors and Suppliants*, 244.

[84] The Diplomatic Association, "China at the Peace Conference," in *Far Eastern Political Science Review* (August 1919), 141.

[85] FO to Jordan, May 21, 1919, BA: FO 371/3683/16.

[86] Koo Memoir (Columbia University Oral History Project), reel 2/vol. 2.

[87] Chinese memorandum, April 23, 1919, in Wilson Papers, Ser. 6: Peace Conference documents, 6A/minutes; see also Jin, *China at the Paris Peace Conference*, 22; and Chinese Delegation's Memorandum to the Conference, Paris, April 23, 1919, in Quai d'Orsay, A-Paix, vol. 198, microfilm no. 1515, 116–18.

[88] Gu Weijun, "Bali Hehui De Huiyi," *Zhuanji wenxue*, 7:6 (1965).

refusal. When Wilson found out that the Chinese did not sign the peace treaty, he was deeply worried. He told Robert Lansing that "That is most serious. It will cause grave complications."[89] He was clearly right on this prediction, but it was too late for him.

China's failure to regain Shandong led to an outburst of anger by influential Chinese against the United States and Wilson. The bitter reality also forced China to recognize that power still prevailed over justice and right. They complained that Wilson's new world order had not come to China.[90] This so-called new order, wrote one Chinese pamphleteer, was "admittedly sound, but up to the present all that China has received is the vibration of the sound but not the application of the principles."[91] One newspaper article published in Jinan, the capital of Shandong Province, commented that the United States only "pretended to love peace and justice. It actually has a wolf's heart." The same newspaper attacked Wilson personally the next day, calling him a "hypocrite," "useless," and "selfish."[92] Mao Zedong, who had once dreamed of a close relationship with the United States, had had high hopes for the Paris Conference. But after the betrayal of Versailles, he concluded that "in foreign affairs all past alliances or Ententes were the union of international bullies," and only revolution could rectify the irrational and unjust international system.[93] In an article he wrote on the treaty, Mao described Wilson in Paris as behaving "like an ant on a hot skillet":

> He didn't know what to do. He was surrounded by thieves like Clemenceau, Lloyd George, Makino, and Orlando. He heard nothing except accounts of receiving certain amounts of territory and of reparations worth so much in gold. He did nothing except to attend various kinds of meetings where he could not speak his mind. . . . I felt sorry for him for a long time. Poor Wilson![94]

As for Chen Duxiu, soon to turn to Marxism, he now saw Wilson as an "empty cannon" whose principles were "not worth one penny."[95] Chen wrote: "It is still a bandits' and robbers' world, it is still a world where justice is overpowered by might."[96] Students across China openly expressed their disappointment at the failure of Wilsonianism. At Peking University, some cynically joked that Wilson

---

[89] Link, ed., *The Papers of Woodrow Wilson*, 61: 326.

[90] Wilson himself actually realized the challenge to achieve his ideals. As early as November 26, 1918, Wilson personally told Wellington Koo that "it was comparatively easy to form principles for a peace, but their practical application was quite a task." See Link, ed., *The Papers of Woodrow Wilson*, 57: 632.

[91] Chinese Patriotic Committee, New York City, "Might or Right? The Fourteen Points and the Disposition of Kiao-Chau," May 1918, National Archive, State Department Records Relating to the Political Relations between China and Other States, 7-18-5/m341/roll 27/743.94/875.

[92] *Jinan Ribao* (*Jinan Daily*), May 16, 17, 1919, Clips in National Archive, State Department Records Relating to the Political Relations between China and Other States, 7-18-5/m341/roll 28.

[93] Mao Zedong, "The Great Union of the Popular Masses (1), July 21, 1919," in Schram, *Mao's Road to Power*, 1: 378–81.

[94] Mao, "Poor Wilson, July 14, 1919," in Schram, *Mao's Road to Power*, 1: 338.

[95] *Meizhou Ping lun*, 20 (May 4, 1919).

[96] Chen Duxiu, "Wei Shandong wenti jinggao ge fangmian" ("Our Position on the Shangdong Issue"), in *Duxiu Wencun* (*Surviving Writings of Chen Duxiu*) (Hong Kong: Xianggang yuandong tushu gongsi, 1965), 2: 629.

had discovered a jolting new formula with his Fourteen Principles and idealistic world order: "14 = 0."[97] Even the American philosopher John Dewey, who was in China at the time, supported the decision not to sign the treaty.[98] In a letter of July 2, Dewey wrote: "Today the report is that the Chinese delegates refused to sign the Paris treaty; the news seems too good to be true, but nobody can learn the facts."[99] "You can't imagine what it means here for China not to have signed. The entire government has been for it—the President up to ten days before the signing said it was necessary. It was a victory for public opinion, and all set going by these little schoolboys and girls. Certainly the United States ought to be ashamed when China can do a thing of this sort."[100]

These "little schoolboys and girls," as Dewey admiringly but condescendingly called them, led protests that would galvanize into a larger political and social movement and lead to the downfall of the Chinese liberal republic and its replacement by a Leninist party state.[101] Student groups in Peking had planned a march on May 7 in support of the March First Korean student movement for independence, but once news of the failure to win back Shandong reached Chinese shores, they decided not to wait. On May 4, over 3,000 students from across Peking rallied and tried to meet with the Allied diplomats in the capital to appeal to them on their country's behalf.[102] Chinese trust in the West was soon replaced by feelings of betrayal and disillusionment, and by a determination to find their own way.[103] Thus, the May Fourth Movement marked the end of China's all-out efforts to join the liberal Western system, efforts that had begun when it sought to join the First World War. The movement explicitly linked Chinese domestic politics to international affairs and launched China's search for an alternative world order and its place there.[104] The movement conceived itself as the product of a double betrayal and a huge identity vacuum: having first rejected their own traditions

[97] Zhong Guo She hui ko xue yuan Jing dai shi yan jiu so, ed., *Wu Si Yun Dong Hui Yi Lu* (*Recollections of the May Fourth Movement*) (Beijing: Zhong guo she hui ko xue chu ban she, 1979), 1: 222.

[98] For details on Dewey in China, see Xu, *Chinese and Americans*.

[99] John Dewey, Alice Dewey, and Evelyn Dewey, *Letters from China and Japan* (New York: E. P. Dutton Company, 1920), 258–9.

[100] Dewey, *Letters from Japan and China*, 266.

[101] John Fitzgerald, *Big White Lie: Chinese Australians in White Australia* (Sydney: University of New South Wales Press, 2007), 230.

[102] Liang Jingqun, "Wo Su Zhidao De Wusi Yundun," *Zhuanji wenxue*, 8:5 (1966).

[103] For the broad impact of the May Fourth Movement in Chinese history, see Rana Mitter, *A Bitter Revolution: China's Struggle with the Modern World* (Oxford: Oxford University Press, 2004).

[104] The best studies on the May Fourth Movement include the following books: Chow Tse-Tsung, *The May Fourth Movement: Intellectual Revolution in Modern China* (Cambridge, MA: Harvard University Press, 1960); Benjamin I. Schwartz and Charlotte Furth, eds., *Reflections on the May Fourth Movement: A Symposium* (Cambridge, MA: Harvard University Press, 1972); Lin Yu-sheng, *The Crisis of Chinese Consciousness: Radical Anti-traditionalism in the May Fourth Era* (Madison, WI: University of Wisconsin Press, 1979); Vera Schwarcz, *The Chinese Enlightenment: Intellectuals and the Legacy of the May Fourth Movement of 1919* (Berkeley: University of California Press, 1986); Yeh Wen-Hsin, *Provincial Passages: Culture, Space, and the Origins of Chinese Communism* (Berkeley: University of California Press, 1996); Chen Mao, *Between Tradition and Change: The Hermeneutics of May Fourth Literature* (Lanham, MD: University Press of America, 1997); and Milena Dolezelová-Velingerová, Oldrich Král, and Graham Martin Sanders. *The Appropriation of Cultural Capital: China's May Fourth Movement* (Cambridge, MA: Harvard University Asia Center, 2001).

and civilization, the Chinese found their aspirations thwarted by the West; China had become a country without roots or external support. According to Zhang Yongjin, the May Fourth Movement successfully transferred Chinese "discontent into a national rejection of an international order imposed upon China by the Powers."[105] This double betrayal compelled the Chinese to confront challenging questions: what did it now mean to be Chinese? Where was the country heading? What values should the Chinese government adopt? In short, what shape should China's national identity take? Thus, the key theme of May Fourth was "recreating civilization."[106] The great modernist writer Lu Xun compared his countrymen to people sleeping in a house made of iron. The house was on fire and the sleepers would die unless they woke up. But if they did wake, would they be able to get out? Was it better to let them perish in ignorance or die in the full knowledge of their fate? For all their doubts, Lu Xun and other radical intellectuals of his generation did try to wake China; they made it their responsibility to speed change by clearing away the debris of the past and forcing the Chinese to look to the future. They published journals with names such as *New Youth* and *New Tide*. They wrote satirical plays and stories scorning tradition. Their prescription for China was summed up in a slogan touting "Mr. Science and Mr. Democracy"—with science representing reason and technology, while democracy was what they thought China needed to create unity between the government and the people, and thus make China strong.

During the era of the First World War but before their betrayal in Paris, the Chinese had experienced something of a national euphoria stemming from expectations of renewal and full dignity in the new world order. But the May Fourth Movement prompted their search for a third way, a way between Western ideas and Chinese traditional culture. Zhang Dongsun (1886–1973) declared that the First World War indicated the collapse of the "second civilization" (the West),[107] and he advocated a "third civilization," by way of the introduction of socialism. Li Dazhao agreed. He argued that Russia, geographically and culturally situated at the intersection of Europe and Asia, was the only country that could undertake "the creation of a new civilization in the world that simultaneously retains the special features of eastern and western civilizations, and the talents of the European and Asian peoples."[108] For Li, the October Revolution heralded a world in which

[105] Zhang Yongjin, *China in the International System, 1918–20: The Middle Kingdom at the Periphery*, 76.

[106] Chen Qitian, "Shen me shi xin wenhua de zhen jingshen" ("What Is the Real Spirit of New Culture"), in *Shaonian Zhong Guo (Young China)* 2:2 (August 1920), 2. Lucian Bianco also argues that "The importance of the May Fourth movement should by now be apparent. Intellectually, the Chinese revolution originated in the challenging of China's cultural heritage by Western civilization. The May Fourth Movement was the culmination of that challenge of the brutal, wholesale repudiation of Confucianism, the symbol of Chinese culture and Chinese history." Lucian Bianco, *Origins of the Chinese Revolution, 1915–1949* (Stanford, CA: Stanford University Press, 1971), 28.

[107] "Xuan yan" (Declaration), "Di san zhong wen min" ("The Third Civilization"), and "Zhong guo zhi qiantu: de guo hu? Wo guo hu?" ("Model for China; Germany or Russia?"), in *Jie fang yu Gai zhao (Liberation and Reform)*, 1 (1919); 2:14 (July 15, 1920).

[108] Quote from Maurice Meisner, *Li Ta-Chao and the Origins of Chinese Marxism* (Cambridge, MA: Harvard University Press, 1967), 46–7, 64.

weak nations would regain their independence.[109] At this point, Mao Zedong, then just another young educated Chinese person from the provinces, concluded that Russia was "the number one civilized country in the world."[110]

This convergence, or perhaps clash, of events explains why many Chinese, in the wake of their disillusionment with the West, responded enthusiastically to Russian diplomatic initiatives. The Russian Revolution offered an example of a traditional society, not unlike China's, which had apparently skipped ahead to the future in one bold and glorious move. In light of their dismal experience with Western-style democracy after 1911, their rejection of Confucian tradition, and their disappointment after the war, the Chinese saw the clear alternative presented by communism as the solution to China's problems.

Further confirmation came in an unprecedented gesture by the new Bolshevik commissioner for foreign affairs, who offered in the summer of 1919 to give up all the territories and concessions squeezed out of China in the days of the tsars.[111] The young Chinese admired Soviet Russia, not only because it had declared its intention to relinquish its unequal rights in China, but more importantly, because the Russians had showed a spirit of humanism and internationalism contrary to the power politics of the West.[112] Russia's denunciation of imperialism and secret diplomacy struck a deep chord in China. Russia's diplomatic initiatives demonstrated more than the empty promises of the West. Soon, the Chinese Communist Party was founded under Russian direction in 1921. Many of the leading demonstrators from May 1919 were to become members. The dean of humanities who had handed out leaflets was the party's first chairman. Sun Yat-sen's Guomindang (Nationalist Party) also aligned itself with Russia in the early 1920s.[113] As Benjamin Schwartz explains, "Paradoxically, one can actually assert that one of the main appeals of Marxism-Leninism to young Chinese was its appeal to nationalistic resentments. The Leninist theory of nationalism provided a plausible explanation for China's failure to achieve its rightful place in the world of nations."[114]

Even as it embraced this new way to define its position in the world, China remained part of the trend to internationalization and still looked to the West. Socialism, after all, is a Western idea. Moreover, interest in socialism was a global phenomenon in the wake of the Great War. The American people in 1919 were "eagerly urged into what are called socialistic experiments."[115] Arif Dirlik points to

---

[109] Hans J. Van de Ven, *From Friend to Comrade: The Founding of Chinese Communist Party, 1920–1927* (Berkeley: University of California press, 1991). 27–8.

[110] John King Fairbank and Albert Feuerwerker, ed., *The Cambridge History of China: 1912–1949* (Cambridge: Cambridge University Press, 1986), 13, 802.

[111] For the record, the Bolshevik government never actually delivered on that promise, but the Chinese at the time were deeply impressed by a generosity that no other power showed to them.

[112] *Shaonian Zhong Guo (Young China)*, 2:2, 2.

[113] Regarding Sino-Russo relations in the 1920s, please see Akira Iriye, *After Imperialism: The Search for a New Order in the Far East, 1921–1931* (Chicago: Imprint Publications, 1990).

[114] Benjamin I. Schwartz, "Chinese Perception of World Order," in John K. Fairbank, ed., *The Chinese World Order: Traditional China's Foreign Relations* (Cambridge, MA: Harvard University Press, 1968), 286.

[115] Albert W. Atwood, "Our Forgotten Socialism," *The Saturday Evening Post*, 192:4 (1919), 16.

the kinds of experiences China shared with the rest of the world. He wrote that for Chinese intellectuals, socialism already appeared "as a rising world tide in the aftermath of World War I, as was dramatized in the worldwide proliferation of revolutionary social movements of which the Russian revolution was the most prominent."[116] The emergence of a communist movement in China, according to Dirlik, "resulted from a conjuncture of internal and external developments. In 1918–19, socialism appeared as a world political tide, nourished by the successful October Revolution in Russia, labor, and social revolutionary movements in Europe and North America, and national liberation movements in colonial societies that found inspiration in socialist ideas."[117] In other words, though China decided against aligning itself with the capitalist West, the Chinese were still motivated by a Western sense of internationalization. For instance, China remained committed to its membership in the League of Nations even after its failure to get back Shandong. Sir Beilby Alston, Jordan's successor in China, was right when he wrote to Lord Curzon in his 1920 annual report: "The rising tide of international esteem began to flow when China refused, weak as she was, to be bullied into signing the treaty of Versailles. Though the momentary political victory at that time went to Japan, the moral victory remained with China, and has since culminated in her obtaining one of the temporary seats on the Council of the League of Nations."[118]

The May Fourth Movement in China sparked a series of anti-Japanese protests and a boycott of Japanese goods. Katō Takaaki, the aristocratic president of the Kenseikai, a Japanese opposition party, who as foreign minister had issued the Twenty-one Demands in 1915, demanded that the Japanese government force the Chinese government to suppress the anti-Japanese boycotts. "If the Chinese government is too weak to suppress it," Katō declared, "then the Japanese government should use our military force on behalf of the Chinese government." Anti-Japanese boycotts continued on and off until 1923 and started to die down after 1924. The direct cause was the great earthquake in Japan in 1923. On September 11, 1923, Ito Takeo, chief of the Peking branch office of the South Manchuria Railway, observed: "There is no room to doubt the sincerity of the sympathy shown by various societies in Peking for the difficulties the great earthquake has caused the Japanese people." The Chinese were simply too humane to continue the boycotts in the face of this great disaster.[119]

JAPANESE DISAPPOINTMENTS

Japan had won what it wanted most: Great Power status and Shandong. Even so, the Japanese came away disappointed with the gathering and with the results of the

---

[116] Arif Dirlik, *The Origins of Chinese Communism* (New York: Oxford University Press, 1989), 142.

[117] Dirlik, *The Origins of Chinese Communism*, 253.

[118] Alston to Lord Curzon: 1920 Annual Report, BA: FO 405/229/2.

[119] Banno Junji, "Japanese Industrialists and Merchants and the Anti-Japanese Boycotts in China, 1919–1928," in Peter Duus, Ramon Hawley Myers, and Mark R. Peattie, eds., *The Japanese Informal Empire in China, 1895–1937* (Princeton, NJ: Princeton University Press, 1989), 316–21.

Great War. Many in Japan were critical of their delegates to Paris and the delegates acknowledged their failures. Baron Saionji apologized in his formal report to the emperor: "I am sad that we could not accomplish our wishes in total."[120] There was a widespread feeling that Japan, as in 1895 and 1905, had been outmaneuvered by the Europeans and Americans. Japan had sustained deep wounds to its pride from the world's questioning its intentions in China and Korea, which had put them on moral trial. The Japanese were also embarrassed by the May Fourth Movement in China and the March First Movement in Korea. These humiliations suggest why Japan later developed a go-alone policy and pursued direct expansion into China. What happened in Paris reinforced the Japanese impression that Japan could not get what it wished from the West through peaceful negotiations—"and laid the ground for the Japanese invasion of Manchuria in the 1930s."[121] Japan remained outside the white power club and continued to share second-class status with fellow Asians. Japanese disillusionment extended to both the domestic and external fronts: how the Japanese polity should be shaped; how to deal with the League of Nations, and what to do about Japan's growing isolation in the face of increased Anglo-American solidarity in East Asia and the Pacific. The racial equality issue and the 1924 US Alien Immigration Act also led to a deep sense of disappointment, an area I will discuss in Chapter 7.[122]

Postwar Japan faced a national identity crisis. In the nineteenth century, Japan had proclaimed itself a "pioneer of progress in the Orient" for her successful adoption of the trappings of Western civilization. Official German–Japanese relations went back to 1861, when the Prussian court sent an expedition to Japan and concluded their first bilateral treaty between the nations, and when Prussia engineered the creation of the German nation in 1871, German prestige rose even higher. If China was Japan's former teacher, Germany became the new *sensei*. Japan copied the new German political system, the German constitution, and its military training system. Not long after the Meiji Restoration, the Japanese government expressed its strong desire to "seek close ties with the German Reich and to beg His Majesty the Emperor Wilhelm's government for its special friendship and for its support of Japan in her present difficult period of development."[123] The new Japanese national regime tried to restrict public life and institutions after the Prussian model, including education, medicine, and science, in addition to the political and military systems. As Bernd Martin points out, "The option was clear; in the young and aspiring German Empire the Japanese saw the model of an orderly and politically stable society, or patriotism and, of course, the people's loyalty towards their monarch."[124] In 1882, Ito Hirobumi, the future four-time Japanese prime minister, spent three months in Berlin attending lectures and talking with politicians. Although in 1895 Germany joined the Triple Intervention against

[120] Klaus Schlichtmann, *Japan in the World: Shidehara Kijuro, Pacifism, and the Abolition of War* (Lanham, MD: Lexington Books, 2009), 124.

[121] Mee, *The End of Order*, 191.

[122] Shimazu, *Japan, Race, and Equality*, 171.

[123] Bernd Martin, *Japan and Germany in the Modern World* (Providence: Berghahn Books, 1995), 32.

[124] Martin, *Japan and Germany in the Modern World*, 35.

Japanese territorial gains, which put a damper on the friendship between the two countries, "Meiji Japan had put on a German corset—by taking it off now she would have run the risk of collapsing."[125]

The result of the Great War and the imposition of a new world order forced Japan to conclude that it might have followed the wrong model. Germany's defeat, the immediate revolution, the collapse of the monarchy, and the adoption of a republican constitution had fundamentally shaken Japan's faith. Although the Japanese military largely stuck to the German model, the defeat of German militarism caused many in Japan to rethink the political implications of this model. In Germany, Japan had been known as the "Prussia of the East" after its defeat of China in 1895. After the First World War, one historian wrote: "Accepting the victorious Anglo-Saxon powers' political system would have implied granting more rights to subjects in domestic politics and, in foreign politics, acknowledging the new international order. Both things seemed equally inconceivable to the Japanese. What 'Versailles' was to the Germans, 'Washington' was to them: establishing the political and mercantile predominance of the Anglo-Saxon powers."[126] In domestic politics too, the Japanese parliamentary system during the Meiji period was shot through with German concepts of control. After the war, politics moved outside the circle of emperor, court, and parliament into the electoral system. Parties became more popular, volatile, corrupt, and nationalist. Politicians now had to defend themselves to voters, not to the emperor and their peers.

The Great War markedly increased the Japanese sense of diplomatic isolation. Yukio Ozaki, who was Minister of Justice in the last Okuma Cabinet and known for his progressive thought, said: "Nowhere is a foreign country to be found which will befriend Japan." He claimed that the process "has certainly been a long one; but it has been greatly accelerated by the war, notwithstanding the fact that Japan participated in the latter and sent ships to the Mediterranean Sea to assist the Allies." In Ozaki's view, Japan

> is isolated and solitary, victim within her own borders to the rule of a small oligarchy of bureaucrats and militarists, and beset with labour troubles, unrest in Korea, and domestic difficulties of various kinds; she is weak in armaments, lacking in economic strength, and without intellectual acquisitions; yet she stands opposed to the two strongest nations of the world, and her people pride themselves that she is one of the five Great Powers. It recalls the days when, at Kagoshimi and Shimonoseki, their fathers fought the foreign ships with bows and arrows.[127]

Prince Konoe Fumimaro, a twenty-seven-year-old aristocrat, perhaps expressed the deep sense of disappointment after the Great War the best. In his famous essay, titled "Reject the Anglo-American-Centered Peace," which he wrote when the war was almost over and published in the December 15, 1918 issue of the leading

---

[125] Martin, *Japan and Germany in the Modern World*, 52.
[126] Martin, *Japan and Germany in the Modern World*, 53.
[127] British Embassy, Tokyo, March 21, 1919, BA: FO 608/211.

nationalistic journal *Nihon Oyobi Nihonjin* (Japan and the Japanese), he argued that
the so-called "peace" being proposed at the postwar peace conference was nothing
but maintenance of a status quo that served the interests of the Anglo-American
powers. He was worried that the Anglo-American-centered League of Nations
would do no good for Japan, since the Western Powers would only use it to sanctify
their own interests in the name of humanity. Konoe further suggested that the true
nature of the conflict was actually a struggle between the established powers and
powers not yet established—a struggle between those nations that benefited by
maintaining the status quo and those nations which would benefit by its destruction. The former nations called for peace, and the latter cried for war. In this case,
pacifism did not necessarily coincide with justice and humanity, and militarism did
not necessarily transgress justice and humanity. Konoe's article argued that the
position of Japan in the world, like that of Germany before the war, demanded the
destruction of the status quo. He suggested that in the coming peace conference,
Japan must not blindly submit to an Anglo-American-centered peace; it must
struggle for the fulfillment of its own demands, which were grounded in justice
and humanity.[128] According to his biographer, the ideas expressed in this essay "are
important, for they continued to influence his entire political career."[129] Saionji,
the head of the Japanese delegation, reprimanded Konoe for the article. As an
internationalist, he attached great importance to Japan's relations with Britain and
the United States.[130]

Konoe himself attended the peace conference and afterwards wrote an essay,
"My Impressions of the Paris Peace Conference." In it, he stated that the conference
only revealed the tyranny of the Great Powers. The hope to reform the world based
upon the principles of justice and equity was quashed at the outset. The League
Covenant rejected the principle of racial equality and accommodated the Monroe
Doctrine in the most brazen application of the rule "Power controls." The League
of Nations, Konoe argued, ostensibly set up to maintain world peace based on
justice, was morally obliged to incorporate the principle of racial equality into the
Covenant. But the motion was defeated because Japan, a lesser power, had
proposed it. It seemed to Konoe that Western Powers alone determined the entire
course of the peace conference. Wilson's Fourteen Points, as one example, were
trampled and largely dismissed by European politicians, who were concerned only
with the interests of their own countries. Konoe suggested that the negative results
of the peace conference amply vindicated the view he expounded in his controver-
sial "Reject the Anglo-American-Centered Peace" article.[131] When Konoe returned
to Japan, he found it a sad country. "Everything I see and hear makes me
unhappy."[132] He was clearly disappointed with the postwar world order.

---

[128] Yoshitake Oka, *Konoe Fumimaro: A Political Biography*, trans. by Shumpei Okamoto and
Patricia Murray (Tokyo: University of Tokyo Press, 1983), 10–13.
[129] Oka, *Konoe Fumimaro*, 13.   [130] Oka, *Konoe Fumimaro*, 14.
[131] Oka, *Konoe Fumimaro*, 14–15.   [132] Oka, *Konoe Fumimaro*, 17.

Although Saionji pointed out that Japan's postwar standing in the world was higher than it had been in 1914, one Japanese wrote from Paris: "We are now again disliked by the Powers. Our people again have occasion to sleep on firewood and eat gall.... The League of Nations aims at equality and peace among all nations. Yet it refuses to abolish race discrimination.... By all means it is necessary for us, if this proposition fails, to urge our representatives at Paris to withdraw, and to take up immediately as a people the duty of preparing for revenge ([i.e.] sleeping on firewood and eating gall)."[133]

The Japanese delegates came away from Paris convinced that the United States was out to stop them in China and that the world did not trust Japan. Probably the ultimate reason for Japanese-American disagreements at Paris was "the dichotomy between Wilsonian universalism and unilateralism and... an incipient particularistic regionalism and pluralism which arose from Japanese leaders' perception of the unique position of their own country in East Asia."[134] In November 1918, Japanese Foreign Minister Uchida Yasuya drafted a personal memorandum on Wilson's Fourteen Points as a sort of rough plan for Japanese delegates at the peace conference. Trained under, and a believer in, the principle of old diplomacy and secret diplomacy, he continued to believe that "there are cases in which it is suitable to keep secret the progress of negotiations." He also did not think it was a good idea to remove economic barriers, stating that "it is difficult to say yes or no unless there is discussion of the details of concrete provisions." He did not want armament reduction either and thought it was "inadvisable to be restrained" by arms limitations. However, he also realized that the wind had blown a different way now with rise of the US and Wilsonianism. It seemed to him that "The League of Nations is one of the most important problems and the Japanese government supports its ultimate objective. However, because there still exists racial prejudice between nations today, it is a concern that the methods used to achieve the League objective might cause disadvantages to the Empire."[135] It was no surprise that he became disappointed with Wilson's cherished idea. In these respects, the United States and Japan stood far apart in their views of the world when hostilities in Europe came to an end. Wilson preferred a new world order based on new diplomacy, while Japan tried hard to stick to old diplomacy and imperialism. Edward T. Williams, a Far Eastern technical expert of the American mission, commented that "Japan's objective had been to dominate Asia, and the present cabinet of Takashi Hara is no exception." Williams concluded that "Japan must be restrained if justice is to prevail or liberty survive in the Far East."[136]

According to Harvard historian Akira Iriye, "The main challenge facing Japanese diplomacy after the World War was how best to define its ideological foundations now that the old diplomacy of imperialism was giving way to novel approaches

[133] Ku, *Korea Under Colonialism*, 101.   [134] Kawamura, *Turbulence in the Pacific*, 133.
[135] Rustin Gates, "Out with the New and In with the Old: Uchida Yasuya and the Great War as a Turning Point in Japanese Foreign Affairs," in Toshiro Minohara, Tze-Ki Hon, and Evan N. Dawley, eds., *The Decade of the Great War: Japan and the Wider World in the 1910s* (Leiden: Brill, 2014), 71.
[136] Kawamura, *Turbulence in the Pacific*, 137.

being promoted by the United States, Russia, China and other countries."[137] For one, the postwar American policy was to re-establish order and stability in East Asia, which mandated Japan returning Shandong to China. The Americans also wanted to demolish the existing system of imperialist diplomacy in East Asia. This seemed specifically to target the Japanese.[138] The Anglo-Japanese alliance, which was a cornerstone of Japanese diplomacy since 1902, was abolished. According to Iriye, Japan's participation in the four-power and the nine-power treaties indicated that it was persuaded to recognize the passing of the diplomacy of imperialism.[139] For prominent Japanese historian Nobutoshi Hagihara, the old "center" for Japan was the British Empire, but the end of the Anglo-Japanese alliance after the Great War "left Japan without a sense of direction. Japan became, or had to become, a 'quasi-center' itself and continued to impose its own imperialist designs on Korea and China."[140] Japan was clearly disappointed with the discontinuation of the jewel of its old diplomacy: the Anglo-Japanese alliance which clearly was not compatible with the ideal of the League of Nations. With this excuse, Britain dragged its feet with regard to the renewal of the alliance after the peace conference and indeed intended to terminate it. Japanese Foreign Minister Uchida Yasuya was upset when he learned of the British intention to terminate the alliance.[141] According to Tadashi Nakatani, at the peace conference, Japan tried hard to stick to the old diplomacy and "in taking this position, the peace meant only the end of the 'one chance in a thousand' to Japan."[142]

Japan's victory over Shandong proved costly. Certainly, growing Japanese ambitions in China triggered both Chinese and foreign anger and mistrust. John and Alice Dewey observed how "Japanese are in every town across China like a network closing in on fishes."[143] In a letter to their children, the Deweys reported, "The question which is asked oftenest by the [Chinese] students is in effect this: 'All of our hopes of permanent peace and internationalism having been disappointed at Paris, which has shown that might still makes right and that the strong nations get what they want at the expense of the weak. Should not China adopt militarism as part of her educational system?' "[144] Dewey wrote from Shanghai on May 12, 1919 that "American sentiment here hopes that the Senate will reject the treaty because it virtually completes the turning over of China to Japan."[145] "The apparent lie of the Japanese when they made their splurge in promising before the sitting of the peace

---

[137] Akira Iriye, *Japan and the Wider World: From the Mid-Nineteenth Century to the Present* (London: Longman, 1997), 50.

[138] Iriye, *After Imperialism*, 13–14.   [139] Iriye, *After Imperialism*, 19.

[140] Nobutoshi Hagihara, "What Japan Means to the Twentieth Century," in Nobutoshi Hagihara, Akira Iriye, Georges Nivat, and Philip Windsor, eds., *Experiencing the Twentieth Century* (Tokyo: University of Tokyo Press, 1985), 21.

[141] Rustin Gates, "Out with the New and In with the Old," in Minohara, Hon, and Dawley, eds., *The Decade of the Great War*, 75.

[142] Tadashi Nakatani, "What Peace meant to Japan: The Changeover at Paris in 1919," in Minohara, Hon, and Dawley, eds., *The Decade of the Great War*, 171–2.

[143] Dewey, *Letters from China and Japan*, 171.

[144] Dewey, *Letters from China and Japan*, 180–1.

[145] Dewey, *Letters from China and Japan*, 166–7.

conference to give back the German concessions to China is something America ought not to forget. All these, and the extreme poverty of China is what I had no idea of before coming here."[146] In another letter, he wrote:

> I didn't ever expect to be a jingo, but either the United States ought to wash its hands entirely of the Eastern question, and say "it's none of our business, fix it up yourself any way you like," or else it ought to be as positive and aggressive in calling Japan to account for every aggressive move she makes, as Japan is in doing them. It is sickening that we allow Japan to keep us on the defensive and the explanatory, and talk about the open door, when Japan has locked most of the doors in China already and got the keys in her pocket.[147]

Japan's relations with the British had been damaged, too. Japan "should exert herself for the maintenance of cordial relations with Great Britain and America, as the friendship with the two great nations is the foundation of Japan's international policy after the war," declared Marquis Okuma, the ex-premier, after the war:

> It is my opinion that the most important thing is to dispel all sorts of suspicion of the other nations toward her. Japanese activity in Siberia has caused suspicion on the part of the other Powers, and her diplomacy in China is also received with suspicion by foreigners. Such a state of affairs is indeed lamentable for the future of this country, and it is my opinion that the best and the earliest way to dispel these unnecessary suspicions is to maintain friendly relations with Great Britain and America.[148]

But after the war, the British began to rethink the future of the Anglo-Japanese alliance. The notion that Japan was a "Yellow Prussia" had taken firm root in the West. In the summer of 1919, Curzon lectured Chinda, the Japanese ambassador to London, about Japan's behavior in China. Japan had been unwise to insist on its rights in China; it had created hostility there and apprehension in Britain. Curzon urged the Japanese ambassador to think of the future of the alliance between Britain and Japan, and of the more general question of security in the Far East.[149] In 1922, Japan was forced to leave Shandong and abandon the tremendous influence it had established in China during the war. The Japanese empire was further made to consent to an "open door policy" in China that merely served the interests of the economically strongest powers, the United States and Great Britain. This pressure from the West and rising Chinese nationalism gave Japan little choice.

Even the British, who had been committed to supporting Japan, worried about what they perceived as Japanese arrogance and ambition. They were particularly concerned over Japan's inroads into their economic sphere in the Yangtze valley. The British ambassador in Tokyo warned darkly: "Today we have come to know that Japan—the real Japan—is a frankly opportunistic, not to say selfish, country, of very moderate importance compared with the giants of the Great War, but with

---

[146] Dewey, *Letters from China and Japan*, 176.
[147] Dewey, *Letters from China and Japan*, 179.
[148] "Japanese Views about Peace: Marquis Okuma on Status of Powers after the War," *The Japan Chronicle*, October 31, 1918.
[149] MacMillan, *Paris 1919*, 342.

a very exaggerated opinion of her role in the universe." Britain would not renew the Anglo-Japanese alliance after the war.[150] Japanese officials concluded with some anxiety that an Anglo-American conspiracy to isolate Japan seemed afoot; or in the stronger language of Lieutenant General Tanaka Kunishige, who had been a delegate to the peace conference, there was "an attempt to oppress the non-Anglo-Saxon races, especially the coloured races, by the two English-speaking countries, Britain and the United States."[151] Lord Curzon told the Japanese ambassador:

> In consequence of what had passed in Paris, if public opinion in general, not only in China, but in England, in America, and in other countries, were invited to express its verdict on the recent policy of Japan towards China, or on the conclusions arrived at in Paris, I did not think that its answer would be altogether favourable to the side of Japan. Personally, I had felt myself so much in sympathy with this trend of opinion that I had ventured, not indeed to express an official opinion on behalf of the British Government, but to offer advice to the Japanese Government as to the best method by which they could extricate themselves from a position which was doing no good to them and might end by doing great harm to much larger interests.[152]

The British media even questioned the Japanese contribution to the war. *The Times* wrote, "No Japanese ships were ever sunk by German U Boats," but Japan took over German assets, and used them for her own ends, while China, "For all she had done...was treated like the defeated. It is unfair."[153]

Anti-Japanese feeling certainly ran high in the United States and American-Japanese relations quickly deteriorated. Payson Treat of Stanford University, an American-Japanese relations expert, decried the "very dangerous state of mind" and "reckless criticism" in each country for the other. He pointed out that the effort to "sift out the firm facts from the chaff of suspicion and foreboding" found out "little to excite alarm, except this state of mind," but warned that "in these days when public opinion can influence chancelleries, an unwholesome state of mind is something to be feared by statesmen."[154]

When American legislators were debating how to deal with the Treaty of Versailles and whether to join the League of Nations, Japan became a key instrument with which Wilson's opponents attacked his postwar world order. American public opinion was quite critical of the Shandong decision. Headlines in the United States ran as follows: "Japan the Possessor of Stolen Goods," "The Crime of Shantung," "Far-Eastern Alsace-Lorraine," and "Sold—40,000,000 People." *The Boston Transcript* characterized the Shandong deal as "insolent and Hun-like spoliation." *The New York Call* saw it as "one of the most shameless deeds in the record of imperialistic diplomacy." *The Franklin* (Pennsylvania) *News–Herald* called it a

[150] Miller, *My Diary at the Conference of Paris*, 1: 198–9.
[151] Beasley, *Japanese Imperialism*, 167
[152] Earl Curzon to Mr. Alston, Foreign Office, July 22, 1919.
[153] *The Times*, May 27, 1919.
[154] Shoichi Saeki, "Images of the United States as a Hypothetical Enemy," in Priscilla Clapp and Akira Iriye, eds., *Mutual Images: Essays in American–Japanese Relations* (Harvard University Press, 1975), 105.

"damnable enterprise," an "inexcusable injustice." *The Pittsburgh Dispatch* portrayed it as a "conspiracy to rob." *The Detroit Free Press* saw the "betrayal of China to Japan as the price of the latter's adherence to the League of Nations." *The San Francisco Chronicle* described it as "an infamy."[155] As Robert Lansing commented, "The chief objections raised against the treaty in the United States have been to those articles comprising the covenant of the League of Nations and to those dealing with Shantung."[156] In 1921, the election of Warren Harding as president brought in a still more anti-Japanese American administration. Japan's already difficult relationship with the United States continued to be troubled in the 1920s by disagreements over China—over the loan consortium, for example, of which they were both members—and by continued discrimination against Japanese nationals in the United States.[157]

The Siberian intervention proved to be another major disappointment. For Japan, this was not just a matter of foreign policy, but of Japanese domestic politics under the Meiji constitution.[158] With a toll of 1,480 Japanese combat deaths and another 600 from exposure and disease, the intervention could only be judged a failure.[159] The paper *Tokyo Ashi* ruefully noted: "Compared to the Sino-Japanese and Russo-Japanese wars our pains [in Siberia] have been suffered to no good purpose. Certainly stationing troops for such a long interval has aroused the suspicions of the powers and brought the enmity of the Russian people."[160] Izumi Tetsu had finally concluded that the intervention should be abandoned because "given the great change in world thought today as a result of the Great War...we must bear in mind the danger that we would become the object of distrust by the civilized races."[161]

The widespread unpopularity of the expedition, says historian Paul Dunscomb, cast light on the relationship of the Japanese people to their empire. The public reaction revealed a willingness to downplay imperial expansion as proof of Japanese modernity and to consider instead a vision which put Japan in line with the trends of the times and the world situation.[162] The Siberian intervention, Dunscomb continues, was an important "missing link" in the development of Japanese imperialism and its domestic support system rather than an "aberration caused by a unique alignment of events." The international situation at the end of the First World War challenged assumptions about what would make Japan a powerful and modern state. The defeat of the Central Powers, the triumph of Western democratic states, and the overthrow of Russian Tsarism seemed to mark the end of an historical epoch. The apparent triumph of liberal democratic over militarist, autocratic imperialism

---

[155] "The Uproar over Shantung," *The Literary Digest*, 62:5 (1919).

[156] Robert Lansing, *The Big Four and Others of the Peace Conference* (London: Hutchinson & Co., 1922), 75.

[157] MacMillan, *Paris 1919*, 342.

[158] Paul E. Dunscomb, *Japan's Siberian Intervention: 1918–1922: A Great Disobedience Against the People* (Lanham, MD: Rowman & Littlefield, 2011), 2.

[159] Dunscomb, *Japan's Siberian Intervention*, 192.

[160] Dunscomb, *Japan's Siberian Intervention*, 215.

[161] Dunscomb, *Japan's Siberian Intervention*, 215.

[162] Dunscomb, *Japan's Siberian Intervention*, 214.

gave pause to imperial realists and even some unilateralists. The trends of the time gave new credibility to advocates who rejected the pursuit of empire through conquest in favor of cooperation with the Allies, arms limitation, and non-interference on the Asian continent. Dunscomb cites Yoshino Sakuzō, who wrote that the "new trend of the world is, in domestic policy, the perfection of democracy. In foreign policy, the establishment of international egalitarianism."[163]

In 1921, the sharp electoral instincts of Prime Minister Hara told him that Japanese imperialism had reached a critical stage:

> If the old order had truly come to an end, as the new diplomacy seemed to promise, the nation had no reason to persist in an aggressively expansionist policy. With a few adjustments, Japan might 'graciously' relinquish some of its more recent claims in China. On balance, then, moderates found the idea of accommodating the new order palatable, and the declining influence of the army made such a policy politically feasible."[164]

The prime minister and his colleagues thus pressed for a large step back from the expansionist commitments that had preoccupied a generation of national leaders. The Eastern Conference in May 1921 ratified withdrawal from Shandong and Siberia. This new policy posture soon allowed the Japanese to accept the conditions devised at the Washington Conference, which had started in November 1921. According to Dunscomb, "Anti-imperialist critiques of Japan's foreign policy, like those of the little Japanists, gained a certain degree of respectability and the new spirit of internationalism became fashionable among intellectual circles. Simultaneously the appeal of 'militarism' plunged to new lows."[165]

These tectonic shifts in the diplomatic terrain left standing the worst disappointment of the peace conference for Japan: the dismissal of its racial equality proposal by the Western Powers. That story will be told in Chapter 7.

---

[163] Dunscomb, *Japan's Siberian Intervention*, 214–15.
[164] Dunscomb, *Japan's Siberian Intervention*, 145.
[165] Dunscomb, *Japan's Siberian Intervention*, 216.

7

The Japanese Dream of Racial Equality

In 1899, the European treaty powers renounced their extraterritorial privileges in Japan, and by 1911, Japan had also won back control over its tariffs. In other words, with the "unequal treaties" completely abrogated, Japan gained recognition as a "civilized" country. In 1905, by defeating Russia, Japan had entered international society as a "civilized" power with which to be reckoned. Japan had reason to feel proud, since it was the first non-Western country to achieve "civilized" status. It took Turkey until 1923 and China until 1943 to complete their respective abrogations of extraterritoriality. Japan hoped to be finally accepted into the white man's club at the Paris Peace Conference, but the Powers summarily rejected the Japanese proposal for a racial equality clause in the Covenant for the League of Nations. Japan was forced to choose between vain attempts to promote racial equality and the gain of territory in China. According to the prominent Japanese diplomat Viscount Kikujiro Ishii, Japan had been "singled out for discrimination" after being recognized by "common consent as one of the civilized powers of the world." In other words, although Japan had fulfilled the standard of "civilization," the other "civilized" nations "were disregarding the standard in their treatment of Japan."[1] The result was trouble at home and abroad. Japanese success in the war fueled anti-Japanese feelings in the West, especially in the United States.[2] When the discredited Japanese delegation returned home, crowds protested their failure to push through the racial equality clause, undermining popular support for future cooperation with the West. Yet even in failure, the racial equality issue highlights a complex strand of history. While the Chinese, Indians, and Vietnamese all faced discrimination from Europeans, the Japanese themselves treated Koreans as an inferior people and harbored racist prejudices against the Chinese. The Japanese treatment at the Paris Conference was in many ways a continuation of the longstanding agitation against the Chinese and Japanese in the United States going back to the 1850s and the "White Australia" policies and other restrictions throughout the British Empire and Dominions.[3] The US Anti-Japanese Immigration Act of 1924 helped set the stage for the massive struggle that would follow.[4]

---

[1] Gerrit W. Gong, *The Standard of "Civilization" in International Society* (Oxford: Clarendon Press, 1984), 198–9.

[2] Roger Daniels, *The Politics of Prejudice: The Anti-Japanese Movement in California, and the Struggle for Japanese Exclusion* (Berkeley: University of California Press, 1962), 65–78.

[3] Daniels, *The Politics of Prejudice*, 16.

[4] For a recent study on this issue, see Izumi Hirobe, *Japanese Pride, American Prejudice: Modifying the Exclusion Clause of the 1924 Immigration Act* (Stanford, CA: Stanford University Press, 2001).

THE PUSH WITHIN

One might say that Japan suffered from a national inferiority complex, but that any "inferiority" was imposed from the outside. With the launching of the Meiji Restoration in 1868, reformist Japanese elites at first idealized the white race and Western civilization and openly suggested that Japan leave its Asian identity behind. Inoue Kaoru, an influential Japanese politician, declared: "We must make our nation and people into a European nation and European people."[5] Still, progressive Japanese debated whether to develop a unique national identity that would be a model for the rest of Asia or to imitate dominant white cultures, with the hope that one day Western nations would accept Japan as an equal. Japan enjoyed startling military successes, defeating China in 1895 and imperial Russia in 1905. But the Japanese faced many of the same hurdles and forms of discrimination as their fellow Asians. Even though its defeat of China made Japan an empire in typical Western fashion, the Western Powers forced the newborn empire to give back the Liaodong Peninsula. Japan joined the ranks of the major Powers in 1905, yet the Western nations still refused to even let Japanese citizens immigrate to their countries and colonies as equals, and treated the Japanese as not good enough to associate with whites, own land, or become citizens. The racism of Western countries fed the vortex of mutual distrust that led to Pearl Harbor.

One such country was the United States. According to Akira Iriye, "The self-conscious antagonism between Japanese and Americans came to a climax during World War I."[6] In 1913, the state of California passed the Alien Land Bill, which prohibited aliens who were ineligible for citizenship from owning agricultural land; the only groups in that category were the Chinese, Indians, Japanese, and Koreans. The Japanese were also an obvious target and were affected the most, given the fact that the American Congress had passed the Chinese Exclusion Act as early as 1882, followed by a series of laws tightening restrictions. A law that had been passed just one year before the First World War was renewed in 1920, one year after the conclusion of the Treaty of Versailles. The Japanese ambassador to the US, Viscount Sutemi Chinda, expressed "painful disappointment" and protested that the bill was both "unfair and discriminatory." Chinda explained that the Californian statute was "mortifying" to both his government and the people of Japan because the racial discrimination "inferable from these provisions" was hurtful to their "just national sensibilities." Japan's foreign minister, Baron Makino Nobuaki, also declared that he was unwilling to "acquiesce in the unjust and obnoxious discrimination."[7] Foreign observers in Japan noted how deeply the Californian legislation offended Japanese national sensibilities. The Tokyo-based correspondent for *The Times* reported that the issue was one "the significance of which every Japanese feels keenly." The man in the street "went straight to the root of the question" and knew that the conflict affected "the position of his race in the world."

---

[5] Iriye, *Japan and the Wider World*, 5.   [6] Iriye, *Across the Pacific*, 131.
[7] Marilyn Lake and Henry Reynolds, *Drawing the Global Colour Line: White Men's Countries and the International Challenge of Racial Equality* (Cambridge,: Cambridge University Press, 2008), 271–2.

The Californians had publicly refuted the Japanese "claim of equality with Occidentals." The cause had thus become one of national honor and feelings ran high. In 1913, the issue of racial equality was a topic of widespread discussion. Prime Minister Okuma Shigenobu told an audience at Waseda University that the "white races regard the world as their property and all other races are greatly their inferiors. They presume to think that the role of the whites in the universe is to govern the world as they please. The Japanese are a people who have suffered by this policy, and wrongfully, for the Japanese are not inferior to the white races, but fully their equals." In 1915, Okuma further declared that a satisfactory solution to the discrimination against Japanese in the West "will date the harmonization of different civilizations of the east and the west, thus making an epoch in the history of human civilizations."[8] On the eve of the Great War, the Japanese demand for equality of status with the Western Powers had created a far-reaching international disturbance.[9]

The Great War was primarily fought among nations of the white race and was perhaps even a civil war among the Western Powers. The British sought support from the Japanese, Chinese, and Indians; France from the Vietnamese and Chinese; while Japan was courted by Britain and others, and chose to enter the war as a British ally. When the war was over and Wilson announced his blueprint for a new and fair world order, the Japanese had high hopes for finally winning recognition of racial equality. A writer in *The Japan Times* hoped that the Great War had disrupted conventional ideas of racial solidarity and that perhaps the war had "shed a new ray of hope on this extremely difficult problem showing how it might solve itself." The Japanese publicist K. K. Kawakami (Kiyoshi Karl Kawakami), an American-educated Christian who often reflected Japanese official positions, warned that future world peace depended on racial reconciliation.[10] A November 1918 article in Tokutomi Soho's *Kokumin* wrote that the main object of the projected League of Nations was the "equalization of the races of the world," but that its role in the world could not be fully realized "so long as Japanese and other coloured races are differentially treated in white communities."[11] An extract from November 30, 1918 runs: "A justice and humanity which fails to solve the racial question is merely spurious. A world league of peace built upon a spurious justice and humanity is a house built on sand."[12]

How the proposed League of Nations would deal with racial discrimination was of key importance for the Japanese. Some expressed hope for Wilsonian ideals. *Kokumin* noted: "It is most gratifying that Mr. Wilson and Monsieur Clemenceau, protectors of mankind, take their stand upon the ideal of world peace. If this (racial) problem is solved, such questions as Tsingtao and the South Sea Islands are not worth mentioning. We desire to urge Marquis Saionji to find a satisfactory solution

[8] Paul Gordon Lauren, "Human Rights in History: Diplomacy and Racial Equality at the Paris Peace Conference," *Diplomatic History*, 2 (1978), 259–60.

[9] Lake and Reynolds, *Drawing the Global Colour Line*, 273–5.

[10] Lake and Reynolds, *Drawing the Global Colour Line*, 282–3.

[11] Cited by Naoko Shimazu, *Japan, Race, and Equality*, 55.

[12] *Kokumin*, November 30, 1918.

for this problem in conjunction with Messrs. Wilson and Clemenceau."[13] In its November 3 issue, *Kokumin* stated: "The main objects of Mr. Wilson's League are the perpetuation and the freedom and equalization of the races of the world." It pointed out that "there is nothing to choose between economic barriers as a cause of international strife and racial discrimination as a cause of international antagonism," since the purpose of the League of Nations is to establish, simultaneously with world peace, the principles of the freedom and equality of all nations. The article reminded its readers that Wilson himself stated in his first Article for the League that "impartial justice" for all peoples must involve the abolishment of discrimination; there must be no favoritism, and no standard set up but the equal rights of the several peoples. The article also hoped that once Japan joined the League, racial discrimination in America and Australia would, as a matter of course, be removed. Under the principle of equality for all peoples, the Japanese should enjoy the same rights as other foreigners. "We do not doubt the President's sincerity . . . If the President's idea of a League of Nations materializes we look forward to the policy towards the Japanese in America undergoing a modification." According to Naoko Shimazu, Japanese newspapers in November 1918 had started treating the racial issue as a potential time bomb. By early December, the three major Japanese newspapers—*Tokyo Nichi Nichi Shimbun*, *Yomiuri Shimbun*, and *Asahi Shimbun*—had launched an all-out offensive on the racial equality issue, demanding that the government propose a solution at the peace conference. In the eyes of the Japanese public, the entire legitimacy of the League of Nations was linked to the fate of the racial equality proposal. And Japan had a moral duty as the non-white Great Power to demand that equality for the sake of greater international justice.[14]

Not everyone was hopeful. As mentioned in Chapter 6, Prince Konoe Fumimaro published an article, "Reject the Anglo-American-Centered Peace," five days after the Japanese delegation left for Paris, doubting whether the Anglo-American-dominated world order would honor the principle of racial equality. Though he believed that the "sense of equality" among races was the "fundamental moral doctrine for the human community," it seemed to him that the proposed peace treaty would preserve the dominance of the leading Western nations and their control of the world's resources by shutting out foreigners from their "colonial areas." Konoe suggested that unless the "discriminatory treatment of Asian peoples by Caucasians" and the Western Powers' economic imperialism were removed, Japan should not join the League of Nations. Konoe declared: "At the coming peace conference we must demand this in the name of justice and humanity. Indeed the peace conference will provide the opportunity to determine whether or not the human race is capable of reforming the world on those principles."[15]

Other leading Japanese, however, suggested that if Japan made a forceful effort at the peace conference, it just might succeed. Dr. Kaiichi Toda, a professor in the College of Law at Kyoto Imperial University, wrote in *Tokyo Asahi* on January 1–3,

---

[13] British Embassy, Tokyo, December 2, 1918. BA: FO 608/211.
[14] Shimazu, *Japan, Race, and Equality*, 55–6.
[15] Oka, *Konoe Fumimaro*, 11–13.

1919 that the Japanese demand for the abolition of racial discrimination was based not on its economic benefit to Japan, but on the principle of the equal right to exist. In particular, he wrote:

> Our objection to this discrimination against coloured immigration is not simply that we are being treated differently from the white man, because our opposition would still remain if coloured and white immigration were forbidden altogether or rigidly limited to an equal degree for both.... Prejudice against the coloured races is unjust not merely because of the fact of discrimination but because it is contrary to the principle of the joint utilization and development of wealth. The monopolization of resources is economic imperialism and is no less unjust than militarism or military imperialism. Indeed seeing that modern economic imperialism requires militarism to make it effective it is not at all necessary to discriminate between the two. Before militarism can be fundamentally destroyed, economic imperialism must also be destroyed.... If racial discrimination is not done away with a League of Nations would simply degenerate into a means of oppression of the coloured races by the white.[16]

Other opinion-makers were equally adamant. The racial discrimination question "must be fought to the last," declared the editor of *Yamato*. The elimination of that "unjust practice" was the "greatest of Japan's missions." Discrimination meant the "usurpation of rights and interests on the part of the white race." If Japan did not rise to curb them, who would be there to "check the unbridled selfishness and domination of the white people?"[17] The editor of *Nichi Nichi* expressed hope that the Allies would deal with the question of racial equality with "sincerity and justice."[18] Referring to Wilson's talk of universal brotherhood, the *Yorozu* thought it "unimaginable" that he would retreat from his cherished ideals.[19] The Japanese delegate Baron Makino appealed to Australian Premier William Morris Hughes on behalf of Japan's racial equality proposal, in spite of Hughes' staunch support for White Australia. Makino spoke certain truth when he told Hughes: "my country-men feel so strongly about this clause that if I go back and tell them it has been rejected, they may kill me."[20]

In late 1918 and the early months of 1919, public opinion in Japan was mobilized by newly formed interest or pressure groups. One of the largest was the League to Abolish Racial Discrimination, which started off as a group of military and public officials who wanted to push the importance of racial equality to Japan's peace policy. The League for People's Diplomacy delivered a memo to the government on December 6, 1918, demanding the abolition of racially preju-diced politics in the British and American territories. Racial equality dominated the editorials of Japan's leading national newspapers.[21] The Japan-America Associ-ation, the Association for Publicists of Peace Issues, the League for People's

---

[16] "Prejudice Against the Immigration of the Coloured Races, by Dr. Kaiichi Toda," Conyngham Greene to London, January 10, 1919, BA: FO 608/211.
[17] Greene to London, March 27, 1919, BA: FO 608/211.
[18] Greene to London, December 3, 1918, BA: FO 608/211.
[19] Greene to London, December 3, 1918, BA: FO 608/211.
[20] William Morris Hughes, *Policies and Potentates* (Sydney: Angus and Robertson, 1950), 247.
[21] Shimazu, *Japan, Race, and Equality*, 51–4.

Diplomacy, and the Sun and Stars Association all held public meetings and impressed on the government the importance of racial equality. The League to Abolish Racial Discrimination brought together representatives from the major political parties, the bureaucracy, the armed services, and thirty-seven other public associations. Following a mass meeting in Tokyo in February 1919, the League cabled Georges Clemenceau, expressing its expectation that the Peace Conference would abolish all forms of racial discrimination. At a second mass meeting in March, it was resolved to oppose the establishment of a League of Nations if it was not based on the abolition of racial discrimination.[22] The Japanese community in Hawaii sent Clemenceau a petition in March 1919 and asked him to "spare no effort to have a clause inserted in the Peace Treaty and in the Covenant for the League of Nations, declaring, in accordance with the principles of Justice, Right-eousness and Humanity, the right of Japanese nationals to immigrate into all the territories of the High Contracting Parties and to enjoy therein without discrim-ination the rights of naturalization and civil and political rights."[23]

Commenting on the public ferment, K. K. Kawakami observed that the racial equality question was forced on the government by "the masses of Japan." It was "the proposal of sixty million souls of the Mikado's Empire."[24] As the Japanese leaders departed for France, they were sent off with a united chorus of newspaper commentaries. The *Kokumin* hoped the delegation would not betray the trust placed in it by the country. The elimination of racial discrimination was as important an objective as the formation of the League of Nations. *Asahi* agreed: "No other question was so inseparably and materially interwoven with the per-manency of the world's peace as that of unfair and unjust treatment of a large majority of the world's population. And Japan could not have set forth her views with greater propriety and more just contention than in vindication of the wrong suffered by other races than the whites."[25]

Japanese domestic opinion was divided into those who supported the League and those who opposed it, with the latter being more representative of the national sentiment. Prime Minister Hara supported Japan's entry into the League of Nations. The Hara Cabinet laid out guiding principles for its delegates with the following priorities: (1) conditions of peace in which "Japan alone has interest independently from the Allied and Associated Powers," which included the transfer of rights pertaining to the former German colonies of Qingdao and the Pacific islands north of the equator; (2) conditions of peace in which Japan "has no direct interest," in which case, Japan should be vigilant and try to contribute whenever possible; and (3) conditions of peace in which Japan "has common interest with the allied and associated powers," for which the delegates are instructed to coordinate as much as possible with the other Allied Powers. In other words, the main focus as far

[22] Ian Hill Nish, *Alliance in Decline: A Study in Anglo-Japanese Relations, 1908–1923* (London: Athlone Press, 1972), 269; Shimazu, *Japan, Race, and Equality*, 51–3.
[23] "Japanese Rights of Immigration," BA: FO 608/211.
[24] K. K. Kawakami, *Japan and World Peace*, 46.
[25] Lake and Reynolds, *Drawing the Global Colour Line*, 285–6.

as the government was concerned was the legitimatization of its control of German interests in Asia, especially those in China.[26] Joining the League presented no obstacle to that goal and could be a useful lever in the face of resistance.

But according to Naoko Shimazu, "It can be reasonably construed that the racial equality proposal had the role of appeasing opponents by making Japan's acceptance of the League conditional on having a racial equality clause inserted into the covenant of the League."[27] Contrary to the general perception that the Japanese held a uniform position on the racial equality proposal, the Japanese government remained internally divided over the issue of the League of Nations. Shimazu argued that "it is reasonable to suggest that the racial equality proposal can be seen as a means of appeasing the sceptics who did not share Hara's conviction that Japan needed to court the Anglo-Saxon powers at the peace conference in order to avoid international isolation of Japan."[28] While Japanese society was consumed with discussing racial equality in the postwar world order, officials in the Japanese Foreign Ministry and members of the prestigious Advisory Council on Foreign Affairs were concerned that racial prejudice might jeopardize Japan's position at the projected League of Nations. Draft guidelines prepared by the Foreign Office for the delegation in Paris urged that plans for such an organization be shelved "in view of the racial prejudices which have not yet entirely been banished from among the nations," and which could only produce results "gravely detrimental to Japan." If, however, the League became a fait accompli, Japan could not afford to be on the outside, and the delegates should make efforts to secure suitable guarantees against disadvantages arising from racial prejudice. Only then could Japan be confident that the Western Powers would not use the new body to "freeze the status quo."[29] The instructions of both the Cabinet and the Advisory Council were clear: the country's participation in the new international organization was contingent on the inclusion of a racial equality clause either in the body or the preface of the planned Covenant of the League of Nations.

As Naoko Shimazu has noted, the Japanese government was concerned with attaining equality with the Western Powers, but its focus was the discrimination suffered by its own nationals in other countries. Their demand was "a highly particularistic and nationalistic" expression of Japan's desire to prevent its nationals, and thereby itself, from suffering the "humiliation of racial prejudice in the League of Nations."[30] But once the genie was out of the bottle and became public, the Japanese delegation had to make the proposal for racial equality at the peace conference, no matter how difficult it might be to pull it off. As Japanese Ambassador to Washington Ishii told the Americans, the racial equality issue was "too close to the heart of every Japanese," so he had to pay close attention to Japanese public opinion.[31]

[26] Shimazu, *Japan, Race, and Equality*, 45.   [27] Shimazu, *Japan, Race, and Equality*, 39.

[28] Shimazu, *Japan, Race, and Equality*, 50.

[29] Noriko Kawamura, "Wilsonian Idealism and Japanese Claims at the Paris Peace Conference," *Pacific Historical Review*, 66:4 (1997), 515; Lesley Connors, *The Emperor's Adviser: Saionji Kinmochi and Pre-war Japanese Politics* (London: Croom Helm, 1987), 70, 233.

[30] Shimazu, *Japan, Race, and Equality*, 113–15.

[31] Link, ed., *The Papers of Woodrow Wilson*, 56: 188.

THE PROPOSAL

Scholars have largely insisted that Japan was not sincere in pushing this racial equality proposal and it was merely advancing it as a bargaining lever. And there can be little doubt that the racial equality issue was used that way, and to some extent was intended as such. But the evidence presented here strongly indicates that there was also Japanese sincerity behind this proposal, and that they regarded it as of the greatest importance. Aware of the likely difficulties the proposal faced, the delegates Makino and Chinda made preliminary approaches to the Americans, talking in particular to President Wilson's trusted advisor, Colonel Edward M. House.

The Japanese first raised the racial equality issue with Colonel House on February 2, 1919, and informed him of the general Japanese position regarding the abolition of racial discrimination. House had been entrusted by Wilson with negotiations on the race issue and the Japanese believed he was friendly to Japan, as discussed in Chapter 6. Makino and Chinda submitted four different draft proposals to House between February 5 and 12.[32] Colonel House spent many hours talking with them and always appeared supportive. The initial draft included the following language: "The equality of nations being a basic principle of the League of Nations, the High Contracting Parties agree that concerning the treatment and rights to be accorded to aliens in their territories, they will not discriminate, either in law or nationality." House rejected that proposal, but accepted a second one, which reads as follows: "The equality of nations being a basic principle of the League of Nations, the High Contracting Parties agree that concerning the treatment of aliens in their territories, they will accord them, as far as it lies in their legitimate powers, equal treatment and rights, in law and in fact, without making any distinction on account of their race or nationality." David Miller wrote in his February 9 diary entry:

> Colonel House called me in and talked to me about the Japanese proposal. While I was discussing it Mr. Balfour came in. There was a general discussion of the matter between Colonel House and Mr. Balfour . . . Colonel House said that he did not see how the policy toward the Japanese could be continued. The world said that they could not go to Africa; they could not go to any white country; they could not go to China, and they could not go to Siberia; and yet they were a growing nation, having a country where all the land was tilled; but they had to go somewhere.[33]

House seems to have indeed been sympathetic to the Japanese situation.

Encouraged by House's friendly responses, the Japanese decided to take their proposal to the League of Nations' Commission, where discussions on the draft Covenant were nearing completion. Japan first submitted the racial equality proposal at the tenth session of the Commission on February 13. Makino proposed adding the declaration regarding racial equality as an amendment to Article 21 of the Covenant, which guaranteed religious freedom. The idea of

---

[32] "From the Diary of Colonel House," February 4 and 5, 1919, in Link, ed., *The Papers of Woodrow Wilson*, 485, 500; see also Shimazu, *Japan, Race, and Equality*, 17.
[33] Miller, *The Drafting of the Covenant*, 1: 183–4.

religious freedom came from Wilson, who called for the equal treatment of all religious minorities. Wilson had in mind, specifically, the equal treatment of the Jews under immigration laws around the world. The Japanese wished to have the phrase read: "religious and racial equality." Makino proposed: "The equality of nations being a basic principle of the League of Nations, the High Contracting Parties agree to an accord as soon as possible to all alien nationals of states, members of the League, equal and just treatment in every respect making no distinction, either in law or in fact, on account of their race or nationality."[34] In his speech introducing this proposal, Makino said "race discrimination still exists, in law and in fact, is undeniable, and it is enough here simply to state the fact of its existence." He suggested that "an immediate realization of the ideal equality of treatment between peoples is not proposed" in this Japanese proposal.[35] Makino's appeal to a shared wartime experience failed to win over the Commission. While it made sense, since the matters of religion and race discrimination could well go together, rather than accept the Japanese proposal, President Wilson decided to withdraw the proposed "religious equality" article.[36] The decision to delete the entirety of Article 21, including the Japanese amendment, was carried. David Miller suggested that the contributing cause for Wilson dropping the "religious" article was Makino's "equality" amendment. By killing the Japanese amendment, Wilson made it impossible to include any article on religious liberty in any form.[37] The very next day, when the draft Covenant was presented to a Plenary Session of the Conference without the Japanese proposal, Makino made a reservation that Japan would again submit another proposal for the consideration of the Conference.

Having been rebuffed in February, the Japanese delegation returned to its task in late March, fortified by fresh instructions from Tokyo and news of growing public anger at home over the question of racial discrimination. On March 30, Hara asked the diplomatic advisory council to consider a possible course of action in case of the proposal's rejection. Hara personally believed that "it was not a big enough problem to [justify] withdrawal from the League of Nations." And the Advisory Council on Foreign Affairs unanimously concluded that the government should not, in any event, lose face over the issue. Hence, new instructions outlined an option to declare the specified passage as an appendix to the League Covenant.[38]

During March, the Japanese had continued to seek the support of American and British delegates for an amendment to the preamble of the Covenant. Over a four-week period, Makino and Chinda had more meetings with the Americans, the British, and the Dominion leaders, including Smuts from South Africa, Sir Robert Borden from Canada, and William F. Massey from New Zealand.[39] Japan's case was even presented by Ambassador Ishii directly to the American people when he

[34] "Minutes of the Commission of the League of Nations," in Miller, *The Drafting of the Covenant*, 2: 324.
[35] Link, ed., *The Papers of Woodrow Wilson*, 55: 138–40.
[36] Miller, *The Drafting of the Covenant*, 1: 269; 2: 273, 323–5.
[37] Miller, *The Drafting of the Covenant*, 1: 269.
[38] Shimazu, *Japan, Race, and Equality*, 26–7.
[39] Kajima, *The Diplomacy of Japan*, 3: 395–418.

gave an address at a dinner of the Japan Society in New York on March 14, 1919. Ishii made a strong plea for the inclusion of a provision against racial discrimination in the Covenant of the League of Nations, and indicated clearly that this was the policy of his government. But he did not state or even imply that his government would insist on equality of immigration.[40] However, Japanese delegates in Paris informed Colonel House: "they would reserve the right or propose equality of immigration in any discussion of the League constitution."[41]

The Japanese seized an opportunity at the meeting of the Covenant Commission on the April 11, where Makino proposed inserting in the preamble of the Covenant a phrase endorsing "the principle of equality of nations and just treatment of their nationals." In his introductory statements, Makino emphasized the shift from demanding "equality of races" to "equality of nations," arguing that "my amendment to the Preamble is simply to lay down a general principle as regards the relationship at least between the nationalities forming the League, just as it prescribes the rules of conduct to be observed between the Governments of the State Members. It is not intended that the amendment should encroach on the internal affairs of any nation. It simply sets forth an aim in future international intercourse." According to Makino, the new modified proposal did not fully meet Japanese wishes but "was the outcome of an attempt to conciliate the view-points of different nations." Makino explained that the Japanese proposal tried to secure recognition of the equality of all nations and their subjects: "all aliens who happen to be the nationals of the States which were deemed advanced enough and fully qualified to become Members of the League," making no distinction on account of race or nationality.

Makino also called attention to the fact that the race question was a standing grievance which might become acute and dangerous at any moment; thus, it was important that a provision dealing with the subject be included in the League Covenant. He stated: "We did not lose sight of the many and varied difficulties standing in the way of a full realisation of this principle. But they were not insurmountable." Since as matters stood, serious misunderstandings between different peoples might grow to an uncontrollable degree, the Japanese hoped that the issue would be taken up now, when what had seemed impossible before was about to be accomplished. The Japanese proposal also argued that since the question was of a delicate and complicated nature, involving the play of a deep human passion, the immediate realization of equality was not proposed; instead, the clause presented just laid out the principle and left the actual working of it in the hands of the different governments concerned. It was up to the governments and peoples concerned to examine the question more closely and devise a fair means to meet it. The Japanese argued that since the League had been devised as insurance against war, in cases of aggression, nations must be prepared to defend the territorial integrity and political independence of a fellow member, and this meant that a national of a member state must be ready to share military costs for the common

---

[40] Link, ed., *The Papers of Woodrow Wilson*, 56: 62.
[41] Link, ed., *The Papers of Woodrow Wilson*, 56: 60.

cause, including the sacrifice of his own person. In view of these duties, each national would naturally feel, and in fact demand, that he be on an equal footing with the people he undertakes to defend, even with his own life.[42]

In the ensuing debate, the Japanese were backed by some of the most prominent personalities at the Conference—Orlando of Italy, Bourgeois of France, Venizelos of Greece, and Wellington Koo of China. Eleven votes out of seventeen were recorded in favor of the amendment. French delegate Bourgeois said that it was impossible to vote against "an amendment which embodied an indisputable principle of justice."[43] But Robert Cecil, who was now Undersecretary of State under Balfour, refused to accept the amendment, acting, as he said, under instructions from his government. Wilson, chairman of the meeting, was supported by Cecil and opposed the proposal, saying that he was afraid of the controversies "which would be bound to take place outside the Commission." So the Japanese proposal was defeated under the unanimity principle. For Wilson to accept the proposal, better than majority support was needed.[44] Wilson declared that none of those present wished to deny the principles of either the equality of nations or the just treatment of nationals. But the discussion had already lit "burning flames of prejudice," which it would be unwise to allow to flare in public view. He might have been responding to a note Colonel House handed to him as the discussion proceeded, which read: "The trouble is that if this Commission should pass it, it would surely raise the race issue throughout the world."[45] Wilson thus used procedure to kill the Japanese proposal. House's secretary, Auchincloss, reported on the vote in a telegram dated April 13 to the US Undersecretary of State, Frank Polk: "Inasmuch as the inclusion of a clause in the draft covenant required the unanimous consent of the members of the Commission, the Japanese proposal was rejected. Lord Robert Cecil's flat objection made it unnecessary for us to vote on the question."[46] Observing this scene, David Miller thought that Cecil behaved as though he were performing a difficult and disagreeable task. After making his statement, he sat with eyes fixed on the table and took no further part in the debate.[47] Nevertheless, Japan's second official attempt at introducing racial equality to the League Covenant was killed.

But the Japanese did not give up. After further discussions between Makino, House, Border, Smuts, and others failed to resolve the matter, the Japanese decided to put their proposal to the final meeting of the Commission. On April 28, Makino decided to return to the first racial equality proposal submitted on February 13; he presented it to the plenary session of the Paris Peace Conference with the following speech:

> The principle which we desire to see acted upon in the future relationship between nations was set forth in our original amendment as follows: The equality of nations

[42] Link, ed., *The Papers of Woodrow Wilson*, 57: 259–61; Kajima, *The Diplomacy of Japan*, 3: 395–418.
[43] Miller, *The Drafting of the Covenant*, 2: 390.
[44] Link, ed., *The Papers of Woodrow Wilson*, 57: 261.
[45] Miller, *The Drafting of the Covenant*, 1: 461–3.
[46] Lake and Reynolds, *Drawing the Global Colour Line*, 300.
[47] Miller, *The Drafting of the Covenant*, 1: 461.

being a basic principle of the League of Nations, the High Contracting Parties agree to
accord, as soon as possible, to all aliens nationals of States Members of the League equal
and just treatment in every respect, making no distinction, either in law or in fact, on
account of their race or nationality. It is our firm conviction that the enduring success
of this great undertaking will depend much more on the hearty spousal and loyal
adherence that the various peoples concerned would give to the noble ideals underlying
the organisation, than on the acts of the respective Governments that may change from
time to time. In an age of democracy, peoples themselves must feel that they are the
trustees of this work and, to feel so, they must first have a sure basis of close harmony
and mutual confidence. If just and equal treatment is denied to certain nationals, it
would have the significance of a certain reflection on their quality and status. Their
faith in the justice and righteousness which are to be the guiding spirit of the future
international intercourse between the Members of the League may be shaken, and such
a frame of mind, I am afraid, would be most detrimental to that harmony and
cooperation, upon which foundation alone can the League now contemplated be
securely built. It was solely and purely from our desire to see the League established
on a sound and firm basis of goodwill, justice, and reason that we have been compelled
to make our proposal. We will not, however, press for the adoption of our proposal at
this moment. In closing, I feel it my duty to declare clearly on this occasion that the
Japanese Government and people feel poignant regret at the failure of the Commission
to approve of their just demand for laying down a principle aiming at the adjustment of
this long-standing grievance, a demand that is based upon a deep-rooted national
conviction. They will continue in their insistence for the adoption of this principle by
the League in the future.[48]

Makino's final bid to have a racial equality clause included in the preamble of the
Covenant of the League of Nations was eloquent and moving. He pointed out that
the idealism that shaped the League had "quickened the common feelings" of
people all over the world, given birth to hopes and aspirations, and strengthened
the sense of unmet but legitimate claims. The grievances of oppressed nationalities
and the "wrongs of racial discrimination" were the subject of deep resentment; if
the reasonable and just claims in the Japanese proposal were denied, it would cast a
lasting shadow over the status of peoples across the world. The consequences had to
be borne in mind, "for pride is one of the most forceful and sometimes uncontrollable causes of human action."[49] David Miller thought the Japanese presentation
"carefully prepared" and "admirably done." It secured the sympathy of almost
everyone present.[50] Writing to Lloyd George a few days later, Cecil observed that
the Japanese had made speeches of great moderation, and he too thought that
practically every member of the Commission supported them.[51] Would the Western Powers accept the Japanese proposal this time? How would fellow Asians
respond?

[48] Miller, *The Drafting of the Covenant*, 2: 702–4.
[49] Miller, *The Drafting of the Covenant*, 2: 702–4.
[50] Miller, *The Drafting of the Covenant*, 1: 461.
[51] Lake and Reynolds, *Drawing the Global Colour Line*, 300.

The Chinese, although deeply resentful of Japan's actions in China, shared Japan's cry for racial equality. As early as 1899, Liang Qichao had written that Japan and China should cooperate to protect the independence of the yellow race.[52] At Paris, each time the Japanese submitted the racial equality proposal, the Chinese delegates expressed their support.[53] When the Japanese first submitted the proposal, Wellington Koo stated that he was naturally in full sympathy with the spirit of the proposed amendment. But pending the receipt of instructions from his government, he would reserve his right of discussion for the future, and request that the reservation be recorded in the minutes.[54] On March 26, Koo asked David Miller whether the Japanese planned to resubmit and told Miller that "the Chinese of course would have to support the proposal if it came up."[55] And indeed, when the Japanese again submitted proposal, Koo told the conference assembly, "I should be very glad indeed to see the principle itself given recognition in the Covenant, and I hope that the Commission will not find serious difficulties in the way of its acceptance."[56] The Indians at the conference also expressed their support. After all, of all the Asians, the Indians and Chinese were particular targets of Western immigration policies.

The West remained the stumbling block. At the conference, the Japanese were seated at the far end of the long table, opposite representatives of Guatemala and Ecuador. But it was not merely the physical distance from where the Great Powers huddled that prompted Clemenceau to complain of not being able to hear Makino—and the terrible fate of being trapped with "ugly" Japanese in a city full of attractive blonde women. Clemenceau was not alone. The Australian Prime Minister Hughes hated interviews with Makino and Chinda, whom he referred to as "two little fat Japanese noblemen in frock coats and silk hats, neither much more than five feet high."[57] He did not seem to remember that it was the Japanese fleet that protected the troopships conveying the Australian and New Zealand armies to the Middle East.

THE RESPONSES

The Japanese quest to get their proposal heard and accepted met with obfuscation and opposition. The British firmly opposed the Japanese proposal. While discussing the draft proposal with Colonel House, British Foreign Secretary Balfour announced that while he sympathized with the Japanese, he could not accept the

---

[52] Liang, *Yin Bing Shi He Ji*, 29: 19b.

[53] Miller, *My Diary at the Conference of Paris*, 1: 205; see also Miller, *The Drafting of the Covenant*, 1: 336.

[54] Miller, *The Drafting of the Covenant*, 2: 325.

[55] Miller, *The Drafting of the Covenant*, 1: 336.

[56] For Koo's support, see "Lu Zhengxiang telegram to Waijiaobu," February 13, April 12, 1919, in Zhongguo she hui ke xue yuan, Jin dai shi yan jiu suo, Jin dai shi zi liao bian ji shi, and Tianjin shi li shi bo wu guan, eds., *Mi Ji Lu Cun (Collections of Secret Documents)*, 82–3, 129.

[57] Lake and Reynolds, *Drawing the Global Colour Line*, 296.

principle of racial equality. Although the draft proposal borrowed ideas from the American Declaration of Independence such as the idea that "all men are born free and equal," Balfour rejected it and claimed the idea was now "outmoded." While all men of a particular nation might be considered to be born free and equal, he was far from convinced that an African "could be regarded as the equal of a European or an American."[58]

Realizing the strength of British opposition, the Japanese delegation moved to negotiate directly with Balfour and Cecil instead of relying on House. On behalf of the British government, Robert Cecil had expressed his objection to the Japanese racial equality proposal in the early February. Chinda then replied that Japan had not broached the question of race or immigration, but asked for nothing more than the principle of the equality of nations and just treatment for their nationals. These words might have broad significance, "but they meant that all the members of the League should be treated with equality and justice." "If the Japanese amendment were accepted and were written into the Preamble, a clause relative to religious liberty might also be introduced."[59] The Japanese argued that acceptance of their amendment would mean only that the League of Nations was to be founded upon justice. Japanese public opinion was so strongly behind this amendment that the Japanese delegate asked the Commission to put it to the vote. If the amendment was rejected, "it would be an indication to Japan that the equality of members of the League was not recognised and, as a consequence, the new organisation would be most unpopular."[60]

The racial equality proposal and its corollaries were doomed from the very beginning. Before the peace conference, one high-ranking British official wrote:

> We do not even know whether the Japanese will raise the question of Japanese immigration into India and the British Dominions at the Peace Conference. If they do, it seems to me that they should be met, not on the basis of Resolution XXI of the War Conference, which might be modified later by the Dominions, but with the simple statement that His Majesty's Government will not be in a position to discuss the question of foreign immigration with foreign Governments until definite arrangements have been made with regard to the migration of British Asiatics between the component parts of the British Empire.[61]

With regard to the entry of Japanese into the British Dominions, Lord Milner agreed:

> The question whether the British Empire Delegates at the Peace Conference should put forward the general policy laid down by the Resolutions of the Imperial War Conference Nos. 22 of 1917 and 21 of 1918 as a defence against any Japanese claims for further rights of immigration and as an alternative to any existing rights which Japan may possess might appropriately be raised by the Indian representatives at any meeting of the British Empire delegates at which the question of Japanese claims was

---

[58] Bonsal, *Unfinished Business*, 38.   [59] Miller, *The Drafting of the Covenant*, 2: 389–91.
[60] Miller, *The Drafting of the Covenant*, 2: 390.
[61] Letter to R. Macleay, Foreign Office, February 10, 1919, BA: FO 208/211.

discussed, on the ground that the acceptance *qua* Japan of the policy would make it much easier for India to fall into line with the rest of the Empire in resisting further Japanese claims. British Empire delegations at the conference should maintain the following stand: the treatment within the British Empire of any particular class of British subjects was a domestic matter and it would be difficult for any foreign Government to demand that its subjects should have the same favours as those granted to British subjects. On the other hand it was not necessarily a good answer to claims of foreign governments that certain classes of British subjects were subject to special restrictions as to right of entry.[62]

The Australian Prime Minister Hughes wrote later that if the Japanese racial equality proposal had not been stifled at birth, "it would have meant the end of the Australia we know." [63] If the Americans hid behind the British to block the Japanese proposal, Robert Cecil used the Dominions' objection as an excuse when he told the Japanese it was an Australian matter and not an issue of fundamental importance to the Empire as a whole. Indeed, though the Dominions might think they were the "top dogs" in discussions of immigration issues, British officials cleverly used the Dominions as their running dogs as well.[64] So even given the moderate tone of Japan's February 13 proposal, the British delegation would not give its support, and many other Western countries took the same position. Facing especially strong objections from the Australians, the Japanese submitted the revised proposal of March 22 to the Australian Attorney General, Robert Garran, which simply said: "By the endorsement of the principle of equality of all nationals of States members of the League."[65] Hughes still objected.

On March 23, Makino and Chinda called on Sir Robert Cecil. Cecil explained that while he personally favored the proposal, he could not make a definite reply because the question was "after all an Australian one."[66] At a meeting the following day, Cecil indicated that Hughes and the other Dominion leaders remained adamant and that direct negotiations with them were necessary. At a March 25 meeting between the Dominion premiers and the Japanese delegates, the Japanese explained that they were under great pressure from the public at home but sought to allay fears about immigration to the Dominions. The Dominion leaders explained the difficulties that would arise if the provision was applied to the Chinese and the Indians and stated that they could not agree to it unless the world "equal" was deleted. The Japanese refused to budge; the word was central to their proposal. Sir Robert Borden from Canada worked out a compromise, revised wording that would recognize "the principle of equality between nations and just treatment of their nationals." Hughes alone opposed it. New Zealand Prime Minister William F. Massey was willing to go along with the compromise, but only if Hughes concurred. Hughes declared that as the representative of Australian public opinion, he had no choice but to oppose it

---

[62] A. E. Collins confidential letter to foreign office, January 25, 1919, BA: FO208/211.
[63] Hughes, *Policies and Potentates*, 244.
[64] Lake and Reynolds, *Drawing the Global Colour Line*, 301.
[65] Shimazu, *Japan, Race, and Equality*, 24.
[66] Lake and Reynolds, *Drawing the Global Colour Line*, 297.

absolutely. What mattered was not the wording of the proposal, but the "underlying idea itself, which ninety-five out of a hundred Australians rejected." Pressed by his colleagues to come up with a compromise, Hughes walked out of the meeting.[67]

Largely due to Hughes, the British Empire delegation was united in opposing the Japanese proposal. On April 11, even with the agreed upon language, Cecil of Britain rejected the amendment on the following grounds:

> The British Government realized the importance of the racial question, but its solution could not be attempted by the Commission without encroaching upon the sovereignty of States members of the League. One of two things must be true: either the points which the Japanese Delegation proposed to add to the Preamble were vague and ineffective, or else they were of practical significance. In the latter case, they opened the door to serious controversy and to interference in the domestic affairs of States members of the League.[68]

The Japanese proposal for racial equality was thus quashed by the British, who felt obliged to heed the violent objections of Australia. Hughes continued to insist that Japan's proposal flew in the face of the "White Australia" policy of his government, and he cited the anti-Japanese sentiment on the Pacific coast of the United States as support.

Racist attitudes were widespread within the British Empire, including its dominions, Australia, New Zealand, Canada, and South Africa, which exercised great influence within the British delegation to the peace conference. These white dominions had been accorded separate representation at Paris while also comprising part of the British delegation. As David Miller observed, Australia "had more influence with London than Tokyo."[69] Moreover, Hughes threatened a public attack on the whole of the League of Nations should such a clause be inserted in the preamble.[70] From the moment he became aware of the Japanese proposal, in February 1919, until its final defeat in April, Hughes remained implacable and vociferous in his opposition. When pressed by Colonel House to accept a compromise, Hughes scribbled a reply saying that he would sooner "walk into the Seine—or the Folies Bergeres with my clothes off."[71] When one of Hughes' most able officials, Major E. L. Piesse, suggested in a memo written in preparation for the peace conference that, as regards "the greater part of the Japanese nation," there was little reason for applying discrimination not thought necessary with the "less advanced European nations," Hughes crossed the comments out and scrawled "Rot" in the margin.[72] An American official, Colonel Stephen Bonsal, who was an assistant to Colonel House at Paris, recorded in his diary on March 16 how Hughes "Morning, noon, and night bellows at poor Lloyd George that if race equality is recognized in the

---

[67] Henry Borden, ed., *Robert Laird Borden: His Memoirs* (Toronto: MacMillan, 1938), 927–8.

[68] Link, *The Papers of Woodrow Wilson*, 57: 261–2.

[69] Godfrey Hodgson, *Woodrow Wilson's Right Hand: the life of Colonel Edward M. House* (New Haven: Yale University Press, 2006), 210.

[70] Lake and Reynolds, *Drawing the Global Colour Line*, 299.

[71] MacMillan, *Paris 1919*, 319.

[72] Lake and Reynolds, *Drawing the Global Colour Line*, 295.

preamble or any of the articles of the Covenant, he and his people will leave the Conference bag and baggage." The usually reserved Wilson even described Hughes as "a pestiferous varmint."[73] As Lake pointed out, other Australians in the delegation shared Hughes' anxiety. John Latham, writing to his wife, Ella, told her of the Japanese attempt to get "something" into the Covenant about racial equality. He observed that Hughes was fully aware of the fact that "no government could live for a day if it tampered with a White Australia." The delegation's strong anti-racial equality attitude at Paris reflected widespread Australian public opinion. Deputy Prime Minister W. A. Watt sent a telegram to Hughes on April 4, following a Cabinet meeting in Melbourne, reaffirming the government's view that "neither people nor Parliament of Australia could agree to principles of racial equality."[74]

Colonel House warned Makino that if Hughes spoke out against the Japanese proposal, President Wilson would be forced to side with him because of his concern for public opinion on the West Coast of the United States.[75] Makino replied that Japan could not tolerate a situation in which the strong opposition of Hughes alone defeated their proposal.[76] In his memoir, *Policies and Potentates*, published in 1950, Hughes claimed that on the night before the vote was taken, he met American reporters from the western states and urged them "to protest against this evil, this wicked clause," which "would bring disaster to the people of the Pacific slopes and gravely imperil those in adjoining States."[77] In a subsequent meeting with the Japanese press in Paris, "Hughes pointed to the role of the United States in defeating racial equality. Australia had no vote at the Commission and the Japanese shouldn't take at face value Wilson's avowed support for their position. Alarmed at the prospect of growing anti-American feeling in Japan, House responded to Hughes' press conference by immediately sending a cable to the United States ambassador in Japan, asking him to make an appropriate reply in the Japanese press."[78]

The Americans were happy to let the British, and in particular Hughes, take responsibility for the defeat of the racial equality clause. Wilson, however, not only supported Hughes, but was a strong racist himself. In January 1917, Wilson argued that America should stay out of the war in order "to keep the white race strong against the yellow—Japan for instance." Wilson told Robert Lansing that he believed "white civilization and its domination of the planet rested largely on our ability to keep this country intact."[79] As a matter of fact, in 1913, when he ran for the White House, Wilson was quoted as saying "in the matter of Chinese and Japanese coolie immigration . . . , I stand for the national policy of exclusion." In the same telegram, Wilson stated: "We cannot make a homogeneous population out of a people who do not blend with the Caucasian race."[80]

[73] Bonsal, *Suitors and Suppliants*, 229.
[74] Lake and Reynolds, *Drawing the Global Colour Line*, 294.
[75] Kajima, *The Diplomacy of Japan, 1894–1922*, 3: 407–8.
[76] Lake and Reynolds, *Drawing the Global Colour Line*, 299.
[77] Hughes, *Policies and Potentates*, 247.
[78] Lake and Reynolds, *Drawing the Global Colour Line*, 302.
[79] Mishra, *From the Ruins of Empire*, 197–8.
[80] Daniels, *The Politics of Prejudice*, 55.

Wilson embraced the hierarchy of race. He recognized new nations in Europe, but not elsewhere. The mandate system of the new League provided an alternative to becoming traditional European colonies for those peoples who, in his view, had not reached the developmental stage to become independent nations. At Paris, Wilson was caught in the same stance as at home. According to historian Lloyd Ambrosius, Wilson had endorsed the melting pot theory of assimilation in the United States, but only for peoples of European ancestry. Native Americans and African Americans might live in the country, but not as equal citizens. Similarly, he wanted Japan in the new League, which he viewed as an organic community of nations, but he still opposed racial equality for people of color. Wilson hoped to subordinate non-Western nations, such as Japan, in the postwar world community in much the same way that he sought to dominate racial minorities in the United States. He rejected genuine pluralism or equality for all peoples around the world. In this regard, "Wilson's internationalism derived from his Americanism."[81] Seth P. Tillman has concluded that Wilson, fearing an outburst of hostile opinion in the western states of the United States, submitted to Hughes' threats rather than stand up for his principles.[82] But Wilson's commitment to Anglo-Saxon solidarity and white supremacy were all important and meshed with his national political interests. His personal physician, Dr. Cary T. Grayson, observed in his diary that concealed in the apparently simple Japanese request was "the nucleus of serious trouble in the United States should it be adopted," inasmuch as it would allow Asians to demand the repeal of discriminatory laws in California and other western states.[83] California politicians and newspapers had made their opposition to the Japanese proposal absolutely clear. Indeed, when news of the Japanese proposal reached California, opposition was immediate and vociferous. United States Senator J. D. Phelan launched a powerful propaganda campaign that besieged the delegation in Paris with angry telegrams. Any declaration on the subject of racial equality or "just treatment," he warned, could be construed as giving jurisdiction to an international body over immigration, naturalization, the voting franchise, land ownership, and marriage. Western senators would oppose any measure by which "Oriental people" would gain equality with the white race. It was, he declared, in a now familiar vein, "a vital question of self-preservation."[84] Regardless of Wilson's own racist ideas, Wilson as the politician also could not support the Japanese racial equality proposal. He knew "no American Senate would ever dream of ratifying any covenant which enshrined so dangerous a principle."[85]

Wilson was certainly sensitive to public opinion and the sensibilities of the voters. Colonel House sent a copy of Japan's racial equality clause to Senator Elihu Root, Theodore Roosevelt's Secretary of State, asking for his comment.

[81] Lloyd Ambrosius, *Wilsonianism: Woodrow Wilson and His Legacy in American Foreign Relations* (New York: Palgrave Macmillan, 2002), 28–9.

[82] Seth P. Tillman, *Anglo-American Relations at the Paris Peace Conference of 1919* (Princeton, NJ: Princeton University Press, 1961), 304.

[83] "From the Diary of Dr. Grayson, April 11, 1919," in Link, *The Papers of Woodrow Wilson*, 57: 239–40.

[84] Shimazu, *Japan, Race, and Equality*, 138.   [85] Nicolson, *Peacemaking 1919*, 145.

Root, a supporter of the Immigration Restriction League, replied with an emphatic "Don't let it in, it will breed trouble." Wilson would have trouble gaining support for the League of Nations, but with the racial equality clause attached, it would "get nowhere in the Senate." On the Pacific coast, they would certainly think that lurking behind it was "a plan for unlimited yellow immigration."[86] There was also concern that American opposition to the amendment might lead Japan to abandon the voluntary restrictions on emigration to America in the so-called "Gentlemen's Agreement" Root had worked out in 1907.

The Japanese initially thought Colonel House was supportive and trustworthy; however, House's support for the Australian position would be crucial in the defeat of the Japanese bid for racial equality. House prided himself on his diplomatic skills, which were nowhere more evident than in his negotiations with the Japanese and the British over the proposed racial equality clause. House noted in his diary on February 9: "I had a good many callers today, including Viscount Chinda and Baron Makino, who came again upon the inevitable race question. I have placed them 'on the backs' of the British, for every solution which the Japanese and I have proposed, Hughes of the British delegation objects to."[87] In her recent study of the Paris Peace Conference, historian Margaret MacMillan has questioned the sincerity of American support for the Japanese position. While Makino and Chinda repeatedly appealed to House, she suggests that they were looking in the wrong quarter. Wilson was not prepared to fight for a policy he did not support and which was unpopular in the United States. Privately, he was delighted that the British were forced by Hughes to oppose the racial equality clause. "It has," wrote Wilson's right-hand man, "taken considerable fitness to lift the load from our shoulders and place it upon the British, but happily it has been done."[88]

With their Shandong and racial equality goals in jeopardy in late April, the Japanese had to choose one battle and use the other as a bargaining chip. The Japanese official position jelled in mid-March, when the Japanese government had decided to forgo its push for racial equality in favor of its claims in China. According to Balfour's report to the Council of Four on his April 26 meeting with Makino and Chinda, Makino went to call on Balfour that day. With great delicacy but perfect clearness, Makino indicated that Japan wanted a decision on both its claims as a whole. Regarding the racial equality issue, it seemed that the Western Powers wanted Japan to join the League of Nations but refused to grant it equality of treatment. Makino told Balfour that public opinion in Japan was much concerned over this question. But he also informed Balfour that Shandong was crucial to Japan's position in the peace conference and that the Shandong issue must be sewn up before that afternoon's plenary session on the League of Nations. He conveyed to Balfour that if Japan received what she wanted in

[86] Bonsal, *Unfinished Business* (Garden City: Doubleday, Doran and Company, Inc., 1944), 142.

[87] Charles Seymour, ed., *The Intimate Papers of Colonel House* (London: Ernest Benn, 1928), 4: 324.

[88] "From the Diary of Dr. Grayson, March 22, 1919," in Link, ed., *The Papers of Woodrow Wilson*, 56: 164; see also MacMillan, *Paris 1919*, 319.

regard to Shandong, Japanese representatives would content themselves regarding the inequality of races, and Japan then would merely register a protest when its racial equality clause was rejected. If, however, Japan was "ill-treated" over Shandong, Makino told Balfour he was unable to say "what line the Japanese Delegates might take."[89] In other words, Japan might walk away from the conference and the League of Nations.

From the very beginning, some Westerners thought the Japanese had introduced the racial equality proposal as a sort of blackmail. After House met with Balfour on February 10, Balfour wrote:

> Colonel House showed me a sheaf of papers, each one of which embodied an attempt to find a formula on the subject of Immigration which would satisfy the Japanese. In the absence of such a formula, the Japanese had intimated that they would find it difficult, or impossible to join the League of Nations. I observed that this was very much like an attempt at blackmail on the part of our Ally—to which Colonel House assented.... Speaking for myself, I did not believe that any of the English-speaking communities would tolerate a great Japanese flow of immigration.[90]

C. T. Wang (Wang Zhengting), an influential Chinese delegate, declared:

> China knows that equality of the races forms the foundation of the League of Nations. Japan's demand to include such a phrase in the Covenant was pure camouflage. It was a smoke-screen to cover a real objective. The idea was to press this hard, knowing that President Wilson would refuse it; but after he had refused it the Japanese then pointed to Kiaochou, and said, "Well, give us that anyhow." And President Wilson said, "Well, I guess we'll have to give those Japanese something."[91]

Wilson did just that. As Chair of the League of Nations Commission, Wilson eventually blocked the inclusion of the racial equality clause in the Covenant. To save his League of Nations and keep Japan in it, Wilson agreed to give Japan Shandong.

So on April 30, Japan "lost" its battle on racial equality and won Shandong. In his address to the Australian federal parliament, Prime Minister Hughes was pleased to announce: "White Australia is yours. You may do with it what you please; but, at any rate, the soldiers have achieved the victory, and my colleagues and I have brought that great principle back to you from the Conference."[92] In a similar vein, Senator Phelan declared to the United States Congress that he was "very glad" that the president had stemmed the "insidious movements of the Japanese" to establish the principle of racial equality, "under which they would have flooded this land."[93] But how did the Japanese accept the failure of their racial equality proposal?

---

[89] "Notes of a Meeting held at Wilson's Residence in Paris with Lloyd George, Clemenceau and Wilson," April 28, 1919 at 11.00 a.m., in Wilson Papers, Ser. 6: Peace Conference Documents/6A/Minutes.

[90] Shimazu, *Japan, Race, and Equality*, 19.   [91] Shimazu, *Japan, Race, and Equality*, 146.

[92] Commonwealth Parliamentary Debates, House of Representatives, vol. LXXXIX (1919), 12175.

[93] Rubin Francis Weston, *Racism in US Imperialism: The Influence of Racial Assumptions on American Foreign Policy, 1893–1946* (Columbia: University of South Carolina Press, 1972), 33.

Japan's failure in the end was not only due to the Western Powers' white supremacy policies, but also to Japanese double standards. According to the former Minister of Justice and influential politician Yukio Ozaki, Japan's racial equality proposal was bound to fail. He declared in March 1919: "How can Japan, which herself practices a policy of exclusion towards the Chinese and ill-treats the people of the newly annexed country of Korea, expect of others what she herself refuses to do?"[94] There was an argument as to whether Japan simply used the racial equality issue to cover their invasion of other Asian countries. Thomas F. Millard, in a report from Paris, explained that the Japanese stand in favor of racial equality was simply a pretext, useful to the pan-Asian propaganda that Japan had for a number of years been purveying in all Asiatic countries, whose most current expression was "race equality."[95]

THE DISAPPOINTMENT

The Japanese had long resented the widespread anti-Japanese sentiments in North America, and with the war over, the immigration issue was bound to come back. The failure of the racial equality proposal was a profound disappointment, whose import was thought to be not "properly understood in the West." For some Japanese, racial equality should serve as "a fundamental principle of an association of nations." In this sense, "The noble words of President Wilson were apparently turned into mockery by sinister deeds."[96] Tokutomi Soho wrote in the *Kokumin* that the failure in Paris was a "disgrace to the country" and disproved Japan's confidence that it had been accepted as a Great Power.[97] The failure of its racial equality proposal reminded the Japanese that no matter how much had been gained in territorial expansion or diplomatic rank, Japan had still not achieved equal footing in the West-dominated world order. In this sense, Japan remained outside the great white power club, a fate it shared with fellow Asians. Japan's sense of disillusionment deepened. The Japanese had no confidence in the League of Nations; they were suspicious of increasing Anglo-American solidarity in East Asia and the Pacific; and they chafed at the 1924 Alien Immigration Act.[98]

The Japanese were plainly more disappointed with others than with themselves. Their high hopes and expectations for Wilson were dashed. Wilson took advantage of his position as Chair of the League of Nations Commission to block the inclusion of a racial equality clause in the final treaty. As Erez Manela wrote: "Perhaps the most glaring contradiction to the universalist message of Wilson's wartime pronouncements on self-determination was his record on race relations in the domestic

---

[94] British Embassy, Tokyo, March 21, 1919, BA: FO 608/211.
[95] Thomas F. Millard, "Japan, 'Race Equality' and the League of Nations," April 6, 1919, in Houghton Library, Harvard University: Immigration Restriction League Papers, MS AM 2245 (1069).
[96] Payson J. Treat, *Japan and the United States, 1853–1921* (Boston: Houghton Mifflin Company, 1921), 234, 242.
[97] *The Japan Times*, 16 April 1919.   [98] Shimazu, *Japan, Race, and Equality*, 171.

American context," which was full of racial assumptions and racist attitudes.[99] Some Japanese called Wilson "an angel in rhetoric and a devil in deed."[100] The Ōsaka *Mainichi* went so far as to charge that the President had a "female demon within him."[101] The editor of *Yorozu* remarked that the failure of the racial equality proposal made a mockery of President Wilson's "contentions for humanity."[102] One editorial summarized the prevailing Japanese feeling: "The world had great expectations of Wilson but he has proven to be self-interested and we are getting tired of it all."[103] With the Wilson administration's support for the "idea of white hegemony in all disregard of humanity and international justice," those Japanese who had relied on the American spirit of justice and humanity had "built a castle of idealism in America, and it collapsed." The Japanese nationalist writer Tokutomi Soho declared that the many Japanese appeals to American goodwill, sympathy, and a sense of justice had all been pointless, and he launched a campaign against what he called "white snobbery." He wrote that the other races "must make the whites realize that there are others as strong as they."[104] Tokutomi Soho's 1921 book, *Japanese-American Relations*, sold 300,000 copies and went through twelve editions in a few months. It stressed Japan's disappointment and disillusionment over American racial hostility, which seemed now to be universal in that country. Japan itself had yet to win the equal treatment accorded the human race in general.

In *Japan, Race, and Equality*, Naoko Shimazu observed that the question of racial equality dominated domestic debate in Japan from November 1918 until May 1919 because of its symbolic importance as an expression of Japan's fears and expectations of the new international order.[105] Public opinion in Japan was inflamed by the failure to achieve the amendment to the Covenant and so remove the "badge of shame" imposed on Asians and Africans by the white race.[106] *Nichi Nichi* believed that the spirit of the League Covenant was dead due to "Anglo-Saxon dominance in defiance of racial equality." Japanese commentators considered themselves to be leading an idealistic crusade; the editor of *Asahi* compared Makino's and Chinda's diplomacy with Britain's insistence in 1815 that the delegates at the Treaty of Vienna condemn the slave trade. Racial discrimination, the newspaper declared, occupied precisely the position in the contemporary world that slavery had one hundred years before. Being the leading non-white power, Japan had the responsibility to fight for two-thirds of the world's population and could not find a "nobler cause." Japan thus "must endeavour to make the Peace Conference leave behind a glorious record of putting an end to an inhuman and anti-civilization practice as did the Vienna Conference a hundred years ago."[107]

[99] Manela, *The Wilsonian Moment*, 26.
[100] Manela, *The Wilsonian Moment*, 197.
[101] Bailey, *Woodrow Wilson and the Lost Peace*, 276.
[102] Lake and Reynolds, *Drawing the Global Colour Line*, 303.
[103] Shimazu, *Japan, Race, and Equality*, 58.
[104] Lake and Reynolds, *Drawing the Global Colour Line*, 272–4.
[105] Shimazu, *Japan, Race, and Equality*, 51.
[106] Lauren, "Human Rights in History," 265.
[107] Lauren, "Human Rights in History," 266.

Even more humiliating, Japan had been betrayed by its own wartime allies. Britain had distanced itself and moved closer to America. And the Japanese felt betrayed by Western models which they worked so hard to learn from and follow. *The Japan Times* wrote that it could not "suppress its anger" at the Anglo-Saxons who thought they could control the wealth of the world and subjugate other races.[108] A long editorial in *the Japan Times* claimed that the failure of Japan to achieve the acceptance of racial equality had caused the "sorest disappointment. . . . A most careful and comprehensive survey of the feelings of typical and leading thinkers shows that they learnt of the fact with the profoundest regret. All agree in feeling that rejection of a demand formally made by a nation is tantamount to a snub and humiliation." The failure of the Japanese racial equality proposal had exposed and placed on record the real truth concerning the attitudes of whites toward non-whites.[109] Japanese commentators continued to discuss the racial equality question after the Peace Conference concluded. In an essay, "My Impressions of the Paris Peace Conference," Prince Konoe Fumimaro argued that he was fully justified in believing that power alone determined the course of international affairs. The racial equality proposal, he argued, had been defeated because Japan, a lesser power, had proposed it. The hope that the world would be reformed based upon principles of justice and equality had been dashed.[110] But the most authoritative commentary regarding Japanese disappointment with the West was provided by the eighty-three-year-old former prime minister Marquis Okuma in an article in *Asian Review*, entitled "Illusions of the White Race." Okuma argued that if the Japanese were to see racial equality prevail in the world, the nation must devote itself to the cause with unswerving determination. "The Whites," he observed, "were obsessed with the mistaken theory that they are superior to all other races." Such a belief was based neither on science nor evidence of any kind. It was "mere superstition, backed by historical prejudices," but it was the most serious obstacle in the way of the realization of racial equality. "Some Whites," Okuma declared, "regard the development of Japan as an unjustifiable encroachment upon their own rights and aim to organise a league of white nations to perpetuate white supremacy in the world." Most Asian nations were "fully peers of European nations, yet they are discriminated against because of the colour of their skin. The root of it lies in the perverted feeling of racial superiority entertained by the whites. If things are allowed to proceed in the present way, there is every likelihood that the peace of the world will be endangered."[111] When the news of the racial equality proposal's failure reached Japan, meetings were being held all over Japan to protest against the "badge of shame" imposed by the so-called "white" upon the so-called "colored" races. The lower house of the Japanese Diet became "the scene of a significant demonstration" against Japanese submission to "a Western abuse."[112]

---

[108] *The Japan Times*, 26 April 1919.   [109] *The Japan Times*, 19 April 1919.
[110] Oka, *Konoe Fumimaro*, 14–15.
[111] K. K. Kawakami, ed., *What Japan Thinks* (New York: Macmillan, 1921), 6–7, 161, 170.
[112] Patrick Gallagher, *America's Aims and Asia's Aspirations* (New York: The Century Co., 1920), 323.

Liberal, internationally-minded Japanese were as dismayed as the nationalists. The liberals believed they had shown themselves ready to participate in the international community on its terms. They were worried that the rebuff could become an important factor in turning the country toward aggressive nationalist policies.[113] According to Shimazu, the failure of the racial equality proposal contributed to Japan's general sense of disillusionment with the West, and especially the Anglo-Saxon powers. Yet the early 1920s postwar governments, under the banner of the "Shidehara diplomacy," adopted the policy of emphasizing international cooperation with the United States and Britain. However, it became evident in the process of pursuing this policy that Japan was becoming secondary to Anglo-American hegemony in East Asia and the Pacific, which emerged as a result of the Washington Conference of 1921–2. Moreover, the 1924 United States Immigration Act undermined Shidehara diplomacy by challenging the wisdom of cooperating with the Americans, who did not hesitate to humiliate the Japanese. Overall, the apparent domestic consensus around international cooperation was possibly not as strong as has been suggested in the past.[114]

In retrospect, it is ironic that the racial equality proposal, which was originally created by the pro-internationalists within the Japanese government as a means to demand Japan's equality with the West, indirectly contributed to making their pro-Western policy less and less tenable. Matsuoka Yosuke, the Japanese representative who executed the dramatic withdrawal from the League of Nations in 1933, referred to the failure of racial equality as an example of the West's bullying Japan at Paris. Naoko Shimazu has concluded that the rejection of Japan's proposal and the unwillingness to acknowledge Japan as an equal had deeper psychological effects than has generally been understood, and left an indelible mark on its foreign policy.[115] Japan's disappointment at the Paris Conference was reflected in the Showa emperor's linking the principal legacy of the conference with that rejected clause. Combined with anti-Japanese immigration sentiment in California, the rejection of the racial equality language was "enough to anger the Japanese people"; it was sufficient to argue in his 1946 declaration, "The Background Causes to a Greater East Asia War," that the root of the Second World War "lies with the contents of the peace treaty signed at the end of the First World War."[116]

The racial equality proposal began as a means for Japanese nationals overseas to achieve equal treatment, but in time it came to represent a human rights initiative of global significance. The whole Asian world shared the Japanese dream. As an American reporter at the Paris Conference wrote: "United Asia asks [for] national equality."[117] The Japanese idea of racial equality in the heady, idealistic moment at the end of the Great War—the Wilsonian moment—became a universal one

---

[113] MacMillan, *Paris, 1919*, 319–21.   [114] Shimazu, *Japan, Race, and Equality*, 175–6.
[115] Shimazu, *Japan, Race, and Equality*, 179–81.
[116] Kenneth Pyle, *Japan Rising: The Resurgence of Japanese Power and Purpose* (New York: Public Affairs, 2007), 158.
[117] Gallagher, *America's Aims and Asia's Aspirations*, 317–23.

after the second conflagration to be called a "world war."[118] Supporters and opponents alike came to see bringing an end to racial discrimination as a universal crusade. In his groundbreaking study of Indian and Chinese responses to Wilson's promise of self-determination, Erez Manela criticized existing scholarship for remaining "rather single-mindedly focussed on Europe."[119] The struggle over the racial equality clause was closely watched in other parts of the non-European world. Chinese delegate V. K. Wellington Koo told Patrick Gallagher, an American foreign correspondent at Paris for *The New York Herald*, that he had received letters and telegrams from Chinese all over the world, including major American cities, Java, South Africa, and Australia urging him to support the Japanese proposal. At the conference, Koo went on record as being in favor of the proposal and wanting to support the Covenant to give recognition to the Japanese principle.[120] Koo and his fellow delegate, C. T. Wang, who were American-educated cosmopolitans, wrote a pamphlet in English to put forward the Chinese case for "a new order of things which would ensure universal peace." Memory of the defeat of the racial equality clause weighed heavily on the delegates who gathered at San Francisco in 1945 to draft a Charter for the United Nations. This time, the assembly embraced human rights for all, regardless of race, nationality, ethnicity, religion, or gender. Among the delegates was Wellington Koo.[121]

In November 1920, the new Russian socialist leader V. I. Lenin, who was vigilant for cracks in the Great Wall of capitalism, asked "are there any radical antagonisms in the modern capitalist world that must be utilized?" It seemed to him that the racial issue might bring the US and Japan to eventual war.[122] If Lenin here thought about a war within the capitalist world, we can make a further link between the race issue and a clash of civilizations. To a great extent, the widespread idea of the decline of the West contributed to the rising anti-Japanese feeling in the West. For many anti-Japanese Westerners, the future of Western civilization depended on its white racial purity: "White civilization is to-day coterminous with the white race."[123] When Japan went to Paris to take part in making decisions for a new world order, Japan, as a recently accepted "civilized" nation, hoped for a "civilized" status as equal as anyone in the world. However, even to attain "civilized" status, as Japan discovered at Paris Peace Conference, was not necessarily to become equal—"The 'civilized' had a way of becoming more 'civilized' still." As Gerrit W. Gong argued, progress toward "civilized" status was necessary and possible for the less "civilized" to achieve, but "complete and perfect equality was not." Gong wrote that "in a world governed by the principle of self-help, Japan was naïve to assume that attaining 'civilized' acceptance meant attaining equality. Still,

[118] For the most recent study of the optimism unleashed by the "Wilsonian moment," see Erez Manela, "Imagining Woodrow Wilson in Asia: Dreams of East-West Harmony and the Revolt against Empire in 1919," *American Historical Review*, 111:5 (December 2006), 1327–51.
[119] Manela, "Imagining Woodrow Wilson in Asia," 1328–9.
[120] Gallagher, *America's Aims and Asia's Aspirations*, 321–2.
[121] Manela, "Imagining Woodrow Wilson in Asia," 1348.
[122] Daniels, *The Politics of Prejudice*, 65.   [123] Daniels, *The Politics of Prejudice*, 67.

while such equality as symbolized by the denial of the racial equality clause in 1919, may have been a mirage, it was only after Japan declared the fountains of international law to be dry that it embarked on its own revisionist course."[124] With the failure of its racial equality dream in Paris, Japan "had difficulty recognizing that it had entered an international society that was still both anarchical and hierarchical."[125] Eventually, and ironically, the failure of its racial equality initiative in Paris contributed to Japan's ultimate decision to go it alone or expand its empire in the name of a so-called Asian way. Chapter 8 will tell that story.

[124] Gong, *The Standard of "Civilization" in International Society*, 63.
[125] Gong, *The Standard of "Civilization" in International Society*, 199.

PART IV

TOWARD A NEW ASIA
AND WORLD?

8

Asia Rethinks Its Relation to the World

The entire twentieth century was shaped by the Great War's massive moral and physical destruction. British philosopher and pacifist Bertrand Russell discovered to his amazement that in Britain "average men and women were delighted at the prospect of war."[1] Few understood what lay ahead, but around the world many pondered its meaning and its impact. As Edward Grey, the British foreign secretary, famously declared, "The lamps are going out all over Europe; we shall not see them lit again in our lifetime."[2] H. G. Wells titled a 1915 article for *The New York Times* "Civilization at the Breaking Point"—"civilization," of course, meant Western civilization. Americans largely viewed the Europeans through Henry James's spectacles:

> Europe was complex, cunning, riven with plots and double-dealing, culturally rich but morally and politically decadent; America was bright, forward-looking, innocent, resistant to cabals, still fresh with promise. The average American knew little of the outside world and cared less. There was an unspoken understanding that a foreign policy was strictly unnecessary, or was simply a rhetorical flourish, useful for inaugurals and Independence Day speeches.[3]

THE GREAT WAR AND WESTERN CIVILIZATION

As early as August 1917, with incomprehensibly barbaric fighting bringing appalling destruction, the American educator and philosopher John Dewey exclaimed: "The world is dead; long live the world! A great civilization has just passed away; we are being swept at lightning speed into an altogether new and strange form of society. It will be as different from the society of four years ago as that society was different from the Middle Ages." Dewey admitted it was difficult to think through the war's true significance, but he could still point out:

> Just now we are fighting for democracy. Democracy is a fact in the minds of most Americans. They think, at least, that they know what it means. It seems certain that the Allies will be victorious and I believe they will find democracy. But that democracy will be as different from the democracy of their concepts as the New World was different from the Orient which Columbus sought. . . . We are fighting to do away with the rule

---

[1] Bertrand Russell, *Autobiography* (London: Routledge, 1998), 239.
[2] Edward Grey, *Twenty-five Years, 1892–1916* (London: Hodder and Stoughton, 1925), 2: 223.
[3] Quoted from Brian Morton, *Woodrow Wilson, USA* (London: Haus, 2008), 69.

of kings and Kaisers. When we have finished the job we may find that we have done away with the rule of money and trade. We are fighting for freedom to transact business; but this war might easily be the beginning of the end of business.

Dewey speculated that even the family might soon "cease to exist."[4] Such new inner doubts fueled predictions of collapse, and the German scholar Oswald Spengler's *The Decline of the West* stormed bestseller lists worldwide.[5]

The carnage on the Western Front made a mockery of the conceit that discovery and invention necessarily delivered progress and benefit to humanity. The Great War had become "an industry of professionalized human slaughter" and technology could be equated with tyranny. The future of Western civilization was threatened by the very machines it had created. Bertrand Russell and Sigmund Freud suggested that years of bloodshed in the heartland of their civilization demonstrated that Europeans were as susceptible to atavistic responses and primeval drives as were any colonized people. According to Michael Adas, a historian of South Asia, "This mechanized slaughter undermined the credibility of most of the ideals and assumptions upon which Europeans had based their sense of superiority and from which they had fashioned that ideological testament to their unprecedented hubris, the civilizing mission."[6]

Yet the corrosive effects of the Great War on those who carried the civilizing mission to the colonies "were felt only with the passage of time, and then quite unevenly."[7] Prasenjit Duara, another distinguished Asia scholar, has observed that the First World War era fundamentally transformed the relationship between nations and civilizations: "Western Civilization had forfeited the right to represent the highest goals of humanity," and in Asia "the new national movements sought to turn towards their own civilizational traditions—often reconstructed in the image of Civilization—to found the ideals of the new nations and the right to sovereignty."[8]

Ideas of East versus West that emerged during the Great War were premised upon this idea of civilizational spirituality. The war had demonstrated massive problems with the Western version of civilization and the world seemed to be searching for a new template. Writer after writer in Asia and around the world denounced the materialism and destructiveness of the West. At the same time, the war settlement at Versailles and the new balance of power jump-started the beginning of decolonization, the emergence of new nation-states, and the

[4] John Dewey, "Sunday World, August 5, 1917," typed manuscript, in Rare Book and Manuscript Library, Columbia University: central file, box 321, folder 13: John Dewey.

[5] The two volumes of the German edition were published, respectively, in 1918 and 1922 by C. H. Beck'sche Verlagsbuchhandlung, Munich. It was soon translated into many other languages.

[6] Michael Adas, "The Great War and the Decline of the Civilizing Mission," in Laurie J. Sears, ed., *Autonomous Histories, Particular Truths: Essays in Honor of John R. Smail* (Madison, WI: University of Wisconsin Center for Southeast Asian Studies, 1993), 109.

[7] Adas, "The Great War and the Decline of the Civilizing Mission," in Sears, ed., *Autonomous Histories, Particular Truths*, 117–18.

[8] Prasenjit Duara, "The Imperialism of 'Free Nations': Japan, Manchukuo, and the History of the Present," in Ann Laura Stoler, Carole McGranahan, and Peter C. Perdue, eds., *Imperial Formations* (Santa Fe: School for Advanced Research Press, 2007), 214.

ascendancy of anti-imperialism. These new political forces had little use for Civilization. Duara further argues that the critique of Civilization launched by both Western and non-Western intellectuals centered on "the betrayal of the universalizing promise of the 'civilizing mission'—a mission which exemplified the desire not (simply) to conquer the other, but to be desired by the other."[9]

The Great War for the first time forced people of different races, regions, and religions to think about their roots and how they fit into this new idea of the world. The war launched new nationalist projects. Harvard-educated W. E. B. DuBois was in Paris during the peace conference, where he lobbied for pan-Africanism. He deplored the conference's failure to adopt Japan's racial equality amendment, which confirmed his view of white arrogance and underlined the need for a world congress in which black and brown and yellow could curb the "selfish nations of white civilization."[10] DuBois elaborated this view in *Darkwater*, a collection of essays published in 1920. In his classic essay "Souls of White Folk," DuBois declared that the recent "shameful" war, a white civil war in Europe, was nothing compared with the fight for freedom which the "black and brown and yellow men must make and will make unless their oppression and humiliation and insult at the hands of the White World cease."[11] DuBois' greatest achievement in Paris was to convene a First Pan-African Congress. He had tried to win support from Woodrow Wilson, but only got as far as the president's gatekeeper, Colonel House, who gave him a "sympathetic but non-committal hearing"—but that was more than other activists and nationalists received.[12]

For Asians, as for Africans, the Great War was a white man's war, a European war, but it forced them to reflect on who they were and their position in the world. The Great War helped them to reconsider the values of Western civilization that many had innocently embraced.[13] This chapter addresses the war's cultural and political effects in Asia.[14]

---

[9] Prasenjit Duara, "The Discourse of Civilization and Pan-Asianism," *Journal of World History*, 12:1 (Spring 2001), 104–6.

[10] For details, see W. E. B. DuBois, "The League of Nations," *Crisis*, May 1919.

[11] W. E. B. DuBois, *Darkwater: Voices from Within the Veil* (New York: Harcourt, Brace and Howe, 1920), 35, 49.

[12] For DuBois' recollections, see DuBois, "The Pan-African Congresses: The Story of a Growing Movement," in David Levering Lewis, *W. E. B. DuBois: A Reader* (New York: Henry Holt and Company, 1995), 670–5; Lake and Reynolds, *Drawing the Global Colour Line*, 306.

[13] South Asian scholars' work was presented in the panel "The Internationalist Moment: South Asia, Worlds, and World Views, 1919–1939" at the Annual Conference on South Asia, Madison, WI, October 2009. See also Michele L. Louro, *At Home in the World: Jawaharlal Nehru and Global Anti-Imperialism* (PhD thesis, Temple University, 2011), 15.

[14] Regrettably, there is not enough material for an adequate discussion of Korean or Vietnamese reflections on the war. Ho Chi-minh did comment on postwar Asian thinking, however. For instance, he published an article in *La Revue Communiste* of May 15, 1921, which reads, "Asians—although considered backward by Westerners—understand better, however, the need for total reform of the present society. And here is why... The great Confucius (551 B.C.) advocated internationalism and preached the equality of wealth. He says that world peace comes only with a universal Republic. One should not be afraid of having little, but of not having equally." Brocheux, *Ho Chi Minh: A Biography*, 20.

NEW THINKING IN JAPAN

The Great War and its aftermath provided ample food for thought in Japan. Tokyo Mayor Sakatani Yoshiro suggested that a general European war meant conflict "in the heart of world civilization, in the heart of world finance, in the heart of world transportation." It was like "succumbing to an illness in the most precious organs of the heart and lungs." Asada Emura, a staff writer for the popular monthly *Taiyo*, noted in September 1914 that "the high level of civilized living that they boasted for so long is quickly being demolished, without apology, in the face of the bloodcurdling ferocity of war."[15]

With war ravaging Europe, the Japanese began thinking of the broader picture. As A. Morgan Young, editor of the English-language Kobe daily *The Japan Chronicle*, observed: "By the end of July 1914 developments on the other side of the world, perhaps for the first time in Japan's history, eclipsed more local interests."[16] Observers in Japan as well as in Europe anticipated the most fundamental consequences of a general European conflagration: an epic transformation of international politics and culture. At the very least, such a conflict would mark the end of European centrality in modern civilization. Given the overwhelming importance of European models in the construction of the modern world, the war threatened profound repercussions. At issue now was a global standard of civilization.

If the Great War raised desperate questions about European ideas of "civilization," it also presaged an alternative order. From an early date, Japanese policy-makers and opinion leaders considered the rise of the United States to be a natural corollary to European decline. The US had, after all, followed just behind the European powers in imperial politics and posed the greatest challenge to Japan's burgeoning continental interests. As Yoshino Sakuzō noted in 1917, Wilson's ideas would "have an important bearing on the advance of civilization after the war." For the Seiyukai Party President Hara Takashi, it was evident that "world affairs will completely change" under pressure from the new American belligerence.

The new definition of civilization made it necessary to retool beyond simple physical transformation, and much of this reconstruction occurred far from the flattened fields of Flanders. Japan specialists have generally described the interwar years as an era of leisure, but just as historians of the nineteenth century have written about a culture of Western fads, fashions, and gadgets that accompanied Japan's dramatic modernization, one might view interwar Japan as something more than a random assortment of reforms or obsession with the pleasures of exotic technologies. Just as the founders of modern Japan in the Meiji Restoration were inspired to base their modernization on Western "civilization and enlightenment," the architects of New Japan responded to the ruin of the Somme with a concerted effort to embrace a new culture of peace. As elder statesman Saionji Kinmochi declared in September 1919, it was "time for Japan to invest wholeheartedly in the

[15] Dickinson, *World War I and the Triumph of a New Japan*, 19–20.
[16] Dickinson, *World War I and the Triumph of a New Japan*, 20.

arts, industry and commerce, to become an active contributor to the new global peace project (*heiwateki jigyo*)."[17]

Many Japanese agreed that their country should seize the momentum and the moment. After 1919, Japan again embraced a spirit of change and reform. Many have made explicit parallels with the Meiji transformation of the state. For the first time in the fifty years since the Meiji Restoration, noted Hara Takashi, "it is time for a national renovation." Yoshino Sakuzō felt so strongly about parallels between Japan after the Great War and the late nineteenth-century reforms that he and several Tokyo University colleagues embarked upon an enormous compilation of Meiji documents, titled *A Study of Meiji Culture*. Journalist and politician Tagawa Daikichiro described the Paris Peace Conference as a global version of the Meiji Restoration: "Now is the time for Japan to rise in the spirit of the first renovation." The biweekly *Nihon Oyobi Nihonjin* reported in September 1919: "Today's key-word is to reform everything." Katō Takaaki argued that Japan should strive to realize "the best of world civilization in politics, industry, wisdom and morality, technology, thought and custom."[18] Even the aristocrat Konoe Fumimaro suggested that one lesson of the Paris Peace Conference was that we "Japanese must now, all the more, nurture knowledge and a general grasp of the world."[19]

From the time of the Meiji Restoration, Japanese elites had tried to make Japan into a Westernized country so it could join the Western ranks. They seemed to have been quite successful until the Great War and the Paris Peace Conference, when Japan's racial equality proposal was rejected. The Japanese were forced to realize that no matter how successful and powerful they became, they would not be treated as equals and could never gain the trust of the West. By emphasizing the geopolitical separation of Asia from the West, they tried to argue that a nation's conduct could be based on principles other than those laid out by the Western Powers. One of the most important repercussions from the racial equality debate of 1919 was the depth of pan-Asian feeling in Japanese public opinion.

According to Frederick Dickinson, the First World War's transformation of modern Japanese life surpassed in many ways the nineteenth-century arrival of the "black ships." "While Commodore Perry spurred a vigorous internal debate by simply making landfall, the First World War, after all, altered Japan from within by dramatically transforming the national economy and catapulting Japan, for the first time in history, to world power status."[20]

After 1919, Japan was ready for change and reform. That zeal for change was embodied in the Imperial Rescript on the establishment of peace of January 1920: "The course of events has completely changed and remains in the process of transformation. It is time to follow a path of great effort and flexibility. You subjects should pursue this deeply and officials of the land should faithfully follow

[17] Dickinson, "Toward a Global Perspective of the Great War," 1154–83.
[18] Dickinson, *World War I and the Triumph of a New Japan*, 27–31.
[19] Dickinson, *World War I and the Triumph of a New Japan*, 31.
[20] Dickinson, *World War I and the Triumph of a New Japan*, 12.

this by attempting to realize, in accordance with the international situation, a League of Nations peace."[21]

THE NATIONALIST ORIGINS OF ASIANISM

"Asianism," or "pan-Asianism," was a political and cultural discourse that conceived and defined Asia as a homogenous region that shared clear and unique character-istics. It emerged directly from the rethinking of Western and Asian civilizations in the face of the West's moral decline. In the beginning, Asianism was an intellectual development widely shared among cultural elites. Unfortunately, it would get a bad name for its association with Japanese aggression and imperialist ambitions.

As the first Asian nation to be accepted as a "civilized" state and a major power in the world, Japan was a hotbed of Asianist thinking and showed what pan-Asianism might achieve. The writer and political thinker Okakura Tenshin (aka Kakuzo) played an important role in articulating its basic ideas. Okakura is the author of *The Ideals of the East with Special Reference to the Arts of Japan* (published in 1903), which famously promoted the idea that "Asia is one."[22] Okakura knew Chinese and Indian cultures well and was deeply versed in the shared Asian religion of Buddhism. He had close connections with fellow Asians who seemed to have shared his ideas, such as Rabindranath Tagore and Ananda Coomarswamy. Tagore and Okakura had a close friendship, and Okakura spent considerable time in India acquiring a deep respect for its arts and culture while introducing Indians to Chinese and Japanese culture.[23] Okakura's ideals had tremendous appeal among educated Indians and Chinese, and were echoed loudly in the wake of the Great War.[24] According to Duara, Japanese pan-Asianism at the turn of the century included imperialistic strains but also egalitarian and compassionate feelings toward fellow Asians who had been exploited and devastated by aggressive cultures. Japanese pan-Asianism articulated the responsibility to raise Asians from their fallen state. Okakura could not refrain from positioning Japan at the head of this new Asia, and his thinking eventually developed into the ideological foundation of Japanese imperialism, endowing it with a mission to lead the region forward.[25]

Another important voice in promoting Asianism was Kodera Kenkichi (1877–1949), a politician and an expert on international relations and international law. In 1916, he published "A Treatise on Greater Asianism" (*Dai-Ajiashugi-ron*), a central work in shaping Asianist ideology. Kodera argued that the Asian

[21] Dickinson, *World War I and the Triumph of a New Japan*, 34.

[22] For details on this, see Rustom Bharucha, *Another Asia: Rabindranath Tagore and Okakura Tenshin* (New Delhi: Oxford University Press, 2006).

[23] Prasenjit Duara, "Asia Redux: Conceptualizing a Region for Our Times," *The Journal of Asian Studies*, 69:4 (November 2010), 969.

[24] For details on this point, see Harald Fischer-Tine, "Indian Nationalism and the 'World Forces': Transnational and Diasporic Dimensions of the Indian Freedom Movement on the Eve of the First World War," *Journal of Global History*, 2 (2007), 325–44.

[25] Duara, "Asia Redux," 970.

nations needed to unite against Western imperialism. To promote his views to a wider audience, Kodera's book was translated into Chinese and published in Shanghai in 1918. The book begins with the following passage:

> Isn't it strange? In Europe, which controls Asia at will and has completely subdued it, these days we hear voices that warn of a yellow peril. However, among the colored races, which are subjugated and threatened by the white race, hardly a peep against the white peril can be heard. Yet while there can be no doubt that the yellow peril is nothing more than a bad dream, the white peril is a reality.[26]

Kodera's main theme was the need for Asians to unite against Western expansionist ambitions and racism, and he, like many of his contemporaries, anticipated a "clash of races." In this coming conflict, Japan was the only possible candidate for leadership of a united Asia. Sven Saaler suggests that "A Treatise on Greater Asianism" was the beginning of a wave of publications that led to the pan-Asian movement and organizations. Kodera's call for a "glorious new Asian civilization under Japanese leadership and guidance" was to be based on close Sino-Japanese cooperation. Japan would become the "educator" of China and indeed of the whole of Asia, and introduce modern civilization to bring about the birth of a "new Asian civilization." It was Kodera who coined the term "Asianism" and who brought the ideology of Asianism closer to Japanese party politics and government circles. Saaler, an expert on Kodera's thought, argues that in Japan, intellectual discourse on "Asia" and Asianism was absorbed by politicians, adjusted to suit political needs, and manipulated and exploited by political actors. In the years after the Meiji Restoration, how to deal with Asian neighbors had been a crucial topic of debate. The government adopted Western imperialist practices, but many in Japan took the opposite side and argued that the Empire should instead support (and eventually unite with) other Asian nations to expel the Western Powers. Saaler demonstrates that by the end of the First World War, a new, rigorous, and systematic ideology with concrete contents had coalesced: pan-Asianism.

In direct opposition to the earlier strategy of "leaving Asia" (*datsu-A*), pan-Asian agitators demanded a "return to Asia" (*Ajia kaiki*). In the wake of the Great War, many Japanese politicians and writers such as Kodera considered Japan capable of challenging the West if it could become the leader of a united Asia. Following on from the concept of regional integration, Kodera argued that the realization of this goal lay in combining a romantic ideology of regional unity with the government's practice of imperialist realpolitik. Saaler maintains that while Kodera's fusion of these two approaches paved the way for a wider acceptance of pan-Asian thought in Japanese politics, it must be seen as the beginning of Japanese appropriation of regionalism for the purposes of its own imperialistic foreign policy. The push for unity eventually led to rivalry over leadership in East Asia, and it was only a small step from Kodera's concept of "Greater Asia" under Japanese leadership to the

---

[26] Quoted from Sven Saaler, "The Construction of Regionalism in Modern Japan: Kodera Kenkichi and His Treatise on Greater Asianism (1916)," *Modern Asian Studies*, 41:6 (November 2007), 1271.

legitimization of imperial expansion, with concept of regionalism playing a purely ancillary role.[27]

Kayahara Kazan (1880–1951) was another influential promoter of Asianism. According to Duara, Kayahara's philosophy sought to synthesize the thought of various Western philosophers such as Hegel, Henri Bergson, and Emerson, as well as the geographical determinism of Henry Buckle and Ratzel. "Kayahara delineated his own stages of civilization, posited the distinction between the dynamic northern civilizations of the Europeans and the 'still' southern civilizations, and explained these in terms of geography and environment. Like other Taisho intellectuals, he too arrived at the necessity of synthesizing the two civilizations."[28]

ASIANISM FROM IDEOLOGY TO POLICY

It was no coincidence that the conclusion to the Great War gave rise to a sense of urgency that fed pan-Asian thought and policy. At Japan's withdrawal from the League of Nations in 1933, the Japanese trumpeted the failure of racial equality in 1919 as justification for pulling away from an unfair international order. In February 1933, one month before Japan's withdrawal, Konoe wrote: "In thinking about it, the Paris Peace Conference was the ideal opportunity to correct the existing irrationalities in the world and to establish a true world peace. This conference was held immediately after the war and the politicians who attended it had all experienced much pain with the horrors of the war. However, the Paris Conference did not recognize the blatant irrationality of discriminating against people by skin colour."[29] This had happened in spite of all that Japan's delegate, Baron Makino, had said about the injustice of the race issue, a problem that might become acute if not seen to.[30]

The Japanese, like everyone else, had read Wilson's "Fourteen Points" of 1918, which eloquently asserted "the principle of justice to all peoples and nationalities, and their right to live on equal terms of liberty and safety with one another." The Japanese assumed this stated goal would allow them to enjoy racial equality, but Korean and Chinese nationalists viewed the Fourteen Points as a proclamation of the right of national self-determination, which in their cases could be aimed squarely at Japanese imperialism. But the Japanese resisted the protests of the Chinese and Koreans just as the West rejected the Japanese cry for racial equality. As Harvard historian Akira Iriye has argued, the postwar world was an Americanized world. Among the Japanese who had been acutely aware of the racial, cultural, and psychological gaps between themselves and the West, "little had changed." Japan's problems with self-definition would not go away. The American

---

[27] Saaler, "The Construction of Regionalism in Modern Japan," 1261–94.
[28] Duara, "The Discourse of Civilization and Pan-Asianism," 113.
[29] Shimazu, *Japan, Race, and Equality*, 179.
[30] S. M. Molema, *The Bantu, Past and Present* (Edinburgh: W. Green, 1920), 352.

immigration law of 1924, which specifically excluded Japanese immigration while giving annual quotas to European countries, confirmed the "seemingly unbridge-able gap separating Japan and the West." At the same time, the Japanese treated Koreans and Chinese as second-class citizens, which indicated that they accepted the prevailing assumptions about racial inequality. "It was simply that they themselves did not want to be considered inferior," Iriye observed.[31]

Until the First World War, Japanese politicians who used pan-Asian rhetoric were still on the fringe, and the government hesitated to give them its backing. Asianism penetrated government circles and official diplomacy only after the war, when it became a practical option for policymakers.[32] Scholar and journalist Nagase Hosuke put it this way in 1921:

> The fate of Asia has to be decided by Asians—this phrase has been heard among officials in our country for quite a while. However, it is a sad fact that, until just prior to the Great War, this kind of statement was not very welcome and it remained in the realm of idealism. But fortunately today the opportunity for the realization [of this notion] has come. I have recently met with representatives from the Bashkirs and the Confucian Tartars for intimate talks, and they, too, stated that they believe that the organization of an Asian League should not be difficult.[33]

Against the backdrop of the Great War, Takebe Tongo, a professor of sociology at the Imperial University of Tokyo, argued that the East Asian concept and practice of *jingi* (morals) was superior to the Western concept *seigi* (justice). He suggested that, whereas *jingi* meant humanitarian fairness based on self-giving love, *seigi* remained a merely legalistic term.[34] Miyazaki Toten (1871–1922), the philosopher who had offered such fervent help to Sun Yat-sen in the 1911 Revolution, declared in 1919:

> There is a good reason that, at the present world peace conference, Japan has fallen into isolation, alienated from the Western Powers. This is because the principles that control Japan follow the so-called gospel of the sword, in imitation of German militarism, and it was these principles that Japan has been applying to China and Korea. But, if anything, this is a natural outcome. The Western Powers, which pride themselves on their Christianity, look down on us as alien beings; they pretend to be sheep but have the greed of tigers and wolves in their hearts, and are ready to pounce whenever an opportunity arises. . . . It is possible that their goal is to deprive Japan of its freedom of movement. . . . But if this is so, how is the Japanese nation to act?[35]

---

[31] Akira Iriye, "Japanese Culture and Foreign Relations," The Richard Story Memorial Lecture, No. 5 (Oxford: St. Antony's College, 1992), 10.

[32] Sven Saaler, "Pan-Asianism in Modern Japanese History," in Sven Saaler and J. Victor Koschmann, eds., *Pan-Asianism in Modern Japanese History: Colonialism, Regionalism and Borders* (London: Routledge, 2007), 6.

[33] Saaler, "Pan-Asianism in Modern Japanese History," in Saaler and Koschmann, eds., *Pan-Asianism in Modern Japanese History*, 7.

[34] Miwa Kimitada, "Pan-Asianism in Modern Japan," in Saaler and Koschmann, eds., *Pan-Asianism in Modern Japanese History*, 27.

[35] Sven Saaler and Christopher W. A. Szpilman, eds., *Pan-Asianism: A Documentary History* (Lanham, MD: Rowman & Littlefield, 2011), 138–9.

Although Japan was certainly in a strong position, there was also anxiety about the nation's direction. With the defeat of Germany and Austria and the collapse of the Ottoman and Romanov empires, along with their monarchs, "Long-held assumptions in Tokyo about the endurance of militarist, autocratic regimes quickly lost their resonance." As financial director of the Kenseikai Party, Tomita Kojiro declared in January 1919: "Germany's surrender has challenged militarism and bureaucratism from the roots. As a natural consequence, politics based on the people, reflecting the will of the people, namely democracy, has, like a race to heaven, conquered the thought of the entire world." Some in Japan then even suggested that "democracy has critical importance in the development of civilization." Seki Kazushi, the Kenseikai's vice chair of policy planning, announced in September 1918: "We hereby declare the eradication of militarism . . . for the prestige of Empire."[36] But Japan could not easily drop the imperial system, since the emperor claimed that his absolute power came from heaven and blood lineage, and militarism was deeply rooted in Japanese culture.

Pan-Asianism began to register in the popular press even before the war's end. As early as August 1914, the journal *Chūō kōron* had highlighted the term "Asian nationality" (*Ajia minzoku*) and called for a new consciousness; sooner or later, Asian people would awaken and demand justice from the rest of the world. The abuse, discrimination, and exploitation Asians suffered at the hands of Western Powers would motivate Asians to be stronger. With the world at a historical turning point, it was time for Asians to work for a better future.[37]

In an article in the April 1917 issue of *Chūō kōron*, scholar Wakamiya Unosuke suggested that pan-Asianism was about kicking out the Western Powers and reclaiming Asia for the Asians, and that it sprang from mistrust of the West and its civilization.[38] By April 1918, Nagai Ryūtarō, a politician and scholar, declared in a *Chūō kōron* piece that it was important for Japan to play a dominant role in China, thus linking Japan's challenge to white civilization with its own aggressive expansion. Only with a Japan made strong at China's expense could Asian civilization break the monopoly of the West and introduce a new era in the history of world civilizations.[39] In other words, the Japanese argument for pan-Asianism had become a sort of Asian Monroe Doctrine that turned the entire region into Japan's backyard.

Back at the very outbreak of war in 1914, a flood of appeals from Japanese patriots had called for prompt action in China. Inoue suggested sending a high-level emissary to Beijing, while the elder statesman Yamagata Aritomo declared that Japanese interests in China were based on the "inseparable spirit" between the two

---

[36] Dickinson, *World War I and the Triumph of a New Japan*, 86–8.

[37] No Author, "To Promote Consciousness of Asian nationality" ("Ajia minzoku no kakugo o unagasu"), *Chūō kōron* (August 1914).

[38] Wakamiya Unosuke, "What is Great Pan-Asianism?" ("Dai Ajia shugi to wa nanizoya?"), *Chūō kōron* (April 1917).

[39] Nagai Ryūtarō, "Sino-Japanese Cooperation as the Pre-condition for Promoting Japan's Great World Mission" ("Waga sekaiteki daishimei o hatasu zentei toshite no Shina teikei"), *Chūō kōron* (April 1918).

countries, and Terauchi devised the "Asian Monroe Doctrine" idea.[40] Over the course of the war, in their search for a more independent and self-assertive policy toward the Asian continent, Japan's leaders gradually developed a pluralistic and regionalist approach to justify Japan's hegemony. Based on the idea that China and Japan had a "special relationship" because of geopolitical, economic, racial, and cultural commonalities, Japanese leaders defended their country's position there and promoted Japanese "tutelage" over China.[41]

For these reasons, the United States and Japan stood far apart in their views of the world when hostilities in Europe came to an end. Wilson preferred a world order based on the new diplomacy, while Japan worked hard to preserve the old style of diplomacy based in imperialism. "When one reads Japanese journals and newspapers published during the period 1918–22, one soon notices that many authors criticized the Western Powers such as Britain and the United States. They used such terms as 'justice' and 'humanity' to denote their moral high ground."[42] Hashikawa Bunzo's work has shown that pan-Asianism in Japan contained a solidarity-oriented, non-dominating conception of Japan's role in reviving Asia, as well as the conception of Japan as, what we might call in short, the harmonizing or synthesizing leader. Pan-Asianism in Japan both fed and resisted Japan's own nascent imperialism.[43]

In the immediate aftermath of the war, a group of Japanese Asianists, in alliance with disaffected Korean elites, worked to establish a utopian, anti-Western government called the Koryo (Gaoli) nation in the borderland between Manchuria and Korea, which had been the location of the ancient Koguryo state. About one million laboring Koreans in the Jiandao region were vulnerable because of their essentially stateless situation. Their leaders drafted a constitution based on Chinese Confucian values, under which Koreans, Japanese, Chinese, and Asian Russians would all be equal citizens.

Historians in China have largely neglected or dismissed such new civilizational discourse and its links to pan-Asianism, due to its association with Japanese imperialism. Ishikawa Yoshihiro argued that the development of East–West civilizational discourse among Chinese intellectuals during the years 1910–19 was closely connected to that in Japan, even though it would take distinctive shape in China. Through the years 1910–19 and the early 1920s, according to Prasenjit Duara, Japan continued to be the principal lens through which the Chinese gained modern knowledge; there was a steady influx of Japanese books and magazines, together with ever-increasing numbers of Western works translated from the Japanese. The new civilizational discourse entered through the same routes and

[40] Dickinson, "Japanese Empire," in Gerwarth and Manela, eds., *Empires at War*, 197–213.

[41] Kawamura, *Turbulence in the Pacific*, 134.

[42] Harumi Goto-Shibata, "Internationalism and Nationalism: Anti-Western Sentiments in Japanese Foreign Policy Debates, 1918-22," in Naoko Shimazu, ed., *Nationalisms in Japan* (London: Routledge, 2006), 66.

[43] Bunzo Hashikawa, "Japanese Perspectives on Asia: From Dissociation to Co-prosperity," in Akira Iriye, ed., *The Chinese and the Japanese: Essays in Political and Cultural Interactions* (Princeton, NJ: Princeton University Press, 1980), 331–41.

brought with it a number of the same assumptions upon which it had been constructed or reconstructed in Japan: the geographical and environmental bases of civilizational differences, the role of linear progressive history, and the binary construction, synthesis formulation, and redemptive character of Eastern civilization, among others.[44]

In short, Japan's interest in the idea of pan-Asianism coincided with the First World War and represented a dramatic change from their long-standing commitment to *datsu-A nyu-O* (escaping from Asia and joining the West) that first took hold during the Meiji Restoration. Although the seriousness with which the Japanese treated the idea of regional unity may be in question, it was certainly a new development in their thinking about themselves and world affairs.

EVOLVING EXPECTATIONS IN CHINA

In China, as in Japan, the war forced many to rethink the relation between Western civilization and their own tradition. Journals like *New Youth* and *New Tide* sprang up like daisies. The New Culture and May Fourth Movements grew out of developments around the Great War. Debates about "new" versus "old" touched upon all manner of issues—social, political, cultural, even civilizational—and generated much attention and activity across Chinese society. In truth, some Chinese thinkers, like their Japanese counterparts, had argued for a sort of Asianism before the outbreak of the Great War. Zhang Taiyan (aka Zhang Binglin), widely considered one of the most powerful intellectuals of late Qing and early Republican China, attended meetings with Indian freedom fighters commemorating the birth of the Maratha warrior Shivaji, who had fought against the Moguls. Zhang was also said to have written the manifesto of the Asian Solidarity Society, which was created in Tokyo around 1907 in support of the idea that Asia was unique and had shared values and traditions. Zhang's commitment to Buddhism and an anti-imperialist position meant that he "saw the threat to peaceful, agrarian societies from warlike Western cultures." But while committed to peace, like Okakura, Zhang acknowledged the necessity of creating a modern nation-state along the Western model to combat the imperialist powers. Duara concludes that "nationalism was a necessary moment in the conception of pan-Asianism."[45]

Others argued for some version of Asian idealism during the Great War. The Malay-born, British- and German-educated scholar Gu Hongming wrote as early as 1915:

> The one and only way for the people of Europe, for the people of the countries now at war, not only to get out of this war, but to save the civilization of Europe . . . is for them now to tear up their present Magna Carta . . . ; in fact to adopt the Religion of good citizenship with its Magna Carta of loyalty such as we have here in China.[46]

[44] Duara, "The Discourse of Civilization and Pan-Asianism," 111–13.
[45] Duara, "Asia Redux," 970–1.
[46] Ku Hung-Ming, *The Spirit of the Chinese People* (Peking: The Peking Daily News, 1915), 168.

Du Yaquan, the editor of *Dongfang zazhi* (*Eastern Miscellany*), wrote in April 1917 that after the war, peoples and societies in the world would face great changes and enter an age of reform. Du believed that the war had revealed obvious and serious problems in the West and symbolized the death of old civilizations and the potential birth of new ones.[47] Du was deeply interested in what kind of new civilization might arise after people realized the current civilizations needed to be reformed.[48] Chen Duxiu declared in 1916 that as China prepared to create a new civilization in the twentieth century, it should not be bound by those of the past, either from the East or West. Chen argued that the Great War would have a deep impact on new Chinese thinking about military, political, intellectual, and other matters. He asserted that the whole world would be transformed by the war and encouraged his fellow Chinese to start anew.[49]

Japan's espousal of Asianism exerted a gravitational pull on Chinese thinking. For instance, Kayahara's impact was considerable, and one Communist Party member even wrote to the young Mao Zedong urging him to fulfill the historical tasks of Lenin and Kayahara. Duara has noted that perhaps Kayahara's most significant impact was upon Li Dazhao, a co-founder of the Communist Party and librarian at Peking University, who collected Japanese magazines that featured Kayahara's writings. In spite of the expansionist ambitions inherent in his ideas, Kayahara influenced Li's conception of history and his own way of synthesizing East and West to create a new civilization. It also seemed to Li Dazhao that the Russian Revolution earned its global significance from being intermediate in both geography and civilization, positioning it to mediate between the East and the West.[50]

Chinese thinking also affected the Japanese. Sun Yat-sen, for example, gave an influential, perhaps even seminal, lecture entitled "Greater Asianism" ("Da Yaxiya zhuyi") to the Prefectural Girl's School in Kobe, Japan, in 1924.[51] Sun informed his Japanese audience that Chinese and Japanese should work in solidarity and appealed to a Confucian pan-Asianism centered on the virtues of the "Kingly Way."[52] He invoked the monumental significance of Japan's victories over Western imperialism, first in overcoming the unequal treaties some thirty years before and, most importantly, in winning the Russo-Japanese War in 1905. Sun drew on the American scholar Lothrop Stoddard's 1920 *The Rising Tide of Color against White World Supremacy* to develop the theme of a racial or color war against the white race. The theme of common colored-ness (*yousede minzu*) among oppressed Asians would be braided

[47] Cangfu, "Dazhan zhongjiehou guoren zhi zijue ruhe" ("How Should Chinese Think About China After the War Has Ended?"), *Dongfang Zazhi*, 16:1 (January 1919), 1–8.

[48] Du Yaquan, "Zhanhou dongxi wenming zhi tiaohe" ("The Fusion of Eastern and Western Civilization After the War"), *Dongfang Zazhi*, 14:4 (April 1917), 1–7.

[49] Chen Duxiu, "1916 nian" ("Year of 1916"), *Qingnian Zazhi*, 1:5.(January 1916), 1–4; Chen Duxiu, "Eluosi geming yu wo guomin zhi juewu" ("Russian Revolution and Chinese National Consciousness"), *Xinqingnian*, 3:2 (April 1917), 1–3.

[50] Duara, "The Discourse of Civilization and Pan-Asianism," 114.

[51] Sun Yat-sen, "Pan-Asianism," in Saaler and Szpilman, *Pan-Asianism*, 2: 78–85, reprinted from Sun Yat-sen, *China and Japan: Natural Friends—Unnatural Enemies* (Shanghai: China United Press, 1941).

[52] Sun, "Pan-Asianism," 81.

into and finally yield to another unity: common culture and cultural resistance. Sun discussed the notion of the Asian Kingly Way (exemplified by the Chinese imperium) versus the hegemonic way of the West: "Oriental civilization is the rule of Right; Occidental civilization is the rule of Might." Toward the end of the speech, Sun returned his attention to Japan: "Now the question remains whether Japan will be the hawk of the Western civilization of the rule of Might, or the tower of strength of the Orient. This is the choice which lies before the people of Japan."[53]

Duara has rightly suggested that in China "the discourse of civilization was not merely an intellectual development but became associated with an astonishingly widespread social movement—a movement whose following exceeded by far the popular base of any modern movements emanating from the May Fourth events." Perhaps even more astonishing is the extent to which this phenomenon—which Duara calls "redemptive societies," that is, homegrown civic movements "determined to save the world from strife, greed, and warfare, and which affected the lives of many millions of followers in the first half of this century"—has remained largely unaccounted for in the historiography.[54] After the Great War, many different types of civic societies popped up in China. One example, the Morality Society, was established in 1918, with the influential public intellectual Kang Youwei as its president until his death in 1927. This society "sought to synthesize the scientific view of the world with the religious and moral visions of Asian thought." Its membership held that "without moral and spiritual regeneration, human evolution would stall and turn even more destructive because of the present trend towards hedonistic materialism."[55]

The question of Chinese civilization versus Western civilization loomed large for the giants of Chinese intellectual life, including Li Dazhao, Liang Qichao, Liang Shuming, Hu Shi, Chen Duxiu, and Zhang Dongsun. The idea that Chinese civilization had value entered China through a "complex global loop." This route revealed not only a new intellectual world, but "the necessity of its recognition by the other in order to be affirmed by the self." The question in China was whether Chinese and, more broadly, Eastern traditional civilization could redeem the West.[56] By the mid-1920s, this discourse and debates around it began to figure in cultural, political, and social practices as well.[57] Wang Hui is right to observe that the Great War injected fresh ideas that shaped the thinking in Chinese minds about their collective future, national identity, and even their civilization; without the Great War, he goes on, the Chinese would not have rooted their thinking in the international scene.[58] Qiu Weijun has also pointed out that the European war was

---

[53] Sun, "Pan-Asianism," 80, 85; Prasenjit Duara, "Transnationalism and the Predicament of Sovereignty: China, 1900-1945," *American Historical Review*, 102:4 (October 1997), 1038–9.

[54] Duara, "The Discourse of Civilization and Pan-Asianism," 117.

[55] Duara, "The Discourse of Civilization and Pan-Asianism," 119.

[56] Duara, "The Discourse of Civilization and Pan-Asianism," 114.

[57] Duara, "The Discourse of Civilization and Pan-Asianism," 115.

[58] Wang Hui, "Wenhua yu zhengzhi de biaozou: zhanzheng, geming yu 1910 niandai de sixiang zhan" ("The Interconnected Nature between Culture and Politics: War, Revolution and Ideological Debates in the 1910s"), *Zhongguo shehui kexue*, 4 (2009).

crucial to China's modern intellectual transformation because it served as a pivot for Chinese national consciousness.[59]

THE JOURNEY OF LIANG QICHAO

If the Chinese were thinking seriously about their country's transformation in the wake of the Great War, they seemed also to be obsessed with the questions "What is China's position in the world?" "What is China?" and "Who are we Chinese?" The wide attention paid to the relative virtues of Western and Eastern civilizations came largely out of the postwar peace conference, where the offhand dismissal of fervent, eloquent, and widely supported Chinese positions left the prestige and attractions of the West in ruins.[60] Historian C. P. Fitzgerald observed that in Paris, the Chinese became at last "completely disillusioned with the false gods of the West. They turned restlessly to some other solution."[61]

The noted public intellectual Liang Qichao struck the same contrast Sun Yat-sen had made when he presented the Oriental "Kingly Way" in opposition to the Occidental "Way of the Hegemon." Liang concluded:

> In international relationships there is the principle of "might is right." This principle still holds sway today as ever. We have heard the principles of justice and humanity. But these are the catch phrases of the strong. If the weak nations, by taking these phrases in their literal sense, hope to be shielded by the strong, they will be quickly disillusioned. . . . Let us rise above our disabilities and be men, and depend upon ourselves for our own salvation. Therein lies our great hope.[62]

Liang and his entourage had left China in late 1918 and would not return until March 1920. He toured France, England, and other parts of Europe. While he was abroad—just as Dewey was visiting China—his correspondence from Paris urged on the May Fourth Movement. Liang came to see the war as "not yet the whole story of a new world history. It is but a mediating passage that connects the past and the future."

Liang's travels led him to an awakening. He found everything in postwar London depressed: "As soon as we landed, what jumped into view was nothing but a picture of impoverishment and desolation in the wake of war." There was no heat in the hotel room although it was very cold; also, sugar and food were difficult to find.[63] Liang and his group had gone to Europe with dreams of bringing about justice and humaneness through diplomacy, but he would leave a disappointed

---

[59] Qiu Weijun, "Ou Zhan yu zhong guo de xiandai xing" ("World War I and China's Modernity"), *Si yu yan*, 46:1 (April 2008), 75–124.

[60] Liang Qichao, "Causes of China's Defeat at the Peace Conference," *Millard's Review*, 9:7 (July 19, 1919), 262–8.

[61] C. P. Fitzgerald, *The Birth of Communist China* (London: Penguin Books, 1964), 54.

[62] Liang, "Causes of China's Defeat," 267–8.

[63] Liang, "Ouyou xinyin lu" ("Impressions from Travels in Europe"), in Liang Qichao, *Liang Qichao quan ji (Complete Collections of Liang Qichao Writings)* (Beijing: Beijing chubanshe, 1999), 5: 2968–9.

man. As Joseph Levenson put it, "From 1919 on, he brought value back to Chinese history, for the West could be revalued." And as he began to revalue Chinese traditional thinking, Liang recognized that the war had driven home the import-ance of international cooperation and peaceful coexistence. He believed that "cosmopolitanism [*shijie zhuyi*] will be the motor from now on."[64]

From the outset, Liang Qichao had expected his postwar travels in Europe to be a learning process; he wrote to his brother that he was "determined to be a student on this trip." But what a learning curve he faced! In his work *Ouyou xinyin lu* (*Impressions from Travels in Europe*), Liang kept track of his experiences and their effect on him:

> I am unable to predict the course of the changes my mind is undergoing. In the past five months, I have met people of all descriptions; I have heard ideas of a variety of schools and observed all kinds of clashes of interest. I am dazzled by paintings and sculptures that capture the inner spirit in the presentation of the outward form, moved by kaleidoscopic and bustling social phenomena and feasted with magnificent and changing natural scenery. Given my nature which is rich in feeling and the desire for continual improvement, try to imagine the stimulation I am experiencing! I feel that my mind is daily fermenting and that it will undergo a great revolution. But what the product of that revolution will be, I am still unable to tell.[65]

He was struck by the fact that Europeans had begun talking about the moral failings of science. "This is a great turning point in modern thought":

> Those who praised the omnipotence of science had hoped that as soon as science succeeded the golden age would immediately appear. Now science is successful indeed; material progress in the West in the last one hundred years had greatly surpassed the achievements of the three thousand years prior to this period. Yet we human beings have not secured happiness; on the contrary, science gives us catastrophes. We are like travellers losing their way in the desert. They see a big black shadow ahead and desperately run to it, thinking that it may lead them somewhere. But after running a long way, they no longer see the shadow and fall into the slough of despond. What is that shadow? It is this "Mr. Science."[66]

Liang came to disparage Darwinian evolution and extreme individualism. Darwinian theory was no longer taken as pure science: "Now, when evil might conceivably be traced to it, it was a cultural exhibit, submitted ... to embarrass the West." As Liang now saw it, after the French Revolution, "the dream of the omnipotence of science" had replaced traditional cultural norms and linkages wrought by the feudal tradition, Greek philosophy, and Christianity. But Darwin's theory of evolution and its concept of the survival of the fittest, or at least a popular distortion of it, had been applied to human society and it became the core of social and political thought, with many evil consequences. Liang concluded that "This great European war nearly

[64] Levenson, *Liang Qichao and the Mind of Modern China*, 198; Liang, "Ouyou xinyin lu," 5: 2969–78.
[65] Liang, "Ouyou xinyin lu," 5: 2969–3048; see Philip C. Huang, *Liang Chi-chao and Modern Chinese Liberalism* (Seattle: University of Washington Press, 1972), 144.
[66] Liang, "Ouyou xinyin lu," 5: 2973–4.

wiped out human civilization; although its causes were very many, it must be said that the Darwinian theory had a very great influence."

Given this, he informed his readers, "All China can count upon is herself and her own undefeatable spirit and courage." Writing about China's humiliation in Paris, Liang observed, "No well-informed man can have any doubt that it will profoundly modify the history of the Asiatic continent, if not the whole world.... China's only crime was her weakness and her belief in post-war international justice. If, driven to desperation she attempts something hopeless, those who have helped to decide her fate cannot escape a part of the responsibility."[67]

Having seen first-hand the war's devastation, Liang was impelled to turn away from the West. He suggested that the East had its own civilizational principles and practices, and in particular was drawn to the traditional values of Chinese culture such as the Confucian ideal of *ren*, which taught harmony and compromise, and which he believed was superior to Western competiveness. According to Philip Huang, "Liang's self-appointed task in the May Fourth period was precisely to discover the 'unique qualities' of Chinese civilization in order to fuse them with 'the better qualities' of the West."[68] Liang continued to stress the primary importance of the foundation of a democratic society—an awakened citizenry. He argued:

> Material life is merely a means for the maintenance of spiritual life; it should never be taken as a substitute for the object which it serves... Our problem is, under the conditions of this unprecedented scientific progress, how can the Confucian ideal of equilibrium be applied so that every man may live a balanced life?

Of the ways to relieve "spiritual famine," Liang recognized the Eastern—Chinese and Indian—to be the best: "Eastern learning has spirit as its departure; Western learning has matter as its point of departure."[69]

Liang hoped to "enrich our civilization with Western civilization on the one hand, and complement Western civilization with our own on the other, so that a new civilization will grow out of this synthesis." This new cultural product of synthesizing and selecting would be extended widely to benefit humankind. He called upon his fellow countrymen with the following moving words: "Our beloved youth! Attention! Forward march! On the other shore of the great ocean are millions of people bewailing the bankruptcy of material civilization and crying out most piteously for help, waiting for you to come to their salvation."[70]

The double course of world history, nationalism and cosmopolitanism, Liang believed, would bring about a new world order in which imperial aggression would not be tolerated. Liang encouraged the Chinese to develop into a "cosmopolitan

---

[67] Liang, "Ouyou xinyin lu," 5: 2968–3048; Levenson, *Liang Qichao and the Mind of Modern China*, 203; Mishra, *From the Ruins of Empire*, 207.

[68] Huang, *Liang Chi-chao and Modern Chinese Liberalism*, 147.

[69] Liang, "Ouyou xinyin lu," 5: 2968–3048; Huang, *Liang Chi-chao and Modern Chinese Liberalism*, 147–9; Mishra, *From the Ruins of Empire*, 212.

[70] Liang, "Ouyou xinyin lu," 5: 2985–7, see also Tang Xiaobing, *Global Space and the Nationalist Discourse of Modernity: The Historical Thinking of Liang Qichao* (Stanford, CA: Stanford University Press, 1996), 193.

nation."[71] But he had to work through a number of contradictions. As Joseph Levinson has noted, "As a nationalist, anxious to strengthen the nation, he is ready to call Chinese errors as he sees them and to advocate corrective measures developed and demonstrated outside of China. But, too, as a nationalist, he must believe in and wish to preserve a Chinese national spirit, which inspired the Chinese past and may be deduced from it. Is Chinese tradition sacrosanct or is it not? Liang is clearly on all sides of this question." In his thinking, breaking with the past was not only difficult, it would be disastrous: "A nation must act in keeping with its national character, which is manifested in language, literature, religion, customs, ceremonies, and laws; for a nation dies when its national character is obliterated." Liang had seen this happen in Annam and Korea: "So many Chinese elements entered their cultures that their national characters could never be more than half-developed. Hence, they fell to aliens."[72]

Others shared Liang's enthusiasm for blending civilizations. After his 1919 visit to China, British philosopher Bertrand Russell concluded that the Great War had showed that something was wrong with Europe and he recommended Chinese civilization as an antidote: "The Chinese have discovered, and have practiced for many centuries, a way of life which, if it could be adopted by all the world, would make all the world happy. We Europeans have not. Our way of life demands strife, exploitation, restless change, discontent, and destruction."[73] Like Liang and Russell, Indian author Rabindranath Tagore also called for a blending of the best features of East and West with his advocacy of Contextual Modernism.

After his many months in Europe, Liang Qichao realized that both Chinese and Western civilizations had their problems. He believed that the best strategy was combining the good parts from both to create something new, and urged the Chinese to use their higher spiritual civilization to salvage what was beneficial in the West's superior material civilization.

The Chinese had turned to Western liberal democracy before 1919 because they could find no other model. But many of them had always been uneasy with the Western stress on individualism and competition. The failure of the Chinese Republic and the spectacle of European nations tearing themselves apart in the war had only deepened that unease. Liang wrote home that Europeans "are like travellers in the desert and have lost their direction.... They are in utter despair.... They once had a great dream about the omnipotence of science. Now their talk is filled with its bankruptcy."[74]

Liang's new thinking influenced many Chinese and his call for self-reliance was widely echoed. One article declared that "the Peace Treaty of Versailles is by no means a document of justice... China must work now to save herself."[75] Carsun Chang (Zhang Junmai) had accompanied Liang Qichao on his European trip, and

[71] Liang, "Ouyou xinyin lu," 5: 2978.
[72] Levenson, *Liang Chi-chao and the Mind of Modern China*, 196–7.
[73] Stephen N. Hay, *Asian Ideas of East and West: Tagore and His Critics in Japan, China, and India* (Cambridge, MA: Harvard University Press, 1970), 140.
[74] Liang, "Ouyou xinyin lu," 5: 2972–4.
[75] No Author, "What the Chinese think of the Shantung Reservation," *Millard's Review of the Far East*, 11:1 (December 6, 1919), 8.

he told friends that through much reflection he had realized that Europeans chased material gains so much that their moral values collapsed. Chang wanted to call upon the Chinese not to repeat Western mistakes and instead to find strength in their own ancient ideas.[76]

"The betrayal at Versailles" made Chinese elites doubt the value and even the possibility of China's identifying with the West in their quest for a modern national identity and internationalization. The moral weight and practical attractions of Western ideas had been deflated, with some Chinese concluding that the Paris treaty testified to the "failure of Wilsonianism and the victory of imperialism." A world system based on the exploitation of Germany and China could not last long,[77] and the League of Nations would do China no good. China must rely on itself.[78]

"ASIANISM" IN CHINA

The Japanese discussion of pan-Asianism had, of course, attracted nervous attention in China. Influential journals such as *Dongfang zazhi* devoted much space to the issue. Li Dazhao was quick to understand that Japan's pan-Asianism was not based on peace, but on aggression, and not on national self-determination, but on imperialism.[79] In response, Li proposed a new Asianism based on national self-determination for the weaker Asian nations and resistance to Japanese aggression.[80]

Acting on inspiration from ideas around Asianism, a Chinese delegate at one of the early League of Nations meetings had made a plea for the inclusion on the Central Council of at least one representative from Asia and the remaining non-Western parts of the world. The League accepted the suggestion in 1922 by adopting a rule that non-permanent members of its Council were to be selected "with due consideration for the main geographical divisions of the world, the great ethnical groups, the different religious traditions, the various types of civilization and the chief sources of wealth." The Indians clearly shared the Chinese view on this matter and at one of the first meetings of the League, called for the "internationalization of ideas and conditions."[81]

This new assertiveness was especially obvious in China itself. In the summer of 1919, John Dewey and his wife, who were traveling and living in China at the time, wrote to their children: "To say that life in China is exciting is to put it fairly.

[76] Weng Hekai, ed., *Zhang Junmai juan (Collected writings of Zhang Junmai)* (Beijing: Zhongguo Renmin daxue chubanshe, 2014), 45–7.

[77] For details, see Gao Yihan, "Wan Guo Lianmeng yu zhuquan," Wang Jingwei, "Zhong guo dui yu wan guo lianmeng zhi xiwang," *Taipingyang* 2:2 (1919), 68–78.

[78] For details, see Geng Sheng, "Wan Guo lianmeng wenti zhi lishi de guancha," *Taipingyang* 2:2 (1919), 4–19; Zheng Dahua and Wang Min, "Ouzhan hou zhong guo zhishi jie dui jianli guoji lianmeng de sikao," *Anhui Daxue xuebao*, 36:1 (2012), 108–19.

[79] Li Dazhao, "Da yaxiya zhuyi yu xin yaxiya zhuyi" (Great Pan-Asianism and New Pan-Asianism), *Guomin Zazhi*, 1:2 (February 1, 1919).

[80] Li Dazhao, "Zailun xin yaxiya zhuyi" ("Second Thoughts on New Pan-Asianism"), *Guomin Zazhi*, 2:1 (November 1, 1919).

[81] Akira Iriye, *Cultural Internationalism and World Order* (Baltimore: Johns Hopkins University Press, 1997), 63.

We are witnessing the birth of a nation, and birth always comes hard."[82] Dewey observed:

> I find... that the Awakening of China has been announced a dozen or more times by foreign travellers in the last ten years, so I hesitate to announce it again, but I think this is the first time the merchants and guilds have really been actively stirred to try to improve industrial methods. And if so, it is a real awakening—that and in combination with the students.[83]

Yan Fu, another influential scholar and authoritative thinker, experienced the developments of the war as a sort of personal awakening. Yan, famous for translating Western philosophical and political books into Chinese, had once strongly believed in social Darwinism. The Great War, says Benjamin Schwartz, gave Yan "a genuine sense of shock." His social Darwinism had prepared him for the more limited wars of the nineteenth century, such as the Boer War, but the enormity and scale of destruction of the First World War filled him with "alternating moods of awe and horror."[84]

Yan Fu advocated a strategic approach to counter China's overwhelming difficulties. When Japan revealed its intention by attacking Qingdao in the fall of 1914 and advancing to Jinan in October, Yan thought the way to deal with the aggression was to "*Ren ru fu tong*" or to bear with the pain and humiliation and wait for a future solution. He argued that if she picked a fight with Japan, China would surely be crushed. It would make more sense to wait and later appeal for justice at the postwar peace conference.[85] After Japan presented the Twenty-one Demands, Yan again thought it would be better to turn to diplomacy and "*Ren ru tui rang*" or bear the humiliation and retreat. He argued that after the war was over, international affairs would undergo great changes, as would political thinking and philosophy, education, finance, and politics.[86]

Possibly at the personal invitation of President Yuan Shikai, between April and June of 1915, Yan translated many news articles about the war exclusively for Yuan and spent at least six hours each day following war news.[87] He clearly advocated China's entry into the war.[88] In 1917, Yan composed a poem about the European

[82] Dewey, *Letters from China and Japan*, 209.

[83] Dewey, *Letters from China and Japan*, 262–3.

[84] Wang Shi, ed., *Yan Fu Ji*, 3: 615–16; Benjamin I. Schwartz, *In Search of Wealth and Power: Yen Fu and the West* (Cambridge, MA: Harvard University Press, 1964), 233–4.

[85] Wang Shi, ed., *Yan Fu Ji*, 3: 617.   [86] Wang Shi, ed., *Yan Fu Ji*, 3: 619–23.

[87] For Yan's close study of the war, see Huang Kewu, "Yan Fu yu Ju ren ri lan," Taiwan shida lishi xuebao, No. 39 (June 2008); Wang Shi, ed., *Yan Fu Ji*, 3: 621; Lin Qiyan, "di yi ci shijie dazhan qijian Yan Fu de guji zhangzhi guan: can zhan sixiang fenxi," in Xi Jinping, ed., *Kexue yu aiguo: Yan Fu sixiang xintan (Science and Patriotism: New Study on Yan Fu's Thoughts)* (Beijing: Tsinghua daxue chubanshe, 2001), 302–18; Wang Xianming, "Yan Fu Yiwen 15 pian kao shi" (A study on 15 recently discovered articles by Yan Fu), in *Tsinghua Daxue Xuebao*, 2 (2001); Sun Yingxiang and Pi Houfeng, eds., *Yan Fu Ji bu bian (Newly Founded Writings of Yan Fu)* (Fuzhou: Fujiang renmin chubanshe, 2004), 339–67.

[88] Chen Youliang and Wang Min, "'Liuxin shiju, juanhuai zongbang:' Yan Fu Ouzhan guan shulun" ("On Yan Fu's Thinking and Ideas about the European War"), in Guo Weidong and Niu Dayong, eds., *Zhongxi jiaorong: Yan Fu lun ji (Fusions of China and the West: Collected Papers on Yan Fu)* (Beijing: Zongjiao chubanshe, 2009), 237–56.

war that lamented the heavy financial losses and human causalities.[89] But at the same time, he called China's entry into the war a "once in a thousand year opportunity" and a decisive moment for China's future. He called on every Chinese to support the government's plan to join the war.[90]

When the war was over, Yan lamented that the West used all its scientific progress and development for barbarian killing and had almost led the world to total destruction. In 1918, he wrote a poem that claimed that the Great War was not a war for justice after all,[91] and concluded that only the venerable Confucian philosophy could save China and the West as well.[92] Benjamin Schwartz has suggested that "until World War I, Yen Fu did not seem ready to abandon the belief that 'liberty, equality, and democracy' in their Anglo-American interpretation were ultimately indispensable elements in the syndrome of factors leading to wealth and power." But during the war, Yan's views began to vacillate between his admiration of Western achievements and a rediscovery of the virtues of Chinese values. Indeed, Yan had not abandoned his former outlook. His conviction that the Allies would win in the end seemed to be linked to the view that they enjoyed "abiding strengths not available to the Germans." At the war's outset, as German power was rolling across Belgium and northern France, Yan assured his protégé, Xiong Chunru, that the Germans would not prevail, despite the fact that "since 1870 they have risen to brilliant heights":[93]

> Such has been the effect on the human race of civilization and science! When I look back on our sacred wisdom and culture, I find that it foresaw this even at an early date and that what it valued was not the same as what these nations [of the West] value.... When I look back on the way of Confucius and Mencius, I find that they are truly the equivalent of heaven and earth and have profoundly benefited the realm.[94]

Yan wrote: "Many thinking people in the West have gradually come to feel this way." He might have pointed to Bertrand Russell, who asserted: "The distinctive merit of our civilization, I should say, is the scientific method; the distinctive merit of the Chinese is a just conception of life.... Those who value wisdom or beauty, or even the simple enjoyment of life, will find more of these things in China than in the distraught and turbulent West."[95]

Yan Fu shared this sense with many Chinese, such as Liang Qichao, Liang Shuming, and others, who now seemed more confident about their own civilization and moral values.[96] Like Liang Qichao, Yan Fu realized that science and technology

[89] Wang Shi, ed., *Yan Fu Ji*, 2: 396.
[90] Lin, "Di yi ci shijie dazhan qijian Yan Fu de guoji zhengzhi guan, in Xi, ed., *Kexue yu aiguo*, 313–14.
[91] Wang Shi, ed., *Yan Fu Ji*, 2: 403.   [92] Wang Shi, ed., *Yan Fu Ji*, 4: 1122–3, 2: 409–10.
[93] Wang Shi, ed., *Yan Fu Ji*, 624–6; Schwartz, *In Search of Wealth and Power*, 229–31.
[94] Schwartz, *In Search of Wealth and Power*, 235.
[95] Mishra, *From the Ruins of Empire*, 213.
[96] For details on this, see Qiu Weijun, "Zhanzheng yu qimeng: Ouzhan dui zhongguo de qishi" ("War and Enlightenment: Revelation of World War One to China"), in *Guoli zhengzhi daxue lishi xuebao*, 23 (May 2005), 91–146.

could not solve China's problems. In a letter to a friend in 1918, Yan wrote that he had witnessed the turmoil of the Chinese Republic for seven years and followed the European war for four years. The bloody war in Europe told him that 300 years of evolutionary progress in Europe had helped Westerners to achieve nothing but four words: selfishness, slaughter, shamelessness, and moral corruption. After the war, the world trend might well turn to Confucian ideas and ideals.[97]

Kang Youwei, who had led the reform movement of the 1890s, was also fascinated by the possibilities of the moment. Early in the war, Kang had believed that Germany would win and had advocated that China should remain neutral.[98] By the time of the armistice, however, Kang had grown intrigued with the League of Nations idea, which he thought would unite all of humanity under its Covenant and thus promote the realization of the traditional Confucian notion of *datong* (great unity), a utopian vision of universal peace, on which Kang himself had elaborated in an essay written some years earlier. Other Chinese who wrote about the League of Nations at the time also typically rendered it in Chinese using the term *datong*. Kang's vision of *datong* might be realized under Wilson's global leadership, since the United States had "achieved a great victory and sponsored a peace conference based on right and justice," where it "would support the weak and small countries." "I never dreamed I would have the good luck to see the formation of a League of Nations in my own day," Kang wrote to his son-in-law in early 1919. "The impossible is about to happen. You can't imagine my happiness."[99] One could argue that the ancient Chinese ideal of *datong* and the unity of Christendom in medieval Europe had elements in common. The Chinese *Tianxia* and the Holy Roman Empire, although both were in fact more aspiration than reality, aimed at a kind of regional connect-edness that we now term internationalism. Thus, Chinese advocacy of a regional Asianism, especially in the shadow of Japanese imperial ambitions, was much weaker than its aspirations for a global vision. And in this effort, it seemed high time that Westerners—as well as Chinese—recognize the value of Confucianism.[100]

In light of wartime developments, another philsopher, Liang Shuming, was able to clarify his own thesis on the advantages of Eastern philosophy and cultures. In his influential 1921 work, *Eastern and Western Cultures and Their Philosophies*, Liang argued that the West had achieved economic growth by successfully con-quering nature, but that it had also cut itself off from a wider conception of humanity that Confucianism still vouchsafed. He asserted that "the fundamental spirit of Chinese culture is the harmony and moderation of ideas and desires."[101] But Liang Shuming disagreed with Liang Qichao's argument for blending East and West. He could not agree that because both Eastern and Western cultures had shortcomings, some ideal could be achieved by choosing the good parts of each. It seemed wrong to combine the fundamental spirits of two cultures. The desire to see

[97] Wang Shi, ed., *Yan Fu Ji*, 3: 691–2.

[98] Xu Guoqi, *China and the Great War: China's Pursuit of a New National Identity and Internationalization* (New York: Cambridge University Press, 2005), 206–7.

[99] Xu, *China and the Great War*, 253–5.

[100] Kung-Chuan Hsiao, *A Modern China and a New World: Kang Yu-Wei, Reformer and Utopian, 1856–1927* (Seattle: University of Washington Press, 1975), 544.

[101] For details, see Liang Shuming, *Dong xi wen hua ji qi zhe xue (Eastern and Western Cultures and their Philosophies)* (Beijing: Shang wu yin shu guan, 1987); Mishra, *From the Ruins of Empire*, 214.

China and the West as equal partners could be the only reason to celebrate blending cultural values and achieving Chinese "equivalency."[102] And in this sense, Liang Qichao seemed to have a point. But Liang Shuming's biographer, Guy Alitto, argues that the reason why he rejected the Liang Qichao formula was "not because he detected Chinese hypocrisy in denying an interest in the national origins of adopted values, but precisely because he felt that no value could be truly borrowed without also taking on the national consciousness that had created it."[103]

Alitto suggests that in Liang Shuming's thinking, China's direction was different from that of the West; science, democracy, and industry were not inevitable there.[104] "The thrust of Liang's 1921 book was that Chinese culture was both on a higher level than Western culture and compatible with modernization." Moreover, his works clearly implied that Confucianism constituted a universal set of values. Liang wrote, "I see the pitiful condition of the Westerners . . . [who], desiring spiritual restoration, are running all over searching. . . . Should I not guide them to this path of Confucius? I also see Chinese slavishly, mistakenly imitating the shallowness of the West . . . [They are also] searching everywhere . . . Should I not guide them to that best and most beautiful of lives, the Confucian one?"[105]

But Liang's ideas faced a stiff attack from liberal scholars such as Hu Shi and Chen Duxiu, who considered his arguments conservative and the very opposite of New Culture thinking. Liang was hurt by such attacks and wrote, "The way [they] talk, I am an obstacle to their thought reform movement. This makes me very sad. I don't feel that I oppose their movement! I applaud and encourage their efforts!"[106]

Hu Shi, a philosopher and educator, called on his young followers to reform the literature by writing in a vernacular style rather than in classical Chinese. Hu himself had received a classical education before traveling to the United States to study. After graduating from Cornell University, he received a PhD from Columbia University, where he studied under John Dewey. Hu espoused the Confucian ideal of the scholar-official, who combined moral principle with practical politics, and thought that Wilson could achieve that ideal on a global scale. Hu saw the American president as a man who made "philosophical ideas the basis of politics, so that although he enters into the political arena, he maintains his uprightness and stresses humane principles in all things." Indeed, Hu's admiration for the president was such that he characterized Wilson, in a phrase that unintentionally echoed Rabindranath Tagore's view of the United States, as "the supreme product of Western civilization."[107] In an article for an edited volume on the postwar world, Hu suggested that the Western model was still the one everyone should follow, and he remained a strong advocate of Westernization in China his whole life.[108]

---

[102] Guy Alitto, *The Last Confucian: Liang Shu-ming and the Chinese Dilemma of Modernity* (Berkeley: University of California Press, 1986), 86.

[103] Alitto, *The Last Confucian*, 86.   [104] Alitto, *The Last Confucian*, 104.

[105] Alitto, *The Last Confucian*, 121–5.   [106] Alitto, *The Last Confucian*, 129.

[107] Manela, *The Wilsonian Moment*, 108.

[108] Hu Shih, "The Civilizations of the East and the West," in Charles A. Beard, ed., *Whither Mankind: A Panorama of Modern Civilization* (New York: Longmans, Green and Company, 1928), 25–41.

Chen Duxiu, for his part, would soon co-found the Chinese Communist Party with Li Dazhao and help to turn China into a socialist country, the antithesis of the liberal democracy model—but even socialism and communism came from the West.

INDIAN TAKES ON ASIANISM

With its defeat of Russia in 1905, Japan suddenly replaced the Western world as the reference point for successful modernization, making Japan, for many educated Indians, the model for a different, indeed Asian, modernity. The Indian press speculated about the establishment of an "Asiatic federation" under Japanese leadership, and prominent Indian nationalists like Lala Lajpat Rai pushed the Asianist argument further by invoking the "fundamental unity between India, China and Japan" to fight back against "Western influences."[109] Thus, between 1906 and 1914, a growing number of patriotic young Indians went to Tokyo instead of attending prestigious European or American universities. Some tried to spread the gospel of Indian nationalism by writing articles for the Japanese public in Japanese newspapers, but they also targeted their fellow students from other Asian countries. Radical Indian nationalists also found their way to Tokyo, where they tried to win Japanese support for the Indian freedom struggle, mostly by appealing to pan-Asian solidarity.

The primary ideological resource drawn upon by the revolutionary Indian expatriate community was pan-Asianism. According to Harald Fischer-Tine, "The idea that there was an underlying Asian quality, a shared mentality of the 'oriental races' was a running trope in Western orientalism. In Japan this idea had found some resonance by the 1880s. In India this idea of Asian specificity was later picked up by various religious reformers of whom Swami Vivekananda and Rabindranath Tagore are just the most outstanding examples."[110] But in its Indian version, it would become an ambivalent ideology, since the original idea was hard to combine with the revolutionary violence preached by Shyamji Krishnavarma and his group.

The conception of an Asia based on the principle of self-determination had been formulated rigorously by Lenin in his search for global support for revolution and fecklessly by Wilson, who had little knowledge of Asia. The concept of self-determination found further support among leaders from diverse backgrounds on the Indian subcontinent after the First World War. The British Empire's wide reach during the war allowed the soldiering bodies of the Indian Army to be transnationalized, and Muslims in the Indian Army in Europe experienced pan-Indian solidarity and the global impact of Islam during the Great War. About

---

[109] Fischer-Tine, "Indian Nationalism and the 'World Forces'," 336.
[110] Fischer-Tine, "Indian Nationalism and the 'World Forces'," 341.

13 percent of all the combatants recruited into the Indian Army were non-Punjabi Muslims, and an even larger percentage were recruited into technical and ancillary units.[111] As early as 1918, Aga Khan, the politically influential imam of the Ismaili Muslims, proposed the creation of a South Asian and West Asian union. Carolien Stolte and Harald Fischer-Tine are right to suggest that the case of the Aga Khan "demonstrates the versatility of the concept of Asianism," for he "vehemently rejected any suggestion of tension between his multiple identities as a Muslim, an Indian, and an Asian."[112] Another Indian nationalist, Mukhtar Ahmed Ansari, firmly put the Khilafat movement that took place immediately after the Great War in the realm of pan-Asianism when he said: "It is, therefore, not only a question of India's honour and freedom, but of a great struggle for the emancipation of all the enslaved Asiatic peoples from the thraldom of the West."[113] Benoy Kumar Sarkar (1883–1949), an Indian economist and nationalist, pressed the idea of Asianism, as well as India's connection to it and other Asian countries during the Great War. He elaborated on his pan-Asian project in *The Futurism of Young Asia*, published in Berlin in 1922. As both Stolte and Fischer-Tine have pointed out, Sarkar envisioned a collective battle of Asians against the political and intellectual dominance of the West: "The leitmotif of Asian cooperation was to him a 'war against colonialism in politics and against *orientalisme* in science.'"[114]

Prominent leaders of the INC also took up an Asianist agenda, including the wish to turn the perceived "fundamental unity of India, China, and Japan" into the basis of a successful struggle against the cultural hegemony of the West.[115] Explicit Asianist tendencies can be found in the INC from early on. In 1921, the possible foundation of an Asian Federation was discussed at the annual meeting, and INC President Chittaranjan Das was convinced that "such a bond of friendship and love, of sympathy and cooperation, between India and the rest of Asia . . . is destined to bring about world peace." Eventually, the spirit of Asianism, having swept the continent during the interwar period, found expression after the Second World War in a series of pan-Asian conferences that deployed the rhetoric of Asianism and confirmed the existence of an Asian identity. The need to jointly fight imperialism anywhere in Asia now had a prominent platform.[116] But the way was hardly smooth.

T. A. Keenleyside noted the difficulties facing the idea of West Asian cultural unity, given the growth of nationalist movements and interstate rivalry among Muslim countries in the twentieth century, even though many Indians, as well as

---

[111] Singh, *The Testimonies of Indian Soldiers and the Two World Wars*, 110.

[112] Carolien Stolte and Harald Fischer-Tine, "Imagining Asia in India: Nationalism and Internationalism," *Comparative Studies in Society and History*, 54:1 (2012), 72.

[113] Stolte and Fischer-Tine, "Imagining Asia in India," 73; for details on the Khilafat movement, see Naeem Qureshi, *Pan-Islam in British Indian Politics: A Study of the Khilafat Movement, 1918–1924* (Leiden: Brill, 1999); Gail Minault, *The Khilafat Movement: Religious Symbolism and Political Mobilization in India* (New York: Columbia University Press, 1982).

[114] Stolte and Fischer-Tine, "Imagining Asia in India," 88–9.

[115] Stolte and Fischer-Tine, "Imagining Asia in India," 70.

[116] Stolte and Fischer-Tine, "Imagining Asia in India," 73–4.

Muslims in other countries, continued to see pan-Islamism as something more than merely "a sentiment of cohesion." Keenleyside continued:

> The idea of a political unity based on the common tie of anti-imperialism—and hence the hope for the creation of an Asian federation—was also premature, considering the real state of inter-Asian relations. In the first place, Japan, the original exponent of Pan-Asian political union, itself became an imperialist power, and its actions in Taiwan, Korea and China gradually dampened the once-ebullient sympathy of nationalist Indians, even though in radical Congress circles there were those (like Subhas Chandra Bose) who continued to advocate collaboration with Japan in the liberation of the East.[117]

Indian Asianists faced serious obstacles. As they watched imperialism emerge in Japan, they also noted a certain ambivalence among their countrymen toward the Nationalist government in China, and they also had to work around the growing anti-Indian sentiment of fellow Asians in South and South East Asia. The paucity of contact between Indian nationalists and their counterparts in other Asian countries complicated and even undermined the efforts to promote Asian solidarity and Asianism among the Indian populace. Once in the wind, however, the pan-Asian ideal was difficult to dispel, and it persisted into the Indian independence period, which only heightened the disillusionment when the concept was finally discredited and abandoned. Keenleyside concluded that "one unfortunate result was the subsequent Indian neglect of the potential for more limited—but more practical— forms of regional cooperation."[118] But the Indian nationalist idea of pan-Asianism, largely developed in association with the new world order after the Great War, would continue to be an important factor in the Indian independence movement and India's future relations with other Asian countries.

Like the Chinese and Japanese, Indian intellectuals and thinkers developed a number of new ways to think about India and the world in the wake of the Great War. Early on, Lajpat Rai had become fascinated by the United States, which he believed had much to teach Indian reformers. Like many Indian nationalists of the early twentieth century, Rai came to consider the US "the freest of all countries of the world," a place, he believed, "where equality, liberty and fraternity reigned and where people were inspired by goodwill and friendship for all peoples of the earth without distinction of colour, creed and caste." He wanted to study the workings of US society and government so that India could "assimilate such of the American idea[s] and ideals as were likely to help her in her aspirations toward freedom, and in her efforts toward national efficiency." He traveled around America during the war and reported his impressions to readers in India in a book entitled *The United States of America: A Hindu's Impressions and a Study*, which was published in Calcutta in 1916.[119]

That book was received with acclaim in India. Going far beyond the expected "contrasts between East and West," it was said to provide a "quiet, careful study" of

---

[117] T. A. Keenleyside, "Nationalist Indian Attitudes Towards Asia: A Troublesome Legacy for Post-Independence Indian Foreign Policy," *Pacific Affairs*, 55:2 (Summer 1982), 220.

[118] Keenleyside, "Nationalist Indian Attitudes Towards Asia," 229–30.

[119] Manela, *The Wilsonian Moment*, 86–8.

the United States as a "great, growing nation, on the threshold of imperialism, to find her problems unique and difficult, to behold her as something complex and interesting in the present and full of strange promise and portent for the future, to study her thus as a thing worth studying." However, the book also suggested that Indian civilization should remain Oriental for some time to come. Lajpat Rai, though a committed reformer, found modern civilization too drawn to the pursuit of material things and neglectful of the spirit, and his book concluded with a lament: "I have not yet found a reply to the question, 'What is real civilization?'" His book also touched upon the race issue in the United States and drew parallels with both the status of the lower castes in Indian society and the status of all Indians under British rule. He concluded that, despite widespread discrimination, especially in the South, blacks in America were better off educationally than were Indians under British rule. Another topic of special interest for Lajpat Rai was US rule in the Philippines. He believed that the force of universal principles, once asserted and accepted, could not be confined only to certain regions for long:

> Ideas—universal ideas, have a knack of rubbing off all geographical limitations. It is impossible that the noble truths uttered by President Wilson in his War Message could be limited in their application. Henceforth, his words are going to be the war cry of all small and subject and oppressed nationalities in the world. He has conferred a new charter of democracy and liberty on the latter and the people of Asia are going to make as much use of this charter, if not even more, as are those of America and Europe.

Many Indian intellectuals like Lajpat Rai thought that American participation in the war had thrown "the Imperial Powers of Europe into the shade," and they would have no choice but to go along with Wilson's plan for the postwar international order. The credibility of Wilson's pronouncements was bolstered by the common perception of the United States as a society that reflected a more progressive version of Western modernity than the aggressive imperialism of the European powers. But when those pronouncements were betrayed in the postwar power negotiations, the Indians, too, came to realize they would have to look elsewhere. Jawaharlal Nehru commented that the Wilsonian moment "has passed and for ourselves it is again the distant hope that must inspire us, not the immediate breathless looking for deliverance." The discrediting of Wilson, he observed, had raised "the spectre of communism" all over Asia.[120]

Mohandas K. Gandhi insisted on the superiority of the spiritual Indian civilization over the materialist civilization of the West:

> The pandemonium that is going on in Europe shows that modern civilization represents forces of evil and darkness, whereas the ancient, i.e. Indian civilization, represents in its essence the divine force. Modern civilization . . . employs human ingenuity in inventing or discovering means of production and weapons of destruction; ours is chiefly occupied in exploring spiritual laws. . . . Many of us believe, and I am one of them, that through our civilization, we have a message to deliver to the world.[121]

---

[120] Mishra, *From the Ruins of Empire*, 203, 208.
[121] Nanda, *Gandhi: Pan-Islamism, Imperialism, and Nationalism in India*, 152.

Although his inspiration derived mainly from strong indigenous roots, Gandhi's political ideas "spanned East and West" and also drew upon humanist and radical strands in Western thought. While the Chinese and Japanese were debating Asianism, Gandhi used Christianity and Hinduism to promote his non-cooperation independence movement among Indians.[122]

RABINDRANATH TAGORE'S ASIANISM

Even before the outbreak of the war, the Bengali poet and Nobel laureate Rabindranath Tagore was one of the most widely known Indians to advocate new thinking about the future of India and the world. In the wake of the Great War, Tagore acknowledged that while "the shifting sands of neglectful centuries" concealed the evidence of the ancient unity of Asia, he still believed that there was "an inner human bond" among Eastern peoples that awaited rejuvenation—the same bond of spirituality that he believed distinguished Indian from materialist Western civilization. Belief in the cultural and spiritual oneness of Eastern Asian countries was based primarily on their common Buddhist heritage.[123] Tagore published his collection of English-language poems called *Gitanjali* before the Great War broke out. One of them perhaps reveals Tagore's expectations of India:

> Where the mind is led forward
> By Thee into ever-widening thought and action
> Into that heaven of freedom, my Father,
> Let my country awake.[124]

In 1917, Tagore published the following poem:

> The day is come
> But where is India?
> Strike the blow at her self-suspicion and despair.
> Save her from the dread of her pursuing shadow, O Lord,
> Ever awake.[125]

Tagore shared the idea of Asianism and was certainly influenced by the Japanese. He stayed in touch with Okakura until the latter's death in 1913, and made Japan the focal point of his attempts to establish a collective Asian identity. As a self-appointed spokesman for the intellectual and political elites of India, he delivered a

[122] Masselos, *Indian Nationalism*, 151.
[123] Keenleyside, "Nationalist Indian Attitudes Towards Asia," 211.
[124] The poetry collection Gitanjali (Song Offerings) was published in 1913 in London by Macmillan and helped him to win a Noble Prize for literature in 1913, the first one for an Asian. Uma Dasgupta, *Rabindranath Tagore: A Biography* (New Delhi: Oxford University Press, 2004), 9.
[125] It was published in *The Modern Review*, 22 (September 17, 1917), ed. Ramananda Chatterjee (Calcutta: Prabasi Press Private, Limited, 1917), 232.

speech titled "The Message of India to Japan" during his first visit to the Imperial University of Tokyo. Tagore told the Japanese that Asia had a long, superior, and glorious history and civilization, while the West was obsessed with a soulless and materialistic approach. Asia had the responsibility and reason to respiritualize the shallow and self-destructive Western civilization and Japan should assume a leadership in this mission. He appealed to the Japanese elites to distinguish themselves clearly from the West, and to refuse those acquisitions of "European modernity" that might have a dubious impact:

> Of all countries in Asia, here in Japan you have the freedom to use the materials you have gathered from the West according to your genius and to your need. Therefore your responsibility is all the greater, for in your voice Asia shall answer the questions that Europe has submitted to the conference of Man. In your land the experiments will be carried on by which the East will change the aspects of modern civilization, infusing life in it where it is a machine, substituting the human heart for cold expediency, not caring so much for power and success but for harmonious living.

However, Tagore became disappointed with Japan. His second trip there occurred in 1924, which was ironically the same year Sun Yat-sen came to Kobe and called upon Japan to follow the "Kingly Way" of ancient China. Tagore denounced the Japanese aspirations to become a Great Power in forceful words:

> I have come to warn you in Japan, the country where I wrote my first lectures against Nationalism at a time when people laughed my ideas to scorn. . . . Let Japan find her own true mind, which will not merely accept lessons from others, but will create a world of her own, which will be generous in its gift to all humanity. Make all other people of Asia proud in their acknowledgement of your greatness, which is not based on the enslavement of victims [and] upon the accumulation of material wealth.

Although his hope for "a synthesis of cultures of India and China" seemed also to be a failure, Tagore's vision of an Asian civilization as a spiritual "anti-Europe" and world-redeemer is still too important to ignore.[126]

Tagore's 1922 essay "East and West" expressed his criticisms of an overly nationalistic and imperialistic Europe, as well as his concerns that violent nationalistic factions might emerge as a result of Indian decolonization. Western colonialism was damaging Asia and other colonized peoples, as well as Europe itself.[127] "There is," he wrote to the French pacifist novelist Romain Rolland in early 1919, "hardly a corner in the vast continent of Asia where men have come to feel any real love for Europe."[128]

True, he initially expressed trust in America and Wilson. He wrote in 1913 that the United States was "rich enough not to concern itself in the greedy exploitation of weaker nations" and was therefore free, and perhaps ready, to "hold up the torch of freedom before the world." The United States was "the best exponent of Western

---

[126] Stolte and Fischer-Tine, "Imagining Asia in India," 77–9.
[127] Rabindranath Tagore, "East and West," in Krishna Dutta and Andrew Robinson, eds., *Rabindranath Tagore: An Anthology* (New York: St. Martin's Press, 1997), 203–14.
[128] Mishra, *From the Ruins of Empire*, 192.

ideals of humanity," and had the potential to achieve "some higher synthesis" of the best of both East and West and to hold up "the banner of Civilization." Touring the United States in 1916, Tagore would denounce what he called "the new god of the Nation."[129]

Indian and other anticolonial leaders and intellectuals were willing to downplay even the most glaring contradictions between Wilson's avowed principles and US practices at home and abroad. Tagore, over the course of his extensive lecture tours in the United States during the war, noted rampant racial prejudice, but he believed that this was something that would eventually be alleviated. America, Tagore wrote, was "the only nation engaged in solving the problems of race intimacy" and might eventually solve "the problems of the human race, national, political, religious." But after the war, he wrote that "The poison that civilized Europe had pushed down the gullet of such a great country as China has severely impaired its own forever.... The torch of European civilization was not meant for showing light, but to set fire."[130] He warned against obscuring "our vision of the wider world with the dust raised by political passion ... Our present struggle to alienate our hearts and minds from the West is an attempt at spiritual suicide."[131] In 1921, Tagore wrote: "Those who live ... away from the East, have now got to recognize that Europe has completely lost her former moral prestige in Asia. She is no longer regarded as the champion throughout the world of fair dealing and the exponent of high principle, but rather as an upholder of Western race supremacy, and the exploiter of those outside her own borders."[132] He recognized that China's protesting students might not agree:

This is one section of the youth of Asia which denies the value of ancient Asian civilization and follows the ideas in Western civilization, trying its best to absorb them. This is a great mistake.... Western civilization is simply interested in material things, and has many defects in its spiritual life. This point is obvious when we look at the bankruptcy of European culture after the World War.[133]

Romain Rolland wrote of Tagore in his diary: "Despite his charming politeness, one sees that he is perfectly convinced of the moral and intellectual superiority of Asia—above all, of India—over Europe."[134] Rolland, having greatly admired Tagore's speech "Message from India to Japan," wrote to Tagore in April 1919 to ask for his help in bringing "the intelligence of Asia" into closer touch with European thinkers. "My dream will be that one day we may see the union of these two hemispheres of the Spirit; and I admire you for having contributed towards this more than anyone else."[135] After receiving a sympathetic reply, Rolland wrote once again in the same strain: "After the disaster of this shameful world war which marked Europe's failure, it has become evident that Europe alone cannot save herself. Her thought is in need of Asia's thought, just as the latter profits from

129 Mishra, *From the Ruins of Empire*, 210. 130 Mishra, *From the Ruins of Empire*, 210.
131 Nanda, *Gandhi: Pan-Islamism, Imperialism, and Nationalism in India*, 241.
132 Mishra, *From the Ruins of Empire*, 186. 133 Hay, *Asian Ideas of East and West*, 148.
134 Hay, *Asian Ideas of East and West*, 132. 135 Hay, *Asian Ideas of East and West*, 128.

contact with European thought. These are the two hemispheres of the brain of mankind; if one is paralyzed, the whole body degenerates. It is necessary to re-establish their union and their healthy development."[136]

When Liang Qichao welcomed Tagore to China in 1924, he described India as China's "nearest and dearest brother.... Both of us bear lines of sorrow on our face, our hair is grey with age, we stare with a blank and vacant look as if we are just awakened from a dream, but as we gaze on each other, what recollection and fond memories of our early youth rise in our mind, of those days when we shared our joys and sorrows together."[137] Tagore later wrote that Asians like himself who "believed with all our simple faith that even if we rebelled against foreign rule we should have the sympathy of the West," were simply nursing a delusion. While visiting Japan in 1916, Tagore told the prime minister and other dignitaries that "I sincerely hope that the Japanese people will not forget the old Japan. The new Japan is only an imitation of the West. This will ruin Japan."[138]

Still, Tagore, Gandhi, and Nehru have all been described as both nationalist and internationalist figures.[139] Gandhi was reported to say that it was impossible for one to be an internationalist without being a nationalist, and he always asserted that "my nationalism is intense internationalism." Gandhi believed that nationalism was a necessary step on the way to internationalism because "the struggle for India's freedom was thus part of a larger world movement concerning all mankind."[140] The scholar Mool Chand concluded that "Nehru's internationalism was progressive and political, whereas Gandhi's was humanitarian and religious, and that of Tagore spiritual and cosmopolitan."[141]

But perhaps another poet, Muhammad Iqbal, best summarized Indian thinking about the West at the time, in this satirical verse:

> The West develops wonderful new skills,
> In this as in so many other fields
> Its submarines are crocodiles
> Its bombers rain destruction from the skies
> Its gasses so obscure the sky
> They blind the sun's world-seeing eye.
> Dispatch this old fool to the West
> To learn the art of killing fast—and best.[142]

[136] Hay, *Asian Ideas of East and West*, 129.

[137] Rustom Bharucha, *Another Asia*, 74.

[138] Krishna Dutta and Andrew Robinson, *Rabindranath Tagore: The Myriad-Minded Man* (New York: St. Martin's Press, 1996), 203.

[139] For this point, see Chand Mool, *Nationalism and Internationalism of Gandhi, Nehru, and Tagore* (New Delhi: M. N. Publishers and Distributors, 1989).

[140] Chand, *Nationalism and Internationalism of Gandhi, Nehru, and Tagore*, 2, 116–17.

[141] Chand, *Nationalism and Internationalism of Gandhi, Nehru, and Tagore*, 9.

[142] Mishra, *From the Ruins of Empire*, 210.

INDIAN PAN-ISLAMISM AND PAN-ASIANISM

India's new thinking about Asia included a widespread pan-Islamism. According to Selcuk Esenbel, a coalition between Japanese Asianists and Muslims formed with the 1905 Russo-Japanese War and became part of the Japanese claim to Asia in the wake of the Great War. A shared critique of the West helped establish the basis for an anticolonial stance against the Western Powers, yet the Japanese use of Islam for an "Asian awakening" promoted only a pan-Asianism that operated under Japanese control.[143] After the outbreak of the war, it was in fact *pan-Islamism* that drove Indian Muslims closer to the national politics, not nationalism.[144] How did this happen?

Like the Chinese and Vietnamese, some Indian Muslims were convinced that the Russian Bolsheviks were in their corner and opposed imperialism; they also believed that socialism might defeat the British. As they discovered similarities between Islam and Bolshevik ideology, they found a way that eased their eventual transition to socialism.[145] K. H. Ansari contends that the stance of the Indian Muhajirin was transformed when they discovered that the new government in Russia seemed to favor Muslim causes. The Muhajirin looked to the Bolsheviks for support, leading some to espouse socialism. These Muslim socialists argued that India should free herself, but "we pray Russia to hold out to us the hand of help that we may gain freedom."[146] Maulana Barkat-Allah, though a staunch Muslim, was steadfast in developing this new relationship with the Bolsheviks. Though he never claimed to be a Bolshevik, probably because he could not free himself from his attachment to Islam, his views on most secular matters became almost identical to those of the Bolsheviks. "In India," he declared, history had "matured the same prerequisites of revolution which existed in Russia in October 1917." In *Bolshevism and the Islamic Body Politick*, which was printed in several languages and circulated throughout Central Asia and India, he appealed to the Muslims of the world to "understand the noble principles of Russian socialism and to embrace it seriously and enthusiastically." "Oh, Muhammedans," he wrote, "listen to this divine cry. Respond to this call of liberty, equality and brotherhood which Comrade Lenin and the Soviet Government of Russia are offering to you." In March 1919, he went to Moscow as an "ambassador extraordinary" of Amir Aman-Allah to establish permanent relations and to see how willing Soviet leaders were to support a struggle against the British. This led India to form a long partnership with the Soviet Union in its freedom struggle.[147]

---

[143] Selcuk Esenbel, "Japan's Global Claim to Asia and the World of Islam: Transnational Nationalism and World Power, 1900–1945," *American Historical Review*, 109:4 (October 2004), 1140–70.

[144] For details on this point, see Chakravorty, *Indian Nationalism and the First World War*, 37.

[145] K. H. Ansari, "Pan-Islam and the Making of the Early Indian Muslim Socialists," *Modern Asian Studies*, 20:3 (1986), 510.

[146] Ansari, "Pan-Islam and the Making of the Early Indian Muslim Socialists," 517–18.

[147] Ansari, "Pan-Islam and the Making of the Early Indian Muslim Socialists," 519–20.

Ansari thus concluded that passionate fighters for Islam were among the first Muslims to become socialist, that men who left India to defend Islam against the advance of the West within a few years paradoxically embraced socialism, a Western doctrine, because they recognized basic similarities between socialism and Islam. Their primary aim was to oust the British from India and socialism seemed to be the most effective instrument to mobilize the people.[148]

TOWARD A CONCLUSION

Pan-Asianism represented the collective search for new directions in national development and values that could replace the once dominant but now war-tainted civilizational narratives of the West. Still, pan-Asianism was flawed and bound to fail.

The root of that failure might be found in Japan's dominant role. Japan was a primary inspiration for Asianism but also a devoted practitioner of imperialism. Koreans and Chinese suffered from Japanese aggression, while Vietnamese and Indians who were under yoke of Western imperialism naturally had problems with the paradox of Japanese policy and its pan-Asian arguments. Indian students first attracted to Japan for study were frequently discriminated against by the Japanese public and disappointed by Japan's alliance with Great Britain. Japan's ascent to intra-Asian colonial power soon dampened pan-Asianist aspirations in India. Japan's annexation of Korea, the imposition of the Twenty-one Demands on China in 1915, and its insistence on retaining German territory in China at the Paris Peace Conference made it seem like a bad actor among fellow Asians. Japanese imperialist policies thus undermined the rhetoric of pan-Asianism.

Another problem was that pan-Asianism could not be sustained by the political societies of the region. As Duara has suggested, the ideas of race, culture, anti-imperialism, and imperialism to be found in pan-Asianism all ran perilously close to matters of rising nationalism. In the case of Japan, pan-Asianism was easily absorbed into Japanese imperialism; in China, national self-determination took priority; while in India, Tagore's anti-nationalist pan-Asianism made him and his ideas irrelevant to many Chinese and Japanese.[149] Writing about nationalism in Japan, Tagore observed:

I have seen in Japan the voluntary submission of the whole people to the trimming of their minds and clipping of their freedoms by their governments . . . The people accept this all-pervading mental slavery with cheerfulness and pride because of their nervous desire to turn themselves into a machine of power, called the Nation, and emulate other machines in their collective worldliness.

---

[148] Ansari, "Pan-Islam and the Making of the Early Indian Muslim Socialists," 537.
[149] Duara, "Asia Redux," 972–3.

Tagore was committed to an alternative cosmopolitanism also drawn from Asian traditions, but was bitterly disappointed by growing nationalism in his homeland.[150]

Although liberal internationalism did not disappear in China, Japan, Korea, India, or Vietnam after the Great War, the emergence of pan-Asianism was a direct response to Western capitalist modernity and materialism. As Timothy Cheek observed, "The point of Pan-Asianism for all concerned [in Asia] was precisely how to copy what 'the West' had brought to East Asia over the past half century." What the West had brought was "that destabilizing mix of imperial aggression . . . and fabulous technological developments, all inflected by the ethno-nationalism of late nineteenth century Euro-America and frank racism of the economically and militarily privileged white representatives of these imperial regimes in Asia."[151] The complex forms this new thinking took reflected common aspirations complicated by circumstances on the ground in each country.

Ironically, though the Japanese were the first to promote the pan-Asian idea, they also killed it by using it to justify the invasion of China and Korea. India and Vietnam, both colonies of Western Powers, faced their own long-term struggles as they worked out just how to assert their independence. Elite Chinese, who had for many years argued for following the West, now faced the historic question of where to turn after the discrediting of Western ideals and values. The new thinking eventually prompted Japan to withdraw from the League of Nations and precipi-tated conflicts that turned China and Vietnam into socialist countries. Frederick Dickinson argued that the Great War demonstrated the rise of Japan as a twentieth century world power, and that China's experience in it provided a foundation for a twentieth and twenty-first century China.[152] The war and its aftermath served as turning points for Indian, Korean, and Vietnamese national awakening and inde-pendence movements, helping them to articulate a new and modern national identity and status. Therefore, the postwar ideas embraced across Asia were not so much a clash between those of Asian and Western civilizations as a driver in the search for a better future for Asians and the rest of the world, on a new and more equal footing.

---

[150] Duara, "Asia Redux," 971.

[151] Timothy Cheek, "Chinese Socialism as Vernacular Cosmopolitanism," *Frontiers of History in China*, 9:1 (March 2014), 118.

[152] Dickinson, "Toward a Global Perspective of the Great War," 1154–83.

Conclusion

Asian involvement made the *Great* War into the First *World* War, and the First World War changed the world. The Asians' part in the war and the part the war played in the collective development of Asia represent the first steps of the long journey to full national independence and international recognition. As a consequence of the war, China and eventually Indochina/Vietnam would follow a socialist path, while in Japan it gave rise to a new sense of national pride that would eventually lead the Japanese to challenge the West outright. The war had a powerful impact on national identity: for Japan, the war provided confirmation as a world power; for China, the war finally sparked a fundamental cultural and political revolution and a burning desire for a new national identity. The war clearly inspired visions of independence in India, Vietnam, and Korea. All of these states but Korea physically participated in the war.

As I presented the way each country—China, Japan, India, and Indochina—directly took part in the European war efforts, I have looked at these still largely unrecognized stories through the lens of comparative and international history. I have also paid attention to how the war experiences of both people and political communities in these countries still shape their national identities and their places in the world order that has defined the twentieth century. I further examined how the Great War served as a turning point in each country's national development and introduced the notion of fusing civilizations, East and West. I have also addressed a number of questions not usually posed in connection with the war, such as why China and Japan were so eager to press the opportunities the war presented to advance their respective dreams of national renewal and international prestige; how Germany became a great convenient catalyst for China and Japan to jump into the European war; and why China eventually declared war on the same side as its enemy Japan, even though resisting Japan was its real goal. Moreover, I have explained how the war played a role in India's eventual independence and democracy while elsewhere planting the seeds of communism.

The Great War affected the thinking and political ideas of the future leaders of these five nations, Mao Zedong in China, Ho Chi-minh in Vietnam, Korea's Syngman Rhee, India's Gandhi, and Japan's Konoe Fumimaro. During the second of these two "world wars," these leaders all either played an active political role or were somehow involved in the war and postwar world order. Mao wrote about the war and Paris Peace Conference, and even considered going to France in the footsteps of the Chinese laborers sent there to support the Allies. Ho Chi-minh was already in Paris, where he personally lobbied for the homeland that the French had conquered and divided. Gandhi's rise as a leader for Indian national independence began during the war and took off after the Paris Peace Conference. Rhee, exiled to the United States, tried to use his connections to Wilson and his knowledge of American political rhetoric to push for Korean independence; he desperately wanted to go to Paris to work directly for the Korean cause. Konoe Fumimaro was a member of the Japanese delegation to Paris and had his thinking about Japan's place in the world changed by the Allied rejection of the racial equality clause in the League of Nations Charter.

The disparate histories written in the West and Asia make clear that there are different and sometimes incompatible perceptions and understandings of the war. Asian peoples had their own journeys in connection with the war: some of their experiences ran parallel with each other, some were interconnected, but no matter what their different historical backgrounds or trajectories, all were significantly affected and experienced the trademark paradoxes of the conflict.

The story of Asia in the First World War is full of irony, paradox, and contradictions. In order to realize their nationalist dream of independence, Indians enthusiastically supported the war efforts of their imperial rulers. The issue of neutrality was played in opposite ways. Britain, for instance, used German violations of Belgian neutrality to legitimize its entry into the war; but intentionally violated the neutrality of China and so aided Japanese aggression there. The war was all to do with empires. China dissolved its long-standing empire to struggle toward becoming a republic and a nation-state. A Han Chinese politician (Yuan Shikai) for a brief moment dreamed of ascending the empty imperial throne, and when that did not work, the last Manchu emperor returned to that throne for an even briefer moment.[1] The war promoted Japan to the top rank of world powers, but the postwar world order increased the Japanese sense of mistreatment and fear of inferiority, and Japan was badly stung by the failure of its racial equality initiative and the worldwide denunciation of its empire-building aspirations. The final contradiction was between defeat and victory: China, a stalwart on the side of the Allied victors, was treated like one of the vanquished; Japan's gains as a victor carried the seeds of its eventual destruction in another world war.

The war affected Japan's domestic politics and international relations and played an important role in reshaping modern Japan. The same might well be argued for China. On the surface, the war seemed not to affect Chinese lives very much. But from a long and comparative historical perspective, we can see that the Great War was key to China's transformation and national development. Perhaps no foreign policy initiative had a stronger impact on China's domestic politics than its policy on the First World War. But instead of enjoying the fruits of China's first major independent diplomatic initiative, the Chinese people tasted only bitter social disorder, political chaos, and national disintegration. Disputes around war participation fed the flames of factionalism, encouraged warlordism, and put China on the road to civil war.

---

[1] For details on this, see Xu Guoqi, "China and Empire," in Gerwarth and Manela, eds., *Empires at War*, 214–34.

For the three colonized countries, India, Korea, and Indochina, the war's political repercussions helped inspire their rugged journeys toward independence and modern nationalism. All three took the occasion of the war and the discredit it brought for Europe to try to escape their imperial masters' control. The Indians, Vietnamese, and Koreans all saw the war and the postwar peace conference as a moment in which they could advance their national development and international status, and all had high hopes for the postwar world. They all ended up deeply disillusioned but determined to find stronger weapons.

To understand today's Asia, we have to travel back to the war that broke out one hundred years ago. Over those last hundred years, China, India, Korea, Vietnam, and even Japan have become different structures and the structure of the international system has transformed as well. When the Great War broke out, China was poor, weak, sick, and unorganized. The national government, barely functioning at best, was hamstrung by financial rot and the overwhelming burdens inflicted by its so-called allies through indemnities, pernicious loans, and unequal treaties that constrained growth and development. Today, a powerful centralized government controls a China that boasts the world's second largest economy, the status of largest trading nation, and a substantial middle class. Japan, which became a world power during the First World War, today faces major difficulties as China claims dominance in Asia and undermines Japan's status, but remains a prosperous and influential nation. India, Korea, and Vietnam, all colonies during the Great War, won their independence and are prospering on their own terms.

Now, as the world commemorates the First World War, it is time to think deeply about its legacy and its significance. The one lesson in common that countries across Asia took from the war was that they were weak and that they could never achieve their dreams unless they created power and used it. Asians would no longer go hat in hand to request politely that Western leaders grant equitable treatment and human rights. Force was the key. Leaders and social groups in each country fought with each other for power in brutal and destructive ways, but they disagreed only over strategy and tactics, not over the now fundamental goal of building political organizations that had the power to achieve independence, prosperity, and social justice. Japan tried diplomacy, and when that failed, turned to militarism and expansion as forceful means to idealized ends. In China, Vietnam, and (northern) Korea, traditional Confucians gave way to ruthless leaders who adopted the organizational weapons of Leninist revolution, while in India, Gandhi discovered that force without violence was nonetheless force. Once these nationalist organizations were successful in achieving power, the world saw once again that "power corrupts," but that is another story, one that also began with the Great War.

In the countries examined in this book, the Great War seems to have been largely forgotten. The milestones of memory were lost, and its moment remains a cipher. In the scholarly world, the First World War has been appraised as a "lost," an "ignored," or a "forgotten" war. Even before the war was over, some people confessed that they did not know much about India's involvement. Lord Hardinge, viceroy of India until 1916, later wrote that "It is very difficult to describe the course of the war, as far as India was concerned, and the effort made by India in every quarter where war was in progress."[2] A French painter took the time to visit Indian camps in France during the war and jotted down her thoughts. In her diary, she hoped that the world would not soon forget these soldiers "from a distant land, who have come from the other end of the world to fight our common foe for the triumph of right and justice."[3] At the end of the Great War, James Willcocks, Commander-in-Chief of Indian troops in Europe, wrote a special plea not to forget India's involvement in the war: India's soldiers, he soberly wrote, "will furnish no writers to thrill the generations to come; they will just pass with the great masses of India, content that they have done their duty and been faithful to their salt."[4]

Despite Willcocks' worried plea, nearly one hundred years later, we are still not sure we can close the knowledge gap. The complete story, with the recognition of all the actors and their shared experience, is yet to emerge. No wonder Indian scholar Santanu Das recently declared: "There is a general cultural amnesia about the participation and contribution of more than one million Indian men, including soldiers and labourers, in the Great War," yet he adds that "under the Eurocentric surface of the First World War and modern memory lurk traces—in sites of public commemoration, in archives as well as in literature—of the global nature of the conflict. Once spotted, they appear everywhere."[5] Hagihara Nobutoshi, a renowned Japanese historian, has likewise noted that "Japan did not really experience World War I," so the "Japanese were unable to cope with the ideas and forces released by the war." Hagihara further suggested that "If the Great War opened the twentieth century, Japan remained outside until 1945."[6] Like India and Japan, the Chinese, Vietnamese, and Korean memories of the war are thin and little contemplated, and the studies too few.

It is my hope that this small book has begun to address these gaps and bring the Great War more fully into Asian history, as well as and Asians into the international history of the war. I also hope this book gives the people of Asia a better understanding of their shared history in order to lay the groundwork for a healthy and peaceful journey into a future that can only be shared, not lived separately.

    [2] Lord Hardinge of Penshurst, *My Indian Years, 1910–1916*, 99.
    [3] Massia Bibikoff, *Our Indians at Marseilles* (London: Smith, Elder & Co., 1915), 160.
    [4] Omissi, *Indian Voices of the Great War*, 1.
    [5] See Santanu Das, "Imperialism, Nationalism and the First World War in India," in Jennifer D. Keene and Michael S. Neiberg, eds., *Finding Common Ground: New Directions in First World War Studies* (Leiden: Brill, 2011), 85; Das, "Ardour and Anxiety," in Keene and Neiberg, *Finding Common Ground*, 341; Vedica Kant, *India and the First World War: "If I Die Here, Who Will Remember Me?"* (New Delhi: Lustre Press/Roli Books, 2014).
    [6] Nobutoshi, "What Japan Means to the Twentieth Century," in Nobutoshi, Iriye, Nivat, and Windsor, *Experiencing the Twentieth Century*, 20. See also Nakatani, "What Peace Meant to Japan," in Minohara, Hon, and Dawley, *The Decade of the Great War*, 171–2.

Select Bibliography

Aksakal, Mustafa. *The Ottoman Road to War in 1914: The Ottoman Empire and the First World War.* Cambridge Military Histories. Cambridge: Cambridge University Press, 2008.

Alexander, Jeffrey W. *Brewed in Japan: The Evolution of the Japanese Beer Industry.* Honolulu: University of Hawaii Press, 2013.

Ali, Asghar. *Our Heroes of the Great War.* Bombay: The Times Press, 1922.

Alitto, Guy. *The Last Confucian: Liang Shu-ming and the Chinese Dilemma of Modernity.* Berkeley: University of California Press, 1986.

Ambrosius, Lloyd E. *Woodrow Wilson and the American Diplomatic Tradition: The Treaty Fight in Perspective.* New York: Cambridge University Press, 1987.

Ambrosius, Lloyd E. *Wilsonian Statecraft: Theory and Practice of Liberal Internationalism During World War I.* Wilmington, DE: SR Books, 1991.

Ambrosius, Lloyd E. *Wilsonianism: Woodrow Wilson and His Legacy in American Foreign Relations.* New York: Palgrave Macmillan, 2002.

Armitage, David. *The Declaration of Independence: A Global History.* Cambridge, MA: Harvard University Press, 2008.

Bailey, Thomas Andrew. *Woodrow Wilson and the Lost Peace.* New York: Macmillan, 1944.

Bailey, Thomas Andrew. *Woodrow Wilson and the Great Betrayal.* New York: The Macmillan Company, 1945.

Baldwin, Frank P. *The March First Movement: Korean Challenge and Japanese Response.* PhD thesis, Columbia University, 1969.

Bao, Tianxiao. *Chuan Ying Lou Hui Yi Lu.* Taibei Shi: Long wen chu ban she, 1990.

Barley, Nigel. *Rogue Raider: The Tale of Captain Lauterbach and the Singapore Mutiny.* Singapore: Monsoon, 2006.

Barua, Pradeep. *The Army Officer Corps and Military Modernisation in Later Colonial India.* Hull: University of Hull Press, 1999.

Barua, Pradeep. *Gentlemen of the Raj: The Indian Army Officer Corps, 1817–1949.* Westport, CT: Praeger, 2003.

Basu, Bhupendranath. *Why India is Heart and Soul with Great Britain.* London: Macmillan and Co., 1914.

Beard, Charles A. *Whither Mankind: A Panorama of Modern Civilization.* New York: Longmans, Green and Company, 1928.

Beasley, W. G. *Japanese Imperialism, 1894–1945.* Oxford: Clarendon Press, 1987.

Beckett, I. F. W. *1917: Beyond the Western Front.* Boston: Brill, 2009.

Bharucha, Rustom. *Another Asia: Rabindranath Tagore and Okakura Tenshin.* New Delhi: Oxford University Press, 2006.

Bhattacharya, Sabyasachi. *Rabindranath Tagore: An Interpretation.* New Delhi: Viking, Penguin Books India, 2011.

Bibikoff, Massia. *Our Indians at Marseilles.* London: Smith, Elder & Co., 1915.

Bianco, Lucien. *Origins of the Chinese Revolution, 1915–1949.* Stanford, CA: Stanford University Press, 1971.

Birdsall, Paul. *Versailles Twenty Years After.* New York: Reynal & Hitchcock, 1941.

Bley, Helmut, and Anorthe Kremers. *The World During the First World War*. Essen: Klartext, 2014.

Bloom, Irene, and Joshua A. Fogel. *Meeting of Minds: Intellectual and Religious Interaction in East Asian Traditions of Thought: Essays in Honor of Wing-Tsit Chan and William Theodore De Bary*. New York: Columbia University Press, 1997.

Bloxham, Donald. *The Great Game of Genocide: Imperialism, Nationalism, and the Destruction of the Ottoman Armenians*. Oxford: Oxford University Press, 2005.

Bonsal, Stephen. *Unfinished Business*. Garden City: Doubleday, Doran and Company, Inc., 1944.

Bonsal, Stephen. *Suitors and Suppliants: The Little Nations at Versailles*. New York: Prentice-Hall, 1946.

Borden, Henry, ed. *Robert Laird Borden: His Memoirs*. Toronto: Macmillan, 1938.

Bourne, Kenneth, ed., *British Documents on Foreign Affairs: Reports and Papers from the Foreign Office Confidential Print*, vol. 23: *China, January 1919–December 1920*. Frederick, MD: University Publications of America, 1994.

Brocheux, Pierre. *Ho Chi Minh: A Biography*, trans. Chaire Duiker. New York: Cambridge University Press, 2007.

Brown, Edwin A. *Singapore Mutiny: A Colonial Couple's Stirring Account of Combat and Survival in the 1915 Singapore Mutiny*. Singapore: Monsoon, 2015.

Brown, J. M., and W. M. Roger Louis, eds. *Oxford History of the British Empire*, vol. 4. Oxford: Oxford University Press, 1999.

Buttinger, Joseph. *Vietnam: A Political History*. New York: Praeger, 1968.

Cai, Shangsi. *Cai Yuanpei*. Nanjing: Jiangsu ren min chu ban she, 1982.

The Carnegie Endowment for International Peace, ed., *Shantung: Treaties and Agreements*. Washington, DC: The Carnegie Endowment for International Peace, 1921.

Cao, Rulin. *Yi Sheng Zhi Hui Yi*. Hong Kong: Chun Qiu chu ban she, 1966.

Chakravorty, U. N. *Indian Nationalism and the First World War, 1914–18*. Calcutta: Progressive Publishers, 1997.

Chand, Mool. *Nationalism and Internationalism of Gandhi, Nehru, and Tagore*. New Delhi: M. N. Publishers and Distributors, 1989.

Chen, Daode, Zhang Minfu, and Rao Geping, eds. *Zhong Hua Min Guo Wai Jiao Shi Zhi Liao Xian Bian (1911–1919)*. Beijing: Beijing daxue chu ban she, 1988.

Chen, Duxiu. *Duxiu Wencun (Surviving Writings of Chen Duxiu)*. Hong Kong: Xianggang yuandong tushu gongsi, 1965.

Chen, Duxiu. *Duxiu Wencun (Surviving Writings of Chen Duxiu)*. Hefei: Anhui renmin chu ban she, 1987.

Chen, Mao. *Between Tradition and Change: The Hermeneutics of May Fourth Literature*. Lanham, MD: University Press of America, 1997.

Chen, Sanjing. *Hua Gong Yu Ou Zhan*. Taipei: Zhong yang yan jiu yuan jin dai shi yan jiu suo, 1986.

Chen, Sanjing. *Lü Ou Jiao Yu Yun Dong*. Taipei: Zhong yang yan jiu yuan jin dai shi yan jiu suo, 1996.

Chen, Sanjing, Lu Fangshang, and Yang Cuihua, eds. *Ouzhan Huagong shiliao*. Taipei: Zhong yang yan jiu yuan jin dai shi yan jiu suo, 1997.

Chen, Xiaoming. *From the May Fourth Movement to Communist Revolution: Guo Moruo and the Chinese Path to Communism*. Albany: State University of New York Press, 2007.

Chen, Zhiqi, ed. *Zhong Hua Min Guo Wai Jiao Shi Liao Hui Bian*. Taipei: Bo hai tan wen hua gong shi, 1996.

Chi, Madeleine. *China Diplomacy, 1914–1918*. Cambridge, MA: East Asian Research Center, distributed by Harvard University Press, 1970.

Chow, Tse-Tsung. *The May Fourth Movement: Intellectual Revolution in Modern China*. Cambridge, MA: Harvard University Press, 1960.

Chung, Henry. *Korean Treaties*. New York: H. S. Nichols, 1919.

Chung, Henry. *The Oriental Policy of the United States*. New York: Fleming H. Revell Co., 1919.

Chung, Henry. *The Case of Korea: A Collection of Evidence on the Japanese Domination of Korea, and on the Development of the Korean Independence Movement*. New York: Fleming H. Revell Company, 1921.

Clapp, Priscilla, and Akira Iriye, eds. *Mutual Images: Essays in American-Japanese Relations*. Cambridge: Harvard University Press, 1975.

Clark, Christopher M. *The Sleepwalkers: How Europe Went to War in 1914*. New York: HarperCollins, 2013.

Connors, Lesley. *The Emperor's Adviser: Saionji Kinmochi and Pre-war Japanese Politics*. London: Croom Helm, 1987.

Craft, Stephen G. *V.K. Wellington Koo and the Emergence of Modern China*. Lexington: University Press of Kentucky, 2003.

Dalton, Dennis. *Indian Idea of Freedom: Political Thought of Swami Vivekananda, Aurobindo Ghose, Mahatma Gandhi, and Rabindranath Tagore*. Gurgaon, Haryana: Academic Press, 1982.

Dane, Edmund. *British Campaigns in Africa and the Pacific, 1914–1918*. London: Hodder and Stoughton, 1919.

Daniels, Roger. *The Politics of Prejudice: The Anti-Japanese Movement in California, and the Struggle for Japanese Exclusion*. Berkeley: University of California Press, 1962.

Daniels, Roger. *Asian America: Chinese and Japanese in the United States since 1850*. Seattle: University of Washington Press, 1988.

Daniels, Roger, and Spencer C. Olin. *Racism in California: A Reader in the History of Oppression*. New York: Macmillan, 1972.

Das, Santanu. *Race, Empire and First World War Writing*. Cambridge: Cambridge University Press, 2011.

Das, Santanu. *1914–1918: Indian Troops in Europe*. Ahmedabad: Mapin Publishing, 2015.

Dasgupta, Uma. *Rabindranath Tagore: A Biography*. New Delhi: Oxford University Press, 2004.

Dessingué, Alexandre, and J. M. Winter. *Beyond Memory: Silence and the Aesthetics of Remembrance*. New York: Routledge, 2016.

Devji, Faisal. *Muslim Nationalism: Founding Identity in Colonial India*. PhD thesis, University of Chicago, 1993.

Devji, Faisal. *The Impossible Indian: Gandhi and the Temptation of Violence*. Cambridge, MA: Harvard University Press, 2012.

Devji, Faisal. *Muslim Zion: Pakistan as a Political Idea*. Cambridge, MA: Harvard University Press, 2013.

Dewey, John, Alice Dewey, and Evelyn Dewey. *Letters from China and Japan*. New York: E. P. Dutton Company, 1920.

Dewey, John, and Jo Ann Boydston. *The Middle Works, 1899–1924*. Carbondale: Southern Illinois University Press, 2008.

Dickinson, Frederick R. *War and National Reinvention: Japan in the Great War, 1914–1919*. Cambridge, MA: Harvard University Press, 1999.

Dickinson, Frederick R. *World War I and the Triumph of a New Japan, 1919–1930*. Cambridge: Cambridge University Press, 2013.

Ding, Wenjiang. *Liangrengong Xiansheng Nianpu (Life Chronology of Mr. Liang Qichao)*. Taipei: Shijie shuju, 1959.

Dirlik, Arif. *The Origins of Chinese Communism*. New York: Oxford University Press, 1989.

Dodwell, H. H., ed. *The Cambridge History of India*. Delhi: S. Chand & Co., 1964.

Dolezelová-Velingerová, Milena, Oldrich Král, and Graham Martin Sanders. *The Appropriation of Cultural Capital: China's May Fourth Movement*. Cambridge, MA: Harvard University Asia Center, 2001.

DuBois, W. E. B. *Darkwater: Voices from Within the Veil*. New York: Harcourt, Brace and Howe, 1920.

Duchesne, A. E. *Asia and the War*. Oxford Pamphlets No. 59. London: Oxford University Press, 1914.

Duiker, William J. *The Rise of Nationalism in Vietnam, 1900–1941*. Ithaca: Cornell University Press, 1976.

Duiker, William J. *Ho Chi Minh*. New York: Hyperion, 2000.

Dunscomb, Paul E. *Japan's Siberian Intervention, 1918–1922: A Great Disobedience Against the People*. Lanham, MD: Rowman & Littlefield, 2011.

Dutta, Krishna, and Andrew Robinson. *Rabindranath Tagore: The Myriad-Minded Man*. New York: St. Martin's Press, 1996.

Dutta, Krishna, and Andrew Robinson, eds. *Rabindranath Tagore: An Anthology*. New York: St. Martin's Press, 1997.

Duus, Peter, Ramon Hawley Myers, and Mark R. Peattie. *The Japanese Informal Empire in China, 1895–1937*. Princeton, NJ: Princeton University Press, 1989.

Eckert, Carter J., Ki-Baik Lee, Young Ick Lew, Michael Robinson, and Edward W. Wagner. *Korea, Old and New: A History*. Cambridge, MA: Harvard University Press, 1990.

Ellinwood, DeWitt C., *Between Two Worlds: A Rajput Officer in the Indian Army, 1905–21: Based on the Diary of Amar Singh of Jaipur*. Lanham, MD: Hamilton Books, 2005.

Ellinwood, DeWitt C., and Cynthia H. Enloe. *Ethnicity and the Military in Asia*. New Brunswick, NJ: Transaction Books, 1981.

Ellinwood, DeWitt C., and S. D. Pradhan, eds. *India and World War 1*. New Delhi: Manohar, 1978.

Fairbank, John K., ed. *The Chinese World Order: Traditional China's Foreign Relations*. Cambridge, MA: Harvard University Press, 1968.

Fairbank, John K., and Albert Feuerwerker, eds. *The Cambridge History of China: 1912–1949*. Cambridge: Cambridge University Press, 1986.

Feng, Gang, et al. eds. *Minguo Liang Yansun Xiansheng Shiyi Nianpu (Life Chronology of Mr. Liang Shiyi)*. Taipei: Commercial Press, 1978.

Fifield, Russell H. *Woodrow Wilson and the Far East: The Diplomacy of the Shantung Question*. Hamden, CT: Archon Books, 1965.

Fitzgerald, C. P. *The Birth of Communist China*. London: Penguin Books, 1964.

Fitzgerald, John. *Big White Lie: Chinese Australians in White Australia*. Sydney: University of New South Wales Press, 2007.

Fogarty, Richard Standish. *Race and War in France: Colonial Subjects in the French Army, 1914–1918*. Baltimore: Johns Hopkins University Press, 2008.

Fogel, Joshua A. *The Role of Japan in Liang Qichao's Introduction of Modern Western Civilization to China*. China Research Monograph, vol. 57 Berkeley: Institute of East Asian Studies, University of California Berkeley, Center for Chinese Studies, 2004.

Fogel, Joshua A. *Crossing the Yellow Sea: Sino-Japanese Cultural Contacts, 1600–1950*. Norwalk: EastBridge, 2007.

Fogel, Joshua A. *Articulating the Sinosphere: Sino-Japanese Relations in Space and Time*. Cambridge, MA: Harvard University Press, 2009.

Frattolillo, Oliviero, and Antony Best. *Japan and the Great War*. New York: Palgrave Macmillan, 2015.

Fridenson, Patrick. *The French Home Front, 1914–1918*. Providence: Berg, 1992.

Fromkin, David. *Europe's Last Summer: Who Started the Great War in 1914?* New York: Vintage, 2005.

Fung, Edmund S. K. *The Intellectual Foundations of Chinese Modernity: Cultural and Political Thought in the Republican Era*. New York: Cambridge University Press, 2010.

Gallagher, Patrick. *America's Aims and Asia's Aspirations*. New York: The Century Co., 1920.

Gao, Pingshu. *Cai Yuanpei Nian Pu Chang Bian*. Beijing: Ren min jiao yu chu ban she, 1996.

Gerwarth, Robert, and Erez Manela, eds. *Empires at War: 1911–1923*. Oxford: Oxford University Press, 2014.

Godshall, Wilson Leon. *Tsingtau under Three Flags*. Shanghai: The Commercial Press, 1929.

Gong, Gerrit W. *The Standard of "Civilization" in International Society*. Oxford: Clarendon Press, 1984.

Grey of Fallodon, Edward Grey. *Twenty-Five Years, 1892–1916*. London: Hodder and Stoughton, 1925.

Griffin, Nicholas. *Use of Chinese Labour by the British Army, 1916–1920: The "Raw Importation," its Scope and problems*. PhD thesis, University of Oklahoma, 1973.

Grigg, John. *The Young Lloyd George*. Berkeley: University of California Press, 1974.

Gu, Weijun. *Gu Weijun Hui Yi Lu (Wellington Koo Memoir)*. Vol. 1. Beijing: Zhonghua shu ju, 1983.

Hagihara, Nobutoshi, Akira Iriye, Georges Nivat, and Philip Windsor, eds. *Experiencing the Twentieth Century*. Tokyo: University of Tokyo Press, 1985.

Hall, John Whitney. *The Cambridge History of Japan*. Cambridge: Cambridge University Press, 1988.

Hardinge of Penshurst, Charles Hardinge. *Old Diplomacy; the Reminiscences of Lord Hardinge of Penshurst*. London: J. Murray, 1947.

Hardinge of Penshurst, Charles Hardinge. *My Indian Years, 1910–1916: The Reminiscences of Lord Hardinge of Penshurst*. London: John Murray, 1948.

Hardinge of Penshurst, Charles Hardinge, and Ernest Marshall. *Loyal India; an Interview with Lord Hardinge of Penshurst*. London: Hodder & Stoughton, 1916.

Harper, R. W. E., and Harry Miller. *Singapore Mutiny*. Singapore: Oxford University Press, 1984.

Hay, Stephen N. *Asian Ideas of East and West: Tagore and His Critics in Japan, China, and India*. Cambridge, MA: Harvard University Press, 1970.

Henn, Katherine. *Rabindranath Tagore: A Bibliography*. Metuchen, NJ: Scarecrow Press, 1985.

Hess, Gary R. *Vietnam and the United States: Origins and Legacy of War*. Boston: Twayne Publishers, 1990.

Hewett, Sir J. P. *The Indian Reform Proposals*. London: Indo-British Association, 1918.

Hirobe, Izumi. *Japanese Pride, American Prejudice: Modifying the Exclusion Clause of the 1924 Immigration Act*. Stanford, CA: Stanford University Press, 2001.

Ho Chi Minh, and Walden F. Bello. *Down with Colonialism*. London: Verso, 2007.

Hodgson, Godfrey. *Woodrow Wilson's Right Hand: The Life of Colonel Edward M. House*. New Haven: Yale University Press, 2006.

Hogan, Patrick Colm, and Lalita Pandit. *Rabindranath Tagore: Universality and Tradition*. Madison, NJ: Fairleigh Dickinson University Press, 2003.

Hopkirk, Peter. *On Secret Service East of Constantinople: The Plot to Bring Down the British Empire*. London: John Murray, 1994.

Horne, John. *Labour at War: France and Britain, 1914–1918*. Oxford: Clarendon Press, 1991.

Hoyt, Edwin P. *The Fall of Tsingtao*. London: A. Barker, 1975.

Hsiao, Kung-Chuan. *A Modern China and a New World: Kang Yu-Wei, Reformer and Utopian, 1856–1927*. Seattle: University of Washington Press, 1975.

Hsiao, Kung-Chuan. *A History of Chinese Political Thought*. Princeton, NJ: Princeton University Press, 1979.

Hu, Guoshu. *Cai Yuanpei Ping Zhuan*. Zhengzhou: Henan jiao yu chu ban she, 1990.

Huang, Kewu. *Yi Ge Bei Fang Qi De Xuan Ze: Liang Qichao Tiao Shi Si Xiang Zhi Yan Jiu*. Taipei: Zhong yang yan jiu yuan jin dai shi yan jiu suo, 1994.

Huang, Kewu. *Zi You De Suo Yi Ran: Yan Fu Dui Yuehan Mi'er Zi You Si Xiang De Ren Shi Yu Pi Pan* Shanghai: Shanghai shu dian chu ban she, 2000.

Huang, Kewu. *The Meaning of Freedom: Yan Fu and the Origins of Chinese Liberalism*. Hong Kong: Chinese University Press, 2008.

Huang, Kewu. *Wei Shi Zhi An: Yan Fu Yu Jin Dai Zhongguo De Wen Hua Zhuan Xing*. Taipei: Lian jing chu ban shi ye gu fen you xian gong si, 2010.

Huang, Philip C. *Liang Chi-chao and Modern Chinese Liberalism*. Seattle: University of Washington Press, 1972.

Hughes, William Morris. *Policies and Potentates*. Sydney: Angus and Robertson, 1950.

Iriye, Akira, ed. *The Chinese and the Japanese: Essays in Political and Cultural Interactions*. Princeton, NJ: Princeton University Press, 1980.

Iriye, Akira. *After Imperialism: The Search for a New Order in the Far East, 1921–1931*. Chicago: Imprint Publications, 1990.

Iriye, Akira. *China and Japan in the Global Setting*. Cambridge, MA: Harvard University Press, 1992.

Iriye, Akira. *Cultural Internationalism and World Order*. Baltimore: Johns Hopkins University Press, 1997.

Iriye, Akira. *Japan and the Wider World: From the Mid-Nineteenth Century to the Present*. London: Longman, 1997.

Iriye, Akira. *Global Community: The Role of International Organizations in the Making of the Contemporary World*. Berkeley: University of California Press, 2002.

Iriye, Akira. *Across the Pacific: An Inner History of American-East Asian Relations*. Chicago: Imprint Publications, 2005.

Ishikawa, Yoshihiro, and Joshua A. Fogel. *The Formation of the Chinese Communist Party*. New York: Columbia University Press, 2013.

Jarboe, Andrew Tait. *Soldiers of Empire: Indian Sepoys in and beyond the Imperial Metropole during the First World War, 1914–1919*. PhD thesis, Northeastern University, 2013.

Jeans, Roger B. *Democracy and Socialism in Republican China: The Politics of Zhang Junmai (Carsun Chang), 1906–1941*. Lanham, MD: Rowman & Littlefield Publishers, 1997.

Jin, Wensi. *Woodrow Wilson, Wellington Koo, and the China Question at the Paris Peace Conference*. Leyden: A. W. Sythoff, 1959.

Jin, Wensi. *China at the Paris Peace Conference in 1919*. Jamaica, NY: St. John's University Press, 1961.

Johnson, Gordon. *Provincial Politics and Indian Nationalism: Bombay and the Indian National Congress*, Cambridge: Cambridge University Press, 1973.

Joll, James. *The Origins of the First World War*. London: Longman, 1984.

Kajima, Morinosuke. *A Brief Diplomatic History of Modern Japan.* Rutland, VT: C. E. Tuttle Co., 1965.

Kajima, Morinosuke. *The Emergence of Japan as a World Power, 1895–1925.* Rutland, VT: C. E. Tuttle Co., 1967.

Kajima, Morinosuke, and Kajima Heiwa Kenkyujo. *The Diplomacy of Japan, 1894–1922.* Tokyo: Kajima Institute of International Peace, 1980.

Kale, Vaman Govind. *India's War Finance and Post-war Problems.* Poona: The Aryabhushan Press, 1919.

Kant, Vedica. *India and the First World War: "If I Die Here, Who Will Remember Me?"* New Delhi: Lustre Press/Roli Books, 2014.

Karnow, Stanley. *Vietnam: A History.* New York: Penguin Books, 1997.

Kawakami, Kiyoshi Karl. *Japan and World Peace.* New York: Macmillan, 1919.

Kawakami, Kiyoshi Karl, ed. *What Japan Thinks.* New York: Macmillan, 1921.

Kawamura, Noriko. *Turbulence in the Pacific: Japanese–U.S. Relations During World War I.* Westport, CT: Praeger, 2000.

Keene, Jennifer D., and Michael S. Neiberg. *Finding Common Ground: New Directions in First World War Studies.* Leiden: Brill, 2011.

Keylor, William R. *The Legacy of the Great War: Peacemaking, 1919.* Boston: Houghton Mifflin, 1998.

Kiernan, V. G. *The Lords of Human Kind: Black Man, Yellow Man, and White Man in an Age of Empire.* New York: Columbia University Press, 1986.

Kipling, Rudyard, and Thomas Pinney. *100 Poems: Old and New.* Cambridge: Cambridge University Press, 2013.

Kitchen, James E., Alisa Miller, and Laura Rowe. *Other Combatants, Other Fronts: Competing Histories of the First World War.* Newcastle upon Tyne: Cambridge Scholars, 2011.

Koo, Wellington et al., *China and the League of Nations.* London: G. Allen & Unwin Ltd., 1919.

Krenn, Michael L. *Race and U.S. Foreign Policy from 1900 through World War II.* New York: Garland, 1998.

Kripalani, Krishna. *Rabindranath Tagore: A Biography.* New York: Oxford University Press, 1962.

Kripalani, Krishna. *Rabindranath Tagore: A Biography.* Calcutta: Visva-Bharati, 1980.

Ku, Dae-yeol. *Korea Under Colonialism: The March First Movement and Anglo-Japanese Relations.* Seoul: The Royal Asiatic Society Korea Branch, 1985.

Ku, Hung-ming. *The Spirit of the Chinese People.* Peking: The Peking Daily News, 1915.

Kuwajima, Sho. *The Mutiny in Singapore: War, Anti War and the War for India's Independence.* New Delhi: Rainbow, 2006.

Lake, Marilyn, and Henry Reynolds. *Drawing the Global Colour Line: White Men's Countries and the International Challenge of Racial Equality.* Cambridge: Cambridge University Press, 2008.

Lansing, Robert. *The Peace Negotiations: A Personal Narrative.* Boston: Houghton Mifflin Company, 1921.

Lansing, Robert. *The Big Four and Others of the Peace Conference.* London: Hutchinson & Co., 1922.

Lawrence, Walter R. *The India We Served.* Boston: Houghton Mifflin Company, 1929.

Lee, Chong-sik. *The Politics of Korean Nationalism.* Berkeley: University of California Press, 1963.

Lee, Chong-Sik, and Michael Langford. *Korea, Land of the Morning Calm*. New York: Universe Books, 1988.

Lee, Ki-Baik. *A New History of Korea*, trans. Edward W. Wagner with Edward J. Shultz. Cambridge, MA: Published for the Harvard-Yenching Institute by Harvard University Press, 1984.

Levenson, Joseph Richmond. *Confucian China and its Modern Fate: A Trilogy*. Berkeley: University of California Press, 1968.

Levenson, Joseph Richmond. *Liang Qichao and the Mind of Modern China*. Berkeley: University of California Press, 1970.

Lewis, David Levering. *W. E. B. DuBois: A Reader*. New York: Henry Holt and Company, 1995.

Lewis, Michael. *Rioters and Citizens: Mass Protest in Imperial Japan*. Berkeley: University of California Press, 1990.

Li, Dazhao. *Li Ta-Chao Hsüan Chi*. Beijing: Ren min chu ban she, 1962.

Li, Dazhao. *Li Dazhao Wen Ji (Collections of Li Dazhao Writings)*. Beijing: Ren min chu ban she, 1984.

Li, Dazhao. *Li Dazhao Quan Ji*. Shijiazhuang: Hebei jiao yu chu ban she, 1999.

Liang, Qichao. *China's Debt to Buddhist India*. New York: Maha Bodhi Society of America, 1900.

Liang, Qichao. *China and the League of Nations*. Peking: Society for the Study of International Relations, 1918.

Liang, Qichao. *Dun Bi Ji*. Taipei: Wen hai chu ban she, 1966.

Liang, Qichao. *Xin Da Lu You Ji*. Changsha: Hunan ren min chu ban she, 1981.

Liang, Qichao. *Yin Bing Shi He Ji (Collected writings of Liang Qichao)*. Beijing: Zhonghua shu ju, 1989.

Liang, Qichao. *Liang Qichao quan ji (Complete Collections of Liang Qichao Writings)*. Beijing: Beijing chubanshe, 1999.

Liang, Shuming. *Dong xi wen hua ji qi zhe xue (Eastern and Western Cultures and their Philosophies)*. Beijing: Shang wu yin shu guan, 1987.

Liang, Shuming. *Liang Shuming Quan Ji*. Jinan: Shangdong ren min chu ban she, 1989.

Liang, Shuming. *Liang Shuming Ji*. Beijing: Qun yan chu ban she, 1993.

Liang, Shuming. *Liang Shuming Juan*. Shijiazhuang: Hebei jiao yu chu ban she, 1996.

Liebau, Heike, et al., eds. *The World in World Wars: Experiences, Perceptions and Perspectives from Africa and Asia*. Leiden: Brill, 2010.

Lin, Yu-sheng. *The Crisis of Chinese Consciousness: Radical Anti-traditionalism in the May Fourth Era*. Madison, WI: University of Wisconsin Press, 1979.

Link, Arthur Stanley, ed. *The Papers of Woodrow Wilson*. Princeton, NJ: Princeton University Press, 1981.

Link, Arthur Stanley. *Woodrow Wilson and a Revolutionary World, 1913–1921*. Chapel Hill: University of North Carolina Press, 1982.

Littrup, Lisbeth. *Identity in Asian Literature*. Studies in Asian Topics. Richmond, Surrey: Curzon Press, 1996.

Lord Sydenham of Combe. *India and the War*. London: Hodder and Stoughton, 1919.

Luo, Guang. *Lu Zhengxiang Zhuan (Biography of Lu Zhengxian)*. Taipei: Shangwu yi shu guan, 1966.

Lynn, Hyung-Gu. *Critical Readings on the Colonial Period of Korea 1910–1945*, vol. 1. Leiden: Brill, 2013.

Mackenzie, Dewitt. *The Awakening of India*. London: Hodder and Stoughton, 1918.

MacMillan, Margaret. *Paris 1919: Six Months that Changed the World.* New York: Random House, 2002.

Maddox, Robert James. *The Unknown War with Russia: Wilson's Siberian Intervention.* San Rafael, CA: Presidio Press, 1977.

Manela, Erez. *The Wilsonian Moment: Self-Determination and the International Origins of Anticolonial Nationalism.* New York: Oxford University Press, 2007.

Marr, David G. *Vietnamese Anticolonialism, 1885–1925.* Berkeley: University of California Press, 1971.

Martin, Bernd. *Japan and Germany in the Modern World.* Providence: Berghahn Books, 1995.

Masselos, Jim. *Indian Nationalism: An History.* New Delhi: Sterling Publishers, 1985.

Masselos, Jim. *Struggling and Ruling: The Indian National Congress, 1885–1985.* New Delhi: Sterling Publishers, 1987.

Masselos, Jim. *India, Creating a Modern Nation.* New Delhi: Sterling Publishers, 1990.

Mee, Charles L., Jr. *The End of Order: Versailles, 1919.* New York: Dutton, 1980.

Meisner, Maurice J. *Li Ta-Chao and the Origins of Chinese Marxism.* Cambridge, MA: Harvard University Press, 1967.

Miller, David Hunter. *My Diary at the Conference of Paris, with Documents.* New York: Printed for the author by the Appeal Printing Company, 1924.

Miller, David Hunter. *The Drafting of the Covenant.* New York: G. P. Putnam's Sons, 1928.

Minault, Gail. *The Khilafat Movement: Religious Symbolism and Political Mobilization in India.* New York: Columbia University Press, 1982.

Minohara, Toshihiro, Tze-Ki Hon, and Evan N. Dawley, eds. *The Decade of the Great War: Japan and the Wider World in the 1910s.* Leiden: Brill, 2014.

Mishra, Pankaj. *From the Ruins of Empire: The Intellectuals Who Remade Asia.* New York: Farrar, Straus and Giroux, 2012.

Mitter, Rana. *A Bitter Revolution: China's Struggle with the Modern World.* Oxford: Oxford University Press, 2004.

Molema, S. M. *The Bantu, Past and Present.* Edinburgh: W. Green, 1920.

Morrow, John Howard. *The Great War: An Imperial History.* London: Routledge, 2004.

Morton, Brian, *Woodrow Wilson, USA.* London: Haus, 2008.

Morton-Jack, George. *The Indian Army on the Western Front: India's Expeditionary Force to France and Belgium in the First World War.* New York: Cambridge University Press, 2014.

Moulik, Achala. *Rabindranath Tagore: A Man for All Times.* New Delhi: Har-Anand Publications, 2011.

Mukherjee, Kedar Nath. *Political Philosophy of Rabindranath Tagore.* New Delhi: S. Chand, 1982.

Nanda, B. R. *Mahatma Gandhi: A Biography.* Boston: Beacon Press, 1958.

Nanda, B. R. *Socialism in India.* Delhi: Vikas Publications, 1972.

Nanda, B. R. *Gokhale: The Indian Moderates and the British Raj.* Princeton, NJ: Princeton University Press, 1977.

Nanda, B. R. *Essays in Modern Indian History.* Delhi: Oxford University Press, 1980.

Nanda, B. R. *Gandhi: Pan-Islamism, Imperialism, and Nationalism in India.* New Delhi: Oxford University Press, 2002.

Nanda, B. R. *In Search of Gandhi: Essays and Reflections.* New Delhi: Oxford University Press, 2002.

Nicolson, Harold. *Peacemaking, 1919.* Boston: Houghton Mifflin Company, 1933.

Ninkovich, Frank A. *The Global Republic: America's Inadvertent Rise to World Power.* Chicago: The University of Chicago Press, 2014.

Nish, Ian Hill. *Alliance in Decline: A Study in Anglo-Japanese Relations, 1908–23*. London: Athlone Press, 1972.

No Author. *Our Indian Army: A Record of the Peace Contingent's Visit to England, 1919*. London: Issued for the India Office by Adams bros. & Shardlow Ltd., 1920.

No Author. *Korea's Appeal to the Conference on Limitation of Armament*. Washington, DC: Government Printing Office, 1922.

No Author. "100 Years after 1914, Still in the Grip of the Great War," *The Economist*, March 29, 2015, 20.

No Author. *The Korean "Independence" Agitation, Articles Reprinted from the "Seoul Press," 1919*, No publishing data.

O'Neill, H. C. *The War in Africa and in the Far East*. London: Longmans, Green and Co., 1919.

Oka, Yoshitake. *Konoe Fumimaro: A Political Biography*, trans. Shumpei Okamoto and Patricia Murray. Tokyo: University of Tokyo Press, 1983.

Omissi, David. *The Sepoy and the Raj: The Indian Army, 1860–1940*. London: Macmillan, 1994.

Omissi, David. *Indian Voices of the Great War: Soldiers' Letters, 1914–18*. New York: St. Martin's Press, 1999.

Ouyang, Zhesheng. *Cai Yuanpei Juan*. Shijiazhuang: Hebei jiao yu chu ban she, 1996.

Paine, S. C. M. *The Sino-Japanese War of 1894–1895: Perceptions, Power, and Primacy*. Cambridge: Cambridge University Press, 2003.

Pearl, Cyril. *Morrison of Peking*. Sydney: Angus and Robertson, 1967.

Peycam, Philippe M. F. *The Birth of Vietnamese Political Journalism: Saigon, 1916–1930*. New York: Columbia University Press, 2012.

Pinney, Thomas, ed. *Cambridge Edition of the Poems of Rudyard Kipling*. Cambridge: Cambridge University Press, 2013.

Prasad, Yuvaraj Deva. *The Indian Muslims and World War I: A Phase of Disillusionment with British Rule, 1914–1918*. New Delhi: Janaki Prakashan, 1985.

Prior, Robin. *Gallipoli: The End of the Myth*. New Haven: Yale University Press, 2009.

Prior, Robin, Trevor Wilson, and John Keegan. *The First World War*. London: Cassell, 1999.

Purcell, Hugh. *Maharajah of Bikaner*. London: Haus, 2010.

Pusey, James Reeve. *China and Charles Darwin*. Cambridge, MA: Council on East Asian Studies, distributed by Harvard University Press, 1983.

Pyle, Kenneth. *Japan Rising: The Resurgence of Japanese Power and Purpose*. New York: Public Affairs, 2007.

Quinn-Judge, Sophie. *Ho Chi Minh: The Missing Years, 1919–1941*. Berkeley: University of California Press, 2003.

Qureshi, Naeem. *Pan-Islam in British Indian Politics: A Study of the Khilafat Movement, 1918–1924*. Leiden: Brill, 1999.

Rai,Lajpat, and B. R. Nanda. The Collected Works of Lala Lajpat Rai. New Delhi: Manohar, 2003.

Ram, Vangala Shiva, and Brij Mohan Sharma. *India and the League of Nations*. Lucknow: Upper India Publishing House, 1932.

Reinsch, Paul Samuel. *An American Diplomat in China*. Garden City: Doubleday, Page & Company, 1922.

Reynolds, Michael A. *Shattering Empires: The Clash and Collapse of the Ottoman and Russian Empires, 1908–1918*. Cambridge: Cambridge University Press, 2011.

Rhee, Syngman, and Han-Kyo Kim. *The Spirit of Independence: A Primer of Korean Modernization and Reform*. Honolulu: University of Hawaii Press, 2001.

Rhee, Syngman. *The Syngman Rhee Correspondence in English, 1904–1948*, 2 vols., eds. Young Ice Lew, Young Seob Oh, Steve G. Jenks, and Andrew D. Calhoun. Seoul: Institute for Modern Korean Studies, Yonsei University, 2009.

Riddell, George. *Lord Riddell's Intimate Diary of the Peace Conference and after, 1918–1923*. London: V. Gollancz, 1933.

Riddell, George. *Lord Riddell's War Diary, 1914–1918*. London: I. Nicholson & Watson, 1933.

Rogan, Eugene L. *The Fall of the Ottomans: The Great War in the Middle East, 1914–1920*. London: Allen Lane, 2015.

Roy, Franziska, Heike Liebau, and Ravi Ahuja. *When the War Began We Heard of Several Kings: South Asian Prisoners in World War I Germany*. New Delhi: Orient Blackswan Pvt. Ltd., 2011.

Roy, Kaushik. *The Indian Army in the Two World Wars*. Boston: Brill, 2012.

Roy, R. N. *Rabindranath Tagore, the Dramatist*. Calcutta: A. Mukherjee & Co., 1992.

Rumbold, Algernon. *Watershed in India, 1914–1922*. London: Athlone Press, 1979.

Russell, Bertrand. *Autobiography*. London: Routledge, 1998.

Saaler, Sven, and J. Victor Koschmann, eds. *Pan-Asianism in Modern Japanese History: Colonialism, Regionalism and Borders*. London: Routledge, 2007.

Saaler, Sven, and Christopher W. A. Szpilman. *Pan-Asianism: A Documentary History*. Lanham, MD: Rowman & Littlefield, 2011.

Sareen, Tilak Raj. *Secret Documents on the Singapore Mutiny, 1915*. New Delhi: Mounto Pub. House, 1995.

Sarraut, Albert. *La Mise en valeur des Colonies Françaises*. Paris: Payot, 1923.

Saxena, Shyam Narain. *Role of Indian Army in the First World War*. Delhi: Bhavna Prakashan, 1987.

Schlichtmann, Klaus. *Japan in the World: Shidehara Kijuro, Pacifism, and the Abolition of War*. Lanham, MD: Lexington Books, 2009.

Schoppa, R. Keith. *Revolution and its Past: Identities and Change in Modern Chinese History*. Upper Saddle River, NJ: Pearson Prentice Hall, 2006.

Schram, Stuart R., ed. *Mao's Road to Power: Revolutionary Writings, 1912–1949*. Armonk, NY: M. E. Sharpe, 1992.

Schwarcz, Vera. *The Chinese Enlightenment: Intellectuals and the Legacy of the May Fourth Movement of 1919*. Berkeley: University of California Press, 1986.

Schwartz, Benjamin I. *In Search of Wealth and Power: Yen Fu and the West*. Cambridge, MA: Harvard University Press, 1964.

Schwartz, Benjamin I. *China and Other Matters*. Cambridge, MA: Harvard University Press, 1996.

Schwartz, Benjamin I., and Charlotte Furth, eds. *Reflections on the May Fourth Movement: A Symposium*. Cambridge, MA: Harvard University Press, 1972.

Sears, Laurie J., ed. *Autonomous Histories, Particular Truths: Essays in Honor of John R. Smail*. Madison, WI: University of Wisconsin Center for Southeast Asian Studies, 1993.

Seymour, Charles, ed. *The Intimate Papers of Colonel House*. London: Ernest Benn, 1928.

Sharma, Saroj. *Indian Elite and Nationalism: A Study of Indo-English Fiction*. Jaipur: Rawat Publications, 1997.

Shi, Yuanhua. *Hanguo duli yundong yu zhongguo guanxi lunji (Collected papers on the Korean Independent Movement and its Relationship with Chin)*. Beijing: Minzu chubanshe, 2009.

Shimazu, Naoko. *Nationalisms in Japan*. London: Routledge, 2006.

Shimazu, Naoko. *Japan, Race, and Equality: The Racial Equality Proposal of 1919*. London: Routledge, 2009.

Shotwell, James T. *At the Paris Peace Conference*. New York: Macmillan, 1937.

Singh, Ajai. *Rabindranath Tagore: His Imagery and Ideas*. Ghaziabad: Vimal, 1984.

Singh, Gajendra. *The Testimonies of Indian Soldiers and the Two World Wars: Between Self and Sepoy*. London: Bloomsbury, 2014.

Sinha, S. P. *The Future of India: Presidential Address to the Indian National Congress by Sir S. P. Sinha on the 27th December 1915*. London: Jas. Truscott & Son, 1916.

Sisson, Richard, and Stanley A. Wolpert. *Congress and Indian Nationalism: The Pre-Independence Phase*. Berkeley: University of California Press, 1988.

Smail, John, and Laurie J. Sears. *Autonomous Histories, Particular Truths: Essays in Honor of John R. W. Smail*. Madison, WI: University of Wisconsin Center for Southeast Asian Studies, 1993.

Starling, John, and Ivor Lee. *No Labour, No Battle: Military Labour during the First World War*. Stroud: Spellmount, 2009.

Stoler, Ann Laura, Carole McGranahan, and Peter C. Perdue, eds. *Imperial Formations*. Santa Fe: School for Advanced Research Press, 2007.

Su, Wenzhuo, ed. *Liang Tan Yuying Ju Shi Suo Cang Shu Han Ying Cun*. Hong Kong: Su Wenzhuo, 1986.

Summerskill, Michael. *China on the Western Front*. London: Michael Summerskill, 1982.

Sun, Yat-sen. *China and Japan: Natural Friends—Unnatural Enemies*. Shanghai: China United Press, 1941.

Sun, Yat-sen. *Sun Zhongshan Xuan Ji*. Beijing: Ren min chu ban she, 2011.

Sun, Yat-sen, Julie Lee Wei, Ramon Hawley Myers, and Donald G. Gillin. *Prescriptions for Saving China: Selected Writings of Sun Yat-Sen*. Stanford, CA: Hoover Institution Press, 1994.

Sydenham of Combe. *India and the War*. London: Hodder and Stoughton, 1915.

Tagore, Rabindranath. *Nationalism*. London: Macmillan and Co., 1918.

Tagore, Rabindranath. *The Home and the World*. New York: Penguin, 1985.

Tagore, Rabindranath, and Anthony Xavier Soares. *Lectures and Addresses*. London: Macmillan, 1936.

Tai, Hue-Tam Ho. *Radicalism and the Origins of the Vietnamese Revolution*. Cambridge, MA: Harvard University Press, 1992.

Tang, Qihua. *Beijing Zheng Fu Yu Guo Ji Lian Meng, 1919–1928 (The Beijing Government and the League of Nations)*. Taipei: Dong da tu shu gong si, 1998.

Tang, Qihua. *Bali He Hui Yu Zhongguo Wai Jiao,* Beijing: She hui ke xue wen xian chu ban she, 2014.

Tang, Xiaobing. *Global Space and the Nationalist Discourse of Modernity: The Historical Thinking of Liang Qichao*. Stanford, CA: Stanford University Press, 1996.

Tang, Xiaobing. *Chinese Modern: The Heroic and the Quotidian*. Durham, NC: Duke University Press, 2000.

Tang, Zhenchang. *Cai Yuanpei Zhuan (Biography of Cai Yuanpei)*. Shanghai: Shanghai ren min chu ban she, 1985.

Thu, Trang. *Những hoạt động của Phan Chu Trinh tại Pháp*. Paris: Sudestasie, 1983.

Thu, Trang-Gaspard. *Hồ Chí Minh à Paris (1917–1923)*. Paris: Editions L'Harmattan, 1992.

Tillman, Seth P. *Anglo-American Relations at the Paris Peace Conference of 1919*. Princeton, NJ: Princeton University Press, 1961.

The Times. The Times *History of the War, 1914*. London: *The Times*, 1914.

Tooze, J. Adam. *The Deluge: The Great War, America and the Remaking of the Global Order, 1916–1931*. New York: Viking Adult, 2014.

Tran, Nhung Tuyet, and Anthony Reid, eds. *Viet Nam: Borderless Histories*. Madison, WI: University of Wisconsin Press, 2005.

Treat, Payson J. *Japan and the United States, 1853–1921*. Boston: Houghton Mifflin Company, 1921.

Trevelyan, Ernest John. *India and the War*. London: 1914.

Tyau, Min-Chien T. Z. *China Awakened*. New York: Macmillan, 1922.

United States. Department of State. *Papers Relating to the Foreign Relations of the United States: The Paris Peace Conference, 1919*. Washington: US Government Printing Office, 1942.

United States. Department of State, and Robert Lansing. *The Lansing Papers, 1914–1920*. Washington: US Government Printing Office, 1939.

Van de Ven, Hans J. *From Friend to Comrade: The Founding of the Chinese Communist Party, 1920–1927*. Berkeley: University of California Press, 1991.

Verma, D. N. *India and the League of Nations*. Patna: Bharati Bhawan, 1968.

Vu-Hill, Kimloan. *Coolies into Rebels: Impact of World War I on French Indochina*. Paris: Les Indes savantes, 2011.

Walworth, Arthur. *Wilson and His Peacemakers: American Diplomacy at the Paris Peace Conference, 1919*. New York: Norton, 1986.

Wang, Guanhua. *In Search of Justice: The 1905–1906 Chinese Anti-American Boycott*. Cambridge, MA: Harvard University Asia Center, distributed by Harvard University Press, 2001.

Weng, Hekai. *Xian Dai Zhongguo De Zi You Min Zu Zhu Yi: Zhang Junmai Min Zu Jian Guo Si Xiang Ping Zhuan*. Beijing: Fa lu chu ban she, 2010.

Weng, Hekai, ed., *Zhang Junmai juan (Collected writings of Zhang Junmai)*. Beijing: Zhongguo Renmin daxue chubanshe, 2014.

Weston, Rubin Francis. *Racism in US Imperialism: The Influence of Racial Assumptions on American Foreign Policy, 1893–1946*. Columbia: University of South Carolina Press, 1972.

White, John Albert. *The Siberian Intervention*. New York: Greenwood Press, 1969.

Willcocks, James. *With the Indians in France*. London: Constable and Company, Ltd., 1920.

Williams, L. F. Rushbrook. *India in 1919: A Report Prepared for Presentation to Parliament in Accordance with the Requirements of the 26th Section of the Government of India Act*. Calcutta: Superintendent Government Printing, 1920.

Winegard, Timothy C. *Indigenous Peoples of the British Dominions and the First World War*. New York: Cambridge University Press, 2011.

Winter, J. M. *Dreams of Peace and Freedom: Utopian Moments in the Twentieth Century*. New Haven: Yale University Press, 2006.

Winter, J. M. *Remembering War: The Great War between Memory and History in the Twentieth Century*. New Haven: Yale University Press, 2006.

Winter, J. M., ed. *The Legacy of the Great War: Ninety Years On*. Columbia, MO: University of Missouri Press, 2009.

Winter, J. M. *The Cambridge History of the First World War*. Cambridge: Cambridge University Press, 2014.

Winter, J. M. *Sites of Memory, Sites of Mourning: The Great War in European Cultural History*. Cambridge: Cambridge University Press, 2014.

Winter, J. M., and Blaine Baggett. *The Great War and the Shaping of the 20th Century*. New York: Penguin Studio, 1996.

Winter, J. M., and Antoine Prost. *The Great War in History: Debates and Controversies, 1914 to the Present*. Cambridge: Cambridge University Press, 2005.

Winter, J. M., and Emmanuel Sivan. *War and Remembrance in the Twentieth Century*. Cambridge: Cambridge University Press, 1999.

Winter, J. M., Geoffrey Parker, and Mary R. Habeck. *The Great War and the Twentieth Century*. New Haven: Yale University, 2000.

Wolpert, Stanley A. *Massacre at Jallianwala Bagh*. New Delhi: Penguin Books, 1988.

Wolpert, Stanley A. *Tilak and Gokhale: Revolution and Reform in the Making of Modern India*. Delhi: Oxford University Press, 1989.

Wolpert, Stanley A. *A New History of India*. New York: Oxford University Press, 2009.

Wrigley, Chris, ed. *The First World War and the International Economy*. Cheltenham: Edward Elgar, 2000.

Xi, Jinping, ed. *Kexue yu aiguo: Yan Fu sixiang xintan (Science and Patriotism: New Study on Yan Fu's Thoughts)*. Beijing: Tsinghua daxue chubanshe, 2001.

Xia'an hui gao nian pu bian yin hui, ed. *Ye Xia'an Xianshen Nianpu*. Shanghai: Xia'an hui gao nian pu bian yin hui, 1946.

Xu, Guoqi. *China and the Great War: China's Pursuit of a New National Identity and Internationalization*. New York: Cambridge University Press, 2005.

Xu, Guoqi. *Strangers on the Western Front: Chinese Workers in the Great War*. Cambridge, MA: Harvard University Press, 2011.

Xu, Guoqi. *Chinese and Americans: A Shared History*. Cambridge, MA: Harvard University Press, 2014.

Yamasaki, Kakujiro, and Gotaro Ogawa. *The Effect of the World War upon the Commerce and Industry of Japan*. New Haven: Yale University Press, 1929.

Yan, Fu, and Wang Shi, ed. *Yan Fu Ji*. Beijing: Zhonghua shu ju, 1986.

Yanaga, Chitoshi. *Japan since Perry*. New York: McGraw-Hill Book Co., 1949.

Yang, He. *Wu Si Yun Dong Yu Min Zu Fu Xing: Ji Nian Wu Si Yun Dong 90 Zhou Nian Ji Li Dazhao Dan Chen 120 Zhou Nian Li Lun Yan Tao Hui Xue Shu Lun Wen Ji*. Beijing: Beijing da xue chu ban she, 2010.

Yavuz, M. Hakan, and Feroz Ahmad. *War and Collapse: World War I and the Ottoman State*. Salt Lake: The University of Utah Press, 2015.

Yeh, Wen-hsin. *Provincial Passages: Culture, Space, and the Origins of Chinese Communism*. Berkeley: University of California Press, 1996.

Yu, Young Ick. *The Making of the First Korean President: Syngman Rhee's Quest for Independence, 1875–1948*. Honolulu: University of Hawaii Press, 2014.

Zhang, Junmai, and Wenjiang Ding. *Ke Xue Yu Ren Sheng Guan*. Jinan: Shandong ren min chu ban she, 1997.

Zhang, Junmai, Kejian Huang, and Tao Wang. *Zhang Junmai Juan*. Shijiazhuang: Hebei jiao yu chu ban she, 1996.

Zhang, Junmai, Kejian Huang, and Xiaolong Wu. *Zhang Junmai Ji*. Beijing: Qun yan chu ban she, 1993.

Zhang, Li. *Guo Ji He Zuo Zai Zhongguo: Guo Ji Lian Meng Jiao Se De Kao Cha, 1919–1946*. Taipei: Zhong Yang Yan Jiu Yuan Jin Dai Shi Yan Jiu Suo Zhuan Kan, 1999.

Zhang, Yongjin. *China in the International System, 1918–20: The Middle Kingdom at the Periphery*. New York: St. Martin's Press, 1991.

Zheng, Dahua. *Zhang Junmai Juan*. Beijing: Zhong hua shu ju, 1997.

Zhong gong zhong yang dang shi yan jiu shi. *Li Dazhao Yan Jiu Wen Ji*. Beijing: Zhong gong dang shi chu ban she, 1991.

Zhong Guo She hui ko xue yuan Jing dai shi yan jiu so, ed. *Wu Si Yun Dong Hui Yi Lu*. Beijing: Zhong guo she hui ko xue chu ban she, 1979.

Zhong yang yanjiu yuan jindai shi yanjiu suo, ed. *Zhong ri guanxi shi liao: Ouzhan yu Shandong wenti*. Taipei: Zhong yang yanjiu yuan jindai shi yanjiu suo, 1974.

Zhong yang yanjiu yuan jindai shi yanjiu suo, ed. *Zhong ri guanxi shi liao: ershiyi tiao jiaoshe (Documents on Sino–Japanese Relations Regarding the Twenty–one Demands Negotiations)*, 2 volumes. Taipei: Institute of Modern History, Academia Sinica, 1985.

Zhongguo Cai Yuanpei yan jiu hui. *Cai Yuanpei Quan Ji*. Hangzhou: Zhejiang jiao yu chu ban she, 1997.

Zhongguo she hui ke xue yuan Jin dai shi yan jiu suo. Jin dai shi zi liao bian ji shi and Tianjin shi li shi bo wu guan. *Mi Ji Lu Cun*. Bejing: Zhongguo she hui ke xue chu ban she, 1984.

Index

Abe, Shinzo 2
Adams, Brooks 25
Adas, Michael 214
Aden 33, 75
Africa 5, 73, 97, 192
African
  colonies 111
  culture 105
  troops 74
Africans 105–6, 198, 206
Alien Immigration Act 7, 176, 185, 205, 208
Alien Land Bill 186
Allied Games 47–8
Allies 6–8, 11–12, 20, 26, 33–5, 39, 43–5,
    47–8, 51, 71–2, 74–5, 81, 86, 119, 126,
    130, 138, 141, 157, 161–2, 165–6,
    169–70, 172, 177, 184, 189, 190, 213,
    233, 247–8
Alsace-Lorraine 95, 182
Alston, Sir Beilby 175
Aman-Allah, Amir 244
Ambrosius, Lloyd 202
America/United States 8, 24, 29, 34, 36, 39, 43,
    48–50, 55, 79, 85–6, 89, 91–2, 110,
    114–16, 119, 122–30, 132, 136, 139–41,
    144, 147–8, 155, 159, 162–3, 171–2, 175,
    178–83, 185–6, 188, 200–8, 213, 216,
    223–5, 238–9, 241–2, 248
American
  army 106, 132
  Declaration of Independence 114, 198
  delegation 91, 113, 128, 156, 158, 160–1,
    167–8
  expeditionary forces 48
  government 122, 127, 139, 141, 146
  ideals 121, 158, 238
  immigration laws 24, 154, 220–1
  policy 180
  public opinion 84, 125, 182
  ships 47, 49
American–Japanese relations 182
Americans 22, 26, 91, 106, 120, 126, 128, 140,
    147, 156–8, 168, 176, 180, 186, 191–3,
    199, 201–2, 208, 213
Ampthill, Lord 65
Amritsar (Jallianwala Bagh) massacre 60,
    84, 93
An, Changho 125
Andrews, C. F. 82
Anglo-American
  -centered peace 178, 188
  conspiracy 182
  hegemony 208

powers 178
solidarity 7, 176, 205
Anglo-German Brewery 21, 36
Anglo-Japanese alliance 20, 25, 180–2
Annam 13, 96, 114, 230
Annamites 94, 102–3, 110, 112–13, 115
Ansari, K. H. 244–5
Ansari, Mukhtar Ahmed 237
Asada, Emura 216
Asian Federation 237–8
Asianism, see pan-Asianism
Asquith, Herbert 60
Assam 69
Association for Publicists of Peace Issues 189
Association of Annamite Patriots 111
Association of Workers of the Saigon
    Arsenal 109, 117
Australia 155, 158, 185, 188–9, 199–201,
    204, 209
Australian
  parliament 204
  public opinion 199, 201
  troops 33, 197
Austria 60, 165, 168–9, 222
Austrians 22, 29
Austro-Hungarian Empire 52, 114
Austro-Hungarian troops 22, 32

Bailey, Thomas 156
Baker, Ray Stannard 127, 159–60, 168
Baldwin, Frank P. 126–7
Balfour, Arthur 50, 145, 155, 170, 192, 195,
    197–8, 203–4
Balkans 2, 34, 84, 103
Bao, Tianxiao 23
Barkat-Allah, Maulana 244
Barnett, Eugene 162
Barres, Maurice 72
Barua, Pradeep 73
Basu, Bhupendranath 61, 78
Beijing, see Peking (Beijing)
Belgian neutrality 35, 248
Belgium 34, 48, 73, 75, 77, 146, 233
Bengal 62, 80
Besant, Annie 62–3, 80, 84, 86, 90
Birdsall, Paul 114
Bliss, Tasker 160
Bolsheviks 34, 83, 117, 174, 244
Bonsal, Stephen 147, 158, 200
Borden, Sir Robert 193, 199
Bose, Subhas Chandra 238
Boxer Movement 24, 33, 162–3, 165
Briand, Aristide 99

Index